Adult Attachment

A Concise Introduction to Theory and Research

Adult Attachment
A Concise Introduction to Theory and Research

Omri Gillath
Department of Psychology, University of Kansas
Lawrence, KS, USA

Gery C. Karantzas
School of Psychology, Deakin University
Burwood, Victoria, Australia

R. Chris Fraley
Department of Psychology
University of Illinois at Urbana-Champaign
Champaign, IL, USA

ELSEVIER

AMSTERDAM • BOSTON • HEIDELBERG • LONDON
NEW YORK • OXFORD • PARIS • SAN DIEGO
SAN FRANCISCO • SINGAPORE • SYDNEY • TOKYO
Academic Press is an imprint of Elsevier

Academic Press is an imprint of Elsevier
125, London Wall, London EC2Y 5AS, UK
525 B Street, Suite 1800, San Diego, CA 92101-4495, USA
50 Hampshire Street, 5th Floor, Cambridge, MA 02139, USA
The Boulevard, Langford Lane, Kidlington, Oxford OX5 1GB, UK

British Library Cataloguing-in-Publication Data
A catalogue record for this book is available from the British Library

Library of Congress Cataloging-in-Publication Data
A catalog record for this book is available from the Library of Congress

ISBN: 978-0-12-420020-3

For information on all Academic Press publications
visit our website at https://www.elsevier.com/

Publisher: Nikki Levy
Acquisition Editor: Emily Ekle
Editorial Project Manager: Timothy Bennett
Production Project Manager: Caroline Johnson
Designer: Mark Rogers

Typeset by Thomson Digital

Dedications

To the love of my life Irit, and my amazing kids Yoav and Yael, for everything they are and everything they do. To my mother Nurit, my father Haim, and my sister Dana for helping me become the person I am. To my mentors, Gurit Birnbaum, Silvia Bunge, Mario Mikulincer and Phil Shaver for teaching me and shaping my academic endeavor. And finally to my coauthors who helped me make this dream come true.

Omri

To my two most precious girls Kellie and Mary, I experience no greater joy than when we're together. To Mum, Dad, and Myra, for providing living proof of what it is to be part of a loving family. To the broadening and building power of mentors—my humbled thanks to Judy Feeney, Pat Noller, Marita McCabe, Jeanette Lawrence, and Jeff Simpson—I so appreciate your support and wisdom.

Gery

To my wife, Caroline, for her patience and support, and my children, Garrett and Mary, for teaching me how to write in extremely noisy locations, my parents and my mentors, Keith Davis, Rick Robins, Phil Shaver, and Niels Waller, for their encouragement and guidance throughout my career.

Chris

Contents

6. How Stable Are Attachment Styles in Adulthood?

7. What Can Social Cognition and Priming Tell Us About Attachment?

10.   What Can Neuroscience, Genetics, and Physiology Tell Us About Attachment?

11.   What Are the Implications of Attachment Processes for Psychopathology and Therapy?

Prologue

*We get old and get used to each other. We think alike. We read each other's minds.
We know what the other wants without asking. Sometimes we irritate each other a
little bit. Maybe sometimes take each other for granted.*

*But once in a while, like today, I meditate on it and realize how lucky I am to
share my life with the greatest woman I ever met. You still fascinate and inspire
me. You influence me for the better. You're the object of my desire, the #1 Earthly
reason for my existence. I love you very much.*

John *(Johnny Cash's 1994 note to his second wife June)*

J.R. "Johnny" Cash (Feb. 26, 1932 – Sep. 12, 2003) was an American singer-
songwriter, guitarist, actor, and author, and is widely considered as one of the
most influential musicians of the 20th century. The letter quoted above was
featured in the 2011 book *House of Cash*, written by his son, John Carter Cash.
The letter is regarded as one of the greatest love letters of all time (Cliff, 2015),
and has received ample exposure and popularity. In his letter, Johnny celebrates
many of the things he appreciates about his partner, June. For example, Johnny
wrote that he and June could read each other's minds and anticipate one another's thoughts. He also indicates that he and June felt safe around each other
and understood one another. Johnny also refers to June as a source of inspiration and fascination for him, and someone who challenged him to be the best he
could be. In short, June was a source of security that allowed Johnny to explore
the world, try new things, and fulfill his potential.

Cash did not have an easy life. After moving to Dyess, Arkansas at the age of
3, he spent the bulk of the next 15 years out in the fields, working alongside his
parents, brothers, and sisters. At the age of 10 he was hauling water for a road
gang, and at 12 years old he was moving large sacks of cotton. Hardship continued for Cash into young adulthood—even after becoming a famous musician,
his hectic touring schedule and the pressures of fame took a toll. He became a
drug addict, his first wife left him, and in 1966 he got arrested and almost died
due to drug abuse. However, in 1968 he met June Carter and she turned his life
around. One could say love saved his life. Johnny and June were married until
May 2003, when June passed away due to complications from heart surgery.
Johnny died a mere 4 months later. The official "cause of death" was attributed
to complications from diabetes. Many people, however, believed that Johnny
died from a broken heart—a theme featured in a song by McRae (2012):

I hear Johnny Cash died of a broken heart
To love like that that the thing just tears you apart

I aint expectin' much from this beat up world
But oh to have a love like Johnny Cash had for her

We chose to open our book with a love letter that Johnny Cash wrote to June because it highlights the powerful role that relationships can play in people's lives. When people have a stable, continuous relationship with someone who cares for them, they feel understood, supported, and able to thrive. But when those relationships are disrupted, people can feel lost and hopeless. In some cases, such as that of Johnny Cash, they may even lose their desire to continue on living.

Social scientists have been studying the role of relationships in people's lives for decades. One of the major theoretical frameworks in this area of research is attachment theory, a framework pioneered by John Bowlby, Mary Ainsworth, and their colleagues. Attachment theory emphasizes the close emotional bonds that people develop towards others in their lives, most notably parents and romantic partners. Moreover, the theory attempts to explain the role that these relationships play in our lives, how they develop, and how they affect human experience and behavior.

There has been an explosion of research on adult attachment over the past few decades. This has been both a boon and a bane. On the one hand, attachment research is alive and well; researchers are continuing to find inspiration in the theory and are continuing to refine our understanding of close relationships, interpersonal cognition, and personality development. On the other hand, the literature has grown so voluminous that there is no way for any one person to read, digest, and integrate it in meaningful ways. Our goal in writing this book is relatively modest. Namely, we wish to present a *concise* overview of attachment theory that hits upon the core concepts and reviews some of the active research areas with which we are most familiar. It is our hope that this book will serve as a useful introduction to attachment theory for curious readers, and provide a useful stepping stone between the core theoretical principles and the vast sea of empirical research that has developed over the past few decades.

There is no shortage of books on attachment these days. What does this book have to offer? Although there are many books on specific areas of research on attachment, such as attachment and psychotherapy (eg, Wallin, 2007), there are few books that are designed to provide a *broad* overview of the field. Feeney and Noller published one in 1996 that served as an outstanding introduction to the field for students and scholars alike. But the field has evolved considerably in the meantime, making that volume less relevant than it used to be. Mikulincer and Shaver (2007a) have also published an excellent book on attachment in adulthood. But that volume aims to be relatively comprehensive and, in our view, is best suited for researchers who want something more than an introduction to the field. Essentially what we wanted was a book that was up to date, like the Mikulincer and Shaver book, but written to be more of an introductory text, like Feeney and Noller's (1996) book. In short, we wanted something that might be useful for those who are seeking brief answers to some of the many questions people often have about the field of adult attachment.

Accordingly, the book structure we adopted is similar to a *Frequently Asked Questions* page. Each book chapter begins with a question (eg, What is an attachment relationship?) that might be commonly asked in a class or seminar on attachment, and then attempts to answer it on the basis of theory and contemporary research. In some cases, it will be apparent that the answers are well understood. In others, we must confess that the field does not yet have good answers to those questions. We will try to be forthcoming in those cases in hope that doing so inspires others to tackle some of the issues themselves.

Whom is this book for? We wrote this book assuming that the primary audience would be advanced undergraduate or graduate students who want to learn about attachment theory and some of the research it has generated. This book might also be of interest to young researchers who study close relationships or personality and individual differences who are seeking a generative theoretical perspective with which to frame their research. Given that attachment theory has deep roots in ethology, cognitive science, developmental science, and information theory, our intuition is that there is something that will be of interest to scholars coming from diverse backgrounds in modern psychology.

We also wrote this book for researchers interested in psychopathology and its underpinnings, and clinicians and therapists who want to learn about attachment and its implications for mental health and psychotherapy. These implications include strategies for working with insecurely attached individuals as well as understanding some of the major pathways that link attachment insecurity to mental health problems. The book will be of interest to people who are not necessarily students, academics, or practitioners, but have a general interest in broadening their horizons on the topics of relationships and human behavior.

Readers who are familiar with adult attachment theory are likely aware of the fact that there are two research traditions on adult attachment. One has its origins in developmental psychology and uses the Adult Attachment Interview (AAI; Main, Kaplan, & Cassidy, 1985) as the primary method for assessing individual differences in attachment patterns. The other has its origins in social and personality psychology and tends to rely upon self-report measures for assessing individual differences in attachment patterns. Throughout this book we focus on theory and research inspired by the social-personality tradition. We chose to limit the scope of our review in this way for at least two reasons. Most importantly, we have worked almost exclusively in the social-personality tradition ourselves, and, as such, believe we are better positioned to review that literature. But we also want to ensure that the book serves as a manageable introduction to adult attachment theory. And, if we did not constrain our review in some ways, we would not be able to achieve our goal of providing a succinct, yet informative, discussion of some of the core ideas in adult attachment theory.

WHAT DOES EACH CHAPTER OF THIS BOOK COVER?

Chapter: What is Attachment Theory? briefly reviews the history of attachment theory, and some of the core concepts that make the theory different from other theoretical perspectives. Chapter: What is an Attachment Relationship? addresses the question of what an attachment relationship is and how attachment bonds develop across the lifespan. Chapter: How do Individual Differences in Attachment Develop? discusses the role of early attachment experiences in shaping individual differences in attachment, how those differences are sustained across time, and how they may manifest in the context of adult relationships. Chapter: What Are Attachment Working Models? explains one of the most crucial concepts in attachment theory: internal working models. We discuss several theoretical perspectives on working models and highlight the ways they have been studied in contemporary attachment research. Chapter: How Are Individual Differences in Attachment Measured? reviews some of the most commonly used methods to assess individual differences in adult attachment. We also review what is known about how various assessment methods converge and diverge. Chapter: How Stable Are Attachment Styles in Adulthood? addresses the question of how stable individual differences in attachment are across time and what is known about factors that may promote stability and change.

Chapter: What Can Social Cognition and Priming Tell Us about Attachment? explains the contextual activation of attachment in adulthood. We specifically focus on the enhancement of attachment security (ie, security priming). We also review the various priming methodologies as well as the major findings associated with these socio-cognitive techniques. Chapter: What is the Attachment Behavioral System? and, How is it Linked to Other Behavioral Systems? reviews research on the interplay between the attachment behavioral system and other behavioral systems such as the caregiving, sex, and exploration systems. The chapter discusses the theoretical models related to the functioning of each behavioral system. We also review research demonstrating how changes in one behavioral system can influence the functioning of another behavioral system. Chapter: What are the Effects of Context on Attachment? describes various contextual factors that can influence individual differences in attachment. In particular we review the effects of factors such as: gender, culture, age, relationship status and length. The chapter also examines how the different stages of romantic relationships are contexts in and of themselves that are associated with adult attachment. Chapter: What can Neuroscience, Genetics, and Physiology Tell Us about Attachment? focuses on the neural, physiological, and genetic underpinnings of the attachment system, and the contribution of these factors to the development of attachment style. We review research conducted from both human and animal perspectives. In doing so, we highlight the similarities and differences that emerge from research findings using these distinct perspectives. Chapter: What are the Implications of Attachment Processes for Psychopathology and Therapy? reviews research examining the associations between attachment and various forms of mental health problems and psychopathology. The chapter also discusses how attachment theory can inform therapeutic work. The *Epilogue* outlines our reflections on some of the major issues emerging from writing this book, and reviews some open questions in the field.

Chapter 1

What Is Attachment Theory?

I see now that my insistence on spending that first night alone was more compli-
cated than it seemed, a primitive instinct. Of course I knew John was dead. Of
course I had already delivered the definitive news to his brother and to my brother
and to Quintana's husband. The New York Times *knew.* The Los Angeles Times
knew. Yet I was myself in no way prepared to accept this news as final: there was
a level on which I believed that what had happened remained reversible. That is
why I needed to be alone.

~ Didion, 2005, p. 32

On the evening of Dec. 30, 2003, Joan Didion, an award-winning novelist and
author, was preparing dinner for herself and her husband, John Gregory Dunne.
Shortly after he sat down at the table, he collapsed. The paramedics arrived and
attempted to revive him. By 10:18 pm he was pronounced dead.

Joan Didion and John Gregory Dunne had been married for nearly 40 years
and, in that time, they worked together, traveled together, and raised a daughter
together. The fact that, at one moment John was there and in the next he was
not, unraveled multiple threads in their entwined lives. Didion published a best-
selling book in 2005 that chronicled her efforts to understand the loss. Throughout her book, Didion returns to the phrase "it was an ordinary day" to capture
the idea that loss and tragedy can emerge from nowhere, without warning. But
she also uses this refrain to highlight the ways in which the loss of a loved one
can undo the ordinary. Mundane and perfunctory tasks, such as making dinner,
can become sources of pain and disorganization following a loss. The essence of
the loved one lingers in the ordinary; making efforts to carry on seem, at once,
hopeful and hopeless.

In attempting to find meaning in the events surrounding the loss, Didion
struggles to understand whether she was somehow responsible for John's death
and whether John himself knew what was going to happen. She tried to reconstruct from her memory omens—signs that the death had been foretold, such as
John suggesting that they dine at one of his favorite restaurants, as if it might
be his last opportunity to do so. Her sense is that she missed the telltale signs
and that, if she could turn back time, she could undo certain events and change
John's fate.

Adult Attachment. http://dx.doi.org/10.1016/B978-0-12-420020-3.00001-3

1

Didion characterizes the year following her husband's death as *The Year of Magical Thinking*. She describes a number of superstitious behaviors that appear to represent efforts to bring John back or to undo his death.

> *I could not give away the rest of his shoes. I stood there for a moment, then realized why: he would need shoes if he was to return. The recognition of this thought by no means eradicated the thought. I have still not tried to determine (say, by giving away the shoes) if the thought has lost its power. (p. 37)*

> *"Bringing him back" had been through those months my hidden focus, a magic trick. By late summer I was beginning to see this clearly. "Seeing it clearly" did not yet allow me to give away the clothes he would need (p. 44).*

Didion's book is a masterful exploration of loss by one of America's most celebrated writers. Part of what makes the book compelling is that she is able to articulate clearly a set of confusing experiences that are common among those who lose someone important to them. Many people who lose someone experience profound distress and despair. And their efforts to find their way without that loved one are some of the most challenging that people may face in their lives. Why should the loss of a loved one have such a profound impact on people's lives? Why do the bereaved behave in ways that, to others, may seem hopelessly lost, inexplicable, and even superstitious? Why do people engage "magical thinking" to bring their loved ones back?

ATTACHMENT THEORY

According to attachment theory (Bowlby, 1969/1982, 1973, 1980), the reactions described previously are mature and natural—not immature or magical—responses of a motivational system that originally emerged in the context of infancy. Specifically, attachment theory holds that the desire to be reunited with someone we love—someone who seems distant or inaccessible—is a manifestation of an instinct that evolved originally to keep infants in close proximity to potential caregivers.

Although attachment theory has been a popular theoretical framework for understanding infant–caregiver relationships for many years (eg, Karen, 1994), the theory has also become a prominent framework for understanding personality processes and close relationships in adulthood. One of the unique features of attachment theory—a feature that sets it apart from other theories in modern psychology—is its assumption that *the same kinds of dynamics that play out in infant–parent relationships also govern the way adults function in their close relationships.* For example, adults, like children, are more confident exploring the world when they believe that there is someone who is there to support and encourage them. Moreover, like children, adults get restless and anxious when they are separated from their loved ones for a prolonged period of time. And, just as some children are more secure in their relationships with their parents, some adults are more secure than others in their adult relationships, including those they have with parents, friends, and romantic partners.

The purpose of this book is to review contemporary theory and research on the way in which attachment dynamics play out in adulthood. Although we opened this chapter with a tale of loss, we should be clear from the outset that attachment theory is not merely a theory of grief; it is a theory of love, emotional connection, and psychological well-being. According to attachment theory, we all have a desire to be loved—to have a warm and supportive relationship with someone who understands us and advocates for us. Having such a relationship provides people with a sense of security, and facilitates their positive social and emotional development. But grief and love have something in common. Namely, they are both extraordinarily powerful emotional experiences that are governed by attachment processes. John Bowlby, the creator of attachment theory, articulated this theme well in the following oft-quoted passage:

> Many of the most intense emotions arise during the formation, the maintenance, the disruption, and the renewal of attachment relationships. The formation of a bond is described as falling in love, maintaining a bond as loving someone, and losing a partner as grieving over someone. Similarly, threat of loss arouses anxiety, and actual loss gives rise to sorrow; whilst each of these situations is likely to arouse anger. The unchallenged maintenance of a bond is experienced as a source of security, and the renewal of a bond as a source of joy. Because such emotions are usually a reflection of the state of a person's affectional bonds, the psychology and psychopathology of emotion is found to be in large part the psychology and psychopathology of affectional bonds. (Bowlby, 1980, p. 40)

In the current book we explain what attachment relationships are, how they develop, and how they contribute to adaptive—or maladaptive—interpersonal functioning. In addition to reviewing the core ideas underlying attachment theory, we also highlight some of the exciting new research developments that have taken place over the past decade, including the integration of attachment and social neuroscience, experimental interventions that can be used to probe attachment dynamics, and the implications of attachment theory for understanding psychological well-being and psychopathology in adulthood. Attachment theory has the potential to address many of the themes that are of interest to contemporary psychologists. Our goal is to highlight the current state of the art, illustrate the relevance of the theory for contemporary discourse, and, hopefully, inspire the next generation of scholarship.

The Origins of Attachment Theory

Bowlby's ideas regarding the profound effects of love and loss began to take shape in the early 1930s. While working in a home for delinquent boys, Bowlby was struck by the difficulties that many of the children experienced in forming close emotional bonds with others. After studying the family histories of the children, Bowlby learned that a disproportionate number of them had experienced severe disruptions in their early home lives. Many of the children had experienced the loss of their mother, had been separated from her repeatedly, or had been passed from one foster home to the next (Bowlby, 1944). Bowlby gradually came to believe that having a continuous, warm, and supportive relationship with a mother or mother-figure is essential for the development of mental health.

Bowlby proposed this hypothesis in a report commissioned by the World Health Organization (Bowlby, 1951). The report generated some controversy, but, overall, was well-received and helped catapult Bowlby into the international spotlight. Despite receiving recognition for his hypothesis regarding maternal deprivation, Bowlby was unsatisfied with his insights. Although it seemed clear to him that maternal deprivation could have deleterious consequences for social and emotional development, he felt that he did not have a full understanding of why that may be the case (Bowlby, 1969/1982).

Who was John Bowlby?

John Bowlby (1907–1990) was a British psychoanalyst who developed attachment theory. He is ranked as one of the 50 most eminent psychologists of the 20th century (Haggbloom et al., 2002).

Bowlby was born in London in 1907 as one of six children in an upper middle class family. Separation and loss were not merely academic topics for Bowlby. As a child, he did not have much contact with his mother, and most of the childcare in the Bowlby home was relegated to nursemaids in a separate wing of the house. Bowlby became particularly fond of one particular nanny. Unfortunately, she left the family when Bowlby was 4 years old. He was distraught by her departure and felt that he had lost a mother-figure. He did not establish an affectionate relationship with subsequent caretakers. Moreover, because his father was serving as a surgeon in World War I for several years, Bowlby had little contact with him. Bowlby was sent away to boarding school by age 10, further alienating him from his family relationships.

When Bowlby was of college age, he followed in his father's footsteps and went to study medicine at the University of Cambridge. During his studies, however, Bowlby realized he was more interested in understanding human development than medicine. He pursued his newfound interest by working at a school for maladjusted children, Priory Gates. During his work at the school, Bowlby began to appreciate the profound impact of early experiences on the development of children. There were two children in particular who made an impression on him. One child was extremely clingy (referred to as his "shadow;" Bretherton, 1992). This child tended to follow Bowlby around, as if he was starved of affection. The other child, who had been expelled from his previous school, behaved in a much more distant and cold manner toward Bowlby. In some respects, these children became templates for some of his developing views on how attachment behavior can be organized in distinct ways for children.

During his medical training, Bowlby enrolled at the British Psychoanalytic Institute where he worked with Joan Riviere and, eventually, Melanie Klein, who was one of the influential object relations theorists of the era. One of Klein's beliefs was that children's maladjustment was rooted in their fantasies regarding their mother. Bowlby, however, was coming to believe that children's maladjustment was due to actual, rather than imagined, experiences with their caregivers. This particular viewpoint, however, was not accepted by Bowlby's colleagues, and Klein in particular attempted to dissuade him of his views.

During World War II Bowlby was assigned to help with the development of officer selection procedures at the Tavistock Clinic in London. This experience provided Bowlby with an opportunity to learn research methods and statistics to a degree that was unusual for psychoanalysts of his time. This expertise would prove to be crucial for helping Bowlby systematically interrogate research from diverse disciplines as he began to flesh out his ideas on attachment. After the War, Bowlby became head of the Children's Department at the Tavistock Clinic, which he renamed the Department for Children and Parents, and began to pursue his interests in parent–child relationships more actively.

Although Bowlby's ideas about attachment began to be published as early as the 1940s, the "full" theory was presented in a three-volume series, *Attachment and Loss*, the first volume of which, *Attachment*, was published in 1969 and the final volume, *Loss*, published in 1980. His trilogy helped to organize the various ideas he had been developing over his career and provided an accessible means for disseminating his ideas about the importance of early attachment experiences and the role they may play in shaping personality development.

Bowlby began to explore maternal separation in more depth with James and Joyce Robertson at the Tavistock Clinic in the 1950s. The Robertsons had been especially interested in the ways in which otherwise well-adjusted children seemed to break down when separated temporarily from their parents, as might be the case when children were sent to hospital or when a mother was giving birth to a sibling. Indeed, nurseries were often dreary places. When separated from their mothers and placed in hospital nurseries, many children seemed listless and, in other cases, excessively vigilant to signs that their parents were returning (eg, magically transforming the sound of footsteps in the hallway to the sounds of their mother returning).

In their observations, the Robertsons and Bowlby noticed that children who had been separated from their parents often underwent a predictable series of emotional and behavioral reactions (Bowlby, Robertson, & Rosenbluth, 1952). The first stage, which Bowlby referred to as *protest*, was characterized by visible signs of distress, vocalizations (crying), and efforts to bring the caregiver back. Bowlby wrote that "the child appears acutely distressed at having lost his mother and seeks to recapture her by the full exercise of his limited resources. He will often cry loudly, shake his cot, throw himself about, and look eagerly towards any sight or sounds which might prove to be his missing mother" (Bowlby, 1969/1982, p. 27).

After a period of time, protest behavior wanes and the child becomes more listless and resigned to the situation. Bowlby referred to this phase as *despair* to highlight the parallels between the emotional and behavioral state of the child and patterns of depression often observed in adolescents and adults. He noted that the child's preoccupation with his or her mother is still apparent, although the child's behavior may indicate increasing hopelessness. Active physical movements diminish and the child may cry monotonously or intermittently. Bowlby writes that the child "is withdrawn and inactive, makes no demands on people in the environment, and appears to be in a state of deep mourning" (p. 27). According to Bowlby, this phase is sometimes taken as an indicator, often erroneously, of the attenuation of distress.

The third phase, labeled *detachment*, was critical in Bowlby's theorizing. He and his colleagues observed that, as the separation persists, the children would no longer reject the nurses. They would eventually begin to smile toward them, accept their invitations to play, and even initiate sociable interactions. For the nursing staff, this phase was often welcomed as a sign of recovery. But Bowlby observed that such signs sometimes betrayed a defensive maneuver on the part of the child. He wrote "When his mother visits, however, it can be seen that all is not well... So far from greeting his mother he may seem hardly to know her; so far from clinging to her he may remain remote and apathetic; instead of tears there is a listless turning away. He seems to have lost all interest in her" (p. 28). Indeed, in the first volume of his series on *Attachment and Loss*, Bowlby (1969/1982) described this as repression in the making to highlight the fact that the lack of interest in the parent was a defensive strategy on the child's part to divert his or her attention away from the sense of pain and rejection the child felt over the separation.

How can these responses be explained? According to the leading psycho-analytic frameworks of the time, the responses could be understood simply as immature reactions of an ego that has not yet fully developed or, alternatively, an ego that was "stuck" in an early stage of development. In addition, some observers claimed that the apparent distress of the children was due to being in a new environment or a lack of quality care by the hospital or nursery staff. But Bowlby was quick to point out that the children often found the new environment to be a source of adventure when the primary caregiver was present. It was the separation from a parent, in particular, that triggered distress. And in all of the cases that Bowlby and his colleagues observed, the children had more than adequate care and attention from the hospital or nursery staff. In short, Bowlby was not satisfied with common explanations for the behavior of children who had been separated from their parents. Thus, he began a quest to understand why separation is such a powerful force in the lives of children, why children respond in the way they do to these events, and the implications of disruptions in parent–child relationships for personality development. Unbeknown to him, the task he was about to undertake would occupy him in various ways for the rest of his life.

The Fundamentals of Attachment Theory

Why should a young child be so distressed simply by the loss of his mother? Why after return home does he become so apprehensive lest he lose her again? What psychological processes account for his distress and for the phenomenon of detachment? Before all, how do we understand the nature of the bond that ties a child to his mother? (Bowlby, 1969/1982, pp. 33–34)

Drawing on ethological theory, Bowlby (1969/1982) argued that "protest" behaviors, such as crying and searching, function to restore and maintain proximity to a primary caregiver—a strategy that would be adaptive for infants born without the capacity to defend or care for themselves. In the first volume of his trilogy he reviewed an extensive body of research on animal behavior, showing that animals born without the ability to fend for themselves are highly subject to predation and abuse. Bowlby argued that, over the course of evolutionary history, infants who were able to maintain proximity to an attachment figure would be more likely to survive to a reproductive age.

As a result of this evolutionary pressure, infants are born with relatively passive features, such as large eyes and cute smiles, which tend to make them appealing to potential caregivers. As infants get older, they are able to play a more active role in soliciting the attention and care of adults. Gradually, they begin to seek the attention of a specific caregiver, what Bowlby referred to as an *attachment figure*. They may selectively cry or protest when the attachment figure is not holding them, they may maintain visual contact with their caregiver when playing or exploring, and, as they learn to crawl, they will actively move toward a parent and reach upward to be held. Bowlby referred to these behaviors as *attachment behaviors* because (1) they signify an emotional bond that is developing between the infant and his or her attachment figure and (2) they function to maintain and restore a comfortable level of proximity or contact with the caregiver. Once these attachment behaviors have been mobilized and the caregiver attends to the child's attachment needs through the provision of help and support, the child experiences relief and other positive emotions, such as a sense of security.

Harlow's Research on Contact Comfort

When Bowlby was originally developing his theory of attachment, there were alternative theoretical perspectives on why infants were emotionally attached to their primary caregivers (most often, their biological mothers). Bowlby and other theorists, for example, believed that there was something important about the responsiveness and contact provided by mothers. Other theorists believed that young infants feel emotionally connected to their mothers because mothers satisfy fundamental needs, such as the need for food. That is, the child comes to feel emotionally connected to the mother because she is associated with the reduction of primary drives, such as hunger, rather than the reduction of drives that might be relational in nature.

In a classic set of studies, psychologist Harry Harlow (1958) placed young monkeys in cages that contained two artificial, surrogate "mothers." One of those surrogates was a simple wire contraption; the other was a wire contraption covered in cloth. Both of the surrogate mothers were equipped with a feeding tube so that Harlow and his colleagues had the option to allow the surrogate to deliver or not deliver milk. Harlow found that the young macaques spent a disproportionate amount of time with the cloth surrogate as opposed to the wire surrogate. Moreover, this was true even when the infants were fed by the wire surrogate rather than the cloth surrogate. This suggests that the strong emotional bond that infants form with their primary caregivers is rooted in something more than whether the caregiver provides food per se. Harlow's research is now regarded as one of the first experimental demonstrations of the importance of "contact comfort" in the establishment of infant–caregiver bonds, and his work was featured prominently in Bowlby's writings on attachment.

According to Bowlby, attachment behaviors are regulated by an instinctual motivational system, the *attachment behavioral system*, which was gradually "designed" by natural selection to regulate proximity to attachment figures. We elaborate on this concept in detail later in the chapter, but, for now, we note that the psychological dynamics of the attachment system are similar to those of a homeostatic control system, in which a set goal is maintained by the constant monitoring of signals with continuous behavioral adjustment. In the case of the attachment system, the set goal is physical or psychological proximity to an attachment figure and a sense of security (what Sroufe & Waters, 1977a called *felt security*). When a child perceives the attachment figure to be nearby and responsive, he or she experiences security and is more likely to explore the environment and engage socially with others. However, when the child perceives a threat to the relationship or to his or her well-being, the child experiences feelings of anxiety, fear, or distress, and engages in proximity-seeking behavior to gain the attention and comfort of his or her attachment figure. From an evolutionary perspective, these dynamics help to ensure the child's safety and protection, and ultimately his or her reproductive fitness.

Individual Differences in Attachment Organization

Although Bowlby believed that these basic emotional and behavioral responses were representative of the normative functioning of the attachment behavioral system, he recognized that there are individual differences in the way children appraise the accessibility of the attachment figure and how they regulate their attachment behavior in response to threats. However, it was not until his coworker, Mary Ainsworth, began to systematically study infant–parent separations that researchers began to formally study individual differences in the regulation of attachment behavior.

Who Was Mary Ainsworth?

Mary Ainsworth (1913–1999) was an American–Canadian developmental psychologist, ranked among the 100 most influential psychologists of the 20th century (Haggbloom et al., 2002). She earned her BA in 1935, her Master's degree in 1936, and her PhD in developmental psychology in 1939, all from the University of Toronto. At Toronto she took courses with William Blatz who had introduced her to security theory (Blatz, 1940)—a theory that both reformulated and challenged Freudian ideas.

Ainsworth taught at the University of Toronto for a few years before joining the Canadian Women's Army Corps in 1942 during World War II. After getting married, Ainsworth moved to London, England, where she joined Bowlby's team at the Tavistock Clinic. While at Tavistock, Ainsworth became involved with the research project investigating the effects of maternal separation on children's personality development. During this time, she developed her research interests in children's sense of security and set her sights on conducting a longitudinal field study of mother–infant interaction to further examine the development of mother–child relationships in a natural setting. She got her chance to conduct this study in 1954 when she left the Tavistock Clinic to follow her husband to Africa.

Ainsworth studied the interactions of mothers and their infants at their homes in Uganda. She spent approximately 72 hours of observation per dyad. The data from those observations were published years later after she became a faculty member at Johns Hopkins University (Ainsworth, 1967). Ainsworth found that while the majority of the mother–infant interactions involved comfort and security, some were tense and conflicted. She also found evidence that suggested the patterns of interactions between mothers and their infants were related to the level of responsiveness that the mothers showed their infants. Ultimately, this work helped to motivate Ainsworth's development of the strange situation—the first paradigm used for assessing individual differences in the way infants organize their attachment behavior.

Ainsworth, Blehar, Waters, and Wall (1978) developed a procedure called the *strange situation*—a widely used laboratory paradigm for studying infant–parent attachment. In the strange situation, 12-month-old infants and one of their parents are observed in the laboratory as they are systematically separated from and reunited with one another. Of particular interest is the behavior of infants when reunited with their primary caregivers. In the strange situation, most infants (ie, about 60%) become upset when the parent leaves the room, but, when he or she returns, they actively seek the parent and are easily comforted by him or her. Children who exhibit this pattern of behavior are often called *secure*.[1] Other children (about 20% or less) are ill-at-ease

---

1. Initially, Ainsworth et al. (1978) emphasized the classificatory labels Group A, B, and C to refer to the different attachment patterns observed in the strange situation. They did this partly because they did not want the category label to bias the understanding of the category itself. Over time, however, scholars gradually came to use the descriptive labels from Ainsworth's writings. Today, these are often simplified further as secure, resistant, and avoidant.

initially, and, upon separation, become extremely distressed. Importantly, when reunited with their parents, these children have a difficult time being soothed, and often exhibit conflicting behaviors that suggest they want to be comforted, but that they also want to "punish" the parent for leaving. These children are often called *insecure-resistant* or *anxious-ambivalent*. A third pattern of attachment that Ainsworth et al. documented is called *insecure-avoidant*. Avoidant children (about 20%) do not appear overly distressed by the separation, and, upon reunion, actively avoid seeking contact with their parent, sometimes turning their attention to play with objects on the laboratory floor.

Although the Ainsworth et al. (1978) coding system initially resulted in only three categories, additional categories were later added. For example, a fourth classification was added by Ainsworth's student Mary Main (Main & Solomon, 1990) termed *disorganized/disoriented attachment*. Disorganized children exhibit behavior that appears either confused or not coordinated in a way to achieve the goals of the attachment system. Main and Hesse (1990) found that most mothers of children with a disorganized classification had suffered major losses or other trauma shortly before or after the birth of the infant and had reacted by becoming severely depressed.

Ainsworth's work is not without its limitations or criticisms (eg, Lamb, Thompson, Gardner, Charnov, & Estes, 1984; Rothbaum, Weisz, Pott, Miyake, & Morelli, 2000). Nonetheless, her research has been important for at least three reasons. First, she provided one of the first empirical demonstrations of how attachment behavior is patterned in both safe and threatening contexts. Moreover, she provided a systematic procedure that researchers could use to study the conditions that activate and modulate attachment-related behavior. Second, her work led to the first empirical taxonomy of individual differences in infant attachment patterns. Indeed, the majority of attachment research over the past few decades has been inspired directly by this taxonomy. And, although the details of the taxonomic system have changed across time, the emphasis on individual differences led researchers to try to understand what makes some children secure versus insecure and the implications of those patterns for social and emotional development (see chapters: How Do Individual Differences in Attachment Develop?; What Are Attachment Working Models?). Third, Ainsworth demonstrated that these individual differences were related to observations of infant–parent interactions in the home during the first year of life. Children who were classified as secure in the strange situation, for example, tended to have parents who were responsive to their needs. Infants who were classified as insecure in the strange situation (ie, anxious-resistant or avoidant) often had parents who were insensitive to their needs and engaged in inconsistent or rejecting care. Thus, Ainsworth's research was crucial for establishing attachment theory as a framework for understanding personality development and individual differences.

Working Models of Attachment

During the early months of life, the degree of security an infant experiences is believed to depend largely on exogenous signals, such as the proximate availability and responsiveness of primary caregivers. Over repeated interactions, however, children develop a set of knowledge structures, or *internal working models*, that represent those interactions and contribute to the regulation of the attachment system (Bretherton & Munholland, 2008; see chapter: What Are Attachment Working Models?). If caregivers are generally warm, responsive, and consistently available, the child learns that he or she is worthy of love, and that others can be counted upon when needed. Consequently, he or she is likely to explore the world confidently, initiate warm and sociable interactions with others, and feel secure in the knowledge that a caregiver is available if needed (see chapter: How Do Individual Differences in Attachment Develop?). In short, the child develops secure working models of attachment. Conversely, if attachment figures are cold, rejecting, unpredictable, frightening, or insensitive, the child learns he or she is not worthy of being loved, and that others cannot be counted on for support and comfort. This knowledge is embodied in insecure working models of attachment. The child is likely to regulate his or her behavior accordingly—either by excessively demanding attention and care, or by withdrawing from others and attempting to achieve a high degree of self-sufficiency (DeWolff & van IJzendoorn, 1997). Collectively, these experiences are believed to shape two important components of working models: the representations that people develop about themselves (models of self) and the representations they construct about others (models of others). As we explain in the chapter: What Are Attachment Working Models?, these representations can vary in their valence (ie, they can be positive or negative) and organize much of the content underlying people's self-concepts and the attitudes and expectations they have about others.

The working models concept plays a vital role in attachment theory for several reasons. Most importantly, it highlights the role that early experiences play in shaping personality development. As we explain in more detail in the chapter: How Do Individual Differences in Attachment Develop?, many theories in social and personality psychology are focused on individual differences, including differences in basic personality traits, political ideology, social acceptance, and aggressive tendencies. But few theories attempt to explain the developmental antecedents of those individual differences. The working models construct provides a means to describe the kinds of differences that exist, while also providing a means to understand how they come to exist and are sustained across time.

The other reason the working models concept is important is that it provides the theoretical intersection between cognitive science and attachment theory. As we describe in more depth later in the chapter, one of Bowlby's challenges was to create a theory that could not only explain the intense distress experienced by children who had been separated from their caregivers, but could also explain how interpersonal experiences are internalized by children. He imported ideas from cognitive psychology to better understand how interpersonal episodes are encoded and represented in the mind, how memory systems are structured, how attentional processes can be modulated in the service of defensive goals, and how the vagaries of interpersonal experience can lead to both convergence and divergence in the mental representations that children construct (eg, Bowlby, 1980). Indeed, this intersection continues to be alive and well in modern attachment research (eg, Dykas & Cassidy, 2011). In the chapter: What Can Social Cognition and Priming Tell Us About Attachment?, for example, we will review contemporary research on how priming methods have been used to investigate the dynamics of attachment in adulthood.

The Shift to Adult Attachment

Although Bowlby and Ainsworth were primarily focused on understanding the nature of infant–caregiver relationships, they believed that attachment characterized human experience and behavior from "the cradle to the grave" (Bowlby, 1979, p. 129). There are two ways in which this theme has become relevant in modern research.

First, Bowlby believed that attachment-related experiences have implications for social and emotional functioning across the lifespan. In other words, attachment theory is not merely a theory about infant–parent relationships, one that begins and ends in childhood; it is a theory about how attachment-related experiences shape interpersonal functioning across the life course. In his work on juvenile delinquents, for example, Bowlby argued that one reason why the adolescents he studied seemed cold, aloof, and unable to form close emotional bonds was that these children lacked a secure foundation for developing close relationships with others due to disruptions in their early attachment relationships (Bowlby, 1944). For Bowlby, understanding interpersonal and emotional functioning in adulthood required understanding the person's attachment history. Indeed, it is this particular feature of attachment theory that makes it a central one in modern research on personality development and clinical psychology. As we discuss in chapter: What Are the Implications of Attachment Processes for Psychopathology and Therapy?, attachment theory assumes that disruptions in attachment-related experiences, and the internalization of such experiences via working models, have the potential to function as risk factors in the development of psychopathology.

Second, theorists have argued that the attachment behavioral system itself continues to play a role in adulthood; it does not merely recede into the background as children get older. For example, Weiss (1982) suggested that attachment figures in adulthood do not have to be protective figures, but rather they can be seen as "fostering the attached individual's own capacity for mastering challenge" (Weiss, 1982, p. 173). Even in adulthood, Weiss (1982) claimed, attachment relationships provide feelings of safety and security, and without them people feel lonely and restless. Weiss (1975) further suggested that the behavioral elements of attachment in adult life should be similar to those observed in infancy. Indeed, adults do show a desire for proximity to their attachment figure when stressed, increased comfort in the presence of the attachment figure, and anxiety when the attachment figure is inaccessible (see also Ainsworth, 1989).

Building on Weiss's (1975, 1982) ideas, Hazan and Shaver (1987) argued that the emotional bond that develops between adult romantic partners is partly a function of the same motivational system—the attachment behavioral system—that gives rise to the emotional bond between infants and their caregivers. Hazan and Shaver observed that in both kinds of relationship, people feel safe when the other is nearby and responsive; they engage in close, intimate, bodily contact; they feel insecure when the other is inaccessible; they share their discoveries with their attachment figure; they exhibit a mutual fascination and preoccupation with one another; and they engage in "baby talk."

On the basis of these similarities, Hazan and Shaver (1987) and Shaver, Hazan, and Bradshaw (1988) argued that the attachment system underlies adult romantic love. The idea that romantic relationships may function as attachments has had a profound influence on the social psychological study of relationships. Researchers have examined, for example, how attachment-related functions develop in the context of marriage (Creasey & Jarvis, 2009; Kobak & Hazan, 1991), how secure versus insecure people communicate with one another (Feeney, 1994), and how a person's security can shape conflict in marital life (Domingue & Mollen, 2009). Even the process of relationship dissolution itself has come to be understood as an attachment process: one that involves protest, despair, and detachment (Hazan & Shaver, 1992; Weiss, 1975).

Although there are many similarities in the way infant–caregiver and adult romantic relationships function, there are a few crucial differences too (see chapter: What Is an Attachment Relationship?). First, in the context of infant–parent attachment, there is a clear asymmetry in the attachment–caregiving dialectic. Namely, the infant is said to be attached to the parent; it is not assumed that the parent is attached to the infant. This is not to say that the parent does not experience a strong and profound affectional bond toward the infant, but the parent's role is that of a caregiver. In romantic relationships, however, there tends to be a balance between attachment and caregiving. On some occasions, one person may require comfort or support while the other partner provides that support; on other occasions the roles may be reversed. Regardless, in adult romantic relationships both partners are likely to be attached to each other and function as attachment figures for one another.

A second critical distinction concerns sexuality. Many romantic relationships begin not because people happen to find themselves attached to someone; they often begin due to mutual physical attraction or sexual interest. And although certain intimate behaviors, such as holding hands, kissing, and cuddling, might be common in both parent–child and romantic relationships, behavior of an explicitly sexual nature is typically reserved for romantic partners (Hazan & Zeifman, 1994). The bottom line is that, although the bond that links romantic partners often involves attachment, it also involves sexuality, and that alone makes romantic relationships qualitatively different from infant–parent relationships. We discuss the intersection of attachment and sexuality in more depth in the chapter: What Is the Attachment Behavioral System? And, How Is It Linked to Other Behavioral Systems?.

Are Individual Differences in Adult Attachment Similar to Those Identified in Children?

One of the enduring contributions of Hazan and Shaver's (1987) work was the idea that the same kinds of individual differences that characterize infants in the strange situation (ie, secure, anxious-ambivalent, and anxious-avoidant) also characterize the way adults approach close relationships. They observed, for example, that most adults are relatively secure in their relationships: they are comfortable opening up to others, using others for support, and having others depend on them. Other people, in contrast, appear to have difficulty opening up to others and, in many cases, they avoid intimacy as a way to prevent themselves from feeling vulnerable. Yet, others may desire closeness and intimacy, but come across as insecure, prone to loneliness, and excessively clingy. To capture these differences, Hazan and Shaver (1987) created short paragraphs that described the adult analogs of the strange situation types and asked adult participants to indicate which of the three descriptions best captured their thoughts, feelings, and behaviors in close relationships (Table 1.1). In their initial survey work, Hazan and Shaver (1987)

TABLE 1.1 Hazan and Shaver's (1987) Attachment Style Descriptions

____ I am somewhat uncomfortable being close to others; I find it difficult to trust them completely, difficult to allow myself to depend on them. I am nervous when anyone gets too close, and often, others want me to be more intimate than I feel comfortable being. (*Avoidant*)

____ I find that others are reluctant to get as close as I would like. I often worry that my partner doesn't really love me or won't want to stay with me. I want to get very close to my partner, and this sometimes scares people away. (*Anxious-ambivalent*)

____ I find it relatively easy to get close to others and am comfortable depending on them and having them depend on me. I don't worry about being abandoned or about someone getting too close to me. (*Secure*) found that the relative proportions of adults who endorsed secure, anxious-ambivalent, and avoidant descriptions were similar to the corresponding base rates of each attachment pattern in the strange situation (see chapter: How Are Individual Differences in Attachment Measured? for an in-depth discussion).

The study of adult attachment patterns, or what many social and personality psychologists refer to as *attachment styles* (eg, Levy & Davis, 1988), has been one of the most popular areas of adult attachment research. Researchers have examined how attachment styles develop (chapter: How Do Individual Differences in Attachment Develop?), the implications they have for emotion regulation and interpersonal behavior (chapters: What Are Attachment Working Models?; What Is the Attachment Behavioral System? And, How Is It Linked to Other Behavioral Systems?; What Are the Implications of Attachment Processes for Psychopathology and Therapy?), the cognitive processes that characterize the way people with different attachment styles function (chapters: What Are Attachment Working Models?; What Can Social Cognition and Priming Tell us About Attachment?; What Are the Effects of Context on Attachment?), and what kinds of experiences promote stability and change in attachment styles (chapters: How Stable Are Attachment Styles in Adulthood?; What Can Social Cognition and Priming Tell us About Attachment?).

The way attachment styles have been conceptualized and measured over the last 4 decades has evolved considerably; modern researchers rarely study the three attachment types that Hazan and Shaver (1987) emphasized in their early research. We discuss the ways in which these taxonomies and measurement systems have evolved in the chapter: How Are Individual Differences in Attachment Measured?, but for now, we note that one of the common ways of conceptualizing attachment styles is a variant of a model originally proposed by Bartholomew and Horowitz (1991). This model assumes that there are four, rather than three, major styles of attachment: secure, fearful, preoccupied, and dismissing. The secure and preoccupied categories are analogs to Hazan and Shaver's secure and anxious-ambivalent attachment styles, whereas the dismissing and fearful styles reflect a split of Hazan and Shaver's avoidant attachment category. Specifically, *fearful avoidance* reflects a form of avoidance that is rooted in feelings of vulnerability and insecurity. In contrast, *dismissing avoidance* is a form of avoidance that is rooted in a desire to be independent and self-reliant (Bartholomew, 1990).

These four attachment styles are often represented with respect to two major dimensions (Fig. 1.1A), what modern researchers often refer to as *attachment anxiety* and *attachment avoidance* (eg, Brennan, Clark, & Shaver, 1998).[2] Attachment anxiety is characterized by low self-worth and a fear of abandonment and rejection (Brennan et al., 1998; Karantzas, Feeney, & Wilkinson, 2010).

---

2. Different writers have slightly different ways of labeling these dimensions. For example, some writers refer to the anxiety dimension as "attachment-related anxiety" to differentiate it from a more general sense of anxiety. Others refer to it as "anxious attachment" or "attachment anxiety." Despite these subtle differences, the various terms refer to the same key dimensions described here.

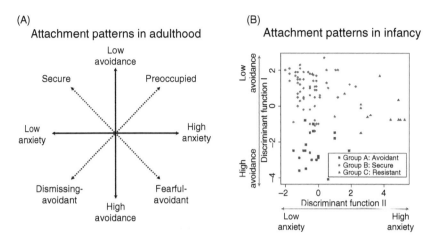

FIGURE 1.1   Attachment patterns in adulthood and infancy. (A) Illustrates the four-category model of adult attachment, based on Bartholomew and Horowitz (1991). In this diagram, the four attachment styles are represented in a two-dimensional space, anchored by the dimensions of attachment anxiety and attachment avoidance. (B) Illustrates the distribution of the three major infant attachment patterns (avoidant, secure, resistant) in a two-dimensional space, based on Ainsworth et al. (1978). The horizontal axis represents variation in anger and resistance, which we have labeled "anxiety" here for continuity. The vertical axis represents variation in proximity seeking versus avoidant strategies, which we have labeled "avoidance."

People high on the dimension of attachment anxiety tend to rely on hyperactivating attachment strategies (Mikulincer & Shaver, 2003, 2007a). Thus, they tend to be hypersensitive to signs of love (Eastwick & Finkel, 2008) or threats of rejection (Mikulincer, Gillath, & Shaver, 2002). When coping with such threats they experience cognitions and emotions that reflect heightened distress and intensify their efforts to seek proximity to an attachment figure (Gillath, Bunge, Shaver, Wendelken, & Mikulincer, 2005).

Avoidant attachment is characterized by a discomfort with closeness, excessive self-reliance, and a lack of confidence in depending on others to meet needs for comfort and security (Brennan et al., 1998; Karantzas et al., 2010). People high on the dimension of avoidance tend to rely on deactivating attachment strategies (Mikulincer & Shaver, 2003, 2007a). Thus, they tend to ignore or suppress cues related to emotions, love, and relationships. When coping with threats they experience cognitions and emotions that reflect either the suppression of or disassociation from distress and the suppression and minimization of proximity-seeking efforts toward an attachment figure.

Importantly, dimensions similar to attachment anxiety and avoidance also exist in the behavior of children in the strange situation (Brennan et al., 1998). When Ainsworth et al. (1978) published their groundbreaking work on attachment patterns, they reported a discriminant function analysis based on a variety of codes of child behavior, including angry-resistant behavior, contact seeking, contact maintenance, and avoidance. The original three patterns they emphasized could be located within a two-dimensional space defined by weighted combination of these behavioral codes (Fig. 1.1B). Fraley and Spieker (2003), analyzing data from a separate sample of strange situation behavior, showed that these dimensions could be construed as *anger and resistance*, which, like attachment anxiety, reflects a hyperactivation of attachment-related behavior and affect, and *proximity seeking versus avoidance*, which, like attachment avoidance in the two-dimensional model, reflects a propensity to seek out others or withdraw from them.

The two-dimensional system has been an influential one in modern attachment research. Thus, we describe it in more depth in chapters: What Are Attachment Working Models?; How Are Individual Differences in Attachment Measured?, along with the history that led to it from the original three-type model proposed by Hazan and Shaver (1987). But, for now, we want readers to be aware of the basics of the most commonly used taxonomy of individual differences in adult attachment research and to appreciate that, despite variation in terminology across different taxonomies, at their core, all systems emphasize secure and insecure patterns of relating to others.

WHAT ARE ATTACHMENT THEORY'S INTELLECTUAL ORIGINS? THE INTEGRATION OF PSYCHOANALYTIC PSYCHOLOGY, ETHOLOGY, AND CONTROL SYSTEMS

Bowlby was originally trained as a psychoanalyst, and, as such, he naturally began developing his theory of attachment from a psychoanalytic perspective. Nonetheless, he gradually came to believe that psychoanalytic theory was not capable of explaining some of the phenomena he was seeking to explain. His psychoanalytic colleagues, for example, often emphasized the role of fantasies and wishes in their efforts to understand dysregulated behavior on the part of children. But it was apparent to Bowlby that real, rather than imaginary, experiences were giving rise to the symptoms he observed. He gradually began to assemble a new theoretical perspective, one that had its origins in psychoanalytic theory, but also brought together emerging themes in ethology (Hinde, 1970), cognitive science (Pantin, 1965), developmental science (Piaget, 1937/1954), and the principles of control systems and information theory (eg, Miller, Galanter, & Pribram, 1960). In this section we explain how his theory developed, how he integrated various ideas from disparate intellectual traditions, and, ultimately, what sets his theory apart from other theories in psychology.

The Departure from Psychoanalysis

Bowlby positioned himself against psychoanalysis by highlighting several key points of departure (Bowlby, 1969/1982). First, psychoanalytic methods were primarily concerned with *retrospective* methodology. A patient presents with a problem and the analyst then attempts to reconstruct the series of events or experiences that may have led to the outcome under investigation. The method is, ultimately, a historical one and, more often than not, based on the recollections of adult patients who are reflecting on their childhood experiences. Although Bowlby was not opposed to the use of retrospective methods per se, his observations suggested that it was possible to study "pathology in the making" among children. Moreover, by starting from real observations of children and tracing the consequences of those experiences, Bowlby believed it would be possible to better understand personality development.

The second key difference, which is not wholly distinct from the first, was to *start with potential pathogenic agents* and uncover their outcomes rather than to start with the outcomes and to attempt to infer their causes. In Bowlby's case, the pathological agent of interest was "the loss of a mother-figure during the period between about six months and six years of age" (Bowlby, 1969/1982, p. 5). As we will illustrate throughout this book, attachment researchers have not limited themselves to the study of separation and loss exclusively; many researchers inspired by the theory have focused on individual differences in the quality of the care received by children—whether their caregivers are responsive and sensitive to their needs. Other researchers have focused on individual differences in the representations (internal working models) individuals have about themselves and significant others. But, for Bowlby, it was absolutely critical to identify a specific experiential factor—regardless of what it was—and to trace the consequences of that experience prospectively.

The third key difference involves the source of the data that are used to understand development. Namely, psychoanalytic sessions largely involve the analysis of associations and meanings, as derived from dreams, free association, and other methods. These associations become the data upon which the causes of pathology were inferred. Bowlby's approach was different. Namely, he wanted to use the *direct observation* of children who had been separated from their mothers as the core source of data to examine the development of pathology.

Due to the differences between Bowlby's approach and that of psychoanalysis, Bowlby's ideas were met with significant resistance by the psychoanalytic community. Nonetheless, it is important to note that Bowlby viewed himself as a steward of Freud's legacy and not an iconoclast (Waters, Crowell, Elliott, Corcoran, & Treboux, 2002). Like Freud, Bowlby was interested in explaining enduring issues pertaining to love, hate, ambivalence, security, mourning, and psychological defense.

Although Bowlby appeared to believe that Freud would agree with many of the revisions he had made to the methods and foundations of psychoanalysis, he recognized that their approaches differed in at least one way that was irreconcilable. Namely, Bowlby abandoned the psychic energy model advocated by Freud and his followers in favor of one that combined ethological approaches on instincts with control theory (later in the chapter). Freud's ideas concerning drive and instinct were at the heart of psychoanalytic metatheory. In Freud's model, energy (eg, sexual energy) builds over time and, eventually, needs to be discharged. When it cannot be discharged in socially appropriate ways, it does not simply dissipate. Instead, it has to be channeled into other outlets, sometimes pathological ones, such that the total amount of energy is held constant. This may lead individuals to get fixated at certain developmental stages, potentially handicapping their emotional development.

Ultimately, Freud was using scientific metaphors (eg, energy and its conservation) that were popular in his time to ground his thinking about the human mind. And this is precisely what Bowlby did too—with full awareness of this fact. Bowlby's objective was to create a new way of thinking about motivation and instinct—one that would enable him to explain why infants develop strong emotional attachments to their primary caregivers, why the disruption of that bond is so stressful, and why the maintenance of that bond is critical for personality development.

Ethology and the Problem of Instinct

To address these issues, Bowlby found inspiration in the emerging ethological theories of instinct and behavior that were gaining popularity in the 1940s. Bowlby was struck by the fact that many behavioral conflicts and pathologies observed in animals who are reared under unusual conditions (eg, away from parents or under stress) had parallels with those observed in humans. Many animals, for example, appear to develop pathological fixations, experience conflict behavior (eg, approach–avoidance conflict), and display displacement activity. Bowlby was also impressed by research on instinct that had been conducted by scholars studying animal behavior. Early ethologists, for example, had conducted extensive experiments on how young animals respond appropriately to specific stimuli without necessarily having learned to do so. Tinbergen (1951), for example, was well-known for his food-begging work in herring gulls. Hatchling birds do not forage for their own food. Instead, they must be fed predigested food from adults. To obtain the food, hatchlings peck at the parent's bill, a behavior that they are capable of exhibiting shortly after hatching. Experimental research by Tinbergen showed that the pecking response could be activated by presenting hatchlings with a red spot, one that is similar in color and contrast to that of a parent's lower mandible. By presenting a variety of models that varied in color, size, and contrast, Tinbergen was able to identify the configuration of stimuli that activated the pecking response, showing that red patterns were often preferred to others, even when presented on disembodied sticks.

Bowlby adopted many ethological ideas into his developing framework. But one of the limitations of ethological models, at least from Bowlby's perspective, was that they often seemed to equate instinctual behavior with behavior that is largely unmodified by experience and learning. As a result, there was a tendency among students of animal behavior to develop separate classes of theoretical models for what they viewed as built-in behavior programs (ie, instinct, drives) and behavior that is acquired (ie, shaped by learning or conditioning processes). Bowlby did not view these as separate classes of behavior. Instead, he believed that classically instinctive and learned behavior represented two ends of a continuum. In his words, the distinction between innate versus acquired needed to be "cast into limbo" (Bowlby, 1969/1982, p. 38), a sentiment that continues to be expressed decades later by behavioral researchers.

In Bowlby's view, *environmental lability*—the extent to which a behavioral response is influenced by the environment—was the critical factor that would determine whether a behavior could be modified. Some behaviors are executed in relatively rigid ways. For example, the funnel-building wasp from Australia lays its larva underground and then builds a connecting stem above the ground with a bell-shaped funnel (see Gould & Gould, 2007). The funnel faces away from the tunnel at an angle that makes it difficult for other animals and insects to gain entrance. If one intervenes and disturbs the funnel, instead of repairing the damage, the wasp will build another funnel on top of it, creating in some cases an endless helix of bell-shaped structures. In short, the wasps' funnel-building program appears to be activated under basic conditions and is executed even in situations in which it is unnecessary. In contrast, other behavioral responses are highly contingent on environmental molding. For example, shortly after hatching, many species of birds will imprint upon the first moving object they see. They will follow the object around and, for all intents and purposes, treat it as the mother. Fortunately, under natural conditions, that object is likely to be their mother. However, as ethologists have demonstrated, if another object is presented to a gosling shortly after hatching, the gosling will follow that object around too, and even attempt to mate with physically similar objects when they reach sexual maturity (Lorenz, 1937, 1970). Like the funnel wasp, there are elements of the gosling's behavior that seem stereotyped and rigid. But, in the latter case, the system requires experience-dependent calibration; it does not have an inherited "template" that it can use to identify the mother after hatching.

A key idea in Bowlby's theory is that the plasticity and rigidity of behavior do not emerge from fundamentally distinct mechanisms (ie, those that are innate vs. those that are acquired). He believed that the same kinds of behavioral programs that enable a funnel wasp to behave in a sequenced and inflexible manner also give rise to more sophisticated and flexible patterns of behavior. It is not that instincts are resilient to environmental inputs and learned behaviors are not, rather instinctual behavior can vary in the extent to which it is organized by feedback from the environment.

According to Bowlby, one reason behavioral systems need to retain some degree of plasticity is that they are designed to function in circumstances that are not fully predictable. The behavior of the funnel-building wasp, for example, is adaptive only to the extent to which humans are not intervening in their architecture to satisfy their scientific curiosity. But in most circumstances, the raw behavioral programs will operate appropriately and very little environmental feedback is required for the nest to be built successfully.

However, many behavioral responses, according to Bowlby, lie somewhere between the extremes of environmental plasticity and insensitivity. We may, for example, have inherited cognitive machinery for communicating with others, but the specific language we speak, the dialect we intone, and the specific words we choose may be largely dependent upon the culture in which we are raised. Likewise, because an infant may not be prewired to know what his or her parent looks like, the instinctual systems underlying attachment must use environmental feedback to gather the appropriate information and fine-tune the system accordingly. In this sense, *learning represents the calibration of instincts*.

Control Systems and Information Theory

How can experiences help calibrate instinctual systems? To solve this problem, Bowlby turned to machines and, more specifically, the concept of control systems. Why machines? When it comes to theorizing about human behavior, intention, and purpose, it is difficult to do so without engaging in circular reasoning. Why does a person eat? Because he or she is hungry. How do we know a person is hungry? Because he or she just ate. One potential solution to this problem is to consider what it would take to build a machine that, ultimately, lacks intention (see Dennett, 1993), but behaves in a manner that is purposeful. To do so, Bowlby turned his attention to the work on cybernetics—an early version of what came to be known as information theory or artificial intelligence.

One of the simplest control systems is that of a regulator. A *regulator* is simply a mechanism that is designed to maintain a constant condition. The example Bowlby (1969/1982) used that is still relevant today is that of a thermostat. A thermostat is designed to maintain a room at a specified temperature. To do so, it compares the actual temperature of the room against a set-value or set-point. When there is a discrepancy between the actual temperature, T, and the set-value, the heater may be powered on. And once the discrepancy has been reduced adequately, the heater is powered off (Fig. 1.2). The comparison process (ie, the comparison of an environmental state against an internalized set-value) is central to the way the thermostat behaves: An environmental signal is compared against a value to determine whether there is a discrepancy and whether certain actions should be invoked.

One of the powerful features of a simple mechanism like this is that it is highly flexible. It can be used to heat or cool a room, for example, by taking into consideration whether the discrepancy is positive or negative. Moreover, the comparator can be modified to take into account rates of change. For example, the cooling mechanism might be amped up in proportion to the discrepancy detected and may be run at a lower level when the discrepancy is trivial. Importantly, the basic machinery can be *replicated*, making it possible to reproduce the same system in ways that can be used by multiple individuals.

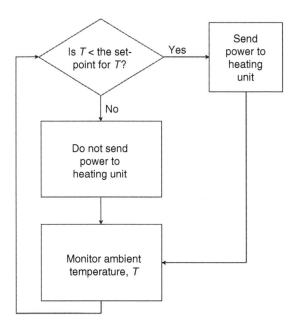

FIGURE 1.2   A control diagram for a simple thermostat.

One of Bowlby's important insights was that instinctual behavior often operates in ways that are similar to a basic thermostat. Namely, instincts that are responsive to environmental inputs are essentially *behavioral control systems* (see chapter: What Is the Attachment Behavioral System? And, How Is It Linked to Other Behavioral Systems?). The core blueprints for their operation are shaped by natural selection rather than human engineers. But the outputs of the systems are not insensitive to environmental inputs; indeed, they are critically dependent upon them. Organisms that behave in ways that directly or indirectly facilitate survival and reproduction are more likely to have behavioral machinery represented in the next generation. The success of the behavioral system is gauged by the extent to which it produces predictable outcomes within a range of environments that are characteristic of the environment in which the system evolved, what Bowlby called the "environment of [evolutionary] adaptiveness" (Bowlby, 1969, p. 47).

Bowlby used this cybernetic framework to explain how attachment behavior is organized, the conditions that activate it, and the conditions that lead to its cessation. At the heart of the *attachment behavioral system* lies a comparison process. It essentially asks the question "Is the attachment figure nearby, accessible, or attentive?" When the attachment figure is judged to be sufficiently nearby or accessible, the person feels secure and, behaviorally, is likely to explore the environment, be sociable, or attend to nonattachment-related concerns. However, when the comparator process determines that the caregiver

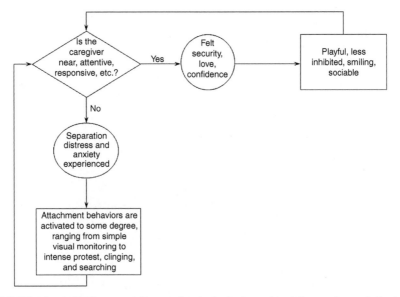

FIGURE 1.3   A simple control diagram for the basic dynamics of the attachment behavior system. (*Adapted from Fraley and Shaver, 2000.*)

is not as accessible as desired, the child experiences varying degrees of anxiety and distress and, behaviorally, engages in attachment-related behaviors, such as scanning the environment for signs of the attachment figure, distress vocalizations, or moving toward the attachment figure's assumed location. If these actions reunite the infant with his or her attachment figure, the discrepancy is reduced. If they do not, a profound sense of distress and hopelessness may set in (Fig. 1.3).

As we elaborate in chapter: What Is the Attachment Behavioral System? And, How Is It Linked to Other Behavioral Systems?, Bowlby also claimed that the attachment system, like any other behavioral system, has a set goal (proximity to a primary caregiver or felt security), a biological function (protection), triggers or activating conditions (eg, separation, illness, fear), and terminating conditions (bodily contact with the attachment object; restoration of security). The important point to appreciate for now is that the control systems framework, combined with an evolutionary context, allowed Bowlby to explain why children behave the way they do when separated from their parents, how the machinery could be replicated across generations, and, importantly, how the operating parameters of the system could be calibrated by actual experience. This enabled him not only to put forth a powerful framework for understanding attachment and its development, but also to situate his work as a modern extension of basic psychoanalytic ideas.

Are Humans Simple Machines?

One of the critiques of using basic control models to understand behavior is that they seem too simplistic. It is hard to imagine how complex behavior, such as a child searching for his or her mother, can emerge from simple processes, such as comparisons and set-values. However, it is possible to create systems that behave in complex ways by adding a few additional components to the cybernetic toolkit. For example, a second kind of control mechanism that Bowlby discussed, a *servomechanism*, can be used to allow the set-value itself to be changed as a function of environmental feedback. Bowlby discussed power steering in automobiles as an example. The axis for the front wheels is designed to be controlled by the steering wheel. In a sense, the steering wheel provides the set-value and various mechanisms function to reduce the discrepancy between the current location of the axis and that implied by the positioning of the steering wheel. But the positioning of the steering wheel can change. And this added complexity allows for much greater plasticity in the behavior of the system. It remains "instinctual" (ie, the automobile is built according to a specific blueprint), but its functioning is determined by feedback from the environment.

One of the most significant features of Bowlby's writings was the concept of the *integration of control systems*—an idea inspired by Miller et al. (1960). In short, it is assumed that the set-value of a system can be determined by the operation and output of other related systems. That is, the interplay between subsystems can create behavior that is not only complex, but purposeful. Bowlby's example of such interplay was antiaircraft guns. The positioning of the cannon is set by information coming from a tracking device, such as a radar system. Thus, one mechanism is designed to detect and track the location of an enemy target and feeds this output into another mechanism that is responsible for moving the cannon to the projected location of the target and firing when ready. The system as a whole is just a machine; it has no purpose, goal, or intention. Nonetheless, it behaves in sophisticated ways—ways that would be difficult to describe without using terms like "purpose," "goals," and "intentions." And it responds to changes in the environment in intelligent and sophisticated ways (see Carver & Scheier, 1998, for a discussion of these ideas in the context of modern research on self-regulation).

The set-goal in this case is a *system-level property*. It characterizes the way in which the system functions at an emergent level. Each of the components is doing something concrete, but none of them are responsible for hitting enemy targets per se. Hitting enemy targets, in this example, is what Bowlby called a "predictable outcome" of the system. And the ability of the system to achieve this goal accurately and efficiently is what may lead to it being used and refined in military operations. When biological systems of this sort are assembled, they are *subject to natural selection at the level of their emergent behavior* and the ways in which it contributes to survival and reproduction.

Goal-Directed Behavior and Primary Versus Secondary Strategies

In complex behavioral systems, behavior does not follow from a stimulus in a rigid manner. Instead, what is inherited is a purposeful system that can select one from many possible behavioral strategies to achieve a goal. A child who is separated from his or her caregiver, for example, has multiple options available to him or her to reestablish proximity, such as crying, searching, and smiling. Depending on his or her experiences, he or she may have learned that some options are more likely to produce the desired outcome than others. Being able to select one strategy among several potential strategies is critical for flexible behavioral control.

In Bowlby's theory, the tendency for children to seek out an attachment figure when distressed is construed as a *primary strategy*. That is, it is the "default" response of the system. Attachment theorists, however, also emphasize *secondary strategies*. Secondary strategies are those that might be used to achieve attachment-related goals (eg, the maintenance of felt security) when the primary strategy is not viable. If it is not possible for a person to seek out their attachment figure for support (perhaps due to an extended separation), the individual may need to rely on alternative means for achieving a state of security (see chapters: What Are Attachment Working Models?; What Is the Attachment Behavioral System? And, How Is It Linked to Other Behavioral Systems?).

If we return to the control model discussed previously in Fig. 1.3, we can see that it only captures the dynamics of what might be called a primary or secure strategy. When the child senses that the attachment figure is inaccessible, he or she experiences distress and, behaviorally, selects behavioral strategies that have the "predictable outcome" of reestablishing proximity to the primary caregiver. But this basic model can be modified to include experience-dependent contingencies (Fig. 1.4). For example, if the child has learned over the course of repeated interactions with the caregiver that crying and persistence are ineffective ways to establish a sense of security, he may downplay those responses and, instead, opt for alternatives. In the diagram in Fig. 1.4, this is represented through the use of deactivating strategies, and when these strategies are successful in regulating anxiety, they may become the foundation for the attachment pattern that the individual develops. Some children, however, may find that exaggerated displays of vulnerability and distress are highly effective in capturing the attention of caregivers and, as a result, employ behavioral strategies that are highly vocal and expressive (ie, hyperactivating strategies).

The distinction between hyperactivating and deactivating strategies plays an important role in modern research on attachment in adulthood. Indeed, as we discuss in the chapters: What Are Attachment Working Models?; What Is the Attachment Behavioral System? And, How Is It Linked to Other Behavioral Systems?), individual differences in attachment are often framed with respect to the way in which these strategies are implemented: avoidant people appear to

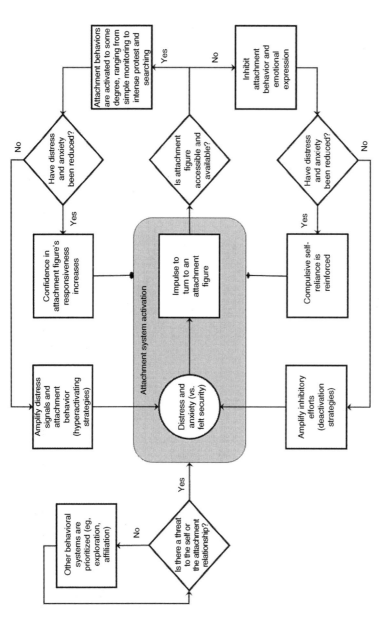

FIGURE 1.4   A modified control diagram of attachment dynamics. According to this model, when there is a threat to the self or the attachment relationship, the attachment system is activated, leading to feelings of anxiety and an impulse to turn to the attachment figure. If the figure is perceived to be accessible, attachment behavior is activated. If that behavior succeeds in reducing anxiety or solving the problem, the system gradually becomes quiescent and the individual's confidence in the availability of the attachment figure and the effectiveness of safe haven base behavior increases. If not, the individual may amplify attachment behavior—a pattern that has the potential to become chronic. If, in contrast, the individual believes that the figure is not accessible, he or she may inhibit attachment behaviors. If this is successful, it has the potential to reinforce a sense of compulsive self-reliance. If it is not successful, deactivating strategies may be amplified, potentially amplifying distress and insecurity.

use strategies that deactivate attachment-related behavior, whereas highly anxious people use strategies that hyperactivate attachment behavior.

IS ATTACHMENT THEORY A "GRAND THEORY"? HOW DOES IT DIFFER FROM OTHER PERSPECTIVES?

A century ago, many major theoretical perspectives in psychology aspired to explain more than just a narrow slice of human behavior. Freud (1900), for example, was not merely trying to understand the meaning of dreams; he was attempting to develop a theory of the mind that could explain love, hate, desire, culture, and taboo. Likewise, Darwin (1859) was not merely attempting to understand why some finches have longer beaks than others; he was seeking an explanation for why variation in the natural world exists and why form and function are so intimately bound. Attachment theory is one of the few modern psychological theories that might be considered a "grand theory" in the spirit of personality theories from yesteryears. Indeed, this may be one reason the theory is so popular. In this final section we briefly consider three features that tend to set attachment theory apart from other theories in contemporary psychology.

Multiple Levels of Analysis and Scientific Explanation

Over 50 years ago, Tinbergen (1963), one of the pioneers of evolutionary approaches to the study of behavior, argued that it is necessary to address four questions when trying to explain behavioral phenomena: those concerning *causation* (ie, what environmental or physiological mechanisms control behavior), *ontogeny* (ie, how does the behavioral pattern develop), *function* (ie, how does the behavior contribute to fitness and what kinds of adaptive problems does it solve), and evolution or *phylogeny* (ie, how did the behavior evolve over evolutionary history)? Contemporary psychologists are largely preoccupied with questions concerning causation, wondering whether specific contextual manipulations lead to immediately observable consequences. As Tinbergen noted, this is a legitimate and important part of trying to understand "why" things are the way they are. But an exclusive focus on causal mechanisms often leaves out other important ways of understanding behavior.

Take grief as an example. Many people who lose someone they love report what, on the surface, may seem to be irrational thoughts and behaviors, as discussed in the Didion example that opened the chapter. For example, they may be unwilling to part with their loved one's possessions, thinking that the deceased may need those items if they were to return. They may also engage in attempts to "undo" the loss, as if these efforts may bring the lost person back. If we wanted to know why some people are inclined to engage in such "magical thinking," we may conjecture that those who do so are more likely to have lost someone who was important to them. We could even evaluate this idea empirically by examining the association between whether people have lost someone recently and rates of such behaviors.

But such an investigation would leave many questions unanswered. Although such a study would help us better understand whether loss, compared to nonloss, predicts such seemingly irrational behavior, it would not shed light on another form of "why"—why is it that people grieve as opposed to, say, simply "move on," in the way they might do if they lost a pencil. That is, knowing the proximal cause of grief does not provide a full explanation for it; it doesn't capture the *meaning* behind the behavior.

To capture the meaning of behavior, we need to be more comprehensive in our inquiry. We could, for example, also inquire about the function of grief: what functions might grief serve in the context of survival and reproduction? According to Bowlby (1980), grief is a manifestation of separation protest behavior—behaviors that function to keep people in close proximity to their attachment figures. And, although certain responses (eg, calling out for one's attachment figure in the night) might lead to the "predictable outcome" of contact and proximity when the separation is temporary, the core components of the system are not necessarily designed to "know" the difference between a temporary and a permanent separation. Thus, when similar behaviors emerge following death, they appear irrational or nonfunctional. But, in fact, they are highly functional in the context in which they were selected: to prevent separations from attachment figures. But this way of understanding the meaning of grief would be difficult to appreciate without considering function; this insight does not emerge naturally as a consequence of studying proximate mechanisms alone.

In short, a grand theory typically goes after more than one kind of "why" when it comes to understanding behavior and experience. Attachment theory is one of only a few contemporary theories in social and personality psychology that attempt to answer "why" questions from multiple timescales and perspectives. As such, it provides novel insights into a variety of questions, including what grief is, why people fall in love, and why human connection is a fundamental part of personality development.

Broad Reach

Second, grand theories offer a unified way to explain a diverse number of phenomena. Attachment theory offers an explanation for many questions about human experience, including:

- Why is relationship between children and their primary caregivers so emotionally powerful?
- Why do some people tend to recreate the same dysfunctional patterns in one relationship after the other?
- Why are some people better able to understand another person's point of view? Why are some people more empathic and compassionate than others?
- Why do people sometimes experience anger toward the people they love?
- Why do adults fall in love with one another, form exclusive pair-bonds, and remain together for prolonged periods of time?

From our point of view, it is noteworthy that there are very few theoretical perspectives in contemporary psychology that have the potential to speak to issues that cut across a variety of disciplinary boundaries, including developmental, clinical, social, and personality psychology. One of the most prominent theoretical perspectives in the study of close relationships, interdependence theory, offers an excellent account of the ways in which the investments people make in romantic relationships give rise to a sense of commitment and relationship persistence (eg, Rusbult, 1980). But interdependence theory has relatively little to say about the nature of love and loss. It does not explain why people are compelled to forge deep emotional connections with others in the first place. Similarly, one of the most prominent theoretical frameworks in the study of personality and individual differences, the Five Factor Model (Costa & McCrae, 2006), offers a nearly comprehensive taxonomy of the ways in which people differ from one another in their thoughts, feelings, and behavior. But the Five Factor Model seems unconcerned with the fact that people live their lives embedded in and negotiating their relationships: seeking love and acceptance, struggling with feeling that they are misunderstood, and trying to find meaning in what they do.

Although we are clearly enthusiastic about the potential for attachment theory to speak to a number of different features of the human condition, we should be explicit in stating that we do not believe it explains everything. Attachment theory, for example, does not explain why men are more likely than women to prefer youthful mates (Buss & Schmitt, 1993). But the fact that attachment theory enters into discussions of gender and mate preferences is evidence of its broad relevance (see chapter: What Are the Effects of Context on Attachment?).

Psychological Adaptation and Well-Being

Finally, at least in psychology, grand theories typically offer a perspective on psychological adaptation: what optimal human functioning entails. One of the core ideas in attachment theory is that security lies at the heart of adaptive functioning. A person who has a history of interpersonal experiences in which he or she has learned that others are available and responsive when needed acquires the autonomy and competency necessary to venture out and explore the world. When things become uncertain, the person knows that he or she can fall back on others.

In short, what actual and internalized supportive relationships do is help establish a sense of confidence and grounded autonomy. A secure person knows they have someone they can turn to—*a safe haven*—when things go wrong. Moreover, they can use the attachment figure as a *secure base* from which to explore the world. As we explain in the chapter: What Is an Attachment Relationship?, these features represent the hallmarks of an attachment relationship, whether that relationship exists in childhood or in adulthood. The presence of a secure base is what enables a sense of autonomy, facilitates the consideration of alternative points of view, and enables people to explore new opportunities (eg, careers).

Many disorders of psychological functioning can be viewed as the breakdown of safe haven and secure base dynamics. For example, the experience of social anxiety can be viewed as uncertainty about the whereabouts of one's attachment figures. This is true, of course, in the short-term (ie, people feel a sense of anxiety and distress when separated from their primary attachment figures or when they are uncertain about their safety or availability). But Bowlby also believed disruptions in attachment relationships can create a more persistent form of uncertainty, which could manifest in a number of ways. Thus, at least in some cases, general patterns of maladaptive functioning may have their origins in specific attachment experiences.

We should be clear that Bowlby did not believe that *all* forms of psychopathology had their origins in attachment-related experiences. It is unlikely, for example, that people who are suffering from posttraumatic stress disorder after serving in combat are symptomatic because of disruptions in early attachment experiences. But, it is possible that those attachment experiences can function as either protective or vulnerability factors, impacting the severity or expression of disorders that have etiologies outside the realm of attachment (see chapter: What Are the Implications of Attachment Processes for Psychopathology and Therapy?).

Chapter 2

What Is an Attachment Relationship?

I think that when we were little, we used to be a lot closer. We used to do everything together. Now that we're older we don't do everything together. We have our own lives, so we have become more independent. It's more like the other one is a fall back. Like I can always fall back onto my [twin] and she can always fall back onto me. Before it was always us... and now that we know other people, we are kind of like a fall back.

—Amy, describing her relationship with her identical twin sister.
Quoted in Tancredy and Fraley (2006, p. 81)

An attachment relationship is said to exist when an individual (1) preferentially seeks out and *maintains proximity* to a specific person and protests separations from that individual, (2) uses that person as a *safe haven* during times of distress, and (3) uses the person as a *secure base* from which to explore the world. The passage above captures well some of the elements of this definition. Amy is discussing the nature of the relationship she has with her twin sister and is reflecting on how that relationship has changed across time. She notes that her cotwin is a "fall back" person—someone she can turn to no matter how difficult life becomes. In this respect, her sister serves as a safe haven. But her sister also functions as a secure base. In some respects, Amy has ventured out into the world and has become more independent, but has done so using her sister as a base for such exploration. Again, the "fall back" theme captures this dynamic well: as long as Amy's sister is accessible, Amy can venture forth, knowing that when things become difficult, her sister will be there to back her up, support her, and renew her confidence.

Theorists describe relationships that serve these three functions as *attachment relationships* and refer to the emotional connection that one may feel for the other as an *attachment bond* (eg, Ainsworth, 1991; Hazan & Zeifman, 1994). The prototypical attachment bond is that which exists between a child and his or her primary caregiver. For example, young children often maintain proximity to their parents, and, when they sense that a separation is imminent, they may protest the separation by crying, clinging, or grabbing hold of their parents. In

Adult Attachment. http://dx.doi.org/10.1016/B978-0-12-420020-3.00002-5

31

addition, young children use their parents as a safe haven; when distressed they turn to parents for comfort, support, and assurance. And, finally, they use their parents as a secure base from which to explore the world. Young children are much more likely to venture out in an uninhibited manner if they know that they can always fall back to their parent when they need them. Attachment relationships play a role throughout the life course, but *who* people use as their primary attachment figures tends to change as people transition from one phase of life to the next. Although children are likely to use their parents for attachment-related functions, such as secure base functions, adults are more likely to use their romantic partners for such purposes (eg, Doherty & Feeney, 2004).

In this chapter we briefly review what attachment theory says about the development of attachment relationships. We will review what has been learned about how various attachment functions (eg, secure base) transfer from one person to the next over the course of development and how they manifest in the context of adult relationships. We review what is known about how long it takes for adult attachment to develop, what happens to the role of parents as peers (eg, friends and romantic partners) begin to assume the role of attachment figures, and the kinds of factors that facilitate and inhibit the development of an attachment relationship. Finally, we will highlight what we perceive to be open questions in this area in hopes that it will inspire future research on attachment relationships.

We begin by noting that, although psychologists have long been interested in the distinction between close and nonclose relationships (eg, communal vs. exchange relationships; Clark & Mills, 1979), an attachment relationship is believed to be something *more* than just a "close" relationship. For example, a child may enjoy spending time with a playmate and may even protest when those play sessions are brought to a close, but it would be unusual for the child, if frightened, to turn to the playmate instead of a parent for comfort and protection. The relationship may be "close" by traditional definitions (the friends enjoy each other's company, the relationship is satisfying), but, in this example, the child's friend does not serve safe haven functions and would not be construed as an attachment figure. Similarly, a child may be attached to his mother, even if she has a history of being unreliable or inconsistent in the care she provides for him. Nonetheless, the child may turn to her—potentially with trepidation—if things go awry. That is, the child may be attached to the parent, despite not having a secure relationship with her. Although most attachments are, in fact, close relationships, not all close relationships are attachments (see also Mikulincer, Gillath, & Shaver, 2002).

HOW DO ATTACHMENT RELATIONSHIPS DEVELOP IN INFANCY?

According to Bowlby (1969/1982), the development of an attachment bond is a gradual process and can be loosely understood as unfolding in a series of stages. In the early months of life, infants are largely indiscriminate in how they direct attachment-related behaviors. Separation from a primary caregiver might not elicit distress, and proximity-seeking behavior may be directed to any number of available individuals. This phase is sometimes referred to as the *initial preattachment* phase (eg, Ainsworth, Blehar, Waters, & Wall, 1978; Bowlby, 1969/1982). Although infants are not selectively discriminating among potential caregivers during this phase, they are nonetheless engaged in behaviors, such as crying, sucking, grasping, and rooting that facilitate proximity to potential attachment figures.

Between 2 and 6 months infants begin to discriminate among caregivers and differentially—and preferentially—respond to them. Bowlby (1969/1982) referred to this as the *attachment-in-the-making* phase. During this period the infant's behavior becomes increasingly diverse and organized. The infant may cry selectively to signal a specific adult, for example, or may only be soothed when specific individuals hold him or her.

Around 7 months of age infants begin to crawl and, as a result, they explore the environment in a more active fashion and are able to seek proximity to specific caregivers. Thus, during this period of time they become capable of expressing fully proximity-seeking, safe haven, and secure-base behavior. As such, this period, combined with the selective preference toward a caregiver and the protest of separation from that individual, is sometimes referred to as the phase in which "clear-cut" or "full-blown" attachment is possible (eg, Ainsworth et al., 1978; Bowlby, 1969/1982).

Bowlby (1969/1982) also discussed the concept of a *goal-corrected partnership* to characterize the way the attachment bond functions when children are approximately 3 years old. As infants get older, they begin to organize their attachment behavior in ways that reflect their greater cognitive sophistication. They understand, for example, that they can negotiate proximity to the attachment figure at both psychological and symbolic levels rather than physical levels alone (eg, the child may take an object that belongs to the parent on an overnight trip as a way of feeling closer to the parent). And, in turn, the caregiver can communicate with the child in ways that allow them to coordinate their behavior and needs and to take each other's plans and intentions into account (eg, although the parent may not be available to the child at the moment due to other obligations, she may promise the child some dedicated time later in the evening). Although this phase is no more representative of attachment than the previous phase, the way the bond is manifested has the potential to be much more sophisticated, making pure behavioral indicators an imperfect way to gauge the presence of an attachment bond. For example, although separation distress is a clear marker of an attachment bond in 12-month-old infants, a 3-year-old child is much less likely to experience or express distress in the face of brief separations.

Who Serves as the Primary Attachment Figure in Childhood?

It is typically assumed that most infants use a parent, typically the mother, as a primary attachment figure (Colin, 1996). But that does not mean that the child does not have several potential individuals who may serve attachment-related functions. Bowlby (1969/1982) and Ainsworth et al. (1978) argued that a child could be attached to multiple individuals and, in fact, in many families it is likely that both parents and potentially even an older sibling or nanny could serve attachment-related functions. To capture some of these ideas, Bowlby described children as having a *hierarchy* of attachment figures.

We discuss the concept of the attachment hierarchy in more depth later in this chapter. But one of the core ideas in attachment theory is that children, despite having many potential attachment figures, often behave as if there is someone in particular that they want when distressed. It is not the case that all potential caregivers are treated as interchangeable; more often than not, there is someone in particular that the child selectively seeks when ill, tired, or scared. This individual is often called the *primary attachment figure*. Bowlby introduced the concept of *monotropy* to capture the idea that there may be a privileged place in a child's attachment hierarchy for a specific caregiver and that, in fact, evolution may have crafted the attachment system to lock-in on a specific figure to help organize and focus behavior during emergencies (Bowlby, 1969/1982). Colin (1987; described in Colin, 1996) adopted the classic and widely used strange situation procedure (see chapter: What Is Attachment Theory?) to examine in a systematic fashion to whom infants would direct attachment behaviors when interacting with both their mothers and fathers. Fifty infants between the ages of 12 and 19 months and their parents visited a laboratory playroom and participated in a sequence of 3-min episodes in which the child was with both parents, with parents and a stranger, alone (with and without stranger), and reunited with parents. Infants were more likely to direct attachment behavior, such as vocalizations and proximity seeking, toward the mother than the father. Moreover, in the final separation and reunion episode, 86% of the infants directed attachment behavior toward the mother rather than the father whereas 12% did not show a clear preference. According to Colin's data, preferences for the father were associated with the father having spent a greater amount of time involved in the child's care. In summary, although children often have more than one individual who may serve attachment-related functions, they appear to have a clear preference for specific individuals when distressed.

Howes, Rodning, Galluzzo, and Myers (1988) assessed infants in the strange situation with their mothers and, separately, their fathers. On the basis of their observations, they concluded that children appear to organize their attachment behavior in meaningful ways with both parents. Moreover, they argued that there are potential benefits of having multiple caregivers, such that having a secure attachment with at least one caregiver can compensate for other insecure attachments in the child's social competence. Thus, although children may show a preference for one particular individual, they often have multiple people in their lives who can fulfill important functions when necessary.

HOW ARE ATTACHMENT-RELATED FUNCTIONS TRANSFERRED FROM ONE PERSON TO ANOTHER?

Although Bowlby (1969, 1973) was specifically concerned with the attachment of a child to his mother figure, he conceived of attachments to other figures as approximating the same model—and he clearly stated that attachments continue throughout the entire life span. Attachment to parent figures may become attenuated as adulthood approaches and may become supplemented and to some extent supplanted by other attachments; but few if any adults cease to be influenced by their early attachments, or indeed cease at some level of awareness to be attached to their early attachment figures.

—Ainsworth et al. (1978, p. 28)

A core developmental milestone is passed in late childhood and early adolescence as children begin to explore and construct their identities in more active ways. They are attempting to figure out where they belong in the world of their peers and, indeed, often become more interested in appealing to real or imagined standards set by their peers than their family. As a consequence, some attachment-related functions begin to shift from parents to peers. Adolescents, for example, may seek proximity to friends at the expense of spending time with parents. In addition, they may begin to share their thoughts and concerns—especially those concerning intimacy and dating—with close friends rather than with their parents.

During this phase children appear to be transferring at least some attachment-related functions from parents to peers. Hazan and Zeifman (1994) suggest that this process takes place in a relatively orderly fashion, such that each of the three functions described previously is transferred sequentially. That is, first, children begin to preferentially seek proximity to peers over parents, then they begin to use peers for safe haven functions, and, finally, may begin to use specific peers as a secure base. Of course, these functions may not be fully transferred in the context of any one relationship. For example, adolescents may elect to spend time with a best friend and may even confide in that individual instead of the parents, but, ultimately, the relationship may serve exploration or affiliation purposes rather than attachment functions. Indeed, in some cases, a new relationship may never come to assume all three attachment functions, despite being an important or meaningful relationship for the person in question. In the sections that follow we review empirical research on how these transference processes take place, among both children and adults, and attempt to answer questions about their timing and the factors that facilitate or inhibit the development of attachment relationships.

Empirical Research on Attachment Transfer in Children and Adolescents

Hazan, Hutt, Sturgeon, and Bricker (1991); Hazan and Zeifman (1994) were the first researchers to systematically examine the ways in which children transfer attachment-related functions from parental to nonparental figures. To do so they

TABLE 2.1 Attachment-Related Functions and Features
Proximity seeking
Who is the person you most like to spend time with?
Who is the person you don't like to be away from?
Safe haven
Who is the person you want to be with when you are feeling upset or down?
Who is the person you would count on for advice?
Secure base
Who is the person you would want to tell first if you achieved something good?
Who is the person you can always count on?

developed the WHOTO interview—a structured interview in which individuals of various ages are asked questions designed to identify who best fulfills various attachment functions. Some example questions are provided in Table 2.1. For example, to assess *who* children use for secure-base functions, they are asked "Who is the person you can always count on?" Children are asked to nominate someone in response to each question.

In their initial research using the WHOTO, Hazan and Zeifman (1994) examined a sample of 100 children who varied in age, ranging from 6 to 17 years of age. They classified the children's responses to the WHOTO questions as falling into one of two categories: parents (eg, mothers, fathers, grandparents, stepfathers) and peers (eg, friends, romantic partners). They found that attachment-related functions appeared to be transferred in an orderly way. Proximity seeking, for example, appears to be easily transferred from parents to peers. For example, approximately 50% of children aged 6−7 years were likely to nominate a peer as someone to whom they sought proximity. But this proportion was as high as 75% among 16−17-year-olds. Other functions, such as secure-base functions, were less prevalent among peer relationships. Approximately 45% of children aged 16−17 indicated that their peers functioned as a secure base.

More recent research has continued to support the original findings reported by Hazan and colleagues. Most of this work uses self-report questionnaires that were inspired by the WHOTO—surveys that instruct people to nominate someone who fulfills each of the core attachment functions (eg, Fraley & Davis, 1997) or which ask people to rate or rank the extent to which various important people in their lives fulfill these needs (eg, Trinke & Bartholomew, 1997). For example, Nickerson and Nagle (2005) examined attachment processes in a cross-sectional sample of 279 North American children in the fourth, sixth, and eighth grades. They found that older adolescents were more likely to use peers for attachment-related functions, such as proximity seeking, than younger children. But the majority of those sampled reported using their parents for

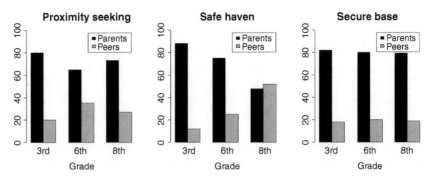

FIGURE 2.1   Who fulfills various attachment functions in children? *(Adapted from Nickerson and Nagle (2005).)*

secure-base functions (Fig. 2.1; see Kerns, Mathews, Koehn, Williams, & Siener-Ciesla, 2015; Rosenthal & Kobak, 2010; and Seibert & Kerns, 2009, for similar findings using different kinds of measures).

Mayseless (2004) examined a sample of 143, 18-year-old Israeli males who were leaving home to fulfill military service requirements. Each participant was administered a self-report version of the WHOTO across two time points. Mayseless (2004) reported that many of these males were using peers for attachment-related functions, but nonetheless continued to use parents for secure-base functions.

In one of the first longitudinal studies of attachment transfer, Friedlmeier and Granqvist (2006) examined a sample of Swedish and German adolescents aged 15−16 years of age. They found that many of the adolescents in their sample had transferred their proximity maintenance, safe haven, and secure-base functions to a peer. They also found that adolescents who formed a romantic relationship between assessment waves were more likely to show transfer from parents to peers compared to adolescents who did not enter into a romantic relationship.

In summary, although the methods used across these various studies differ in some ways, they converge on a common theme: Children between the ages of 10 and 18 are likely to begin seeking proximity to peers more so than their parents. However, the majority of them continue to use their parents—and their mothers in particular—as a primary attachment figure (see Markiewicz, Lawford, Doyle, & Haggart, 2006; and Rosenthal & Kobak, 2010, for similar findings).

Empirical Research on Attachment Transfer in Early Adulthood

There is a growing body of research on attachment figures in college-aged populations. Although college students tend to be the "default" population used in psychological research due to convenience, they are an important population for the study of attachment transfer because the majority of college students are between the ages of 18 and 22 and are living away from home for the first significant period of time in their lives (Larose & Boivin, 1998; Lopez & Gorm-ley, 2002). As such, certain attachment issues may be salient for them (they may miss their parents, they may feel uncertain about being away from home), but they are also meeting new people and exploring new relationships. Much of this research indicates that peers—especially romantic partners—come to play a more salient role in attachment-related behavior in young adult populations.

For example, Fraley and Davis (1997) administered a self-report version of the WHOTO and found that many college-aged students were using their peers (eg, best friends and romantic partners) for attachment-related functions. They found that young adults in their sample were most likely to use parents as a secure base; about 60% nominated "mom" or "dad" in response to two secure-base items. However, young adults were more likely to use peers rather than parents as targets for proximity maintenance (about 78%) and safe-haven func-tions (81%). Zhang, Chan, and Teng (2011) found similar results in a Chinese college student population.

Trinke and Bartholomew (1997) studied a sample of 240 undergraduates (mean age 21) and found that the individuals who were ranked the highest with respect to attachment-related functions were romantic partners, followed by mothers, fathers, siblings, and best friends. They found that the relative order-ing of nonromantic attachment figures was the same for people who were and were not in romantic relationships. Thus, they concluded "when partners be-come attachment figures, it appears as though they bump the other figures to lower places on the hierarchy, but leave the relative positions of these other attachments unaltered" (p. 619).

Similar findings have been reported by others. Pitman and Scharfe (2010) asked college students in romantic relationships to rank a variety of individuals with respect to attachment-related functions. They found that 55% assigned the highest attachment rankings to their romantic partner (followed by their mother, at 31%). Among those not in a romantic relationship, 55% reported their moth-ers first, followed by friends (35%).

Empirical Research on Attachment Transfer in Adulthood

Doherty and Feeney (2004) conducted one of the largest studies to date on at-tachment transfer in adulthood. Although they sampled individuals of a variety of ages ranging from 16 to 90, they studied a large number of people in early to middle adulthood (mean age 35 years) and were able to investigate the way in which attachment processes varied across age. Doherty and Feeney asked adults to rank-order the extent to which various people in their lives fulfilled attach-ment-related functions. They found that, on average, adults were most likely to be attached to their romantic partners. More importantly, when they defined a "full blown attachment" as one in which a target had a specific score for each of the attachment functions, they found that, among adults who were in romantic relationships, up to 74% were judged to be fully attached to that partner.

Doherty and Feeney also classified a person's primary attachment figure as being the individual who had the highest score among the various rankings of attachment-related functions. Using this method, they found that 96% of the sample had a primary attachment figure (4% had a tie between two or more individuals). Among those who had a primary attachment figure, those figures were (in decreasing order) partners, mothers, friends, children, siblings, and fathers.

Summary of Attachment Functions at Different Points in the Life Course

Young children are most likely to use their parents, and, more often than not, their mothers, as primary attachment figures. As they age, they are more likely to begin transferring attachment-related functions from parents to peers (eg, close friends and romantic partners). Indeed, as young adults transition to college, close to half of them are using peers for attachment-related functions. By the time individuals are married adults, the majority of them are more likely to nominate their spouses as being their primary attachment figures rather than their parents. Uncoupled adults are most likely to nominate their mothers or a best friend for attachment-related functions (Doherty & Feeney, 2004; Schachner, Shaver, & Gillath, 2008).

A Cautionary Note on Using Children as Attachment Figures

Doherty and Feeney (2004) reported that some adults in their sample nominated a child as serving attachment functions. Theoretically, however, it is considered dysfunctional for an adult to be attached to his or her young child (Colin, 1996). There are at least two important things to note in the case of Doherty and Feeney's research, however. First, parents tended to nominate their children for the "proximity seeking/maintenance" and "separation distress" functions in particular. In other words, when asked "Who is the person you don't like to be away from?" many parents nominate their children. Does this mean that young children are attachment figures for parents? Not necessarily. One of the complications in assessing the extent to which a relationship is an attachment relationship is that some of the markers of attachment, such as separation distress and proximity seeking, are not unique to attachment. For example, separation distress and proximity maintenance are also crucial features of the *caregiving system*, as evidenced by the powerful feelings of panic and distress that a parent can experience when he or she loses sight of their child (see Kirkpatrick, 1998, for similar examples). Our intuition is that, in most cases where adults nominate their children as serving proximity maintenance functions, this response may be representative of caregiving rather than attachment processes.

Nonetheless, as adults get older, it is not uncommon for their adult children to provide care for them. As a result, parents may, in fact, come to depend on their adult children as attachment figures. They may begin to rely on the adult child as a source of comfort and security and to use the child as a secure base from which to explore the world (see Karantzas & Simpson, 2015). Indeed, in the Doherty and Feeney (2004) study, the age of the respondent was positively correlated with the extent to which people nominated their children for serving attachment-related functions. This indicates that their use of the child as an attachment figure was not necessarily dysfunctional.

CAN PEOPLE HAVE MORE THAN ONE ATTACHMENT FIGURE?

One of the most common ways of studying who it is that people use as attachment figures and how attachment-related functions are transferred across time is through the use of the WHOTO and its derivatives (eg, Hazan & Zeifman, 1994). The WHOTO, however, instructs people to nominate a single individual for each attachment-related function. And, although people can usually perform this task with no trouble, this method obscures the fact that some people may, in fact, have more than one person in their lives who function as attachment figures. Thus, although the WHOTO and its derivatives are useful for studying *who* functions as a person's primary attachment figure, it is not ideal for studying the *hierarchy* of attachment figures that a person has. One cannot use the WHOTO, for example, to determine whether adults tend to have one and only one attachment figure or whether people have multiple attachments. And, if people can have multiple attachment figures, the WHOTO cannot be used to estimate how many attachment figures the typical adult has.

To address some of these issues, Trinke and Bartholomew (1997) developed the Attachment Network Questionnaire (ANQ). Respondents taking the ANQ are first asked to list the "significant people in your life, those people that you currently feel a strong emotional tie to, regardless of whether that tie is positive, negative, or mixed" (p. 609). This name generator is used to make salient for the respondent some of the people they may wish to consider when completing the ANQ. More importantly, however, this listing is designed to emphasize the idea that the quality of the relationship is not necessarily the same thing as its importance. A person can play an emotionally important role in a person's life, even if the relationship is a conflictual one.

Next, respondents are asked a series of questions designed to assess six components of attachment, including the proximity-seeking, safe haven, and secure-base functions described before, but also emotional connection, conflict and strong emotion, and separation distress.[1] Respondents are asked to think about

---

1. Most research on adult attachment defines attachment relationships with respect to proximity-seeking, safe haven, and secure base dynamics (and, as we discuss at the end of the chapter, separation distress). The additional components studied by Trinke and Bartholomew (1997) are not commonly construed as being core features of an attachment relationship but were used by the researchers to help ensure that they were tapping into relationships that were of emotional significance to the respondents.

the people they listed previously and to rank the importance of those people with respect to the items in question. If respondents believe that one or more of the persons listed previously do not pertain to the item in question, they are not required to rank those persons for that item.

Trinke and Bartholomew (1997) administered the ANQ to a sample of 240 undergraduates (mean age 21). They assessed where various targets were placed in people's attachment hierarchies by computing the average ranking for each target across the various components that were assessed. Trinke and Bartholomew found that, on average, partners were ranked 2.1, followed by mothers (2.4), fathers (3.2), siblings (3.7), and best friends (3.9). (Lower numbers indicate greater importance.) Importantly, Trinke and Bartholomew found that adults seem to have approximately 5 attachment figures, on average, and 95% of them seem to have at least one person who emerges at the top of the hierarchy. Thus, although Bowlby's monotropy idea seems to have merit, it is clearly the case that most young adults have a number of secondary attachment figures who may be central in their lives. It is noteworthy that parents tended to be relatively high in the attachment hierarchy, even among subsamples of individuals who were in dating relationships. Thus, although partners were ranked the highest, overall, mothers were ranked a close second.

WHAT KINDS OF FACTORS FACILITATE THE DEVELOPMENT OF AN ADULT ATTACHMENT RELATIONSHIP?

The theory and research we have reviewed up to this point suggest two broad conclusions. First, the majority of children and adolescents are primarily attached to their parents (often their mothers), even if they are beginning to transfer attachment-related functions to peers (eg, romantic partners). Second, most adults tend to use romantic partners as their primary attachment figures. What kinds of factors facilitate the development of an attachment relationship in adulthood?

Bowlby (1969/1982) provided some clues by discussing a few factors that may facilitate bonding in early infancy. For example, he suggested that responsiveness and physical proximity may be key factors that enable a child to target an individual as a primary attachment figure. Theoretically, then, we might expect similar features to facilitate the transfer of attachment-related functions to nonparental targets as adolescents and young adults begin to explore new relationships.

How do Responsiveness and Sensitivity Facilitate the Development of Attachment Relationships?

Fraley and Davis (1997) reasoned that young adults would be more likely to have transferred attachment-related functions from parents to peers to the extent to which those peer relationships were characterized by mutual care, support, and trust. They asked college students to rate the extent to which their best friendships and romantic relationships reflected these qualities, and administered a version of the WHOTO to examine attachment functions. They found that, to the extent to which romantic relationships were characterized by these features, the more likely it was that people had transferred attachment-related functions from their parents to their romantic partners (see also Feeney, 2004). Importantly, Fraley and Davis (1997) also examined best friendships and found that these relationship features also predicted the extent to which people had transferred attachment-related functions from parents to best friends.

How Does Interdependence Facilitate the Development of Attachment Relationships?

One finding that has emerged repeatedly in the literature is that individuals are more likely to report being attached to individuals when their lives are highly interdependent with them. This interdependence can manifest in a variety of ways, including being in frequent contact with the individual or being in a committed relationship with him or her. Doherty and Feeney (2004), for example, found that adults involved in romantic relationships were more likely to use their romantic partner as an attachment figure if that relationship involved a higher degree of commitment; individuals who were living with and/or raising children with their partner were more likely to use that partner as an attachment figure. In a separate sample, Feeney (2004) found that the greater the relationship length, the more likely the romantic relationship was to be an attachment.

Umemura, Lacinová, and Macek (2014) observed a similar finding in a study of over 1000 young adults (age 21) from the Czech Republic. Specifically, they found that people were more likely to use their romantic partners as attachment figures the longer the relationship had lasted. However, they were not necessarily likely to shift attachment functions away from their parents. Stated differently, partners tended to replace friends rather than replacing parents, who remained important figures throughout participants' lives.

How do Individual Differences in Attachment Security Affect the Development of Attachment Relationships?

There is also a growing body of research indicating that people's general attachment styles (chapter: What Are Attachment Working Models?) predict the ways in which attachment functions are transferred across relationships. Fraley and Davis (1997), for example, administered the Relationships Questionnaire (RQ) and a version of the WHOTO to a sample of college students and found that individuals who were relatively secure with respect to attachment in general were more likely to have transferred attachment-related functions from parents to peers (friends or romantic partners). Interestingly, they also found that individuals with dismissing-avoidant attachment styles were more likely to answer "no one" or "myself" to questions that inquired about secure-base functions, such as "Who is the person you can always count on?"

Feeney (2004) reported that individuals who were more insecure were less likely to be attached to their partners, potentially because they fear the kind of intimacy that comes along with being in a close relationship. Similar findings have been reported by Doherty and Feeney (2004) and Mayseless (2004). Rowe and Carnelley (2005), using a measure described in more depth later, found that highly secure people had a greater number of people in their lives who could serve as attachment figures, indicating that a general sense of security may facilitate people's ability to develop and maintain attachment bonds in adulthood.

Do Compensatory Processes Lead People to Develop New Attachments?

One theme that has been present in early and contemporary research is that people may begin to transfer attachment-related functions from parents to peers if their relationships with their parents are unsatisfactory, conflictual, or insecure (see Keefer, Landau, Rothschild, & Sullivan, 2012, for an investigation of this premise using attachment to objects). There are some suggestions in the literature that such compensatory processes can take place. For example, Nickerson and Nagle (2005) found that children who viewed their relationships with their parents as less secure were more likely to select peers to fulfill attachment functions. Friedlmeier and Granqvist (2006) found that self-reports of insecure attachment to mother, combined with high degrees of attachment-related anxiety, were related to a higher degree of attachment transfer from parents to peers. Moreover, Freeman and Brown (2001) found that adolescents who were more generally insecure in their attachment orientation were more likely to nominate their boyfriends, girlfriends, and best friends as attachment figures.

It should be kept in mind that attachment transfer is a normative developmental phenomenon (Bowlby, 1969/1982). Thus, children who are secure in their relationships with their parents should also transfer attachment-related functions from parents to peers (see Feeney, 2004). What should be addressed more carefully in future research is the timing of these processes. It is probably the case that deviations from the typical trajectory are indicative of whether the transfer process represents adaptive developmental processes or whether the acceleration of those processes stems from insecurity.

There is at least one study that speaks to this issue. Fagundes and Schindler (2012) examined longitudinally the timing of romantic attachment formation and its implications for relationship functioning. They found that people who were relatively anxious with respect to attachment concerns began to transfer attachment functions (ie, proximity seeking) to partners earlier than those who were less anxious. Moreover, individuals who began to use their romantic partner as a secure base relatively soon were more likely to break up relative to those who did not. These findings suggest that the timing of attachment processes may be relevant to understanding whether the transference process is a response to an insecure attachment network—an effort at network repair, so to speak—instead of a natural consequence of exploring new relationships from the foundation of a parental secure base.

How Long Does it Take for an Adult Attachment Relationship to Form?

Researchers have concluded that, under normal circumstances, most children have formed an attachment bond to at least one caretaker within the first 7–10 months. And, by the time infants are able to crawl, they are likely to reveal secure-base dynamics in a clear fashion.

Early research on adult attachment, however, suggested that it might take considerably longer for adults to develop an attachment bond toward a nonparental figure. Hazan and Zeifman (1994), for example, suggested that it takes about 2 years, on average, for most young adults to transfer all attachment-related functions from parents to partners. Fraley and Davis' (1997) data supported this claim. They found that among individuals who reported using their romantic partners for proximity-seeking, safe haven, and secure-base functions, those romantic relationships had, on average, lasted 23 months. There are considerable individual differences, however, with some individuals exhibiting all three functions after a few months and some taking as long as 4 years (see also Fagundes & Schindler, 2012).

However, some research is beginning to suggest that romantic attachments can form relatively quickly. For example, Heffernan, Fraley, Vicary, and Brumbaugh (2012) administered a self-report WHOTO measure to a large sample of individuals in romantic relationships and found that people may come to use romantic partners as attachment figures in a much shorter period of time. For example, approximately 50% of respondents (average age 27 years) who had been dating for 3 months reported using their partners as a secure base. Stated differently, a large proportion of adult romantic relationships appear to be attachments when characterized with respect to secure-base functions. And, although people are more likely to use their partner for secure-base purposes as the relationship progresses, they are nonetheless willing or able to do so even in fledgling relationships.

A similar observation was made by Eastwick and Finkel (2008). They noted that one of the core experiential features of falling in love is a preoccupation or fascination with the object of one's affections. This is often accompanied by a sense of anxiety—concern over whether the object is interested in the self or whether he or she will return one's affections. In many ways, these concerns resemble insecurity in the way that it is typically measured in dispositional ways (see chapter: What Are Attachment Working Models?). Eastwick and Finkel argued, however, that this form of insecurity is actually a marker of healthy relationship development in fledgling romantic relationships. Indeed, they showed that individuals who felt more insecure or anxious with respect to a specific partner were more likely to be using that target for attachment-related functions.

WHAT HAPPENS TO PARENTS WHEN NEW ATTACHMENT RELATIONSHIPS DEVELOP? DO THEY SHARE THE STAGE WITH NEW ATTACHMENT FIGURES? OR ARE THEY SUPPLANTED?

Unfortunately, we do not have good answers to this question yet. The question is a difficult one to answer because the way these processes work psychologically might be different from the way they work behaviorally. That is, there are constraints on behavior that do not necessarily exist psychologically, and, as a result, it is sometimes difficult to use behavior as a means to understand psychological processes. As a simple analogy, consider the way people think about their favorite restaurants. If asked, people may indicate that there are several places they consider to be their favorite places to eat and they may genuinely consider some of these places to be equally good. But, when dinner time rolls around, they do not dine at three separate restaurants; they choose one place to eat. Given the structure of the situation and the constraints that exist, people are forced to make a choice. But the fact that they chose one place over others does not always imply that the choice made reveals a hierarchical ordering of preferences. A person who has a clear favorite and a person who has several favorites may nonetheless behave in the same way.

Another reason the question is difficult to answer is that most of the methods we have reviewed for studying attachment hierarchies use either nominations (eg, the WHOTO and its derivatives) or rankings of people (eg, the ANQ). The limitation of ranking methods is that the options are necessarily mutually exclusive. To rank a partner at the top of one's hierarchy, one has to rank someone else second—even if those people are on equal footing psychologically. Tancredy and Fraley (2006) used a continuous rating method to try to get a better handle on this issue. Specifically, for several different targets (eg, mother, father, sibling, partner), participants rated the extent to which the person served attachment-related functions. This method allows the relative distance between people's ratings to be studied in a way that is not constrained by ranking systems. They found that romantic partners and friends tended to be rated highly and were relatively close together, with fathers and siblings being considerably

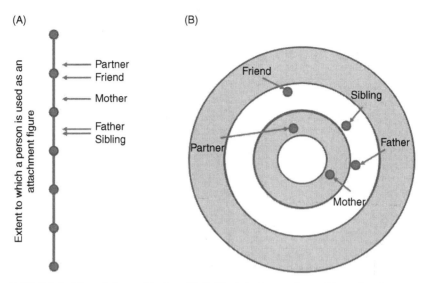

(A)

Extent to which a person is used as an attachment figure

Partner
Friend

Mother

Father
Sibling

(B)

Friend

Sibling

Partner

Father

Mother

FIGURE 2.2   The relative positioning of individuals in the attachment hierarchy when non-ranking measures are used. Part A illustrates the relative positions of targets in Tancredy and Fraley's (2006) research. Part B illustrates the relative positioning from the center of targets in Rowe and Carnelley's (2005) research. (The distance from the center is of interest; the distance of each target from the others is arbitrary in this particular illustration.)

lower in their ratings (see also Karantzas & Cole, 2011). Fig. 2.2 Part A provides a graphical representation of the average relative location of various individuals in the average person's attachment hierarchy based on these data.

Tancredy and Fraley (2006) also examined age-related changes in attachment. They found that older adults were less likely to use their mothers, fathers, and siblings for attachment-related functions across time. Older participants who had romantic partners were more likely to feel attached to their romantic partners compared to younger participants.

Rowe and Carnelley (2005) also used a method for assessing attachment networks that does not require the use of rankings, thereby allowing for a fine-grained mapping of how similar various targets may be in people's representational hierarchies. They used a bull's eye method in which participants are shown three nested concentric circles. Participants are asked to first nominate up to 10 of their "closest and/or most important relationships" (p. 503) and then place a sticker representing each person within the series of circles. Participants are told that the closer they place the sticker to the center, the more central the person is with respect to their core self, but they are not given any special instruction on how to place the stickers relative to one another. The distance, in millimeters, between the center of each sticker and the center of the diagram, is used to quantify the target's position in the attachment hierarchy. Rowe and Carnelley (2005) used this method in a sample of 129 undergraduates in the United Kingdom. They found that mothers (27 mm) and romantic partners (30 mm) tended to be placed closest to the center, followed by siblings (37 mm), fathers (41 mm), relatives (52 mm), and friends (56 mm) (Part B of Fig. 2.2). In a second study they used the bull's eye method in a sample of high-school-aged adolescents and a sample of college-aged students. Importantly, they found that although there were no age differences in how close to the center parents were placed, there were age differences in how close friends were placed to the center. Specifically, older adolescents tended to place their friend closer to their core self than did younger adolescents.

Taken together, these data on continuous ratings rather than rankings and nominations suggest a few conclusions. First, they corroborate previous work showing that romantic partners tend to be people's primary attachment figures in adulthood. But they also reveal that there can be more than one person near the top of the hierarchy. Second, when attachment functions are measured in a more continuous way that does not constrain one person's ranking to be dependent upon another person's ranking, some interesting age-related findings emerge among adults. Namely, adolescents do not appear to consider their parents to be less central, but they do begin to rate their peers as more central (Rowe & Carnelley, 2005). But, among adults, people show a clear and steady decline in the extent to which they relate to their parents as attachment figures (Tancredy & Fraley, 2006). But it does not seem to be the case, at least in any obvious way, that using peers as attachment figures requires pushing parents to a lower location in the attachment hierarchy.

These conclusions are based on the cross-sectional data available to date. Without longitudinal data, it will not be possible to determine exactly how the standing of one particular individual in the attachment hierarchy changes (if at all) as a function of how the status of another individual in the hierarchy changes. The gradual decline in the extent to which people use parents as attachment figures may exist independently of whether people are prioritizing romantic partners in their lives. To understand how change in the placement of one individual (eg, parents) is dependent upon change in the placement of another (eg, partners), it is necessary to investigate these processes in tandem and across time. We hope researchers will address this issue in the future.

We should also note that relatively little is known about how these processes may play out in middle to late adulthood. When adult children reach a point at which they are caring for their aging parents, it is possible that attachment concerns (eg, concerns about the availability of the parental attachment figure) become salient, potentially pushing the aging parent to a higher location in the individual's attachment hierarchy. It is also possible that some people come to realize that their parents cannot function as effective attachment figures anymore and, as a result, the parent's role in the attachment hierarchy stagnates or declines. We believe it would be fascinating to study these issues in future research and to identify factors that may determine individual differences in how attachment functions shift. Finally, we should note that with increasing cultural trends for adult children to live with their parents (Fry, 2014), there could be potential declines in the rate at which children shift attachment-related functions from parents to peers. We hope future work will be able to speak to this question.

WHAT HAPPENS WHEN A RELATIONSHIP ENDS?
FALLING OFF THE LADDER AND CONTINUING BONDS

Much of our discussion up to this point has been concerned with the transfer of attachment-related functions from parents to romantic partners. The research to date seems to indicate that parents do not necessarily become unimportant when a romantic partner emerges as an attachment figure; but parents may no longer be the first people the individual turns to for support.

But what happens when people transition out of a romantic relationship, due to death or a breakup? Although there is not much research on these issues to date, our sense is that different processes are involved in these two kinds of loss. When an attachment figure passes away, people undergo many of the powerful emotions reviewed briefly in chapter: What Is Attachment Theory?. They may cry, feel hopeless and lost, feel restless and despondent, and continue to pine for the lost person. But the lost person does not simply disappear from the attachment hierarchy. The bond still exists, even if the attachment figure is not physically present to serve attachment-related functions. Bereaved individuals often report using the lost person as a safe haven and secure base. For example, they may explore new activities by drawing upon their memories of the deceased as a source of strength or inspiration. They may turn to the deceased for advice, comfort, and solace.

Bereavement scholars refer to this phenomenon as "continuing bonds" to highlight the idea that, although bereaved, many surviving spouses will continue to feel a deep sense of attachment or connection to the lost figure (see Fraley & Shaver, 1999, for an in-depth discussion). Although the process of adaptation to loss may involve coming to terms with living without the loved one, the lost person does not get explicitly removed from the attachment hierarchy. It is possible that another person may come to supersede him or her over time. In this respect, the process may be analogous to the transference process that takes place as adolescents and young adults begin to transfer attachment functions from parents to peers.

Our intuition is that the process of reorganizing one's hierarchy of attachment figures is different for people who break up or divorce. In these situations, some people—especially those who feel scorned—may be taking active steps to remove the former partner from their emotional core. This process may involve a considerable degree of ambivalence and psychological defense. Indeed, this process most closely resembles what Bowlby (1969/1982, 1980) referred to as *detachment*—an active, defensive effort to downplay the emotional significance of an individual. As discussed in chapter: What Is Attachment Theory?, Bowlby and colleagues often observed signs of detachment when children had been separated from their parents for a prolonged period of time. Upon reunion, they would often treat the parent with emotional indifference. But, as Bowlby observed, this was not a genuine experience of indifference and the pattern could easily break down when the children were distressed.

To the best of our knowledge, there is no research on how attachment networks are reorganized when people lose someone they love or when a relationship ends. Our working assumption is that, when people choose to sever ties with an attachment figure, there may be efforts to demote the individual in the hierarchy by downplaying the emotional significance of the individual and minimizing contact with the person. In the case of loss, however, it seems less likely that the former attachment figure is being demoted per se. It seems more likely that part of the process of adaptation involves finding ways to move on while respecting the nature of the lost relationship and even allowing it to continue as a source of security. As a result, the lost partner may continue to serve attachment functions symbolically even as new people come to play an important role in the attachment network.

ARE ATTACHMENT RELATIONSHIPS LIMITED TO PARENTS AND PEERS? WHAT OTHER KINDS OF ATTACHMENT RELATIONSHIPS MAY EXIST?

When measures such as the WHOTO are administered to adolescents and adults, the most commonly identified attachment figures are mothers, fathers, romantic partners, and best friends. However, people also nominate other targets as serving attachment-related functions. Many individuals report that a grandparent serves attachment-related functions. Some people even nominate pets and God (Kirkpatrick, 2005; Kurdek, 2008).

God as an Attachment Figure

God is an interesting figure to consider. Indeed, if one examines Christian views on God, it is clear that God is often portrayed as a father-figure—an older and wiser individual. Christians are encouraged to seek proximity to God, through prayer, worship, and devotion. God is viewed as a safe haven to which people can turn in times of distress. And, importantly, God is conceptualized as a secure base from which one can explore the world. People may feel emboldened, for example, by knowing that God is there when needed and that God is watching over them as they endure trying times (Kirkpatrick, 2005).

God, however, presents a challenge for attachment theory. As noted in chapter: What Is Attachment Theory?, one of the ways in which Bowlby positioned himself against the psychoanalytic models of his time was by emphasizing the importance of observable interactions that take place between infants and their caregivers. Although we can bring infants and their parents into the strange situation to observe their interactions, we cannot do so with God.

But one consequence of the nonphysical relationship people have with God is that individual differences in the quality of the relationship cannot be attributed to actual interpersonal experiences people have had with God. Indeed, Kirkpatrick (2005) suggested that part of what drives the way in which people relate to God (eg, whether they view him as loving and forgiving or wrathful and vengeful) is the nature of the relationship that people have with their parents.

There are at least two ways this could play out, according to Kirkpatrick (2005). One possibility is that people may anchor their relationship with God in their relationship with their parents. Thus, people who are relatively secure with their parents may be more likely to also have a secure view of God (what Kirkpatrick refers to as the *correspondence hypothesis*). And, similarly, people who view their parents as cold, punitive, and unloving may be inclined to view God in similar ways. An alternative model, called the *compensatory hypothesis*, is that people may construct their relationship with God in ways that compensate for perceived deficiencies in their relationships with parents. Thus, someone who feels that their primary caregiver is not as accepting as they would like may construct an image of God that fills that gap. They may come to view God as particularly loving, kind, and accepting.

The empirical research on this issue seems to favor the correspondence hypothesis. Namely, people who have secure relationships with their parents are more likely to view God as a loving and accepting entity whereas people who have insecure relationships with their parents are more likely to view God as unreliable or unjust (see Kirkpatrick, 2005, for a review).

These themes will emerge again in chapter: How Do Individual Differences in Attachment Develop? where we review research on the development of attachment styles in adulthood. The general theme is that the security of one's relationships with parents tends to positively, rather than negatively, predict how secure people will feel with others, whether those others are God, romantic partners, or best friends. It is important to note, however, that these patterns are based on averages. That is, these data do not mean that some people do not, in fact, compensate for weaknesses in one relationship by selecting partners who can do so. It is undoubtedly the case that this takes place in human development, and we reviewed some research previously which suggests that people may be more likely to use peers as attachment figures when they view their parents as being inadequate. But, on average, it is more likely to be the case that people end up in the kinds of relationships to which they are accustomed. Secure experiences beget secure experiences, in the family, with God, and in romantic relationships.

Other Attachment Figures

Scholars have proposed that a large number of targets can serve attachment-related functions. For example, some people have proposed that people can feel attached to places (Scannell & Gifford, 2013), their homeland (Ferenczi & Marshall, 2013), products and brands (eg, Proksch, Orth, & Bethge, 2013), objects (Nedelisky & Steele, 2009; van IJzendoorn et al., 1983), horses (Bachi, 2013), and pets (Kurdek, 2008).

We do not have the space to review all of these possibilities here. Some scholars are skeptical of the idea that *anything*—including pets—could be conceptualized as an attachment figure (eg, Kobak, 2009). In some ways, the concept of "attachment" gets diluted if it is applied to every potential object a person could conceptualize as special or meaningful. But, another way to view the issue is that the drive to form attachments is so powerful that it can permeate many different domains of life. To be clear, it is certainly not the case that everyone is attached to horses. But some people may be. And, to the extent to which that is true, attachment theory may prove to be a powerful framework for understanding the nature of that bond.

WHY DID ATTACHMENT BONDS EVOLVE IN ADULT ROMANTIC RELATIONSHIPS?

It is relatively easy to appreciate why attachment would have evolved in the context of infant–caregiver relationships. Because human infants are born in a highly immature state, their survival depends critically on having someone who can feed them, keep them warm, and protect them from predators. The biological function of attachment in early childhood is protection (see chapters: What Is Attachment Theory? and What Is the Attachment Behavioral System? And, How Is It Linked to Other Behavioral Systems?).

But why would attachment play a role in romantic relationships? Does it serve an obvious evolutionary function? Or is it largely an artifact—what evolutionary biologists sometimes refer to as an *exaptation*—a behavioral and emotional appendage that may have been functional at some point in evolutionary history, but is not necessarily anymore?

At least two functional hypotheses have been articulated in the literature on adult attachment. One is the *paternal care hypothesis*. According to this hypothesis, romantic attachment may facilitate inclusive fitness by helping to keep mates together long enough to provide an additional source of protection and care for vulnerable offspring (Fraley, Brumbaugh, & Marks, 2005). Children might benefit by having access to more resources, distributed care, or additional protection. Consistent with this notion, data on humans indicate that offspring are more likely to survive to a reproductive age if they are raised in families in which the mother and father are pair bonded (Fletcher, Simpson, Campbell, & Overall, 2015). Unpaired women may at times forgo the care of their offspring because of the difficulties of raising the child alone (Hrdy, 1992). There is also evidence that the presence of an invested primate male can deter potential threats by other males (van Schaik & Dunbar, 1990). In short, if infants are at greater risk in the absence of care and protection of both parents, there may have been selection pressures that facilitated pair bonding on the part of mates and a greater degree of parental investment on the father's part.

Another hypothesis—and not necessarily one that is exclusive to the first—is that adult romantic attachment is a by-product of humans' prolonged neotenous state (Bjorklund, 1997; Fraley & Shaver, 2000). In fact, humans are unique in having juvenile characteristics that are retained for an extended period of time. Compared with other primates, for example, the human brain takes longer to develop, humans remain relatively hairless, their teeth erupt at a late age, and their sexual maturation is delayed. These kinds of observations have led some scholars to suggest that one of the mechanisms governing human evolution involves variation in the timing of normative maturational processes. Namely, our rate of development is slower than that of other species and, as a result, we retain many infantile traits into adulthood. Bjorklund (1997) highlights human play as being a prototypical behavioral example of this idea. In many species, play tends to be limited to infancy and early childhood, but, in humans, it characterizes our behavior across diverse contexts—including courtship. The *developmental neoteny hypothesis* holds that the attachment system—a motivational system that originally evolved in the context of infancy—does not become dormant as humans age, in part, because maturational processes proceed at a slower rate in humans. As a result, the attachment system may continue to be sensitive to certain cues (eg, danger) and readily activated in contexts that are similar to infant–parent relationships (eg, involving physically intimate exchanges). This may or may not make it functional per se, but offers one potential explanation for why attachment plays a role in romantic relationships.

Fraley et al. (2005) explored some questions about the evolution of adult attachment by conducting a comparative and phylogenetic investigation into attachment in a variety of species. Specifically, they acquired social, developmental, and morphological data from samples of mammals and primates. They found that, on average, species that exhibited signs of adult attachment were more likely than those who did not to have some degree of paternal care. In addition, species that were rated as being more developmentally neotenous, as indicated by the typical gestation time, the age at which offspring leave the family of origin, etc., were more likely to exhibit adult attachment than species that were less neotenous. These comparative data suggest that romantic attachment is not randomly distributed across living species. It is more likely to be observed among species (1) in which fathers play a role in child care and (2) that exhibit signs of prolonged immaturity.

Fraley and colleagues also attempted to test potential functional accounts by using a method of phylogenetically independent contrasts—an approach that is used in phylogenetic research to determine (1) the extent to which a feature (such as adult attachment) has evolved independently across a phylogenic tree and (2) whether the independent emergence of a trait covaries with instances of another trait (such as paternal care). This method is grounded in the assumption that, if a trait is functional, then independent instances of its emergence in evolutionary time should covary. These analyses indicated that there may be a functional relationship between adult attachment and paternal care. Specifically, on occasions in which adult attachment emerged in species across evolutionary history, it appears that it was more likely than not that paternal care also emerged. However, the covariation between adult attachment and neoteny appeared to be incidental rather than functional. These two attributes appear to covary across species not because they independently coevolved over evolutionary history, but because they happened to coexist in ancestors. Thus, although species that exhibit adult attachment are also more likely to be developmentally immature, it does not appear that these two traits evolved independently across multiple occasions in evolutionary history. Fraley and colleagues also estimated that approximately 26% of mammals and 19% of primates exhibit signs of adult attachment in the context of mating. Adult attachment is not a uniquely human phenomenon and it appears that it may have evolved independently several times in the course of mammalian evolution.

A FEW CAUTIONARY REMARKS

We close by noting a few caveats concerning the definition and measurement of attachment-related features and functions.

Do Attachments Vary in Strength?

Ainsworth et al. (1978) cautioned scholars against thinking about attachment bonds as varying in strength. In the infant attachment literature, there is a tradition of conceptualizing the attachment bond as one that exists or does not exist. This conceptualization has been a useful one because it highlights the distinction between the existence of the attachment bond itself and the quality of that bond (ie, whether it is a secure one or not; chapter: What Are Attachment Working Models?). For example, an infant who would be classified as avoidant in the strange situation may, at first, appear to not be attached to his or her primary caregiver. The infant might not appear to be monitoring the whereabouts of the caregiver in the novel environment and, when he or she leaves the room, the child may not show visible signs of distress. But one would not want to conclude on the basis of these observations alone that the child is not attached to his or her caregiver or that the strength of the bond is lesser than that of a secure child. One can infer the presence of the bond because, as the strange situation progresses, the defensive behavior of the child may give way to visible signs of distress. And although the child may fail to organize his or her behavior in a way that would lead to a secure attachment classification, the child may reveal his or her distress in other ways. Indeed, Sroufe and Waters (1977b) argued that the heart rates of avoidant children in the strange situation are often comparable to those of secure children, suggesting that avoidant children are not merely unaffected by the procedure. They are attached to their caregivers, but organize their behavior to serve different goals.

The other reason Ainsworth and colleagues caution against thinking about the bond as one that varies in strength is that doing so would seem to suggest that anxious-resistant children are "more" attached to their parents than secure children. Behaviorally, anxious-resistant children may engage in more expressions of proximity seeking and separation distress than secure children, creating the impression that they are more strongly attached than secure children. But, theoretically, the intense behavior exhibited by these children reflects secondary strategies for organizing their behavior (chapters: How Stable Are Attachment Styles in Adulthood? and What Is the Attachment Behavioral System? And, How Is It Linked to Other Behavioral Systems?); it does not reflect a "stronger" bond.

Having said that, it is clear that being attached is more than a simple binary affair. Indeed, the way Hazan and Zeifman (1994) and others study attachment in adulthood involves thinking about and measuring the *extent to which a person serves attachment-related functions* (eg, Fraley & Davis, 1997). Thus, although a person who functions as a safe haven and a secure base may be an attachment figure, targets can vary in the extent to which they fulfill these various functions. A peer, for example, may be a target of proximity seeking, but might not function as a secure base. We believe that it is important to take this kind of variation into account, but it is also important to not confuse it with the "strength" of an attachment bond.

Should Separation Distress be Used as a Marker of an Attachment Bond?

It is important to note that the presence of separation distress is often taken to be an indicator of attachment across many species and across many developmental phases. Indeed, Weiss (1975) considered separation distress to be one of the fail-safe indicators of an attachment relationship. However, not all researchers use separation distress as a marker of attachment in empirical research (eg, Fraley & Davis, 1997; Nickerson & Nagle, 2005) because, in practice, it is a difficult one to use for assessment purposes. Brief separations are not as stressful for adults as they are for infants in a strange situation. Moreover, sometimes this distress is most obvious following a severe separation (eg, divorce) or loss, making it an impractical way to gauge the nature of the attachment relationship prior to that point. Our point is not to claim that separation distress is not a marker of an attachment bond; it most certainly is. But our impression is that it is more difficult for adults to self-report accurately on how they would feel if they lost someone. Doing so requires individuals to imagine hypothetical outcomes, whereas reporting on who they actually use for safe haven and secure-base functions does not.

There is also the complication that we alluded to before that separation distress is also a marker of caregiving and not attachment alone. Moreover, although it can be said that an attachment figure serves safe haven and secure-base functions, an attachment figure does not serve "separation protest" functions exactly. Separation protest is a marker of the existence of a bond, but is not a function that an attachment figure serves. Thus, to study the transfer of attachment-related functions, one would not want to include separation protest as a function to be transferred.

To be clear: we are not denying the importance of separation distress in understanding attachment. But we wish to emphasize that it is a difficult criterion to use for assessing the nature of an intact bond in adulthood.

Are All Attachments Alike? Asymmetries Across Relationships

One of the core themes of adult attachment theory is that the attachment system is relevant to adult relationships and personality functioning. And although romantic relationships appear to be the most common kind of attachment in adulthood, there are important differences between the various kinds of attachments that people have across the lifespan. Just because two relationships are classified as "attachment relationships" does not mean that they are equivalent in all possible ways. For example, scholars have highlighted at least two crucial differences between infant–caregiver attachments and adult romantic attachments (see chapter: What Is Attachment Theory?). The distinction between the attached and the caregiver, for example, is clear in infant–caregiver relationships. It is not the parent who is using the infant as a secure base from which to explore the world; it is the child who is using the parent. Moreover, parents do not seek out their children for safety and assurance, but children seek their parents out for these purposes.

In adult romantic relationships, these boundaries are much less clear. At different points in the relationship, one person may function as an attachment figure and the other the attached. And at other times the roles may be reversed (chapter: What Is the Attachment Behavioral System? And, How Is It Linked to Other Behavioral Systems?). It is generally assumed that both individuals in the relationship are mutually attached to one another and that each person is capable of playing either kind of role. (Although their ability to do so competently may vary across individuals.) Second, romantic relationships are rooted in physical attraction and sexuality whereas infant–caregiver relationships are not. Hazan and Zeifman (1994) argued that many romantic relationships are initiated due to feelings of interpersonal attraction and the process of being intimate with others and engaging in persistent physical contact can set in motion the bonding process (see Gillath, Mikulincer, Birnbaum, & Shaver, 2008a). In short, romantic relationships often involve some combination of sexual interest, attachment, and caregiving (Hazan & Shaver, 1994) whereas infant–caregiver relationships lack the sexual component.

Other kinds of attachments in adulthood, of course, may also differ from one another in crucial ways. We discussed attachment to God earlier in this chapter as an example of a potential attachment relationship in adulthood. In fact, this kind of relationship might have more in common with infant–caregiver attachment than it does with adult romantic attachment. The roles of the attached and the attachment figure are much more compartmentalized, for example. One does not provide care and comfort to God, and God does not use people as a secure base from which to explore the world. Similarly, people do not typically have a sexual connection to God in the Christian tradition. We opened the chapter with an example of a twin who was clearly attached to her sibling. Like adult romantic relationships, the roles of caregiving and attachment in twin relationships are more likely to be mutual than asymmetrical, as they are in infant–parent attachments.

Is There Really a Difference Between a Primary and a Secondary Attachment Figure?

A number of interesting questions can be asked about what does and does not constitute an attachment relationship. For example, one may wonder whether a person can only be construed as an attachment figure if he or she serves proximity-seeking, safe haven, and secure-base functions. Or whether a person who serves two such functions is "less" of an attachment figure than a person who serves all three functions. Or whether two or more people can be "primary" attachment figures if they each serve all three functions. Or, what exactly, makes someone a "secondary" attachment figure if that person, in fact, serves all three-attachment functions.

These are challenging questions to answer definitively because there is not a unified way to conceptualize attachment relationships. In fact, the current literature uses a variety of different terms, models, and measures to conceptualize and study attachment relationships. Some theorists, for example, have conceptualized attachment hierarchies in a way that would only leave room for a single individual at the top—as if a pyramid-like structure captures the psychology of attachment relationships (eg, Bowlby, 1969/1982). If this metaphor is appropriate, then only one person can be at the top and, in order for one person to emerge as a new attachment figure, another one must be "dethroned" (see the previous discussion).

Another way of conceptualizing attachment hierarchies, however, is as gradations of attachment-related processes. Thus, although someone could function as an attachment figure (serving all three functions), that person can easily share that privileged position in the hierarchy with others. In such an approach, there is a quantitative and functional difference between someone who serves as a secure base and someone who does not, but there is no natural threshold at which a relationship becomes an "attachment." Moreover, there is no assumption that a person cannot have multiple attachments.

Importantly, the concept of "primary attachment figure" emerges from a conceptualization that assumes a pyramidal structure rather than a graded hierarchical structure. In a graded hierarchical model metaphor, however, it is easier to conceptualize variations in the extent to which people fulfill certain attachment functions and, as a result, it is easier to accommodate the idea that multiple individuals could serve as viable attachment figures. In this framework, it still might be the case that one person is favored and, in such situations, it might be sensible to refer to that individual as the "primary attachment figure" and the others as "secondary attachment figures," but, in some ways, those are just labels that are being used to describe in words the significance of the relationship; they do not reflect hard boundaries or binary categories.

We highlight these issues here to make it clear that there is no "correct" way to think about these issues in the context of contemporary attachment theory. Nonetheless, they are important issues to consider and we hope that future work will focus on solving some of these outstanding issues.

Is It Possible to Develop an Attachment Relationship With Someone who Does not Function as an Effective Secure Base?

Throughout this chapter we have defined attachment relationships as relationships with a person to whom the individual maintains proximity, whom the individual uses as a safe haven during times of distress, and uses as a secure base from which to explore the world. In many respects, this definition assumes that the relationship is a reasonably well-functioning one. After all, it is difficult to imagine that an individual would come to rely on someone as a secure base if, in fact, the person in question has repeatedly failed to be available and responsive when needed.

The clinical literature, however, is replete with examples of individuals who develop attachment relationships with others who do not function as ideal attachment figures. One of the most salient examples concerns emotionally and physically abusive relationships (eg, Henderson, Bartholomew, & Dutton, 1997; Milyavskaya & Lydon, 2013). In these situations, people may be fully aware that the relationship is not a healthy one. But the thought of leaving the relationship can generate anxiety—anxiety that, in turn, has the potential to lead the abused individual to seek proximity to the very same individual who is the source of the distress. Indeed, even in nonabusive relationships where partners are electing to separate or divorce, people often report an emotional gravitational force that keeps them from breaking free (Weiss, 1975).

It is difficult to imagine how an attachment bond could have developed in situations where the potential attachment figure is not responsive, understanding, and supportive—and maybe even abusive. Although we do not fully understand how these kinds of attachments may develop, we believe there may be at least two pathways that could enable their development. First, it may be the case that even suboptimal attachment figures are responsive, understanding, and supportive at some point in the development of the relationship. Indeed, one of the things that people sometimes report when they are separating from or breaking up with a partner is that their partner changed over time; the person the individual married was different—much more caring, kind, and giving (eg, Felmlee, 1995; Weiss, 1975). And some research on attachment and interpersonal attraction suggests that even highly insecure individuals —people who may be unlikely candidates to serve as attachment figures—can be warm, engaging, and charming in initial interactions (Brumbaugh, Baren, & Agishtein, 2014; Brumbaugh & Fraley, 2010).

A second possibility is that, in the absence of an obvious alternative attachment figure, attachment relationships may sometimes develop to whichever individual is most proximate or familiar. The drive to form attachment relationships may be so primal and ingrained that people begin to form attachment bonds even in suboptimal conditions. Indeed, Ainsworth (1991) discussed the ways in which wartime stress has the potential to create enduring and powerful emotional relationships between soldiers—relationships that have many characteristics of an attachment bond. It is possible that suboptimal conditions, such as conditions of danger or risk, may accelerate the proclivity to bond. If so, then people may end up forging attachments to figures who, in many respects, may or may not be ideal attachment figures. They become the person's safe haven and secure base, not because they perform these functions competently, but because no one else is able to do so.

Chapter 3

How Do Individual Differences in Attachment Develop?

Why are some people relatively secure in their attachment styles whereas others are less so? According to attachment theory, these individual differences are reflections of the way in which people's attachment systems have become organized over the course of their lives, beginning with their earliest attachment relationships. But to what extent do early attachment experiences shape later attachment patterns? This question has been at the forefront of developmental inquiry for several decades (see Cassidy & Shaver, 2008, for a review). However, due to the time and expense involved in conducting longitudinal research on personality development, only recently have researchers been positioned to answer this question using multidecade research. The purpose of this chapter is to review what is known about the consequences of early attachment experiences for the development of individual differences in attachment.

We begin by discussing factors that shape individual differences in attachment organization in infancy and early childhood. Readers may wonder, why have a chapter that devotes considerable attention to the development of attachment in childhood when this book is primarily about attachment in adulthood. The answer is that a person's sense of security in adulthood is thought to have its origins in early caregiving experiences. Therefore, it seems sensible to begin at the beginning, so to speak, by reviewing research on how early caregiving experiences may shape individual differences in attachment in infancy and childhood. We then review theory and research on how those early experiences may help scaffold the development of other resources and competencies that might sustain attachment patterns into adulthood.

It is unlikely that early attachment experiences alone fully explain why some people are more secure than others in adulthood. Early attachment experiences are, without a doubt, an important part of the story. But there are many factors that have the potential to influence the organization of attachment as people navigate the life course. Thus, we also review what is known about the various factors that contribute to individual differences in attachment in adulthood, including experiences in relationships with peers. Finally, we close with some caveats and ideas about the kind of research that would be most beneficial in the near future.

Adult Attachment. http://dx.doi.org/10.1016/B978-0-12-420020-3.00003-7

HOW DO EARLY ATTACHMENT EXPERIENCES SHAPE ATTACHMENT PATTERNS IN INFANCY AND EARLY CHILDHOOD?

One of the important goals of research on early attachment experiences is to uncover the antecedents of attachment security (see Belsky & Fearon, 2008, for a review). In Ainsworth's early research, for example, she observed that children who were more confident in exploring the environment had parents who were more supportive and available than children who were less confident in exploring the environment (Ainsworth, 1967). Ainsworth, Blehar, Waters, and Wall, (1978) studied this issue systematically in a sample of parents and children in Baltimore, Maryland. Specifically, they studied approximately 23 infant–mother pairs in their homes. The investigators made notes of how the children behaved, how the mother responded to the child's signals, etc. When the infants were 12 months of age, they were brought to the laboratory to participate in the strange situation procedure as a way of assessing their attachment organization (see chapter: What Is Attachment Theory?).

Children who were classified as secure at 12 months of age were more likely, than those who were not, to have had caregivers who were sensitively responsive to their child's needs in the year prior to the strange situation. Conversely, children who were classified as insecure were more likely to have mothers who were neglectful or inconsistently responsive to their children's needs. This observational research provided some of the first evidence that variations in the early caregiving environment are associated with the ways in which a child's attachment behavior becomes organized in the first year of life.

After the publication of Ainsworth's ground-breaking studies, a number of research teams began investigating factors that may determine whether children develop secure or insecure relationships with their primary attachment figures. One of the key predictors of the attachment patterns children develop is the history of sensitive and responsive interactions between the caregiver and the child (DeWolff & van IJzendoorn, 1997). *Sensitive responsiveness* is typically defined as the extent to which a parent is in-tune with a child's emotional state, is able to decode those signals accurately, and able to respond appropriately and in a timely fashion (Ainsworth et al., 1978). When the child is uncertain or stressed, a sensitively responsive caregiver is one who correctly notes the child's distress and is able to provide the child with comfort or the assistance that is needed. Ainsworth and colleagues believed that the ability of the caregiver to be sensitively responsive to the child is critical for the child's psychological development. Such supportive interactions help the child learn to regulate his or her emotions, give the child the confidence to explore the environment, and provide the child with a safe haven during stressful circumstances.

Evidence for the role of sensitive and responsive caregiving in shaping attachment patterns comes from both longitudinal and experimental studies. For example, Grossmann, Grossmann, Spanger, Suess, and Unzner (1985) studied parent–child interactions in the homes of 54 families, up to 3 times during the first year of the child's life. At 12 months of age, infants and their mothers participated in the strange situation. Grossmann and colleagues found that children who were classified as secure in the strange situation at 12 months of age were more likely than children classified as insecure to have mothers who provided sensitive and responsive care to their children in the home environment.

van den Boom (1990, 1994) developed an intervention that was designed to enhance maternal sensitive responsiveness. van den Boom identified a sample of babies who showed signs of irritability on a newborn behavioral assessment scale. She then randomly assigned half of those babies to an experimental group and the other half to a control group. Mothers in the intervention group were given individualized sessions on sensitive responsiveness—sessions that involved watching video-taped interactions between the mother and her child with coaching and discussion. The control group received no training. When the infants were 9 months of age, the mothers in the intervention group were rated as more responsive and attentive in their interaction with their infants. In addition, their infants were rated as more sociable, self-soothing, and more likely to explore the environment. At 12 months of age children in the intervention group were more likely to be classified as secure than insecure (anxious or avoidant) in the strange situation compared with the control group (see Bakermans-Kranenburg, van IJzendoorn, & Juffer, 2003; van IJzendoorn, Juffer, & Duyvesteyn, 1995, for an in-depth discussion of intervention research).

It is important to note that sensitive responsiveness is embedded in a network of contextual factors (eg, Cowan, 1997). That is, there are a number of factors that can facilitate or impair a parent's ability to provide sensitive and responsive care to a child. If a mother, for example, is experiencing depression, she may not have the psychological resources available to be attentive to her child's needs. Indeed, research shows that the children of parents who experience depressive episodes are more likely to be classified as insecure in the strange situation (Cummings & Davies, 1994; Teti, Gelfand, Messinger, & Isabella, 1995). Likewise, parents who are struggling financially are likely to experience stress. They are also likely to work multiple jobs in an effort to make ends meet, which is likely to add further stress. This stress may carry over into parenting, making it more difficult for the parent to provide a secure base and safe haven for the child. Indeed, research typically finds that the rates of insecure attachment are higher in economically disadvantaged families (eg, Belsky, 1996; Belsky & Isabella, 1998; Scher & Mayseless, 2000). In short, although attachment theorists tend to emphasize the role of sensitive, responsive caregiving in shaping the development of children's attachment patterns, there are many factors that have the potential to influence caregiving quality. Sensitive responsiveness is not viewed as the sole predictor of attachment security; it is regarded as an organizing variable: one that can reflect a broad array of social-cultural and biological influences (eg, Pickles et al., 2013).

WHAT ARE THE CONSEQUENCES OF EARLY ATTACHMENT EXPERIENCES FOR SOCIAL AND PERSONALITY DEVELOPMENT?

One of Bowlby's (1973) arguments was that, as children begin to construct working models of themselves and their interpersonal world, these representations gain traction in shaping the kinds of experiences that children are likely to have. We expand on this theme in chapter: How Stable Are Attachment Styles in Adulthood?, but for now we wish to note that supportive attachment experiences in childhood not only influence the security of the bond that the child develops with his or her caregiver, but have consequences for many outcomes of developmental significance. For example, children who have relatively secure attachment histories are more likely than those who have insecure attachment histories to develop a sense of empathy and the ability to form high-functioning relationships with others (see Berlin, Cassidy, & Appleyard, 2008, for a review). These skills, in turn, are believed to reinforce and sustain the child's working models. As a consequence of these person–environment transactions, early attachment experiences have the potential to set a child on a developmental pathway in which he or she gains momentum across time, ultimately generating individual differences downstream in the ways in which individuals organize their attachment-related thoughts, feelings, and behavior.

In the sections that follow, we review some of the research on how early attachment experiences may impact developmental outcomes (see Fraley & Roisman, 2015, for further discussion of these themes). We focus on two broad outcomes: those concerning social competence and those concerning the quality of peer relationships and friendships. We highlight these outcomes, not because they are the only outcomes that are of interest in understanding social development, but doing so allows us to review the consequences of early attachment experiences for two important domains of human functioning: the intrapersonal and the interpersonal.

How do Early Attachment Histories Shape the Development of Social Competence?

Social competence refers to the broad set of emotional, social, and cognitive skills needed for adaptation to a diverse array of developmental contexts and challenges (Waters & Sroufe, 1983). In this chapter we use the term loosely to capture a wide range of personal skills and competencies, such as emotion regulation skills, self-control, perspective taking, and the capacity for empathy. Bowlby believed that supportive and responsive interactions between parents and their children are crucial for the development of these skills in childhood. For example, he believed that a child's sense of self (ie, whether he or she perceives him or herself as lovable) and his or her ability to regulate emotions in an appropriate way are rooted in the history of a child's interactions with his or her parents.

An important line of work in attachment research concerns the relations among early attachment histories and emotional understanding and perspective-taking skills. Laible and Thompson (1998), for example, had young children watch three puppets enact a variety of dramatic scenes and, at the end of each one, each child was asked questions about the protagonist puppet's feelings. Laible and Thompson (1998) found that children with secure attachment histories exhibited greater emotional understanding compared to children with insecure attachment histories. This suggests that the ways in which children had internalized attachment experiences may have influenced their ability to understand the point of view of others and to better understand the world from someone else's perspective.

Research has also found that secure children are more empathic than others. For example, Kestenbaum, Farber, and Sroufe (1989) studied children's free play interactions and made note of cases in which another child was visibly distressed and how the target child behaved as a result. Kestenbaum and colleagues found that children with secure attachment histories were more likely than those with avoidant histories to behave in emphatic ways in the presence of distressed children.

Children with histories of insecure attachment have been found to behave with more aggression, greater anger, and less empathy across a variety of situations. For example, Troy and Sroufe (1987) found that children with avoidant attachment histories were more likely to victimize their peers. McElwain, Cox, Burchinal, and Macfie (2003) found that, at 36 months of age, children with insecure attachment histories were more likely to exhibit instrumental aggression when interacting with peers.

In summary, these findings are consistent with the notion that early attachment experiences provide a framework for the development of social competence. Children who have a secure attachment history are more likely, than those who have an insecure attachment history, to exhibit the kinds of competencies that might enable them to successfully negotiate a variety of interpersonal tasks. They exhibit greater emotional understanding, are able to take the perspective of other individuals, are more empathic, and express less anger and hostility.

How do Early Attachment Histories Shape the Development of Close Friendship Relationships?

Attachment researchers also believe that early attachment experiences set the stage for the way in which the child navigates interpersonal contexts, including not only his or her relationship with attachment figures, but the way the individual functions in nonparental contexts in which issues concerning trust and intimacy emerge. This can include relations with teachers and mentors

(Ainsworth, 1989), siblings (Teti & Ablard, 1989), and, importantly, close friendships (Furman, Simon, Shaffer, & Bouchey, 2002).

Close friendships serve a number of important developmental functions. For example, friends can provide a context in which one explores new skills and interests, builds alliances, bolsters self-esteem, and reinforces emerging identities (Shulman, Elicker, & Sroufe, 1994). Forming and maintaining a close friendship, however, requires a number of resources. One must be capable of managing conflict, offering support, adopting the other's perspective, and engaging in appropriate levels of self-disclosure and reciprocity. Indeed, research indicates that these kinds of social competencies play a role in facilitating the development of well-functioning friendships (eg, Boling, Barry, Kotchick, & Lowry, 2011; Simpson, Collins, Tran, & Haydon, 2007).

Close friendships are also of special interest from an attachment perspective because they are some of the first extra-familial contexts in which issues concerning intimacy, trust, and support are explored. According to some theorists, close friends are often testing grounds for transferring attachment-related features and functions away from parents (Zeifman & Hazan, 2008; see chapter: What Is an Attachment Relationship?). As such, the experiences that take place in the context of friendship relationships might be a key milestone in the development of expectations for trust, intimacy, and support that are relevant for understanding individual differences in attachment in adulthood.

Research suggests that early attachment experiences may play an important role in shaping the quality of peer interactions and close friendships. Children classified as secure in the strange situation are more likely to have stable play partners, demonstrate greater reciprocity, and exhibit empathy towards peers during the preschool years (Kestenbaum et al., 1989). Research has also found that secure attachment is related to lower levels of child–friend aggression at age 3 (McElwain et al., 2003) and fewer negative interactions with close friends at age 5 (Youngblade & Belsky, 1992).

There are many potential pathways through which early attachment experiences might influence the dynamics of friendships. One pathway that has been investigated extensively by McElwain, Booth-LaForce, and Wu (2011) concerns mental state talk. To be effective in their friendships, children need to take into consideration their friend's desires, beliefs, and feelings. One way in which children can acquire these competencies is through exchanges with caregivers in which they communicate about psychological states in a supportive, uncritical manner. McElwain et al. (2011) examined the association between early attachment experiences and the nature of mind talk in parent–child interactions at 24 months of age. They found that children with secure attachment histories were more likely to have mothers who engaged in cognitive talk (ie, they were more likely to reference appropriately feelings, desires, and plans). In turn, children whose mothers engaged in more cognitive talk at 24 months of age were more likely to have high-functioning friendships at 54 months as indexed by more positive friendship interactions across time.

DO EARLY ATTACHMENT EXPERIENCES HAVE ENDURING CONSEQUENCES FOR SOCIAL AND PERSONALITY DEVELOPMENT?

One of the key ideas in attachment theory is that early experiences have the potential to shape individual differences in adult attachment by providing a *foundation* upon which a variety of skills, competencies, and resources develop. For example, it is possible that sensitive and supportive caregiving in early life has the potential to enable children to acquire interpersonal skills that enable them to relate to others in adaptive ways. These social competencies, in turn, may facilitate children's abilities to develop high-quality friendships (eg, Englund, Kuo, Puig, & Collins, 2011; Simpson et al., 2007) (Fig. 3.1). Although there are a number of specific pathways through which early experiences could shape later outcomes (eg, brain development, emotional regulation, behavioral synchronization), the important theme is that those early experiences provide a starting place for what comes next. The effects of early experiences, whether they are positive or negative, create developmental cascades that have implications downstream for a number of important outcomes (Masten & Cicchetti, 2010; Masten et al., 2005). These ideas are emphasized by the *organizational perspective* on close relationships, a perspective that calls attention to the ways in which new relationship experiences can be shaped by earlier relationship histories (see Simpson, Collins, Farrell, & Raby, 2015).

There is a growing body of research which supports this perspective. For example, Simpson et al. (2007), using data from the Minnesota Longitudinal Study of Risk and Adaptation (MLSRA; see Sroufe, Egeland, Carlson, & Collins, 2005), found that early attachment experiences were related to social competence at ages 6–9, which, in turn, was related to the security of friendship relations at age 16. The security of those friendship relationships predicted interpersonal functioning in romantic relationships (eg, the expression of positive and negative effect in relationships) at ages 20–23. Fig. 3.1 illustrates some of the pathways in question. Using the same data set, Englund, Kuo, Puig, and Collins (2011) found that early attachment histories predicted a variety of

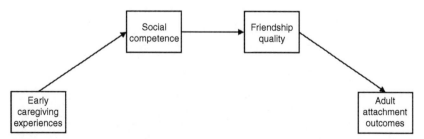

FIGURE 3.1   A basic framework for conceptualizing the way in which early attachment experiences can provide a foundation for social and interpersonal development. (Based, in part, on *Simpson et al., 2007.*)

adaptive outcomes in childhood and adolescence, including peer competence at age 9 and friendship security at age 16. Moreover, those outcomes, in turn, predicted relationship effectiveness at age 23 and global adjustment and functioning at ages 26 and 28. In short, many of the prominent conceptual models for understanding the legacy of early attachment experiences are *intervening variable* or *mediation models*: they assume that early experiences shape later outcomes by providing a foundation for subsequent experiences (Fig. 3.1).

One thing to note about this approach, however, is that it assumes, at least implicitly, that the influence of early experiences may decay across time. This is best illustrated by redrawing the dynamics illustrated in Fig. 3.1 to better reflect the unique pathways that individuals may take as they navigate each developmental task or phase. In Fig. 3.2, for example, each developmental mediator not only functions as a means to help direct an individual along a specific developmental pathway, it also has the potential to create opportunities for divergence from the original pathway. A child entering into a new peer group, for example, may find that he does not fit in, and, as a result, may experience a sense of social isolation. Although having a secure attachment history may buffer him against

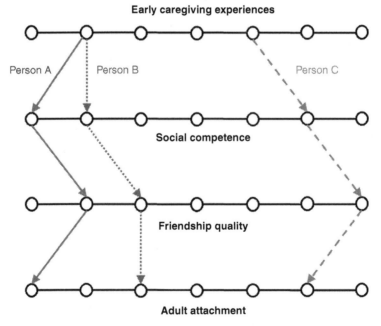

FIGURE 3.2   Cascades in the development of individual differences in adult attachment.
Each horizontal line represents a spectrum of outcomes for a construct, such as friendship quality, that can range from poor (left) to optimal (right). Many models of how early experiences shape later outcomes assume that early experiences are important because they provide a foundation for what is to come next. People who have relatively supportive caregiving experiences in early childhood (Person C), for example, are more likely to develop appropriate social and emotional skills, which in turn may lead to high-quality friendships, and, ultimately, more secure adult attachments compared to people with relatively unsupportive early caregiving experiences (Persons A and B).

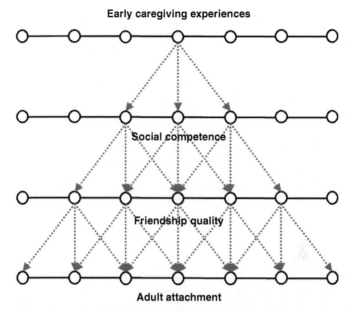

Early caregiving experiences

Social competence

Friendship quality

Adult attachment

FIGURE 3.3   The way in which cascading processes can lead to decreasing levels of predictability across time. In this illustration, people starting at the same place (ie, early caregiving experiences of moderate quality) have the potential to enter into social experiences that are comparable to what might be expected, but there is also a chance they will end up in better or less than ideal circumstances. At each step along the way, however, these junctures create additional opportunities for people to diverge from their initial trajectory. Although the most likely outcome of this process is that people starting at the mid-range of early caregiving quality will be moderately secure as adults, one's ability to forecast a person's actual fate diminishes exponentially each step along the way (eg, Galton, 1894).

this experience relative to someone with an insecure history, the experience of peer rejection can also disrupt his developmental trajectory and undermine his ability to form satisfying relationships in the years to come. Thus, each intervening variable in this framework presents both an opportunity for effects of early attachment experiences to be sustained *and* an opportunity for the effects of early experiences to recede into the background. The consequence of this is that, as people move through life, the impact of early attachment experiences in particular should diminish, even if those experiences initially provided a foundation upon which all subsequent experiences were built (Fig. 3.3).

   Is this, in fact, what we see when we examine the long-term correlates of early caregiving experiences on developmental outcomes? That is, do the consequences of early attachment experiences fade away as individuals reach adolescence and young adulthood? Fraley, Roisman, and Haltigan (2013) attempted to address this question by examining the predictive significance of responsive caregiving early in life for a variety of outcomes assessed at various ages between infancy and age 16. To do so, they used data from the NICHD Study of Early Child Care and Youth Development (SECCYD)—a longitudinal study of approximately 1000 infant–mother dyads who were assessed when the infants were 1 month of age and at a variety of follow-up waves. Fraley and colleagues examined the association between the quality of early attachment experiences in particular (ie, maternal sensitivity in the first 3 years of life) and two outcomes of developmental significance: social competence (as rated by observers and parents) and academic skills (as rated by teachers or as quantified through standardized cognitive tests). They found that the association between early sensitivity and social competence was about 0.27. And, importantly, the association did not decay across time. That is, the legacy of early attachment experiences was manifested in social competence to a similar degree whether children were 5 years of age or 15 years of age (Fig. 3.4). A similar pattern was detected with

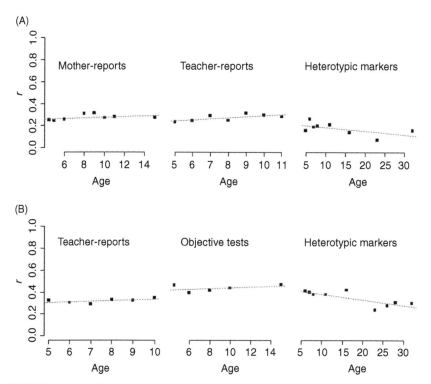

FIGURE 3.4   Associations between early caregiving experiences and various developmental outcomes as a function of the age at which the outcome was assessed. Part A illustrates associations between early caregiving experiences and social competence as assessed via mother-reports in the SECCYD (Fraley et al., 2013a), teacher-reports in the SECCYD (Fraley et al., 2013a), and a variety of heterotypic indicators in the MLSRA (Raby et al., 2015). Part B illustrates the association between early caregiving experiences and academic and educational outcomes as assessed by teacher-ratings in the SECCYD (Fraley et al., 2013a), objective tests in the SECCYD (Fraley et al., 2013a), and objective tests in the MLSRA (Raby et al., 2015). In each of these cases it can be seen that the associations between early caregiving experiences and a broad range of outcomes tend to be relatively stable and are not approaching zero as individuals get older.

cognitive and academic outcomes. Children whose parents were sensitive and responsive in their early caregiving (ie, in the first 3 years of the child's life) were more likely to succeed in school and perform well on cognitive tests and, importantly, the magnitude of that association was relatively invariant across time (Fig. 3.4).

This empirical pattern has now emerged in a number of studies. In one of the most recent ones, Raby, Roisman, Fraley, and Simpson (2015) examined the predictive significance of early caregiving experiences in the MLSRA, using data from a study of approximately 243 individuals who have been followed from birth to age 32. Raby and colleagues operationalized social competence using a variety of developmentally appropriate outcomes. For example, in childhood, social competence was indexed via teacher's ratings of children's interactions with peers. In adulthood (eg, ages 23 and 32 years) social competence was indexed as adaptive functioning in romantic relationships. They found that the association between early supportive caregiving experiences and social competence was relatively constant across time: it did not decay as individuals got older (Fig. 3.4). A similar pattern emerged with indicators of academic and cognitive skills.

What these studies reveal is that early caregiving experiences have the potential to manifest in social, emotional, and cognitive functioning across the first few decades of life. More importantly, these studies raise the possibility that early experiences provide not only a *foundation* for early development, as implied by traditional intervening variable models, but they also provide a *scaffolding* for interpersonal experiences. If early experiences only provided the foundations for subsequent development, we would find that the predictive significance of early attachment experiences would get weaker over time as children begin to accumulate a history of interpersonal experiences that diverge in subtle (or dramatic) ways from their early ones. And, although there is evidence of divergence (the predictive coefficients are not perfect), the fact that the coefficients tend to stay uniform across increasing measurement intervals indicates that early experiences may combine in a way that enables them to continue to guide interpersonal experiences as children develop.

How might this work? How might early attachment experiences continue to play scaffolding effects across time? A variety of hypotheses have been discussed in the literature. Fraley (2002) referred to these ideas collectively as the *prototype* hypothesis because they all hinge on the notion that children develop mental representations of early experiences that are embodied in ways that might be different from the experiences that are encoded and stored later in life. Infants, for example, develop representations of interactions with caregivers before they acquire language. Once children begin to use language, it is possible that the way they come to encode and represent experiences with caregivers' shifts in modality. One potential consequence of this is that the representations that developed in early life are preverbal and more procedural in nature than those that dominate interpersonal dynamics later (Fraley, 2002). Relatedly, scholars have argued that the brain is much more plastic in early life than it is later (Couperus & Nelson, 2008). As a consequence, early experiences have the potential to shape neural development and biosocial organization in a way that is more powerful than similar kinds of experiences that take place later. In the same way that touching an oil painting is more likely to leave an indelible impression when the paint is fresh rather than after it has dried, attachment experiences are more likely to leave an enduring mark on social and personality development when the brain is highly plastic than when it is less so.

Regardless of the specific mechanisms that might enable early experiences to leave a persistent trace on developmental outcomes, many theorists agree that early attachment experiences have the potential to be important in understanding later personal and interpersonal functioning. The idea was expressed most eloquently by Sroufe, Egeland, and Kreutzer (1990, p. 1364) when they wrote that "earlier patterns may again become manifest in certain contexts, in the face of further environmental change, or in the face of certain critical developmental issues. While perhaps latent, and perhaps never even to become manifest again in some cases, the earlier pattern is not gone."

WHAT GIVES RISE TO INDIVIDUAL DIFFERENCES IN ADULT ATTACHMENT PATTERNS?

The studies we have reviewed up to this point suggest two broad conclusions. First, early experiences have the potential not only to provide a foundation for social and personality development, but also to scaffold—in potentially subtle ways—the ways in which later experiences unfold. This raises the possibility that early attachment experiences can have enduring consequences for later outcomes. Second, even if the effects are enduring, that does not mean they are strong. As can be seen from the coefficients in Fig. 3.4, the legacy of early attachment experiences might be persistent, but they do not determine a person's fate. There are plenty of individuals in these samples who, despite having favorable early caregiving histories, are not functioning well in their peer relationships as adolescents or adults. And, similarly, there are plenty of individuals who, although having relatively unresponsive caregivers in early life, are socially and emotionally competent young adults.

The implication of this finding is that individual differences in how people approach their relationships in adulthood must be understood as multifaceted and multidetermined. Attachment theory is sometimes portrayed as a theory that assumes that variation in how adults relate to their romantic partners, for example, can be fully explained by knowing what their attachment histories were like with their parents in infancy (eg, Duck, 1994). Not only is this simplified view unlikely to be correct, but it fails to capture the ideas expressed in Bowlby's writings: early attachment experiences help to shape development, but they do not *determine* development. As such, the degree to which early experiences predict later outcomes is an empirical question; the theory does not make a strong empirical prediction about the answer (see Fraley & Brumbaugh, 2004; Sroufe & Jacobvitz, 1989).

With that as context, in this section we examine some of the research that helps to explain where, in fact, individual differences in *adult* attachment come from. Based on the work we reviewed previously, we suggest that individual differences in adult attachment have their origins in early attachment experiences, and that there may even be some scaffolding effects, as entailed by the prototype perspective. But the theme that we wish to emphasize is that attachment styles can be shaped by a broad array of factors. Although this may not provide readers with a strong sense of closure in helping to identify a smoking gun in personality development, we believe it enriches the mystery. The more ways there are to reach a specific outcome, the more pressing the search becomes.

Attachment theory and research have emphasized a number of factors that might contribute to individual differences in adult attachment styles. Throughout this book we highlight a number of these, including contextual ones, such as sex, culture, and age (see chapter: What Are the Effects of Context on Attachment?) and temperamental or genetic factors (see chapter: What Can Neuroscience, Genetics, and Physiology Tell Us about Attachment?). In the present chapter, however, we limit our discussion to those that have featured most prominently in developmental approaches to understanding the origins of individual differences in adult attachment: (1) the quality of people's caregiving and family environments, (2) the development of social competence, and (3) the quality of peer relationships and friendships. We previously highlighted the role of these factors in early child development. Our purpose in this section is to review what is known about how these factors are related to attachment and relationship functioning in adulthood.

Quality of the Caregiving Environment

A number of investigators have examined the association between early sensitivity and adult attachment styles through the use of retrospective reports. These studies generally reveal that adults who recall warm, loving relationships with their early attachment figures are more likely to rate themselves as secure in attachment. For example, Hazan and Shaver (1987) found that adults who classified themselves as secure were more likely to describe their early experiences with their parents as being affectionate, caring, and loving. Adults who classified themselves as insecure, in contrast, were more likely to describe their parents as cold or rejecting (see also Collins & Read, 1990).

Similar to the findings regarding the effects of context on childhood attachment, theorists have also called attention to a number of contextual factors that may impact the quality of the caregiving environment, and in turn, adult attachment. Maternal depression, for example, interferes with the parent's ability to provide a supportive environment for the child (Cummings & Davies, 1994;

Teti et al., 1995). Mickelson, Kessler, and Shaver (1997) found in a large pop-ulation-based survey that individuals who reported that their parents had experienced depressive episodes when they were young were more insecure in their adult attachment orientation. Similarly, Davila and colleagues have found that young adults who were secure across two assessment waves were less likely than those who were not, to report a history of family psychopathology, including depression (Davila, Burge, & Hammen, 1997).

Moreover, the quality of the relationship between the parents themselves may play a role in shaping the quality of parenting (eg, Rholes, Simpson, & Blakely, 1995; Selcuk et al., 2010) and the attachment styles that the individual develops. Parental divorce, father absence, or high-parental conflicts all have the potential to signal to the individual that other people may not be available, dependable, or reliable. These kinds of ideas have been emphasized most explicitly by attachment theorists inspired by life history perspectives on development (eg, Belsky, Houts, & Fearon, 2010; Simpson & Belsky, 2008). Researchers have found, for example, that adults who indicate that their biological parents divorced are more likely to report insecure attachment styles (Mickelson et al., 1997). In addition, researchers have found that early contextual stressors, broadly defined (eg, father absence, low socioeconomic status), are related to self-report measures of insecure attachment styles in adulthood (eg, Chisholm, Quinlivan, Petersen, & Coall, 2005; Fraley, Roisman, Booth-LaForce, Owen, & Holland, 2013).

Much of the research that has investigated these antecedents, however, has been based on retrospective measures of the interpersonal environment (making the reports subject to reconstructive biases in memory; Scharfe & Bartholomew, 1998) or concurrent associations between attachment and experiences. There are relatively few studies positioned to address these hypotheses in a prospective fashion. Nonetheless, a small number of relevant longitudinal studies have begun to emerge in recent years (eg, Chopik, Moors, & Edelstein, 2014; Zayas, Mischel, Shoda, & Aber, 2011). In one especially rigorous study, Dinero, Conger, Shaver, Widaman, and Larsen-Rife (2008) examined the quality of observed interactions between adolescents and their parents in a sample of over 250 families. Dinero and colleagues found that the quality of parent–child interactions at age 15 predicted self-reports of attachment security at age 25 (rs ranged from 0.05 to 0.21). This study was one of the first to provide longitudinal evidence that parent–child interactions are prospectively related to adult attachment styles, and, importantly, did so using observations of parent–child interactions.

In another longitudinal study involving data from 1070 individuals from the Young Finns Study, Salo, Jokela, Lehtimäki, and Keltikangas-Jaärvinen (2011) it was found that early maternal nurturance, assessed from mothers' reports when their children were an average of 10 years old, significantly predicted children's avoidant attachment 21 to 27 years later ($r = -0.07$). This particular study is noteworthy largely due to the long time interval between assessments and the large sample size.

Fraley, Roisman, Booth-LaForce, et al. (2013b) examined data on over 600 young adults (age 18) who had initially been studied at 1 month of age in the NICHD SECCYD. This study included measures not only of early maternal sensitivity, but of sensitivity assessed across multiple points in time (ie, 6 months, 15 months, 24 months, 36 months, 54 months, Grade 1, Grade 3, Grade 5, and age 15). This provided an unusual opportunity to examine not only how early sensitivity may be associated with adult attachment, but how changes in sensitivity across time are related to adult attachment. Their analyses indicated that self-reported attachment avoidance at age 18 was correlated with both early levels of sensitivity and changes in sensitivity. When both variables were modeled simultaneously, along with other covariates, however, only increases in maternal sensitivity continued to predict avoidance. Specifically, individuals who were more avoidant in attachment at age 18 were more likely than those who were less avoidant to have experienced decreases in maternal sensitivity across time.

Social Competence

The association between social competence and adult attachment has primarily been investigated in social psychological research using concurrent methodologies. Bartholomew and Horowitz (1991), for example, found that relatively secure adults were more likely to have high self-confidence and to express greater interpersonal warmth—qualities that are indicative of social competence. Research has also found that secure adults are more empathically accurate in their relationships (Simpson et al., 2011) and are better able to seek and provide support during stressful and challenging situations (Collins & Feeney, 2000).

There is also longitudinal research linking social competence to relationship functioning. Simpson et al. (2007), for example, examined peer competence and romantic functioning using data from the MLSRA. Peer competence was assessed at Grades 1, 2, and 3 by using teacher ratings of how well target children resembled a prototypical child who "was well liked and respected by peers, had mutual friendships, demonstrated understanding of other children's perspectives and ideas, and constructively engaged peers in activities" (p. 359). Romantic functioning was assessed in a number of ways at ages 20–23, including the emotional tone of the relationship (ie, the relative balance of positive to negative affect) and behavioral observations of couple behavior. They found that individuals who had higher peer competence ratings in childhood had higher romantic relationship process scores, less negative affect, and a higher ratio of positive to negative emotional experiences. Although relationship functioning is not the same "thing" as attachment style, it is an outcome of great significance in attachment theory and is closely related to individual differences in adult attachment.

Using longitudinal data from the NICHD SECCYD, Fraley et al. (2013b) examined trajectories of social competence from early childhood (54 months) through age 15 years. They found that individuals who exhibited greater social competence in early childhood (rated by parents and teachers) were more likely to be secure at age 18 on measures of self-reported attachment styles compared to those who exhibited less social competence in early childhood. In addition, children who became more socially competent across time were more likely to be secure at age 18.

Taken together, these studies indicate that social competence, assessed in a variety of ways in early childhood, adolescence, and concurrently in adulthood is associated with individual differences in attachment and relationship functioning in adulthood.

Friendship Relationships

Importantly, psychologists have not focused exclusively on the family of origin in theorizing about the roots of adult attachment styles. According to many theorists, friendships—especially those that develop in adolescence and early adulthood—play a role in shaping attachment styles (eg, Fraley & Davis, 1997; Furman et al., 2002; Nickerson & Nagle, 2005). Although parents still play an important role in their child's development, peer relationships are some of the first extra-familial contexts in which issues concerning intimacy, trust, and support are explored and negotiated. Some research has suggested that, for many people, close friends can serve important attachment functions (see chapter: What Is an Attachment Relationship?) and that individuals who have higher quality friendships are more likely to be secure in their attachment orientation (eg, Bartholomew & Horowitz, 1991).

Research indicates that the functioning of relationships with friends might shape the way in which romantic relationships function. According to Furman et al. (2002), adolescents develop expectations for and assumptions about romantic relationships based, in part, on their experiences in close friendships. Consistent with this assumption, adolescents who hold relatively secure views of their parents are also likely to hold secure views of close friendships and romantic relationships (Furman et al., 2002). Importantly, however, individual differences in the views people hold of their friendships are associated with views of romantic relationships, even when variation in parental representations is taken into account. Thus, although it is possible that early attachment experiences help set the stage for the functioning of friendship relationships, the unique experiences that adolescents have in those friendships also play a role in shaping expectations and attitudes towards emerging romantic relationships. Indeed, Furman and colleagues conclude that "views of friendships may mediate the links between views of relationships with parents and those of romantic relationships" (Furman et al., 2002, p. 250).

Prospective data that bear on this issue come again from the study by Simpson et al. (2007). Simpson and colleagues assessed the quality of friend relationships in adolescence in the MLSRA through an interview in which participants discussed their close friendships, how much they trusted and disclosed to their friends, and the extent to which they felt that their friends were authentic.

They found that the quality of those friendships was positively correlated with a variety of indices of romantic relationship functioning in early adulthood.

In addition, Fraley et al., 2013b's analysis of data from the SECCYD examined children's perceptions of friendship quality with their self-identified best friend using the Friendship Quality Questionnaire (FQQ; Parker & Asher, 1993), which was administered at Grades 3, 4, 5, and 6 and at age 15 years. The FQQ assesses various aspects of friendship quality, including validation and caring, conflict resolution, help and guidance, and intimate exchange. Using growth curve modeling, they found that individuals who had high-quality friendships early in life were more likely to self-report security in their romantic relationships at age 18 years. In addition, individuals whose friendship relationships increased in quality over time were more likely to report security in their romantic relationships at age 18.

SUMMARY

One of the key ideas in attachment theory is that early attachment experiences play an important role in shaping the development of individual differences. The objective of this chapter was to review some of the research on development and attachment in an effort to better understand how individual differences in attachment emerge. One of the take home messages is that the quality of early caregiving experiences appears to play a role in shaping whether children become secure or insecure in the way they organize their attachment-related thoughts, feelings, and behavior. Moreover, the consequences of early attachment experiences appear to cascade into a number of domains of developmental significance, including the development of social competence and the quality of the friendships that the child develops. Finally, research suggests that these intervening factors, in turn, may be relevant for understanding who becomes relatively secure or insecure in their adult attachment patterns.

A second take home message is that, although adult attachment styles appear to have their origins in early experiences with parents, the associations between early experiences and later outcomes are relatively small. That said, the *history* of experiences across time (eg, whether people are experiencing *more* or *less* parental sensitivity across time) is a critical part of understanding who is secure and who is insecure in adulthood (eg, Fraley et al., 2013b). The implication of this theme is that understanding individual differences in adult attachment styles may require thinking beyond early experiences alone, and require the consideration of a person's developmental history more inclusively (see also Sroufe & Jacobvitz, 1989). When Bowlby (1973) was considering the ways in which developmental processes may shape later outcomes, he asked his readers to consider a railway metaphor. His argument was that if you wish to understand people's final destination, it is useful to know from what station they started. But, importantly, he also suggested that knowing the routes taken along the way—and whether they converge with or diverge from the original path—is necessary for understanding where people end up (see also Shulman et al., 1994). Like Bowlby, we believe that knowing the starting point is useful for understanding later attachment-related outcomes; however, on its own, this information is incomplete. To understand why some adults are secure and others are not requires that we study not only people's early experiences, but also the ways in which those experiences have evolved across people's lives.

A third take home message is that the developmental antecedents of adult attachment do not boil down to any single etiological agent. This is important to understand because a surface reading of attachment theory may seem to suggest that adult attachment styles are fully determined by early caregiving experiences. But as the data make clear, there are many factors that potentially shape individual differences in attachment—more of which will be discussed in chapter: What Are the Effects of Context on Attachment? and chapter: What Can Neuroscience, Genetics, and Physiology Tell Us about Attachment? And, although many of these factors, such as the quality of peer relationships, may have their origins in early caregiving experiences, these factors also represent junctures in the developmental process where a previously established trajectory can diverge. A child with a secure attachment history may be more likely to be relatively secure as a young adult if he or she has well-functioning friendships. But if those friendship experiences are negative (eg, they create tension, fail to establish trust, make one feel unaccepted), they have the potential to undermine the person's developing sense of security. Although the individual may still retain some benefits of supportive early experiences through scaffolding processes, those recent experiences nonetheless have the potential to contribute to a developing sense of insecurity.

We close this chapter with one final thought. We have discussed attachment styles in adulthood as if they refer to a well-known, circumscribed construct. But, as we emphasize in chapter: What Are Attachment Working Models? and chapter: How Are Individual Differences in Attachment Measured?, scholars who study adult attachment emphasize both global attachment patterns as well as relationship-specific attachment patterns. One consequence of this distinction is that the developmental origins of individual differences in how adults relate to their parents may not fully overlap with those that generate individual differences in other attachment relationships in adulthood (eg, attachments to romantic partners). There may be a stronger association, for example, between early attachment experiences and the way in which individuals relate to their parents as adults than the way they relate to their romantic partners (see Steele et al., 2014). Moreover, some of the factors that may shape how secure adults are in their romantic relationships (see chapter: How Are Individual Differences in Attachment Measured?), such as the quality and intimacy of interpersonal interactions (eg, Pierce & Lydon, 2001), may selectively impact attachment orientations in the context of intimate relationships. There is clearly much more research that is needed to fully understand how early attachment experiences shape development and how individual differences in adult attachment patterns may be rooted in—or potentially diverge —from those experiences.

Chapter 4

What Are Attachment Working Models?

In this chapter we discuss one of the central concepts regarding attachment—internal working models (IWMs). Since Bowlby's (1969/1982) early writings on the concept of IWMs, much attention has focused on developing a comprehensive understanding of IWMs. We begin the chapter by explaining the concept of IWMs with an emphasis on their content and structure. We then review research concerning the associations between attachment style and the content and structure of attachment working models.

WHAT ARE ATTACHMENT INTERNAL WORKING MODELS?

Attachment working models are the internalized mental representations (ie, ideas, thoughts, attitudes, expectations, and beliefs) that individuals hold about the self and others (Bowlby, 1973). The model of self represents the extent to which an individual perceives him or herself as worthy of love and support. The model of others refers to the extent that attachment figures (and others more generally) are perceived as reliable, responsive, and trustworthy in meeting one's attachment needs. These attachment needs may relate to desiring comfort and support in the face of distress or the receipt of encouragement in situations of personal growth and achievement (eg, Collins & Feeney, 2000; Feeney, 2004; Feeney & Thrush, 2010).

In describing attachment mental representations as IWMs, Bowlby drew on psychoanalytic concepts such as internalization and object representations but reframed these concepts using theories in cognitive psychology that were current at the time of his writings. Specifically, Bowlby (1969/1982) borrowed the term *internal working models* from Craik (1943) and Young (1964) to describe the cognitive underpinnings of the attachment behavioral system. Craik defined IWMs as "small-scale" representations of external reality—representations that make it possible to evaluate the probability of certain outcomes as a function of executing certain behaviors. Bowlby emphasized the 'working' aspect of attachment mental models to reflect the idea that these representations are not static; they can be manipulated to find optimal solutions to specific problems, such as obtaining the attention of a caregiver. He also emphasized that they can be updated or revised in light of new information. If working models become outdated, or

Adult Attachment. http://dx.doi.org/10.1016/B978-0-12-420020-3.00004-9

77

if they are only partially revised after drastic change in one's environment, then emotional difficulties and mental health problems may ensue (Bowlby, 1988). Bowlby suggested that the conscious processing of model content was indeed necessary to facilitate their extension and revision (Bretherton, 1992).

To date, much of the theoretical and empirical work on attachment working models has focused on their content and structure. Content relates to the cognitive and affective components that are contained as part of IWMs; and structure reflects the organization of these attachment working models in memory.

Unpacking IWMs

One's history of interactions with attachment figures shapes the development of IWMs (Bowlby, 1969/1982; Bretherton, 1990). As a result of these interactions, individuals can vary in the extent that they hold positive or negative mental representations of themselves and others. Individuals that consistently experience support, love, and comfort from attachment figures purportedly develop positive views of the self. The self is viewed as valued and loved, and as competent and capable of dealing with stressful events and life challenges. Positive interactions with attachment figures are also assumed to result in positive views of others, in which people are perceived as caring and trustworthy, and the world is viewed as a safe place.

In contrast, individuals that experience inept or inconsistent care and support, or experience constant rejection, may develop a negative view of the self in which they perceive themselves as not worthy of the love and support of others. They may also develop negative views of others, perceiving others as untrustworthy, and as either unlikely or unable to provide comfort, support, and validation. Furthermore, negative models are likely to exacerbate concerns regarding rejection by attachment figures and people in general. As a function of these negative models, individuals may deem their relationships to be unsatisfying and of limited longevity, and perceive the world to be a lonely and unwelcoming place (eg, Bartholomew & Horowitz, 1991; Kirkpatrick & Davis, 1994).

To this point, we have described IWMs as encompassing two mental representations (models of self and others) and that these representations may be either positive or negative in nature. However, this does not reveal much about the components of IWMs. According to Collins and colleagues (Collins & Allard, 2001; Collins & Read, 1994), IWMs are thought to be comprised of four attachment-related building blocks: (1) memories, (2) beliefs, attitudes, and expectations, (3) goals and needs, and (4) plans and strategies. In the sections that follow, we describe each of these building blocks.

Memories

Attachment-related memories include recollections of specific episodes or interactions as well as people's interpretations of these episodes. These memories contain reflections regarding one's own behavior as well as that of others involved in the interactions. It is important to emphasize that attachment-related memories do not reflect general beliefs, attitudes, or expectations about attachment relationships (see later). Rather, these memories reflect people's interpretation of specific relationship interactions at given points in time.

Beliefs, Attitudes, and Expectations

Beliefs, attitudes, and expectations relate to the knowledge and evaluations that individuals hold about themselves and others. Attachment-related beliefs pertain to principles about oneself, others, and relationships that are perceived as true. An example of a belief is "relationships are a lot of hard work." Attachment-related attitudes pertain to the evaluations that people hold about themselves, others, and their relationships generally. An example of such an attitude is "There's no need for me to waste time with relationships." Attachment-related expectations are future-oriented assumptions regarding one's self, partner, or relationship; an example of such an expectation is "my romantic partner will reject me." According to Collins and Allard (2001), the knowledge inherent in our beliefs, attitudes, and expectations varies in abstraction as a function of the concreteness of social experiences. The more concrete or tangible the social experience, the less abstract the belief, attitude, or expectation that corresponds to the social experience. Further, the concreteness of a social experience is enhanced by: (1) repeated exposure to the social experience (eg, interactions with a caring person) and (2) the time spent reflecting on and reevaluating the social experience.

Goals and Needs

Attachment-related goals and needs reflect highly specific objectives that orient individuals to behave in certain ways that help them obtain their needs for love and comfort (eg, Gillath et al., 2006). The goal of the attachment system is to attain felt security. According to Pietromonaco and Barrett (2000), the achievement of felt security is, in part, dependent upon subgoals (ie, more proximal or immediate goals) that individuals develop about their relationships. Examples of subgoals include seeking intimacy or closeness; maintaining independence and autonomy; and protection of the self from hurt, betrayal, and rejection (see also Gillath et al., 2006). These subgoals could reflect the pursuit or approach of relationship rewards (ie, approach goals) and the avoidance of relationship punishments (ie, avoidance goals, see Gable, 2012). These contrasting subgoals are believed to develop as a function of how successful or unsuccessful a person has been in the past in achieving a state of felt security in attachment relationships. As a result, the individual may develop subgoals that are about minimizing dependence or enhancing one's self-reliance. Individuals whose attachment figures reject them are likely to downplay the importance of having attachment needs met, and thus place these needs lower in priority relative to other social and emotional needs, such as experiencing fun, noncommitted sexual relations, or achieving outcomes at work. To this end, interactions with attachment figures are of critical importance to individuals' attachment-related goals and needs.

Plans and Strategies

Plans and strategies refer to patterns of behavior geared toward the attainment of a particular goal. Collins and Allard (2001) propose that specific plans and strategies for achieving attachment-related goals and needs are encoded as part of working models. As with attachment-related goals and needs, the development of plans and strategies is in part determined by an individual's relationship experiences with attachment figures (Main, 1981). These plans and strategies are varied in nature but can include means for soliciting help (eg, reaching out to another, crying, asking for help) as well as pursuing intimacy, regulating emotional distress, and maintaining independence. Thus, plans and strategies reflect procedural knowledge that individuals maintain about how to navigate their relationships as well as the behaviors necessary to achieve attachment-related goals.

Summary

Attachment working models are mental representations of the self and others. Individuals vary in the degree to which they hold positive or negative views of themselves and others. Furthermore, IWMs are thought to be comprised of four interrelated building blocks: (1) memories, (2) beliefs, attitudes, and expectations, (3) goals and needs, and (4) plans and strategies.

How Are Attachment Internal Working Models Structured?

Do individuals hold one generalized set of mental representations that are indiscriminately applied to all relationships? Or do they hold multiple IWMs that are specific to particular relationships and partners? According to Baldwin, Keelan, Fehr, Enns, and Koh-Rangarajoo (1996) and Collins and colleagues (Collins & Allard, 2001; Collins & Read, 1994) people are likely to hold multiple IWMs as a function of the different interactions, people, and relationships that they experience across their social contexts (eg, families, peers, romantic relationships). Moreover, possessing multiple IWMs is thought to be adaptive as they can help facilitate interactions with different people (eg, Baldwin, Keelan, Fehr, Enns, & Koh-Rangarajoo, 1996; Collins & Read, 1994; Fraley, Heffernan, Vicary, & Brumbaugh, 2011). Not all people interact with us in the same way, and thus, it is adaptive to generate working models that reflect the nuances associated with different relationships (Overall, Fletcher, & Friesen, 2003). To this end, harboring multiple attachment working models is likely to reflect people's propensity to adapt to the threats and rewards associated with forming and maintaining relationships with different people.

A Hierarchical Approach to the Structure of IWMs

Collins and colleagues (Collins & Allard, 2001; Collins & Read, 1994) proposed that attachment mental representations may best be conceptualized as a semantic network of related models that are hierarchically organized. The

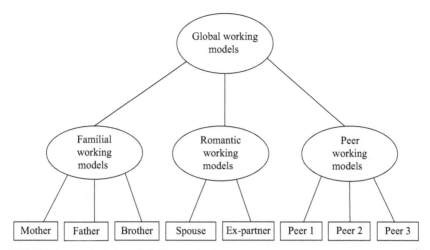

FIGURE 4.1   A depiction of Collins and colleagues' hierarchical structure of attachment IWMs.

proposed hierarchical structure of IWMs is presented in Fig. 4.1. As shown in this figure, at the top of the hierarchy exist people's most general or abstract representations of themselves and others. These *global* IWMs are purportedly derived from relationship experiences across multiple contexts. The common assumption is that these global representations can be considered as a person's default set of IWMs in that they are accessed and guide behavior across diverse social situations including the formation of new relationships with novel individuals. Put another way, theoretically, global working models are activated and govern behavior in the absence of more specific knowledge about a given individual or situation.

Nested under these general IWMs are mental representations that relate to a particular category of relationships. For example, people may hold one set of representations for relationships with family members, another set of representations pertaining to their romantic partners, and yet another pertaining to their peers. At the next level of the hierarchy are highly specific mental representations that pertain to particular individuals within a given relationship category. That is, while individuals may hold a set of familial working models, these are likely to further differentiate into mental representations of one's mother, one's father, one's sibling(s), and other familial relationships such as one's grandmother and grandfather. Likewise, individuals may hold a different set of working models for different friends, and different models for their current romantic partner as well as past romantic partners. Therefore, it is plausible for an individual to hold differentiated mental representations of self and other across specific relationships (eg, secure with one's mother and insecure with one's father). Then again, some people may experience similar relationships with different people (eg, loving and rewarding relationships with their romantic partner and peers) and thus hold more homogeneous mental representations across relationships (Fraley et al., 2011a,b).

The hierarchical conceptualization of attachment working models proposed by Collins and colleagues (eg, Collins & Allard, 2000; Collins & Read, 1994) provides an elegant way of thinking about how IWMs are organized. However, Collins and Allard (2001) noted that "models within the network are probably linked through a rich set of associations and are likely to share many elements" (p. 68). That is, the structure of IWMs is likely to be significantly more complicated than the depiction in Fig. 4.1. So what could this complex structure look like? Given that all forms of IWMs, be they global or specific, reflect knowledge structures about attachment relationships, it may be that models at all levels share direct associations. For example, working models for different relationship types may share direct associations, so too may global working models share direct links with relationship-specific models. In this way, the structural organization of working models may not be strictly hierarchical in nature.

We illustrate some of these possibilities in Fig. 4.2. As can be seen, both figures are hierarchically structured, such that global working models reflect the highest level of abstraction regarding attachment mental representations. Both figures also represent working models tied to different relationship categories as nested at different levels of specificity. However, as part of Fig. 4.2, we add one additional level of specificity pertaining to working models—the level of the interaction. That is, specific interactions with a given individual

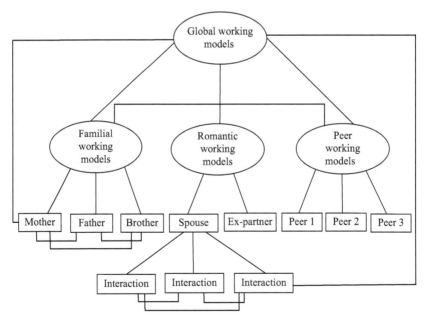

FIGURE 4.2 An additional interpretation of Collins and colleagues' hierarchical structure of attachment IWMs.

may yield distinct knowledge structures about how working models of self and other vary from one interaction to another with this individual. Furthermore, in Fig. 4.2, we propose that relationship-specific working models within a given level of the hierarchical structure may share direct associations. For example, working models about family may share associations with working models about romantic partners. Likewise, working models related to one's attachment relationship with one's father may share associations with working models of one's mother and one's brother (this is illustrated in Fig. 4.2; however, similar associations may exist among relationships nested under romantic partner or peer working models). It is also plausible that working models at any level of the hierarchy share direct associations with one's global working models. In Fig. 4.2 we represent this by illustrating a link between the most specific level of working models (ie, the level of the interaction) and the global working models (though other direct associations are just as plausible across different levels of specificity).

A Connectionist Approach to the Structure of IWMs

One potential limitation of the hierarchical conceptualization of attachment working models is that it does not provide a framework for understanding how specific relationship experiences might coalesce into organized representational patterns. It provides an abstract *description* of how working models of various degrees of specificity are organized. As an alternative framework, Fraley (2007) proposed a connectionist model for understanding the development of working models and how different knowledge structures may emerge as a function of interpersonal experiences.

Although the connectionist framework is similar to the hierarchical framework in several respects, it differs in two ways: First, it assumes that global representations are not separate "things" from relationship-specific representations. Instead, global representations represent an emergent feature of the way in which specific representations are constructed and used in social cognition. Second, and more important for the present purposes, the connectionist framework suggests that, when people are in new situations (eg, interacting with a new potential partner), they do not necessarily rely upon global representations to draw inferences. Instead, they rely on representations of specific others from one's knowledge base that are activated by surface-level (and potentially superficial) similarities between the new target and those specific representations. Those activated specific representations, in turn, are likely to shape the way in which the person relates to a new target.

Regardless of whether attachment IWMs are hierarchical or connectionist in nature, what is clear is that people hold multiple IWMs that are associated through a complex and rich set of interconnections. To this end, we can think of multiple attachment working models that people possess as being distinct but nonetheless related.

What Does Research Reveal About the Content and Structure of Attachment Internal Working Models?

There exists a significant body of research regarding attachment IWMs. Rather than provide an exhaustive review of this body of research, we provide an overview of key findings, and highlight what is or is not known about working models. It is important to note that research on working models is often motivated by the assumption that differences in the cognitive contents and functioning of working models are what give rise to differences in the attachment styles that are typically assessed in social-personality studies. Therefore, in reviewing this work, we emphasize the ways in which the content and structure of IWMs vary across people with different attachment styles.

In terms of the content of IWMs, some research has taken a fine-grained approach by attempting to understand the content contained within each of the building blocks of attachment mental representations (ie, memories; beliefs, attitudes, and expectations; goals and needs; and plans and strategies). In contrast, other research focuses on the content of the working models of self and other without distinguishing between the building blocks of these mental representations. In the sections that follow we draw on both types of studies.

Attachment Styles and the Working Model of Self

Research into the associations between adult attachment and model of the self has focused on: (1) determining the direct associations between attachment style and people's appraisals of the self as related to self-esteem (ie, perceptions of self-worth) and self-efficacy (ie, sense of self-competence or ability) and (2) the cognitive processes used in deriving self-evaluations. A wide array of cognitive processes have been investigated (eg, Wei & Ku, 2007), but the majority of the research has focused on people's attributions and tendencies for verifying information about the self. These cognitive processes can be thought of as mechanisms that help to explain how attachment style is associated with self-evaluations. In this section, we review research on self-esteem, self-efficacy, and the cognitive processes of self-attribution and self-verification.

Self-Esteem and Self-Efficacy

It is generally reported across studies that attachment security (positive model of self) is positively associated with self-esteem and self-efficacy (eg, Corcoran & Mallinckrodt, 2000; Onishi, Gjerde, & Block, 2001; Pietromonaco & Carnelley, 1994; Strodl & Noller, 2003); whereas attachment anxiety (negative model of the self) is negatively associated with both these constructs (eg, Gentzler & Kerns, 2004; Strodl & Noller, 2003). For example, in a large self-report study involving in excess of 1400 participants, Brennan and Morris (1997) found that the higher an individual's attachment security, the higher their ratings of self-esteem; whereas the higher an individual's attachment anxiety, the lower their ratings of self-esteem. Likewise, in a study involving adults across three populations (individuals diagnosed with agoraphobia, individuals diagnosed with depression, and adults with no mental health problems), Strodl and Noller (2003) found that irrespective of population, attachment security was positively associated with self-efficacy while attachment anxiety was negatively associated with self-efficacy.

In terms of attachment avoidance, in studies employing categorical assessments of attachment, individuals classified as avoidant (positive model of self) tend to report higher self-esteem or self-efficacy than individuals classified as anxious (eg, McCarthy, 1999; Salzman, 1996), but appear to be no different from individuals classified as secure (eg, Bringle & Bagby, 1992; Bylsma, Cozzarelli, & Sumer, 1997). For example, Bringle and Bagby (1992) found that young adults classified as secure or avoidant did not differ in achievement-related self-esteem, suggesting that avoidant individuals hold positive views of the self that resemble those of securely attached individuals. Similar findings are reported for self-efficacy (eg, Cozzarelli, Sumer, & Major, 1998; Taubman-Ben-Ari, Findler, & Mikulincer, 2002).

Mikulincer and Shaver (2005, 2007a,b) suggested that an explanation for the positive correlation between avoidance and self-esteem relates to individuals high on attachment avoidance having a propensity for *defensive self-enhancement*. Defensive self-enhancement is thought to emerge as a function of an avoidant individual's tendencies to be compulsively self-reliant as a function of life experiences in which their self-worth has been compromised through rejection and neglect. As such, individuals high on attachment avoidance are forced to cope with stressors on their own. Thus, viewing the self as highly competent, efficacious, and as harboring a high level of self-esteem may create or strengthen the capacity to deal with difficulties alone. In turn, this may lead to overly positive views of the self or perceptions of the self as highly capable.

Various studies point to avoidantly attached individuals' defensive-self enhancement. For instance, research by Mikulincer (1995) in which participants undertook a Stroop task and were exposed to words representing positive and negative self-adjectives, found that individuals with an avoidant attachment style demonstrated a much faster reaction time to positive traits than negative traits. Mikulincer also revealed that avoidant individuals did not integrate different aspects of the self (especially negative personal qualities) particularly well into their self-concept. Thus, they could not articulate how different aspects of the self fitted together or influenced the development of one's self-concept. In contrast, individuals with a secure attachment style responded with reaction times that reflected an acceptance of both positive and negative aspects of the self and a well-integrated sense of self. Similarly, other studies have shown attachment avoidance to be positively associated with high self-esteem and a lack of clarity regarding the self (eg, Pietromonaco & Barrett, 1997).

Some studies, however, find a negative association between attachment avoidance and self-esteem and self-efficacy (eg, Alexander, Feeney, Hohaus, & Noller 2001; Cash, Theriault, & Annis, 2004; Davila, Hammen, Burge, Daley, &

Paley, 1996). For example, in a prospective study of married couples expecting their first child, Alexander et al. (2001) found that attachment avoidance in both men and women was negatively related to self-esteem. The authors suggested that in high-stress situations such as the transition to parenthood, attachment insecurities are heightened to the extent that even avoidant individuals are likely to experience attenuations in self-worth. Yet other studies find no association between avoidance and self-esteem (eg, Gamble & Roberts, 2005; Klohnen, Weller, Luo, & Choe, 2005; Strodl & Noller, 2003).

As a way to reconcile these inconsistencies, we provide two possible explanations. One explanation is that these inconsistencies may simply be a function of studies using different methods to assess attachment and outcomes of self-esteem and self-efficacy. So the inconsistencies observed may be an artifact of measurement imprecision. However, if this were the primary reason underlying the inconsistencies in attachment avoidance, we would expect to see similar inconsistencies in findings pertaining to attachment anxiety and attachment security. Thus, while measurement issues may play a role in the findings related to attachment avoidance, this cannot be the sole explanation for these inconsistencies.

Another explanation is that the inconsistencies related to attachment avoidance may be due to differences in the life domains in which self-esteem or efficacy are studied. Closer inspection of the literature suggests that attachment avoidance is not always associated with self-esteem or efficacy in noninterpersonal contexts (eg, Keating, Tasca, & Hill, 2013; Strodl & Noller, 2003). However, attachment avoidance is often negatively associated with self-efficacy and competence when studied within an interpersonal context (eg, Collins & Read, 1990; Corcoran & Mallinckrodt, 2000; Wei, Vogel, Ku, & Zakalik, 2005). It may be that the interpersonal context taps into questions of self-worth and competence that are at the heart of the insecurities experienced by individuals high on attachment avoidance. That is, the underlying source of their doubts regarding self-worth and competence may be tied to their troubled (and often invalidating) relationships with others rather than domains that sit outside the relationships realm.

Cognitive Processes

While the research reviewed earlier suggests that evaluations of self-worth and competence are tied to individual differences in attachment, this research does not speak to the cognitive processes that securely and insecurely attached people use to arrive at perceptions of the self. To this end, some research has focused on understanding the mechanisms by which attachment style is tied to self-esteem and self-efficacy. In the following sections we outline two mechanisms that have received considerable attention—attributions and self-verification.

Attributions

Research suggests that insecurely attached people, especially those high in attachment anxiety, seem to maintain self-defeating attributions such that they view themselves as hopeless and lacking the skills and abilities to navigate their relationships in a constructive way (Gamble & Roberts, 2005; Kennedy, 1999; Sumer & Cozzarelli, 2004; Williams & Riskind, 2004). This is in line with anxiously attached individuals' negative views of themselves, and their concerns regarding self-worth. In regards to attachment avoidance, some studies have found a positive association between attachment avoidance and self-defeating attributions (Gamble & Roberts, 2005; Sumer & Cozzarelli, 2004; Wei & Ku, 2007), whereas other studies have found that avoidant individuals were less likely to perceive themselves as responsible for negative events compared to securely attached individuals (Man & Hamid, 1998). These findings may again reflect avoidant individuals' tendency to engage in defensive strategies aimed at maintaining a positive (or less negative) view of the self.

Self-Verification

Other studies have investigated the extent to which attachment style is associated with people's tendencies to seek out information that is consistent with (or verifies) their self-appraisals. Interestingly, studies have found that, relative to secure people, insecurely attached individuals (especially individuals high on attachment anxiety) have a preference to receive and endorse negative feedback rather than positive feedback about the self (Brennan & Bosson, 1998; Brennan & Morris, 1997; Cassidy, Ziv, Mehta, & Feeney, 2003). Some studies also find that individuals high on attachment avoidance (ie, dismissing) tend to seek positive feedback from others with regards to one's autonomy (eg, Hepper & Carnelley, 2010). The findings appear to support Swann's (1990) self-verification theory, which assumes that people seek information from others—even negative information—that is in line with their own views of the self. People who are high on attachment anxiety may seek out negative feedback because such feedback reinforces the negative working models they already hold about themselves. For highly avoidant individuals, the seeking out of positive feedback regarding autonomy may feed into established self-perceptions regarding independence and self-reliance, but may also reflect their propensity to engage in defensive self-enhancement.

Attachment Style and Model of Others

As with model of the self, research into the associations between adult attachment and model of others has focused on: (1) determining the direct associations between attachment style and people's appraisals of others and (2) identifying the cognitive processes that shape these evaluations. In terms of the cognitive processes underpinning appraisals of others, research has most commonly investigated partner attributions and self–other distinctiveness.

Perceptions of Others

Studies examining the associations between attachment style and people's perceptions of significant others have largely focused on perceptions of one's parents, romantic partners, and peers. Hazan and Shaver's (1987) seminal work on adult attachment provided the first evidence to suggest that people with an insecure attachment style (either anxious or avoidant attachment) perceive others in a negative light whereas people with a secure attachment style view others in a positive manner. Since this early work, a wide range of correlational, experimental, and longitudinal studies have found that individuals that hold an insecure attachment style report negative perceptions of parents, romantic partners, peers, and even people in general. Specifically, insecurely attached individuals (especially avoidant individuals) view others as untrustworthy and can access memories of trust violations faster than securely attached individuals, perceive others as more distant, rejecting, and hurtful, and as harboring more negative traits and emotions than securely attached individuals (eg, Cyranowski et al., 2002; Hofstra, van Oudenhoven, & Buunk, 2005; Feeney, 2003; Luke, Maio, & Carnelley, 2004). Insecurely attached individuals (especially anxious individuals) also generally perceive others as less supportive, faithful, and dependable than those who are securely attached (eg, Collins & Read, 1990; Feeney & Noller, 1992; Holtzworth-Munroe, Stuart, & Hutchinson, 1997).

Cognitive Processes

Partner Attributions

In general, this research has found that insecurely attached individuals attribute negative partner behavior to more stable and internal characteristics of the partner as opposed to less enduring situational factors. For instance, in an observational study of couples, Pearce and Halford (2008) found that attachment insecurity was positively associated with endorsing negative attributions regarding partner behavior when undertaking problem-solving discussions. In two experimental studies by Collins, Ford, Guichard, and Allard (2006), attachment anxiety was positively associated with endorsing relationship-threatening attributions in hypothetical situations in which partners had engaged in a relationship transgression. In contrast attachment avoidance was more positively associated with endorsing pessimistic attributions in relation to a hypothetical partner's positive behavior compared to a partner's transgressions.

However, it is important to note that while attachment insecurity is generally associated with negative partner attributions, the attributions made by anxiously attached individuals seem to be influenced by contextual factors, namely, mood and relationship satisfaction. Specifically, studies have found that anxiously attached individuals propose less negative or pessimistic explanations for the behavior of others as a function of relationship satisfaction or when not in a negative mood (Collins et al., 2006; Pereg & Mikulincer, 2004). In contrast, the explanations for partner's behavior provided by avoidantly attached individuals appear not to be a function of mood or relationship satisfaction.

For example, in a mood induction study, Pereg and Mikulincer (2004, Study 2) had participants randomly divided into either a neutral affect condition or a negative affect condition in which they either read a story about the development of kites or about a car accident resulting in a girl's death. Participants were then asked to undertake an attribution task involving a scenario detailing a negative relationship event with a hypothetical romantic partner. Individuals high in attachment anxiety exposed to the negative affect prime engaged in more negative attributions of partner behavior than participants exposed to the neutral affect prime. The mood induction, however, did not moderate the association between attachment avoidance and partner attributions.

Self–Other Distinctiveness

Research has also examined the extent to which people's attachment style is associated with how similar to or different from themselves they view others. This research has generally found that attachment anxiety is associated with viewing others as encompassing similar characteristics to oneself, while attachment avoidance is associated with highlighting distinctions between oneself and others (Gabriel, Carvallo, Dean, Tippin, & Renaud, 2005; Lopez, 2001; Mikulincer, Orbach, & Iavnieli, 1998). According to Mikulincer and Shaver (2007a,b), these perceptual biases may reflect false consensus and uniqueness effects. That is, anxious individuals' desires for validation, love, and acceptance may work to bias their perceptions of others toward heightened similarity, thereby fostering greater connectedness and closeness with others. In contrast, avoidant individuals' desires for independence and their emphasis on excessive self-reliance may bias their perceptions such that they see themselves as sharing fewer qualities with others, and thus view oneself as highly distinctive and unique from those around them.

In relation to attachment security, the studies cited earlier suggest that people are less likely to hold perceptions of others that are biased either toward similarity or distinction from oneself. That is, securely attached individuals appear to hold more accurate perceptions of others. Recall that securely attached individuals balance autonomy with relatedness and as such have no desire or motivation to perceive others in a way that makes them feel more similar and close or more unique and distant from oneself. Thus, the lack of such biases means that securely attached individuals can develop relatively accurate perceptions of those around them. This is in line with findings that have demonstrated that attachment security is associated with viewing the self in an authentic and honest way (Gillath, Sesko, Shaver, & Chun, 2010).

Building Blocks of IWMs

Up to this point we have provided an overview of research as it pertains to models of self and others in a general sense. Next, we provide a brief overview of research pertaining to the four aspects of IWMs, according to Collins and colleagues (Collins & Allard, 2001; Collins & Read, 1994).

Memories

Attachment research into memory has generally been conducted in two spheres. The first has investigated the contentions that attachment working models entail a strong cognitive component (Collins & Allard, 2001; Collins & Read, 1994; Pietromonaco & Barrett, 1997). The second has investigated the extent to which individual differences in attachment shape cognitive processes regarding the encoding or retrieval of memories.

The Affective Content of Memories

Research conducted from a social-personality perspective has provided important insights into the emotions that are associated with people's attachment memories. Using a response latency paradigm (methods in which reaction times to the presentation of stimuli are recorded), Mikulincer and Orbach (1995) found that individuals with different attachment styles had different recall times in accessing the emotions attached to childhood experiences. Specifically, people were asked to recall childhood experiences when they felt angry, sad, anxious, and happy. Participants were also asked to rate the extent to which they experienced emotions of anger, sadness, anxiety, and happiness in each of the recalled memories. The time taken to recall the memory was used as a measure of cognitive accessibility (ie, the speed with which a particular thought is brought to mind). The dominant and nondominant emotions associated with each memory were recorded.

The results demonstrated that avoidant people showed the slowest reaction time to sad and anxious memories compared to secure and anxious individuals. In relation to the emotions experienced for each memory, avoidant individuals reported the dominant emotion (eg, sadness when recalling a sad memory) and the nondominant emotion (eg, anger when recalling a sad memory) as far less in intensity than securely attached people. Anxious individuals demonstrated the fastest reaction times to sad and anxious memories, but reported experiencing sadness, anger, happiness, and anxiety as intense across all recalled memories. Securely attached individuals demonstrated reaction times that fell between anxious and avoidantly attached individuals, but reported the dominant emotion as the most intense emotion in a given memory. In terms of the content of the childhood experiences, the findings demonstrated that securely attached individuals were quicker to recall positive as opposed to negative memories, while the reverse association was found for anxiously attached individuals (see Mikulincer, 1998 for a related study).

The studies by Mikulincer and colleagues (Mikulincer, 1998b; Mikulincer & Orbach, 1995), and others (eg, Gentzler & Kerns, 2006; Sutin & Gillath, 2009) provide evidence for the contentions put forward by Pietromonaco and Barrett (2000) that the IWMs include affective content that is intricately woven into the interpersonal memories of individuals. However, these studies also raise questions as to whether attachment style differences in the cognitive-affective processing of memories are associated with the encoding or retrieval of memories. That is, does attachment style influence how a specific event is recorded within one's mind or how it is recalled? In the next section, we describe research that has attempted to address these questions.

Encoding and Retrieval

In terms of the encoding and retrieval of memories, research has largely focused on attachment avoidance in order to understand whether the recording and recalling of interpersonal events reflect defensive cognitive processes. Following on from the work of Mikulincer and Orbach (1995), Fraley, Waller, and Brennan (2000) investigated whether individuals high on attachment avoidance demonstrate difficulty recalling the emotional content associated with memory. In particular, Fraley et al. (2000) examined whether the difficulties experienced by avoidant individuals were due to defensive processes. Specifically Fraley and colleagues were interested in whether cognitive defenses either prevented avoidant individuals from directing attention to the processing of emotional information, prevented the encoding of emotional information, or prevented further elaboration on already encoded information. In other words, Fraley et al. were interested in whether avoidant individuals' defensive processing would cause a reduction in the information encoded and/ or the information recalled.

In two studies, individuals were instructed to listen to an interview about attachment-related issues and were asked to recall details from the interview either immediately after listening to the recording (Study 1) or at variable delays (up to 21 days) after listening to the recording (Study 2). Using forgetting curve methodologies, Fraley and colleagues showed that avoidance was associated with defenses at the level of encoding. Specifically, avoidant individuals, when exposed to the same information as everyone else, were less likely to retain information after variable delays (eg, a day vs. weeks).

In a similar study, Fraley and Brumbaugh (2007) found that, after listening to an emotionally evocative recording, avoidant individuals recalled fewer details than nonavoidant individuals, even when monetary incentives were associated with the memory recall task. Again the findings suggest that difficulties in memory recall are due to the defensive exclusion of affective content at the level of encoding rather than retrieval.

A study by Simpson, Rholes, and Winterheld (2010) investigated how both attachment anxiety and avoidance were associated with changes in people's memories regarding their own actions during discussions with their romantic partners on a conflictual topic. It was found that individuals high on attachment avoidance who were distressed recalled being less supportive of their partners 1 week post the conflict discussion than they had reported immediately after the discussion. The reverse was found for individuals low on attachment avoidance. In relation to attachment anxiety, individuals high on attachment anxiety who were distressed recalled being more emotionally close 1 week after the conflict discussion than immediately following the discussion. Again the opposite effect was found for individuals low on attachment anxiety. Simpson and colleagues suggest that, because the recollections of support behaviors differed over time (ie, a 7-day period), individuals' attachment styles "twisted" the memory of the interaction upon retrieval rather than at the stage of encoding the interaction.

The findings outlined in this section demonstrate how individual differences in attachment may influence the encoding or retrieval of memories—both in terms of the details of these memories as well as their affective content. In particular, the findings point to the idea that individuals high on attachment avoidance tend to limit the encoding of attachment-relevant or emotionally charged episodes and this is largely a result of their defensive cognitive processes. However, it also appears that individual differences in attachment (both attachment anxiety and avoidance) may play a role in the retrieval of memories. As Simpson, Rholes, & Winterheld (2010) note: "In conclusion, what individuals respond to in relationships is not what they actually said or did during an interaction with their partner; rather, what they respond to is memories of the interaction filtered through their working models" (p. 257).

Beliefs, Attitudes, and Expectations

In relation to beliefs about the self and others, research has identified that attachment style is linked to people's beliefs of how central or peripheral certain positive and negative characteristics are in themselves and others. Specifically, Clark, Shaver, and Calverley (1994; as described in Clark & Shaver, 1996) found that while secure adults endorsed positive and negative features regarding their self-concept, the positive features were deemed more central and the negative features more peripheral. In contrast, individuals high on attachment anxiety and avoidance (individuals classified as fearfully attached) demonstrated the complete inverse pattern. These negative beliefs that insecurely attached individuals have about themselves have also been revealed in studies examining people's discrepancies regarding their actual selves and desired selves, as imposed by their own ideals or the ideal of others. In particular, Mikulincer (1995) found that securely attached individuals reported smaller discrepancies between their actual selves and their ideals as noted by oneself and others. Again, the opposite findings were true for insecurely attached individuals.

In relation to expectations, various studies have suggested that individuals store knowledge about their attachment relationships as if–then propositions, and thus reflect the expectations that people have of themselves and others when engaging in social situations. Some of the earliest work to examine the propositional nature of IWMs was conducted by Baldwin, Fehr, Keedian, Seidel, and Thomson (1993). Across a series of experimental studies using explicit as well as implicit (ie, response times to lexical decision-making tasks) assessments of expectations, Baldwin et al. (1993) found that individuals with a secure attachment style held more positive expectations (ie, if–then propositions) and less negative expectations regarding a partner's behavior than both avoidant and anxiously attached individuals. Individuals with a secure attachment style also demonstrated faster response times, and thus great accessibility to positive partner behaviors than negative partner behaviors—a finding that was reversed for insecurely attached individuals. Thus, it appears that people with a secure attachment style not only hold more positive expectations of others' behaviors than insecurely attached individuals, but they are also able to access these positive representations faster than those who are insecurely attached. In contrast, insecurely attached people not only hold more pessimistic expectations of others, but these negative expectations are accessed faster than positive expectations. Similar results are reported by numerous other researchers (eg, Mikulincer & Arad, 1999; Rowe & Carnelley, 2003; You & Malley-Morrison, 2000; Whiffen, 2005).

However, some studies find that when delineating between attachment anxiety and avoidance, negative expectations are somewhat distinct. Anxious individuals report expectations of fear that others will be rejecting combined with expectations that others should provide love and support. In contrast, avoidant individuals doubt the reliability and responsiveness of others to meet their needs (Florian, Mikulincer, & Bucholtz, 1995; Shaver, Schachner, & Mikulincer, 2005).

Goals and Needs

It is assumed that anxious individuals' desire for closeness and validation may manifest in goals and needs geared toward developing very intimate relationships, while avoidant individuals' discomfort with closeness and excessive self-reliance may manifest in goals and needs that downplay closeness and intimacy. Moreover, these goals and needs may influence how insecurely attached people in particular perceive various relationship events such as those that involve self-disclosure or relationship conflict.

Indeed, individuals high in attachment anxiety view high-conflict situations more positively than individuals who do not place such a high premium on intimacy-related goals and needs (Fishtein, Pietromonaco, & Barrett, 1999; Pietromonaco & Barrett, 1997). Pietromonaco and Barrett (2000) suggested that these findings reflect anxiously attached individuals being attuned to the intimacy-promoting aspects of conflict situations. That is, while conflict interactions may be unpleasant on the one hand, they do provide a context to engage with one's partner and to elicit their response that can entail personal disclosure and the expression of emotion—responses that in the eyes of anxiously attached individuals may be deemed as meeting their needs and goals for intimacy and closeness.

In a diary study investigating the associations between attachment style and goals, Locke (2008) investigated four relationship goals (relationship closeness, relationship distance, asserting opinion and views in relationships, and being submissive within relationships). These goals were evaluated in terms of people's tendencies to approach (ie, work toward these goals) or avoid (ie, steer clear from working on these goals). Locke found that attachment avoidance was associated with the avoiding (and not approaching) goals of closeness and submission. The findings pertaining to attachment anxiety revealed an inconsistent goal orientation, specifically, anxiety was associated with avoiding distance but less with enhancing closeness. Moreover, at the individual (ie, within-person) level, attachment anxiety was associated with significant variability. That is, attachment anxiety predicted people's fluctuations in goals related to approaching distance, avoiding closeness, avoiding assertion, and avoiding submission.

In a series of experimental studies of relationship goals regarding self-disclosure and the seeking of support Gillath et al. (2006) found that attachment avoidance was negatively associated with goals pertaining to self-disclosure and the seeking of support from others. In contrast attachment anxiety was positively associated with goals regarding the seeking of emotional support, and while anxiety was unrelated to goals regarding self-disclosure, anxiety was associated with faster responses to self-disclosure items, suggesting less conflict about self-disclosure.

The research to date on goals seems to support Pietromonaco and Barrett's (2000) perspectives regarding how subgoals (ie, proximal goals or more immediate goals) are linked with attachment style to facilitate the achievement of the primary goal of the attachment system (ie, felt security). For example, subgoals around intimacy and independence facilitate the achievement and maintenance of felt security. For anxiously attached individuals, the subgoal of intimacy appears to be activated chronically to provide every possible chance that felt security is achieved. In contrast, for avoidantly attached individuals, subgoals around maintaining independence are chronically activated as a means of suppressing feelings of inadequacy and insecurity (an indirect method for achieving a sense of felt security according to Pietromonaco and Barrett). In contrast, securely attached individuals are likely to harbor subgoals around intimacy and independence, but balance the activation of these goals in a manner that ensures the achievement of felt security as well as continued functioning as an autonomous individual.

Plans and Strategies

The literature on plans and strategies is quite vast, as it largely involves self-report and observational studies in which plans and strategies are operationalized as attachment behaviors—that is the behavioral outputs of the attachment system. Put another way, people's self-reported or observed behaviors are taken as the enactment of people's attachment plans and strategies. From this perspective, research into adult attachment has investigated the associations between attachment style and people's strategies in relation to coping with relationship stressors and stressors in general (eg, Birnbaum, Orr, Mikulincer, & Florian, 1997; Karantzas, Feeney, Bale, & Hoyle, 2015a), support giving and seeking (eg, Collins & Feeney, 2004; Karantzas & Cole, 2011; Mallinckrodt & Wei, 2005; Simpson, Rholes, & Phillips, 1996), relationship conflict (eg, Feeney, Noller, & Callan, 1994; Karantzas, Feeney, McCabe, & Goncalves, 2014; Shi, 2003), sexual functioning (eg, Gillath & Schachner, 2006; Schachner & Shaver, 2004), the formation and dissolution of relationships (eg, Brumbaugh & Fraley, 2010; Collins & Gillath, 2012; Klohnen & Lou, 2003; Pietromonaco & Carnelley, 1994), and more recently, attempts to regulate a partner's behavior

(Simpson & Overall, 2014). Given that we review research on a number of these topics in chapters: How Stable Are Attachment Styles in Adulthood?; What are the Effects of Context on Attachment?, in this section, we specifically focus on literature that directly speaks to people's cognitions regarding plans and strategies.

Research into plans and strategies as they pertain to working models can be grouped into three types of research. One set of studies (largely experimental) has investigated people's narrative descriptions of how they would respond to a particular relationship situation or scenario. Across these studies participants are asked to read various vignettes and describe their response to the given social situation(s). For instance, Collins (1996) asked participants to read a series of vignettes in which their romantic partner behaved in a manner that could be interpreted as negative (eg, "imagine that your partner didn't respond when you tried to cuddle"). Participants were then required to describe in detail how they would respond to the various social interactions. Coding of the descriptions revealed that secure individuals reported less punishing behavior than insecurely attached individuals (see also Gillath & Shaver, 2007).

Other studies have employed implicit experimental methods (specifically lexical decision-making tasks) to assess people's mental accessibility of plans and strategies. For instance, Mikulincer (1998b, Study 5) investigated how attachment style was associated with people's response to trust violations in relationships. Findings demonstrated that individuals with a secure and anxious attachment style responded faster to approach words, such as "talk," when primed with a trust violation compared to individuals with an avoidant attachment style, who responded faster to avoidance words, such as "escape."

In recent years, researchers have used various explicit and implicit experimental methods to examine the extent to which people hold procedural "script-like" knowledge regarding attachment relationships. This script-like knowledge is considered to encompass people's plans and strategies when interacting with attachment figures. This research has focused on unpacking the script-like knowledge of secure and insecurely attached individuals. The first of these studies focused on people's procedural knowledge contained within their "secure-base script" (Bretherton, 1990; Waters, Rodrigues, & Ridgeway, 1998; Waters & Waters, 2006). In short, the secure-base script reflects people's procedural knowledge regarding their history of secure-base support (Waters & Rodrigues-Doolabh, 2004). If the secure-base support received in the past has been consistent, sensitive, and responsive then a coherent, consolidated, and readily accessible script develops regarding one's plans and strategies of how to deal with situations in which the attachment system is activated and the individual needs to work toward reestablishing felt security (see Steele et al., 2014). However, if the secure-base support received in the past has been inconsistent, inept, or ineffective, then the secure-base script is incoherent, and a nonconsolidated script emerges that is likely to be less readily accessible (Steele et al., 2014; Waters & Waters, 2006). In concrete terms, the prototypic secure-base script is conceptualized as a series of if–then propositions, that can reflect the three modules/components of Mikulincer and Shaver's (2003, 2007a) behavioral systems model of attachment dynamics.

The first if–then proposition relates to whether when distress is experienced, an individual can seek out a significant other (ie, a parent, romantic partner, or peer) for assistance ("If I am faced with a challenge or experience distress, I can turn to someone who I know will be available to provide me with support"). The second of these if–then propositions relates to the confidence an individual has in a significant other to be available and provide appropriate support ("If I seek help from someone, then they are likely to be available and provide the support I need"). The third of these if–then propositions relates to the extent that the individual will experience comfort and/or relief as a result of calling upon a significant other to assist in achieving attachment security. To this end, the attachment system is deactivated, and the individual can reengage in daily life ("If I receive support from a significant other, this support will reduce my distress and help me feel better to the extent that I can go back to doing other things").

Thus, the secure-base script provides a coherent plan and strategy for how an individual can/should deal with distressing situations through seeking the help of an attachment figure—whether they be a parent, romantic partner, or peer, or any other person classified as an attachment figure. In many ways, the secure-base script reflects a highly constructive way of dealing with difficult/challenging situations that helps to restore emotional balance (Epstein & Meier, 1989; Mikulincer & Shaver, 2007; Mikulincer, Shaver, Sapir-Lavid, & Avihou-Kanza, 2009). Individuals with a secure attachment style are thought to possess a more accessible, elaborate, and coherent secure-base script than individuals with an insecure attachment style. Actually, some researchers argue that the hallmark of secure attachment is a well-developed secure-base script (Mikulincer & Shaver, 2007; Waters & Rodrigues-Doolabh, 2004; Waters & Waters, 2006).

While developmental research has found support for the secure-base script concept and identified theoretically consistent associations between attachment styles and the content of individuals' secure-base scripts (eg, Dykas, Woodhouse, Cassidy, & Waters, 2006; Steele, Phibbs, & Woods, 2004), little research has explored the secure-base script from the social-personality perspective. However, work by Mikulincer et al. (2009) provided new insights into the content and accessibility of the secure-base script. Across a series of eight studies, Mikulincer and colleagues investigated many of the cognitive aspects of the secure-base script including accessibility and how it effects the processing of attachment-relevant information and memory recall. Their findings suggested that individuals with a secure attachment style were able to more quickly access their secure-base script when asked to engage in a story completion task involving an assumed distressing event or when experiencing a distressing dream compared to individuals with an insecure attachment style (ie, attachment anxiety and/or avoidance). Further, they found that securely attached individuals generated more elaborate and detailed secure-base content as part of their scripts compared to insecurely attached individuals.

When asked to read a fictitious story comprising the main components of the secure-base script (active support seeking, support availability, distress reduction), secure individuals were also found to recall more secure-base script content days after reading the story compared with insecurely attached individuals. In a series of judgment and decision-making tasks in which individuals again read a story that featured secure-base script content, secure individuals were found to more quickly decide whether the characters in the story possessed secure-base qualities and whether arguments about the story were related to the secure-base script compared to individuals who were insecurely attached. Finally, Mikulincer and colleagues demonstrated that when asked to read a fictitious story involving secure-base script content while engaging in a cognitively demanding task (suppress thoughts of a white bear, Wegner, Schneider, Carter, & White, 1987), securely attached individuals could automatically process secure-base script story content more so than insecure individuals.

In complementary research, Ein-Dor, Mikulincer, and Shaver (2011a, 2011b) investigated the extent to which scripts alternative to the secure-base script captured the procedural knowledge associated with the plans and strategies of insecurely attached individuals. In doing so, this research went beyond suggesting that attachment insecurity is associated with less of a secure-base script. In particular, Ein-Dor et al. (2011a) investigated how script-like mental representations guided the processing of and reactions to threatening situations. Across a variety of threatening situations, attachment avoidance was associated with what Ein-Dor and colleagues referred to as the "rapid fight–flight schema" which contains a script involving "… (a) minimize the importance of threatening stimuli; (b) when danger is clearly imminent, take quick self-protective action, either by escaping the situation or by taking action against the danger; and (c) at such times, not worry about coordinating one's efforts with those of other people" (Ein-Dor et al., 2011a, p. 3). In line with this cognitive script, a subsequent study by Ein-Dor et al. (2011b) found that avoidant individuals demonstrated the most rapid response to threat by either fleeing from the threat or confronting the danger, depending on how imminent the threat was.

Ein-Dor et al. (2011a) found that attachment anxiety, in contrast, was associated with a "sentinel" script. The content of this script involves "…(a) to remain vigilant with respect to possible threats, especially in unfamiliar or ambiguous situations; (b) to react quickly and strongly to early, perhaps unclear cues of danger; (c) to alert others about the imminent danger; (d) if others are not immediately supportive, to heighten efforts to get them to provide support; and (e) to minimize distance from others when coping with a threat" (p. 2). Consistent with the sentinel script, Ein-Dor et al. (2011a) found that although anxious individuals were able to detect a threat, they were less likely to respond in an effective manner. Ein-Dor and colleagues suggest that the ineffective behavioral

responses of anxious individuals are a product of their sentinel knowledge structure, which includes "catastrophizing, directing attention to threat-related information, expressing needs and vulnerabilities, and desperately seeking other
people's proximity, support, and comfort" (p. 13).

Empirical Support for the Hierarchical Organization of Attachment Working Models

Some of the first work aimed at understanding the structure of attachment IWMs
was conducted by Baldwin et al. (1996) in which substantial within-person variability was identified when participants were required to report on the mental
representations individuals hold about close others. Specifically, Baldwin and
colleagues found people's self-reported attachments style varied considerably
when assessed in response to thinking about a specific close other. Moreover,
the number of known acquaintances with different attachment orientations varied significantly as a function of whether these connections were romantic or
nonromantic in nature. Specifically, insecurely attached individuals (ie, high
on attachment anxiety or avoidance) reported a significantly lower percentage
of secure romantic relationships than nonromantic relationships. In contrast,
securely attached individuals reported high percentages for both romantic and
nonromantic relationships of a secure characterization. Therefore, this early
work provided some evidence that individuals have the capacity to hold differentiated working models when it comes to attachment relationships.

Since this early research, other studies have demonstrated that the structure
of IWMs is such that it consists of global and relationship-specific attachment
representations. For instance, Cozzarelli, Hoekstra, and Bylsma (2000) and
Pierce and Lydon (2001) found that relationship-specific mental representation
made a greater contribution in explaining people's perceptions of the quality
and intimacy of their social interactions with others, and their self-reported life
satisfaction, than global IWMs. These findings suggest that individuals' IWMs
are organized in such a manner that people distinguish between generalized
cognitions of oneself and others and more relationship-specific or nuanced
IWMs. However, these studies do not attend to the issue of whether IWMs are
hierarchically organized.

Few studies have formally attempted to study the proposed hierarchical
structure of attachment working models put forward by Collins and colleagues
(Collins & Allard, 2001; Collins & Read, 1994). The first study to investigate
this proposed hierarchical structure of attachment working models was conducted by Overall et al. (2003). Overall and colleagues contrasted three models
of how attachment mental representations may be structured. The first model
conceptualized attachment representations encompassing a single global working model. The second model conceptualized IWMs as comprising three sets
of mental representations reflecting different types of relationships—one for
family, another for friends, and another again for romantic partners. The third

model was the most complex of all three models and conceptualized IWMs as consisting of mental representations that reflected working models for each attachment figure, and that these were nested under working models that related to specific types of relationships (ie, family, peer, romantic partner), and these, in turn, were nested under global mental representations.

Statistical comparisons across all three models found that the third and most complex model best represented the hierarchical structure of IWMs for both attachment dimensions: attachment anxiety and attachment avoidance. Further, the hierarchical structure of the third model did not differ as a function of gender or relationship status. Specifically, men and women as well as people in relationships and those that were single appeared to structure their IWMs by way of relationship-specific mental representations nested under general mental representations.

Using a multilevel modeling approach, Sibley and Overall (2008) extended the work of Overall et al. (2003) by examining within- as well as between-person variability in the hierarchical structure of attachment working models. Their findings suggested that relationship-specific IWMs (ie, models of romantic partner, mother, and best friend) were more strongly associated with mental representations of close others that fell into the same relationship type than another type of relationship. That is, relationship-specific models related to a romantic partner were more strongly associated with the representations participants had of different romantic partners than with representations of different peers.

In another study by Klohnen et al. (2005) some relationship-specific mental representations were more alike than others. Specifically models of parents (ie, mother and father) were very similar to each other as were working models of different peers (friends and romantic partner) compared to all other relationship-specific mental representations. Furthermore, models of self demonstrated less variability across relationships than models of other. When examining the relations between specific and global working models, the mental representations relating to romantic partners and friends made the most significant and independent contribution to global working models, and romantic relationship length was found to moderate the association between mental representations of IWMs pertaining to romantic partners and general IWMs. Specifically, the longer individuals had been in a relationship the greater the association between romantic and general IWMs. In relation to the contributions that general and specific models made to self-relevant outcomes, general as well as mother IWMs were associated with emotional stability, self-esteem, and ego-resiliency, while IWMs of romantic partners were associated with emotional stability and self-esteem. In terms of relationship quality (ie, a composite score involving relationship outcomes such as positive relationship experiences, satisfaction, conflict, closeness, and role involvement) associated with each relationship type, only IWMs regarding one's romantic partner were associated with relationship outcomes.

In acknowledging the role of specific attachment relationships to relationship outcomes, mental health, and well-being, Fraley et al. (2011a,b) developed a measure of attachment to assess attachment styles across relationship domains. Termed the Experiences in Close Relationships—Relationship Structures (ECR-RS) questionnaire, the measure yields dimensional assessments of attachment to one's mother, father, romantic partner, and best friend. Using this measure, Fraley et al. (2011a, Study 2) found that all relationship-specific measures of attachment demonstrated greater associations with people's scores on depression and relationship commitment than global measures of the attachment dimensions. Furthermore, the study also investigated whether differentiation in working models (the extent to which people hold heterogeneous or homogeneous attachment mental representations across relationships) was associated with the experience of less satisfaction in relationships and depression. While differentiation appeared to be associated with less relationship satisfaction and more depression, these findings were best explained as being due to insecurity in general: people who are more differentiated are also more likely to be insecure across multiple relational domains.

Fraley and Brumbaugh (2007) investigated the extent to which relationship specific and global IWMs would be activated when individuals are exposed to fictitious people that ideographically resemble either one's parent or current romantic partner. They found that targets that reflected the qualities of a romantic partner were more strongly associated with specific IWMs—those related to romantic partners rather than parents or global IWMs. When exposed to relationship targets that did not exhibit features related to one's parent or romantic partner, global IWMs were found to play an important role (especially IWMs related to attachment anxiety) in addition to IWMs of romantic partners and parents.

In a similar study by Brumbaugh and Fraley (2006) that specifically focused on romantic relationships, participants were exposed to potential dating partners that either did or did not resemble a past romantic partner. In both situations, participants' application of their IWMs for romantic partners was assessed. Results revealed that participants more readily applied their mental representations toward a partner that resembled their past romantic partner. Furthermore, participants experienced more attachment anxiety and less attachment avoidance toward the dating partner who resembled a past relationship. The findings from Brumbaugh and Fraley (2006) and Fraley and Brumbaugh (2007) provide further support regarding the presence and function of both general and specific IWMs, but importantly, provide an understanding regarding the transference of attachment patterns to new or emerging relationships.

Summary

Numerous studies have investigated whether individuals hold general and specific working models of attachment. Research to date provides consistent evidence that individuals maintain differentiated working models that encompass both global and specific IWMs. Findings demonstrate that specific working models make a greater contribution to explaining people's attitudes and behaviors in situations involving a particular type of close relationship compared to global models. That is, in specific relational contexts such as interactions with one's romantic partner, IWMs of romantic relationships are better suited to explaining people's attitudes and behaviors than global working models. Research into the organization of working models is however limited. The research that exists provides some evidence to support a hierarchical structure regarding the organization of working models. But nonetheless, these studies have not tested all plausible organizational structures to equivocally determine whether the hierarchical model as proposed by Collins and colleagues (Collins & Allard, 2001; Collins & Read, 1994) does indeed represent the most appropriate structural mapping of IWMs.

CHAPTER SUMMARY

In this chapter we provided a comprehensive account of the concept of IWMs and research into the content and structure of attachment mental representations. Our social-cognitive discussion of IWMs highlights that attachment mental structures are multifaceted, with models of self and others encompassing atleast four components: (1) memories, (2) beliefs, attitudes, and expectations, (3) goals and needs, and (4) plans and strategies. In terms of the structure of attachment mental representations, research suggests that IWMs demonstrate a degree of differentiation such that people harbor multiple IWMs. We also reviewed alternative theoretical models on the structure and organization of working models by focusing on hierarchical and connectionist frameworks, and the evidence associated with these organizational frameworks.

Chapter 5

How Are Individual Differences in Attachment Measured?

In this chapter we review how social and personality psychologists measure individual differences in adult attachment patterns. We begin with an overview of the history of measurement in this area of research. As we will show, the ways in which theorists conceptualize attachment styles have evolved across time and, not surprisingly, the ways in which researchers have gone about assessing individual differences have evolved as well. Further, we discuss a variety of issues that are relevant to understanding how contemporary assessment systems are used for representing individual differences. Along the way we will address a few challenging theoretical issues (eg, Are the major dimensions underlying attachment orthogonal? Are they sufficient for capturing individual differences in attachment organization?) and provide some practical recommendations on how to best represent individuals within modern two-dimensional systems. Finally, we address one of the most salient questions for researchers new to the area: What is the best way to assess adult attachment styles? We review some of the most commonly used and well-validated self-report measures for assessing adult attachment. But, as we explain, the kinds of questions that researchers ask will dictate the kinds of measures they should use. There is not a "one size fits all" approach to measuring adult attachment. We hope this chapter will serve as a useful guide on how to measure attachment across diverse research contexts, while explaining how those measurements can be mapped to a common theoretical framework.

HOW HAS THE MEASUREMENT OF ADULT ATTACHMENT EVOLVED OVER THE DECADES?

When Hazan and Shaver (1987) began their seminal work on adult attachment, they adopted Ainsworth's three-category typology of attachment patterns in infancy (Ainsworth, Blehar, Waters, & Wall, 1978) as a framework for organizing individual differences in the ways adults think, feel, and behave in romantic relationships (see chapter: What Is Attachment Theory?). In their initial studies, Hazan and Shaver (1987) developed brief multisentence descriptions of the three proposed attachment types, avoidant, secure, and anxious-resistant (Table 1.1). Respondents were asked to think back across their history of

Adult Attachment. http://dx.doi.org/10.1016/B978-0-12-420020-3.00005-0

romantic relationships and indicate which of the three descriptions best captured the way they *generally* think, behave, and feel in romantic relationships. Because participants were asked to make one choice among these three options, this measure is often referred to as a *forced choice measure*.

These descriptions were designed to capture adult analogues to the kinds of psychological dynamics described by Ainsworth and her colleagues based on their research on infants in the strange situation procedure (see chapter 1: What Is Attachment Theory?). For example, the first paragraph captures the kinds of thoughts and feelings that might characterize the adult form of avoidant attachment. This description targets feelings of insecurity, the use of strategies to create emotional distance from close others, and a reluctance to open up to and depend on others. The second paragraph describes secure attachment. Embedded in this description is the secure person's belief that other people are likely to be supportive and responsive. The third paragraph captures the adult analogue of the anxious-resistant infant. It describes a person who is insecure regarding whether or not close others will be available, accessible, and responsive. Moreover, it captures the inherent conflict of anxious-ambivalent children, the desire to be loved and comforted, coupled with the inability to feel adequately loved as well as the frustration and anger that might stem from this conflict.

In their initial studies, Hazan and Shaver (1987) found that people's self-reported romantic attachment pattern was related to a number of theoretically relevant variables, including beliefs about love and relationships (working models of romantic relationships) and recollections of early experiences with parents. For example, people endorsing the secure description were more likely to report warm relationships with their parents and higher levels of happiness and trust in their romantic relationships. People endorsing the avoidant description perceived their mothers as cool and rejecting and, in their romantic relationships, reported a fear of intimacy, difficulty in accepting their partners, and a general belief that romantic love does not last. Anxious-ambivalent adults also reported conflicted relationships with parents and were more likely to report feelings of obsession and jealousy in romantic relationships.

Bartholomew's Four Category Model

In the early 1990s Bartholomew published several important papers that challenged researchers to reconsider the three-category model of individual differences in adult attachment (Bartholomew, 1990; see also Bartholomew & Horowitz, 1991; Griffin & Bartholomew, 1994a). Drawing upon some of Bowlby's writings, Bartholomew argued that people hold separate representational models of themselves (model of self) and their social world (model of others), models that have distinct consequences for the way attachment behavior is organized. As discussed in chapter: What Are Attachment Working Models?, the *model of others* reflects the expectations, beliefs, and strategies that people have concerning close others in general, and attachment figures in particular.

(A)   (B)

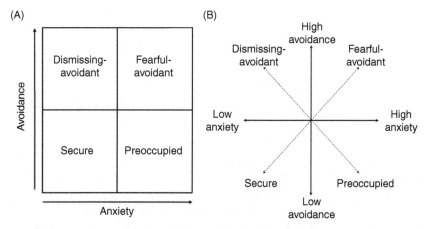

FIGURE 5.1   **Theoretical models of individual differences in adult attachment.** (A) Illustrates the four-category model proposed by Bartholomew and Horowitz (1991). (B) Illustrates the two-dimensional extension of that model in which the four attachment patterns are viewed as regions in a two-dimensional space. Various authors refer to the horizontal dimension as attachment-related anxiety or model of self and the vertical dimension as attachment-related avoidance or model of others.

Individuals with a positive model of others view attachment figures as trust-worthy, reliable, and dependable. Individuals with a negative model of others lack confidence in people's trustworthiness and dependability. The *model of self* reflects the valence of people's views of themselves. People with a positive self-model see themselves as competent, autonomous, and worthy of love. People with a negative self-model lack confidence, harbor self-doubts, and are vulner-able to psychological distress.

Bartholomew argued that when these two kinds of representational models are crossed with valence (ie, the positivity or negativity of model of self and model of others), it is possible to derive four, rather than three, major attach-ment patterns (Fig. 5.1A). She borrowed names for the four patterns from a mixture of Ainsworth's, Hazan and Shaver's, and Main, Kaplan, and Cassidy's (1985) typologies, calling the positive-positive group "secure," the negative-positive group "preoccupied," the positive-negative group "dismissing," and the negative-negative group "fearful." Following Hazan and Shaver's lead, Bar-tholomew (Bartholomew & Horowitz, 1991) developed the Relationship Ques-tionnaire (RQ), a short instrument containing descriptions of each of the four theoretical types. As with Hazan and Shaver's forced choice measure, respon-dents are asked to read each description and select the one that best captures the way they approach close relationships (Table 5.1).

The Bartholomew system is similar to Hazan and Shaver's in several re-spects. For example, both systems contain a secure group as well as an anxious group (preoccupied). The key difference is that the avoidant group from Hazan and Shaver's system is split into two distinct groups in the Bartholomew system.

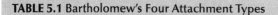

TABLE 5.1 Bartholomew's Four Attachment Types

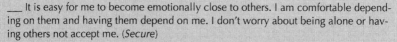

___ It is easy for me to become emotionally close to others. I am comfortable depending on them and having them depend on me. I don't worry about being alone or having others not accept me. (*Secure*)

___ I am uncomfortable getting close to others. I want emotionally close relationships, but I find it difficult to trust others completely, or to depend on them. I worry that I will be hurt if I allow myself to become too close to others. (*Fearful*, or *Fearful-avoidant*)

___ I want to be completely emotionally intimate with others, but I often find that others are reluctant to get as close as I would like. I am uncomfortable being without close relationships, but I sometimes worry that others don't value me as much as I value them. (*Preoccupied*)

___ I am comfortable without close emotional relationships. It is very important to me to feel independent and self-sufficient, and I prefer not to depend on others or have others depend on me. (*Dismissing*, or *Dismissing-avoidant*)

The first kind of avoidance, *fearful-avoidance*, captures the vulnerable, insecure form of avoidance reflected in the Hazan and Shaver avoidant category. Fearful individuals, theoretically, are avoidant of intimacy because they fear being hurt by someone they love. The second kind of avoidance, *dismissing-avoidance*, is not represented in the Hazan and Shaver system. These kinds of individuals avoid intimacy, not because they consciously fear being hurt, but because they consciously value independence and autonomy.

The Evolution of Measurement Systems

By the mid-1990s, there seemed to be consensus in the social-personality literature that the four-category model was better suited for capturing individual differences than the original three-category model. But there was still some lingering concern over whether it was ideal to classify people with respect to attachment style or whether it was more appropriate to scale people with respect to one or more dimensions. The classification system was potentially valuable because it provided a parallel to the infant attachment literature that had also focused on assigning infants to one or more attachment categories. In addition, classification systems were also being used by developmental and clinical psychologists who were studying attachment in adulthood using the Adult Attachment Interview (AAI, see further). Moreover, from a methodological point of view, the analysis of types was made easier by the statistical training of many social psychologists who were accustomed to analyzing categorical data.

Nonetheless, a number of limitations began to emerge with the categorical system. For one, the classifications were not highly stable. Baldwin and Fehr (1995) observed that the test–retest stability of the three-type categorical measure was only 70% (equivalent to a Pearson *r* of approximately 0.40). Some researchers began to wonder if some of that instability was due to attempting to assign people to categories who might, in fact, be somewhere near the boundaries in a dimensional space (see chapter: How Stable Are Attachment Styles in Adulthood? for an extended discussion of this issue). Second, both categorical systems treated the attachment categories as if they were mutually exclusive. That is, they assumed that a person could only fall into one category. But data from continuous measurements suggested that the categories were not mutually exclusive (eg, Collins & Read, 1990). Finally, the categorical system disregarded within-category variance that, in practice, seemed useful for predicting outcomes.

As a result of these tensions, some researchers began to ask respondents to rate items continuously and to use those ratings as a way to scale people in a multidimensional space (eg, Collins & Read, 1990). Nonetheless, two problems quickly emerged. First, there was no principled reason for moving from categories to continua. Moreover, although some researchers used the ratings to scale people on various dimensions, other researchers used the ratings as a means to obtain more accurate classifications. Second, the number of self-report scales that were being developed was growing without bounds. There were an increasing number of scales that researchers could use, some of which emphasized two dimensions and some of which emphasized seven. To make matters more complicated, each of these measurement systems employed slightly different labels, making the conceptual relations among them ambiguous.

Are Attachment Styles Categorical or Continuous?

Although the gradual move from classifications to ratings was an important step towards improving the measurement of adult attachment, these shifts begged a larger theoretical question: Do people vary categorically or continuously with respect to attachment? This question, sometimes referred to as the "types versus dimensions" question, is a critical one for the study of adult attachment. If people actually vary continuously in attachment organization, but researchers assign people to categories, then potentially important information about the way people differ from one another is lost. This loss can have deleterious effects on research, leading to less reliability and less statistical power and precision.

How can one determine whether variation in an unobservable construct, such as attachment organization, is continuous or categorical? Historically, researchers have relied on clustering techniques to identify groupings in data (eg, Collins & Read, 1990; Feeney, Noller, & Hanrahan, 1994). One of the limitations of clustering techniques, such as cluster analysis or latent profile analysis, however, is that they reveal groupings in data regardless of whether natural groupings actually exist. Fortunately, Meehl and his colleagues (eg, Meehl & Yonce, 1996; Waller & Meehl, 1998) developed a suite of techniques that allow one to uncover the latent structure of a domain and rigorously test taxonic (ie, typological) assumptions. Fraley and Waller (1998) adopted two of Meehl's techniques, MAXCOV and MAMBAC, to address the types versus dimensions question in the study of adult attachment. They administered Griffin and Bartholomew's (1994b) 30-item RSQ to a sample of over 600 undergraduates. Their taxometric analyses of the data provided no evidence for a categorical model of attachment. Instead, their results were more consistent with what would be expected if individual differences in attachment were continuously distributed. More recent work by Fraley and his colleagues (eg, Fraley, Hudson, Heffernan, & Segal, 2015) corroborates the dimensionality of individual differences across a number of relational domains (eg, attachment in general, attachment with parents, attachment with romantic partners).

The taxometric results reported by Fraley and his colleagues suggested that dimensional systems might be more appropriate than categorical ones for conceptualizing and assessing individual differences in attachment. The move from categorical to continuous measurement systems, however, raised a number of questions, such as: What is the best dimensional system for conceptualizing variation in adult attachment? We elaborate on these issues further.

What Are the Fundamental Dimensions Underlying Adult Attachment?

In the 1990s a number of investigators began creating multi-item inventories of adult attachment, inventories that could be used to produce continuous attachment scores. Although each of these instruments was rooted in Bowlby and Ainsworth's attachment theory, the designers of these instruments emphasized different constructs and used different methods of test development. Some researchers simply decomposed the items contained in the original Hazan and Shaver paragraphs. For example, Collins's (Collins & Read, 1990) Adult Attachment Scale (AAS) and Simpson's (Simpson, 1990; Simpson, Rholes, & Phillips, 1996) Adult Attachment Questionnaire (AAQ), which are still in widespread use today, were developed by taking the individual sentence fragments in the original Hazan and Shaver descriptions and creating 18 distinct items, each of which was rated on a continuous scale. Based on psychometric analyses of the items, Collins (Collins & Read, 1990) derived three composites: close, depend, and anxiety, while Simpson (Simpson 1990; Simpson et al., 1996) derived two dimensions: attachment anxiety and attachment avoidance. Feeney et al. (1994) took a different approach to generating continuous measures of attachment. Rather than extracting fragments and phrases from the Hazan and Shaver or Bartholomew prototypes, they developed new items designed to capture some of the common themes in attachment theory, such as trust, dependence, and self-reliance. The measure became known as the Attachment Style Questionnaire (Feeney et al., 1994). A factor analysis of responses to their items uncovered five factors: self-confidence, discomfort with closeness, need for approval, preoccupation with relationships, and the belief that relationships are of secondary importance (see also Karantzas, Feeney, & Wilkinson, 2010). Brennan and Shaver

(1995) followed a similar approach, generating a large pool of items which they then factor analyzed. Brennan and Shaver (1995) reported seven factors: ambivalence, anxious clinging to partners, jealousy and fear of abandonment, frustration with partners, proximity-seeking, self-reliance, and trust.

By the mid to late 1990s, researchers new to the field were likely to be overwhelmed by the vast number of self-report instruments in the literature. To address this problem, Brennan, Clark, and Shaver (1998) gathered all of the self-report measures of adult attachment known at the time and administered the nonredundant items to 1086 undergraduates. Factor analyses of the responses revealed two major factors. Based on the content of the items loading on these factors, Brennan and her colleagues labeled them attachment-related *anxiety* and attachment-related *avoidance*. The anxiety factor was defined by items such as "I worry that my partner won't want to stay with me" and "I don't think my partner loves me." The avoidance factor was defined by items such as "I am uncomfortable depending on others" and, at the opposite end, "I turn to my partner for assurance."

The Brennan report was a breakthrough for at least three reasons. First, the analyses that Brennan and her colleagues reported revealed that diverse measures of adult attachment were essentially tapping two fundamental domains, dimensions that are typically referred to as attachment anxiety and attachment avoidance in contemporary research (see chapter: What Are Attachment Working Models?). Second, Brennan and her colleagues showed how measures originally developed with different objectives could be mapped onto a common dimensional framework. This has allowed subsequent scholars to interpret the findings of studies based on different measures within the same two-dimensional system. Finally, Brennan and her colleagues used their data to produce a new questionnaire, the Experiences in Close Relationships (ECR) inventory, a 36-item questionnaire based on the items that best tapped the dimensions of anxiety and avoidance. In their original report, Brennan et al. (1998) showed that the 18 items for each subscale hung together well (alphas > 0.90) and the scales predicted a number of theoretically relevant outcomes, such as the enjoyment of touch, sexual preferences, and emotions experienced in an intimate context. The ECR, along with its derivatives (eg, the ECR-R; Fraley, Waller, & Brennan, 2000), are currently the most commonly used self-report measures of adult attachment and are commonly recommended for use as the primary self-report instruments for assessing adult attachment patterns according to the two-dimensional conceptualization of attachment.

What Do Attachment Anxiety and Avoidance Represent Theoretically?

Although Brennan and her colleagues' analyses indicated that two major factors underlie individual differences in adult romantic attachment, they did not offer an interpretation of the factors that was rooted in a specific model of how the attachment system operates. In fact, there have been several distinct ways of conceptualizing these two factors over the years. Some researchers have favored a "model of self and model of others" interpretation, as put forward by Griffin and Bartholomew (1994a) (eg, Carnelley, Pietromonaco, & Jaffe, 1994; Klohnen & John, 1998). Within this framework, individual differences are conceptualized as differences in the valence (ie, the positivity vs. negativity) of the models people hold of themselves and others. Accordingly, many researchers in this tradition have attempted to examine the content of the beliefs that people hold (eg, Baldwin, Fehr, Keedian, Seidel, & Thomson, 1993; Collins, 1996; Klohnen & John, 1998).

Fraley and Shaver (2000) outlined several limitations of conceptualizing the dimensions within the model of self and others framework. First, the manifest content of the items typically used to assess variation in attachment, both in the ECR and in Bartholomew's original prototype descriptions, is more consistent with a conceptualization that focuses on sensitivity to rejection and strategies for regulating affect. Second, the models of self and others interpretation requires that preoccupied individuals hold positive views of others, views of others as available, responsive, attentive, etc. This characterization is at odds with the empirical literature, which suggests that highly preoccupied individuals are often angry, jealous, and prone to feel that partners are insensitive to their needs (eg, Collins, 1996; Simpson et al., 1996).

As an alternative to the models of self and others interpretation, Fraley and Shaver (2000) put forward an *affective-motivational framework* (see also Fraley & Shaver, 1998; Fraley & Spieker, 2003). From this perspective, the two dimensions can be conceptualized as reflecting variability in the functioning of two fundamental subsystems or components of the attachment behavioral system. One component of the system involves monitoring and appraising events for their relevance to attachment-related goals, such as the attachment figure's physical or psychological proximity, availability, and responsiveness. When the system detects a discrepancy between the current set-goal for sensitivity and proximity and the perceived behavior of the attachment figure, the individual feels anxious and becomes increasingly vigilant to attachment-related cues. Variation in people's threshold for detecting threats to security or cues of rejection corresponds to individual differences in what Brennan et al. (1998) call *attachment-related anxiety*. The second component is responsible for regulation of attachment behavior with respect to attachment-related goals. For example, to regulate attachment-related anxiety, people can orient their behavior towards the attachment figure (ie, seeking contact or support) or withdraw and attempt to handle the threat alone. Variation in this behavioral-motivational component is responsible for individual differences in what Brennan et al. (1998) called *attachment-related avoidance* and, in many respects, reflects whether the person is willing or unwilling to rely on another individual as a safe haven and secure base.

One of the advantages of this framework is that it allows Bartholomew's four theoretical "types" to be conceptualized as linear combinations of the two dimensions of anxiety and avoidance. For example, security and dismissing-avoidance are characteristic of people who have high thresholds for detecting cues of rejection. Preoccupation and fearful-avoidance are characteristic of individuals with low thresholds for detecting such cues, making concerns about love-worthiness and rejection particularly salient. Security and preoccupation characterize people who wish to be close and intimate with their partners. Dismissing-avoidance and fearful-avoidance characterize people who try to deny the importance of close relationships or force themselves not to become vulnerable to them (Fig. 5.1B).

Another advantage of this framework is that it has the potential to be clinically useful. Although it is typically easier to classify a client into one of several distinct categories (eg, secure, dismissing, preoccupied, fearful) than to scale him or her with respect to two or more dimensions (especially given that clinicians are often trained to make categorical diagnoses), it can be much easier to study change in personality organization when the fine-grained distinctions that are available in a dimensional system are made. It is possible, for example, for a client to exhibit gradual gains in security across therapy that would be evident in the use of dimensional measures. However, if clinicians were using classification systems across sessions, those changes might go undetected.

Finally, the fact that the two-dimensional system distinguishes between attachment-related insecurities and the motivational strategies people use to regulate their thoughts and feelings (ie, as reflected in attachment avoidance), enables researchers to make a distinction between different attachment dynamics. It is possible that an individual is relatively secure in the knowledge that his or her partner is available and responsive if needed (ie, he is low in attachment-related anxiety), but that he characteristically relies upon distancing strategies in the relationship (ie, he is high on the avoidance dimension).

We should be clear that the motivational perspective on the dimensions does not claim that people do not hold models of others and the self that vary in valence. Instead, the claim is that commonly used self-report measures appear to be better suited for tapping appraisals and strategies that reflect different ways in which the attachment system may function across individuals. In this sense, they represent a broad-band perspective on individual differences in attachment style. If researchers are interested in assessing models of self and others per se, it might be advisable to use assessment tools that assess self-esteem and confidence (model of self) or general evaluations of the trustworthiness and responsiveness of others. Moreover, if one is interested in assessing the fine-grained aspects of the way in which attachment functions, a tool that highlights specific facets of attachment might be ideal (see further).

Summary

Self-report measures of adult attachment have evolved considerably over the past 30 years. Since landmark article by Hazan and Shaver (1987), the field has moved from classifying people with respect to three categories to scaling people with respect to two dimensions. Although the dimensional system captures the same attachment patterns as the original categorical systems, it allows these patterns to be represented with a greater degree of specificity and fidelity than is possible with classificatory systems. Factor analyses of self-report items indicate that two key dimensions underlie attachment patterns. The first, attachment-related anxiety, captures the extent to which people are insecure about their partner's availability, love, and responsiveness. The second, attachment-related avoidance, captures the strategies that people use for regulating attachment-related behavior, thought, and affect: Some people are comfortable opening up to others in intimate contexts, depending on others, and allowing others to depend on them; other people, in contrast, are more reserved and cautious, guarding themselves and their emotions. We suggest that these two dimensions reflect variation in the basic functioning of the attachment system and that framing them as such can help guide research and theory.

WHERE IS SECURITY IN THE TWO-DIMENSIONAL FRAMEWORK?

A common misconception is that widely used measures, such as the ECR (Brennan et al., 1998), do not capture security per se. One reason for this misconception is that the dimensions are labeled in the "insecure" direction: anxiety and avoidance. Thus, at a glance, it might seem as if security is missing. Another reason for the misconception is that the older categorical models made the various attachment patterns seem as if they were different "things." But as research using continuous measures has demonstrated, the various theoretical patterns are not independent of one another. When people rate the extent to which Bartholomew's four prototypes describe them, ratings of security tend to be negatively correlated with ratings of fearful-avoidance (eg, Fraley & Davis, 1997).

With that as context, it should be clear that security, as it is defined in the Bartholomew and Horowitz (1991) model (see also Griffin & Bartholomew, 1994a), is a combination of the two dimensions that Brennan and her colleagues referred to as anxiety and avoidance. That is, a prototypically secure individual is someone who does not worry about the availability and responsiveness of his or her attachment figures (low anxiety) and is comfortable using others as a secure base (low avoidance). Put in algebraic terms, the security dimension is a 45-degree rotation of the anxiety and avoidance dimensions (Fig. 9.1B). Security anchors one end of this axis, and fearful-avoidance anchors the opposite end.

Sometimes researchers are simply interested in variation in security rather than making a nuanced distinction among multiple dimensions. When this is the case, combining the dimensions of anxiety and avoidance provides a measure of security versus insecurity. Or, more precisely, it provides a measure of security versus fearful avoidance. It is not necessary in these cases to abandon the two-dimensional framework in search of a measure that more explicitly assesses attachment security versus insecurity.

Although the various prototypes are not independent of one another in the two-dimensional system, in this book we often discuss empirical research for security separately from research on anxiety and avoidance. Sometimes we do this out of necessity: The original research findings were based on measures that treated these constructs as if they are unrelated to one another. But sometimes we do it for the convenience of the reader. That is, sometimes it is easier to appreciate the implications of the findings when they can be framed with respect to the psychology of security as well as with respect to the psychology of insecurity. Conceptually, however, it is important to remember that security is the conceptual opposite of fearful-avoidance within the two-dimensional system and, similarly, dismissing-avoidance is the conceptual opposite of preoccupied attachment within that system. As a result, the findings we summarize are not always independent. When we write that highly secure people tend to be more satisfied in their close relationships (eg, chapter: What Are the Effects of Context on Attachment?), that naturally entails that fearful people are not highly satisfied in their relationships, if attachment styles were assessed using dimensional measures.

HOW SHOULD THE ATTACHMENT DIMENSIONS BE USED IN RESEARCH?

Let us assume that a researcher is interested in a relatively basic question, such as: What is the association between attachment style and depressive symptoms? Moreover, let's assume that we have a continuous measure of depressive symptoms. (In other words, we are not classifying people as clinically depressed based on a threshold.)

The categorical approach to this problem is straightforward: One would compute the mean and variance of depressive symptoms within each attachment group and then compare those means across the groups to see if one or more groups scores higher than the others.

The dimensional approach to this problem is also straightforward, but might be less familiar to researchers who are more accustomed to analyzing mean differences. One can model, using multiple regression, the variation in depressive symptoms as a linear combination of anxiety and avoidance. Doing so provides estimates of how depressive symptoms vary as a function of both avoidance and anxiety.

To illustrate more concretely, let's assume that anxiety and avoidance are measured on scales ranging from 1 to 7. But, to make the example easier to discuss, let us assume that both anxiety and avoidance have been standardized, such that their means are both 0.00 and their standard deviations (SDs) are 1.00. We will not assume the symptom measure is standardized. Thus, the intercept in this regression equation will give us an estimate of the mean number of symptoms for people who have average levels of anxiety and avoidance (ie, the intercept represents the expected value of y when the predictors equal 0.00).

Let us assume that we found that the estimate for the intercept was 1.50 and the estimates of the unstandardized regression weight for avoidance and anxiety were 0.20 and 0.40, respectively. What would this mean? First, the intercept would indicate that the average person in the sample reported 1.50 depressive symptoms. Because we have standardized anxiety and avoidance, the typical person in the sample has a value of 0 on both of these dimensions. Thus, the intercept, which is defined as the expected value of y for someone who has values of 0 for each predictor, can be interpreted as a mean. Second, these results would indicate that people who are more avoidant in their attachment orientation are more likely to exhibit depressive symptoms. Specifically, for each 1-unit increase on the standardized avoidance scale, we expect a corresponding 0.20 increase in depressive symptoms. Third, these results would indicate that people who are more anxious in their attachment orientation are more likely than those who are not to exhibit depressive symptoms. Specifically, for each 1-unit increase in anxiety, we expect an increase by almost half (0.40) of a depressive symptom. A common way of graphically depicting the results from this model is shown in Fig. 5.2A. This figure illustrates that symptom levels increase as attachment anxiety and avoidance increase.

This particular formulation emphasizes the two dimensions in particular. However, it is also possible to interpret these findings with respect to Bartholomew's prototypes. Although we previously argued that attachment styles do not represent natural kinds and that people should not be classified with respect to their attachment styles, it can sometimes be helpful to think about the attachment styles as multivariate patterns or configurations in a two-dimensional space (see Griffin & Bartholomew, 1994b). Importantly, this can be done without actually treating them as categories or assigning people to types.

How can these configural patterns be recovered in a multiple regression context? Recall that a person who is relatively secure is low in both anxiety and avoidance. What does "low" mean? One way that researchers often think about this is to define "low" as being 1 SD below the mean on a variable of interest. Thus, a prototypical secure person would be 1 SD below the mean on avoidance and 1 SD below the mean on anxiety (ie, -1 SD avoidance, -1 SD anxiety). Relatedly a relatively preoccupied person would be high in anxiety and low in avoidance (ie, -1 SD avoidance, $+1$ SD anxiety).

To illustrate how these configurations can be examined in our regression example, we can find the expected number of symptoms for a prototypically secure individual by plugging the values of -1 and -1 for avoidance and anxiety respectively into the regression equation.

$$
\begin{aligned}
\text{Expected symptoms} \quad &= \quad 1.50 + 0.20 \times (\text{avoidance}) + 0.40 \times (\text{anxiety}) \\
&= \quad 1.50 + 0.20 \times (-1) + 0.40 \times (-1) \\
&= \quad 0.90
\end{aligned}
$$

Thus, a prototypically secure person (ie, someone who is 1 SD below the mean on both attachment dimensions) has an expected value of 0.90 symptoms.

If we wish, we can do this for each of the theoretical prototypes. For example, to find the expected number of symptoms for someone who is preoccupied,

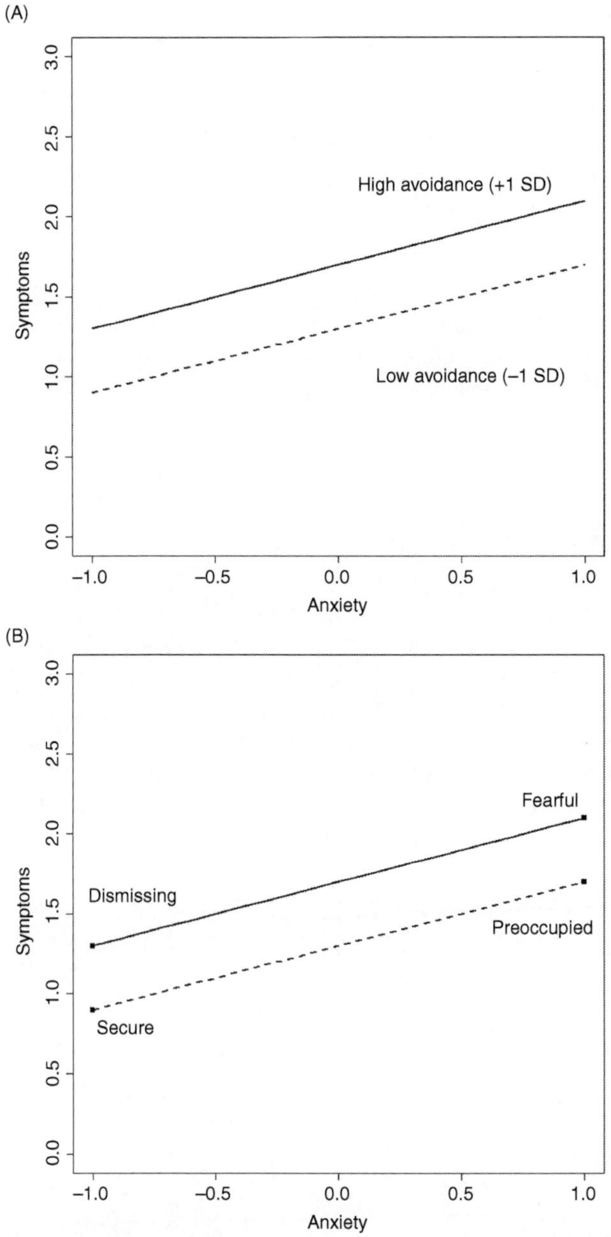

FIGURE 5.2   Visually summarizing regression results, using the two-dimensional model. (A) The first panel illustrates a common way of graphing regression results when there are two predictors; the first is often shown on the x-axis and the second is often shown by plotting separate regression lines at 1 *SD* above and 1 *SD* below the mean. (B) The second panel illustrates the ways in which configural information about the attachment prototypes can be represented in the same fashion, but based on the same multiple regression model rather than a categorical one.

we would plug the values −1 and +1 respectively into avoidance and anxiety. (Keep in mind that the prototypical preoccupied person is low in avoidance and high in anxiety; Fig. 5.2.) Doing so yields:

$$\begin{aligned} \text{Expected symptoms} &= 1.50 + 0.20 \times (\text{avoidance}) + 0.40 \times (\text{anxiety}) \\ &= 1.50 + 0.20 \times (-1) + 0.40 \times (1) \\ &= 1.70 \end{aligned}$$

When we perform all the calculations, we see that prototypically secure people have the fewest number of symptoms (0.90) and that fearful people have the most (2.10). Prototypically preoccupied (1.70) and dismissing (1.30) individuals fall somewhere in between these two extremes. This way of framing the findings is illustrated in Fig. 5.2B. Notice that the graph looks the same as the previous one, but we have annotated it to denote where the configurations lie in the regression space. Because both avoidance and anxiety were positively related to symptom levels, this graph shows that the highest reported symptoms exist among those who are prototypically fearfully avoidant (1 *SD* above the mean on both anxiety and avoidance).

Notice that this interpretation, although it may have a different flavor to it than the two-dimensional one, is summarizing the *same* information. Although we prefer the two-dimensional interpretation, we believe it is important to highlight the fact that the dimensional approach is flexible enough to accommodate both dimensional conceptualizations of individual differences in attachment functioning and the four-prototypes approach. It is important to keep in mind, however, that the prototype approach does not involve four "things." The relevant information is fully contained in the pattern of associations captured by the coefficients for the two dimensions.

SHOULD INTERACTIONS BETWEEN THE DIMENSIONS BE TESTED? ARE THEY NECESSARY?

One common misconception is that it is necessary to test the interaction between the attachment dimensions to truly capture something like security (eg, Shorey, 2010). But, according to the two-dimensional model, each theoretical prototype is an additive combination of anxiety and avoidance (Fig. 9.1B). For example, a prototypically secure person does not worry that his or her attachment figures will be unavailable or inaccessible (ie, he or she is low in anxiety). And such a person is comfortable opening up to others, depending on them, and using others as a secure base (ie, he or she is low in avoidance). The additive combination of the two dimensions fully defines the construct.[1]

---

1. To be clear, we are not suggesting that the two dimensions capture the full range of the construct. One could further refine the assessment of security by assessing additional factors. The point is that there is no further permutation of the two dimensions (eg, their product, their cubic) that contains additional information about the construct itself.

That said, sometimes there are reasons to believe that the *association* between an outcome of interest and the dimensions might be nonadditive. To illustrate, we consider an example from the study of attachment and bereavement where researchers have debated whether the dismissing-avoidant (ie, high avoidance, low anxiety) pattern is associated with poor outcomes (eg, Fraley & Bonanno, 2004). Some writers have hypothesized that the kinds of deactivating strategies that dismissing individuals use may operate to conceal latent vulnerabilities (see chapter: What Are Attachment Working Models?). If this is correct, then we might find that, when confronted with a major life stressor, such as the loss of a loved one, dismissing individuals will experience symptoms of depression that are more comparable to those of insecure people than secure people.

Notice, however, that there is no way to test this specific prediction in a standard additive model. If we were to estimate the regression coefficients in an additive model for avoidance and anxiety and find that both dimensions predict depressive symptoms, such a finding would indicate that dismissing individuals have higher symptoms than prototypically secure people, but not as high as prototypically preoccupied people.

To be more precise, there is no way to draw an axis through the two-dimensional space that equates symptom levels for prototypically dismissing people with other insecure styles. To test this prediction, we would have to add an interaction term to the equation to model both additive and nonadditive combinations of the two dimensions: Outcome = B_0 + B_1 × Anxiety + B_2 × Avoidance + B_3 × Anxiety × Avoidance. The hypothesis implies that B_1 will be positive, B_2 will be positive, and B_3 will be negative.

To illustrate how this works, it is helpful to substitute different values of anxiety and avoidance into the equation to see how the predicted number of depressive symptoms changes. For simplicity, let's assume that the values of B_1, B_2, and B_3 are +1, +1, and −1, respectively. Let's also assume the intercept, B_0, is 5. This implies that, for a person who is average with respect to attachment-related anxiety and avoidance, his or her expected symptom levels are 5. Because a prototypical dismissing individual is high on avoidance and low on anxiety, we can substitute a value of +1 for avoidance and −1 for anxiety into the equation. Doing so yields:

$$
\begin{aligned}
\text{Outcome} &= B_0 + B_1 \times \text{Anxiety} + B_2 \times \text{Avoidance} + B_3 \times \text{Anxiety} \\
&\quad \times \text{Avoidance} \\
&= 5 + B_1 \times (-1) + B_2 \times (+1) + B_3 \times (-1) \times (+1) \\
&= 6
\end{aligned}
$$

Thus, the predicted number of depressive symptoms is 6, on average, for someone who is relatively dismissing. We can plug in the values for the other prototypical attachment patterns too. For example, a relatively secure person is low on both dimensions. Substituting a −1 into avoidance and a −1 into anxiety yields the following:

$$\text{Outcome} = B_0 + B_1 \times \text{Anxiety} + B_2 \times \text{Avoidance} + B_3 \times \text{Anxiety}$$
$$\times \text{Avoidance}$$
$$= 5 + B_1 \times (-1) + B_2 \times (-1) + B_3 \times (-1) \times (-1)$$
$$= 2$$

If we substitute the values for the other prototypes, we find that the inclusion of the interaction term leads secure people to have the lowest number of symptoms (2) and all of the other insecure prototypes (preoccupied, fearful, and dismissing) to have predicted values of 6.

Thus, including an interaction term in this example enables one to model the possibility that the dimensions combine in nonadditive ways to influence the outcomes of interest. In this particular model, relatively secure people exhibit few postloss symptoms of depression, whereas people who are more insecure exhibit a greater number of symptoms. Importantly, this holds true for dismissing people too, whose symptom levels are comparable to those of prototypically preoccupied and fearful people rather than secure people.

We close this section with a cautionary note. Namely, sometimes researchers conjecture that one particular prototype should score higher than the others. For example, researchers might propose that being relatively anxious about the availability and accessibility of one's partner (anxiety) *combined with* the tendency to avoid opening up to and depending on others (avoidance) may lead to a relatively high rate of relationship conflict. This reasoning suggests that fearfully avoidant people will experience conflict at much greater rates than other people.

On the surface, this reasoning might seem to require an interaction term to account for the particular combination of anxiety and avoidance effects postulated and to explain why that particular combination leads fearful people to report the highest rates of conflict. But it doesn't. The notion that the two dimensions "combine" to produce outcomes is implicit in the simple additive model. That is, the assumption that an outcome is a function of both anxiety and avoidance is a natural part of a basic additive model. It is rarely the case that researchers need to further postulate that the way in which the dimensions combine is nonadditive in order to capture the notion that both dimensions are relevant to understanding certain outcomes.

A simple additive model can also lead to the prediction that the combination of the two dimensions produces the greatest (or least) degree of conflict. As we saw in our example regarding depressive symptoms previously, there was a clear rank-ordering among the theoretical prototypes (eg, Fig. 5.2B). One prototype was at highest risk for depression because the dimensions were combining—in additive ways—to produce that outcome.

One reason we believe researchers get confused on this point is because they sometimes theorize at the level of the prototypes rather than the two dimensions themselves. Although we appreciate the appeal of doing so, one potential cost of thinking about the prototypes is that doing so does not always make clear how the component parts of those prototypes combine to lead to specific outcomes. Thinking about the dimensions first helps to make these issues clearer.

To summarize, there were three main points we made in this section. First, the prototypical attachment styles are additive combinations of the two dimensions. Therefore, it is defensible to model outcomes of interest as an additive combination of anxiety and avoidance; there is no need in many circumstances to include an interaction term. Second, there are situations, however, where specific theoretical predictions may entail an interaction term. Adding it in those situations is not only useful, but necessary. Third, researchers sometimes confuse the idea that the dimensions combine to produce outcomes with the idea that they combine in nonadditive ways. The dimensions can combine in additive ways to produce a range of conceptually rich outcomes. Nonadditivity should only be conjectured if there is absolutely no way to accommodate the theoretical expectations on the basis of an additive combination of the dimensions.

ARE THERE MORE THAN TWO DIMENSIONS?

It is almost certainly the case that there are more than two dimensions that are needed to fully capture the kinds of individual differences that exist in adult attachment. The challenge is that, the more fine-grained the assessment system is, the more difficult it becomes to use it efficiently. In our opinion, the two-dimensional model represents a useful middle ground. On the one hand, it is sufficiently complex that it enables distinctions between different forms of avoidance to be made (eg, fearful and dismissing avoidance). Moreover, it acknowledges that security is not a unidimensional phenomenon. On the other hand, the two-dimensional system is not too complex. As a result, it is a relatively easy system for generating and testing hypotheses, graphing results, and examining psychological processes in multidimensional ways.

Some researchers have recommended assessing more than two dimensions. For example, Brennan and Shaver (1995) highlighted seven dimensions that might be useful: ambivalence, anxious clinging to partners, jealous and fear of abandonment, frustration with partners, proximity-seeking, self-reliance, and trust. People who are ambivalent in their relationships are also more likely to report jealousy, fear of abandonment, and frustration with their partners, for example. Karantzas et al. (2010) extended the work of Feeney and colleagues (Alexander, Feeney, Hohaus, & Noller, 2001; Feeney et al., 1994; Fossati et al., 2003a) to also identify seven dimensions of adult attachment. In contrast to Brennan and Shaver (1995), Karantzas et al. (2010) identified the five factors that underpinned Feeney et al.'s multidimensional measure of attachment (confidence, relationships as secondary, discomfort with closeness, preoccupation with relationships, and need for approval), but also uncovered the two primary dimensions: attachment anxiety and attachment avoidance. Karantzas and colleagues suggest that while the broad dimensions provide a more than adequate assessment of attachment, the facet dimensions are likely to be important in counselling and clinical contexts where the efficacy of therapy is in part a function of the therapist's capacity to identify the specific cause of maladaptive interpersonal functioning. For example, while an individual may present with issues of attachment anxiety in session, a practitioner's ability to establish whether the anxiety is rooted in the preoccupation with relationships or in a relentless need for approval will likely result in working on different issues in therapy.

Our general recommendation is that, unless researchers are targeting highly specific aspects of attachment functioning, they focus on the two dimensions commonly studied in attachment research. If they are attempting to zoom in on a specific aspect regarding the way in which the attachment system functions, there may be value in assessing something else in addition to the two dimensions (eg, Karantzas et al., 2010).

ARE THE DIMENSIONS ORTHOGONAL? OR ARE THEY CORRELATED WITH ONE ANOTHER?

Many writers conceptualize and describe the two attachment dimensions as orthogonal (ie, statistically independent). Unfortunately, it is not always clear whether writers do this for convenience (eg, as we have done via the graphs in Fig. 5.2B) or because they are making a theoretical claim about the statistical relationship between the two dimensions.

One reason for the confusion, we suspect, is that, when Bowlby wrote about models of self and others (see chapter: What Are Attachment Working Models?), the language he used might have implied statistical independence. Specifically, he wrote "logically these variables [representations of self and others] are independent" (Bowlby, 1973, p. 204). In our view, what Bowlby meant was that representations of the self and others were *distinct* constructs, that is, they are separable and should not be conflated with one another. We do not think that he was making the statistical claim that they are orthogonal to one another. The fact that he also wrote of the way in which they can be confounded in practice (Bowlby, 1973) seems like a clear indication that orthogonality is not a part of the core theory.

Empirically, the two dimensions tend to be correlated. Cameron, Finnegan, and Morry (2012) conducted a meta-analysis designed to examine the association between anxiety and avoidance. They found that the correlation between the two dimensions tends to be higher with the ECR-R ($r = 0.41$) than the ECR ($r = 0.15$). In addition, Cameron and her colleagues found that the two dimensions tend to correlate more highly in samples of people involved in committed relationships. Samples of older individuals also show stronger associations between the dimensions than younger samples.

Although we believe that the association between the dimensions is not a problem for the theory, it can create problems in practice. If both dimensions correlate with an outcome of interest, it isn't immediately clear whether the association is due to the unique contribution of each dimension or whether one of the dimensions is driving the association and the other is correlated with the outcome simply by virtue of its association with the other dimension.

When the two measures are correlated with one another, it is important to statistically control them both when modeling the outcomes of interest. The examples discussed previously using multiple regression illustrated how to do this. Specifically, when one conducts a multiple regression analysis and includes both anxiety and avoidance in the model simultaneously, one can estimate the association between each attachment dimension and the outcome while controlling for the fact that the two dimensions are related to one another. This provides one means for identifying the unique correlates of each dimension.

ARE SELF-REPORTS AND INTERVIEWS INTERCHANGEABLE WITH ONE ANOTHER?

This chapter has focused on self-report measures of adult attachment for at least two reasons. First, self-report measures are the most commonly used measures in the social-personality tradition to the study of adult attachment. Second, work by Hazan and Shaver (1987) that inspired this particular research tradition, used questionnaire methods to assess attachment styles.

We should be clear, however, that there are alternative means for assessing attachment. Bartholomew, in her original work, for example, developed an interview method for assessing adult attachment styles. Although the interview has been extensively used by Bartholomew and some of her colleagues (eg, Bartholomew & Horowitz, 1991; Griffin & Bartholomew, 1994b; Scharfe & Bartholomew, 1994), it has not been widely adopted in the social-personality tradition.

Similarly, the most common way of assessing individual differences in adult attachment in the developmental tradition is through the use of the Adult Attachment Interview (AAI; Main et al., 1985). The AAI is a semistructured interview that takes approximately 60 min to administer. Participants are asked to describe their early relationships with caregivers and the ways in which these experiences may have shaped their personality development. Those interviews are then transcribed and coded on a number of scales. Each transcript is also classified as autonomous/secure, dismissing, or preoccupied.

Importantly, the AAI is *not* designed to assess the quality of early experiences as inferred from the interview. Instead, the primary construct is the *coherence of discourse*. A person is classified as secure, or autonomous, in the AAI coding system, if he or she is able to characterize his or her early experiences in a coherent manner. In fact, a person can be classified as secure even if he or she describes harsh or neglectful early experiences, if he or she is able to do so in a coherent manner.

Research has shown that attachment classifications based on the AAI and self-reports are weakly related to one another. A meta-analysis reported by

Roisman et al. (2007) showed that self-reported anxious attachment was virtually unrelated to AAI scores and that self-report avoidance was correlated 0.09 with AAI scores. What might explain these discrepancies? There are at least three possibilities. First, the most self-evident explanation is that the two methods rely on fundamentally different methods of assessment: interviews versus self-reports. Although this difference does not fully explain the discrepancy between the methods, research on assessment has shown that different methods for assessing similar constructs rarely converge as strongly as researchers expect (Roberts, Harms, Smith, Wood, & Webb, 2006). Even if the AAI and self-reports were assessing the same constructs, we would not necessarily expect them to converge highly.

Second, the two assessment systems conceptualize security in different ways. In the social-personality tradition, a secure person is conceptualized as someone who is confident in the availability and responsiveness of close others and, importantly, is comfortable opening up to them, depending on them, and using them as a secure base and safe haven. In the AAI, a secure person is conceptualized as someone who can describe his or her early attachment experiences in a coherent manner. Such an individual is able to support his or her descriptions of attachment figures through credible episodic examples and does not become confused or overwhelmed in the process. Although we believe that, conceptually, the kinds of concepts targeted by the AAI and self-reports are logically related, they are not necessarily the same. This conceptual lack of convergence likely helps explain part of the empirical divergence between the methods.

Third, the AAI, although it is often regarded as a measure of generalized attachment representations, specifically probes people about their early attachment experiences with their primary caregivers. It does not, for example, target attachment in romantic relationships, which is what social-psychological measures often target. This is an important point because, when the assessment method is held constant, self-reports of attachment with mothers, fathers, and romantic partners do not converge strongly. For example, Fraley, Heffernan, Vicary, and Brumbaugh (2011) found that people who were relatively secure in their current relationship with their mother were more likely to be secure in their relationship with their romantic partner, but the correlation was between 0.10 and 0.20. In some respects, then, the maximum expected correlation between the AAI and self-reports should be in this range simply due to the fact that these two methods typically target different relational domains.

What is the convergence between the AAI and self-reports when the self-reports specifically target parental attachment rather than romantic attachment? Haydon, Roisman, Marks, and Fraley (2011) examined this issue by administering the AAI and the ECR-RS to a sample of 230 young adults. They used continuous measures of attachment organization for the AAI, focusing on dismissing attachment and preoccupied attachment. They found that the AAI dismissing scale was correlated 0.16 with self-reported avoidance with mother (but only 0.08 with self-reported avoidance with romantic partner). Haydon et al. (2011) also examined continuous measures of the quality of people's experiences with their parents, what are sometimes referred to as the "experience" scales of the AAI in contrast to the "states of mind" scales that are more relevant for attachment classifications. They also found that the correlations between the experience scales of the AAI and the self-reports were markedly higher. AAI mother experience scales correlated 0.24 to 0.30 with self-reported avoidance and anxiety with mothers and the AAI father experience scales correlated 0.41 and 0.22 with the self-reported avoidance and anxiety scales with fathers.

What are the implications of these findings? We believe they suggest that the self-reports and the AAI converge reasonably well when (1) the AAI is scaled for experience and (2) there is specificity in the target being evaluated (ie, parental relationships vs. romantic relationships). It is important to note, however, that the experience scales are not considered relevant for the primary AAI classifications. Specifically, coders are instructed to base their classifications on the coherence of discourse independently of whether people are describing positive or negative experiences with their primary caregivers. Although people who describe positive experiences are more likely to be secure/autonomous in the AAI (eg, Haydon et al., 2011), those experiences are not the primary focus of the assessment and are less central to the meaning of security in the context of the AAI.

To summarize, social psychologists and developmental psychologists tend to rely upon different methods of assessing individual differences. The focus of this book is on the social-personality tradition and, as a result, we have emphasized in this chapter how those differences are assessed. Nonetheless, the convergence, or lack thereof, between these different measures is of theoretical interest. Research shows that there is, at best, a weak association between these alternative measures of attachment. We have argued that this lack of convergence stems from three sources: (1) the use of patently different methods, (2) an emphasis on different constructs, and (3) an emphasis on different relational domains.

WHAT ARE SOME OF THE RECOMMENDED SELF-REPORT MEASURES OF ATTACHMENT?

There are several self-report measures of attachment styles that are in widespread use today. All of these measures exhibit decent psychometric properties and the scores can be easily mapped onto the two-dimensional system described previously. We do not believe that one of these measures is generally better than the others. However, they are likely to be useful for different purposes. We encourage people who are considering assessing attachment to consider one of these measures.

Experiences in Close Relationships (ECR)

The most commonly used measure, the ECR, contains 36 items, 18 of which are designed to assess attachment-related avoidance and 18 of which are

designed to assess attachment-related anxiety (Brennan et al., 1998). The measure is largely construed as a general measure of romantic attachment styles
in adults. By "general" we mean that the measure doesn't target a specific
romantic relationship, but instead asks people to consider their experience in
intimate relationships more generally. Scores on the two ECR scales tend to be
highly reliable (alphas > 0.90). Moreover, the ECR has been used extensively
in empirical research since its publication. Wei and her colleagues created a
shorter version of the ECR, the ECR-S, that contains 12 items (Wei, Russell,
Mallinckrodt, & Vogel, 2007).

The Experiences in Close Relationships, Revised (ECR-R)

The ECR-R is a 36-item variant of the ECR that was developed using the same
item pool as the ECR, but employing item-selection methods based on a combination of factor analysis and item response theory (IRT) (Fraley et al., 2000).
The ECR-R also produces scores for attachment-related anxiety and avoidance
(alphas > 0.90). The ECR and the ECR-R are largely redundant. The ECR-R
was not designed to be an alternative to the ECR per se, but was created as a
means to illustrate how IRT methods can be used in scale construction in the
field of adult attachment. Despite their similarities, however, scores from the
ECR-R dimensions tend to correlate more strongly with one another than scores
from the ECR dimensions (see Cameron et al., 2012).

Adult Attachment Questionnaire (AAQ)

The AAQ was developed by Simpson and his colleagues (Simpson, 1990; Simpson, Rholes, & Nelligan, 1992; Simpson et al., 1996). It contains items from the
original Hazan and Shaver (1987) paragraphs, but it is commonly used these
days to scale people with respect to the two attachment dimensions. The measure consists of 17 items; 9 items measure attachment anxiety while 8 items
measure attachment avoidance. Like the ECR and ECR-R, the AAQ is construed as a measure of general romantic attachment styles.

Relationship Scales Questionnaire (RSQ)

The RSQ is similar to the AAQ and uses items from the original Hazan and
Shaver (1987) paragraphs and the Bartholomew and Horowitz (1991) paragraphs (Griffin & Bartholomew, 1994a). The measure consists of 30 items;
however, only 20 items are used to calculate scores for the four prototypes.
The additional 10 items are used to calculate scores that align with Simpson
et al.'s (1992) dimensions. Although the RSQ was designed, in part, to produce
continuous scores for each of the four prototypes, we caution against that usage
given the theoretical multicollinearity among the four prototypes (see Fraley &
Waller, 1998). We recommend that researchers who use this measure score it

with respect to the dimensions of anxiety and avoidance. Roisman et al. (2007) evaluated several different ways of scoring the RSQ and concluded that the method that maps onto the Simpson et al. (1992) approach works best. Thus, scores generated with this method of scoring the RSQ should be identical to those generated by the AAQ.

Experiences in Close Relationships, Relationship Structures (ECR-RS)

The ECR-RS is a relatively new measure that was modeled after the ECR and the ECR-R (Fraley et al., 2011a). It was inspired by the finding that, when people are asked to self-report their attachment style with specific targets (eg, their mother, their spouse), those reports do not converge strongly (see chapter 4: What Are Attachment Working Models?). This suggests that there is value in attempting to assess attachment in different relationships in a more targeted manner. The ECR-RS is designed to target people's attachment styles in a variety of different relationships, such as current relationships with mothers, fathers, partners, and friends. The ECR-RS contains nine items that are used to assess attachment styles in each of these four relational domains (six items tap avoidance and three items tap anxiety). More recently, Fraley and his colleagues have also used the items to assess attachment more generally (eg, see Fraley et al., 2015).

Attachment Style Questionnaire (ASQ) and Attachment Style Questionnaire-Short Form (ASQ-SF)

The ASQ (Feeney et al., 1994) and its short form the ASQ-SF (Alexander et al., 2001; Karantzas et al., 2010) are widely used measures of adult attachment by researchers who are after an assessment of attachment that extends beyond the two primary dimensions of attachment anxiety and avoidance. Furthermore, because items do not focus on romantic relationships, the measure is best suited to assessing attachment in adolescents and people with little romantic experience. The ASQ consists of 40 items partitioned into five dimensions (confidence, relationships as secondary, discomfort with closeness, preoccupation with relationships, and need for approval). The ASQ-SF consists of a 29-item subset of the ASQ designed to assess the two primary dimensions of attachment anxiety (13 items) and avoidance (16 items, Alexander et al., 2001). In recent years, Karantzas et al. (2010) have identified that both the ASQ and the ASQ-SF can be used to tap into both the broad attachment dimensions as well as the five facet dimensions originally identified by Feeney et al. (1994).

State Adult Attachment Measure (SAAM)

Recently researchers studying attachment have become interested in how attachment changes within an individual due to social or cognitive context fluctuations (eg, Gillath, Selcuk, & Shaver, 2008). The State Adult Attachment

Measure (SAAM; Gillath, Hart, Noftle, & Stockdale, 2009) is a 21-item inventory that was specifically developed to assess state-like fluctuations in working models of attachment. Participants are asked to think about their feelings, attitudes, and beliefs in the present moment and then rate how much they agree or disagree with each item using a 7-point scale. Seven of the items assess state attachment avoidance (eg, If someone tried to get close to me, I would try to keep my distance), seven items assess state attachment anxiety (eg, I wish someone would tell me they really love me), and seven items assess state attachment security (eg, I feel loved). The internal consistency for all three subscales tends to be high (alphas > 0.87). The SAAM structure is more similar to the original Hazan and Shaver (1987) attachment style scale and other early measures of adult attachment, having a separate security factor in it. Xu and Shrout (2013) recently assessed the quality of the SAAM and its ability to capture fluctuations in attachment style as compared with the ECR (Brennan et al., 1998). In two longitudinal studies they found that, even with fewer items, the reliability of change for the SAAM was higher than that of the ECR. Trentini, Foschi, Lauriola, and Tambelli (2015) provide further information on construct and incremental validity of the SAAM, and Bosmans, Bowles, Dewitte, De Winter, and Braet (2014) showed that SAAM scores are sensitive to priming effects.

SUMMARY

Shortly after Hazan and Shaver (1987) introduced attachment theory to social and personality psychologists, there was an explosion of measures developed to assess individual differences in adult attachment. The history of measurement issues in this field has been a bit circuitous, and it may not always be obvious what kinds of theoretical models and measurement instruments modern researchers should be using. Based on our review of the literature, we propose a few broad themes, suggestions, and recommendations that we hope will be useful and that will help provide the foundation for the ideas discussed in the remainder of this book.

First, many researchers who are studying adult attachment styles tend to ground their work in a two-dimensional system, one that has its origins in Bartholomew and Horowitz's (1991) four-prototype model. Although there are subtle differences in the ways in which people describe these dimensions (ie, some people discuss self- and other models, some people discuss anxiety and avoidance), it seems clear that these two dimensions cut across the content domain of most measurement approaches and represent a "common denominator" in attachment research.

Second, there is some nuance that needs to be considered when working with multidimensional measurement systems. It is not always obvious how a concept that people tend to think about categorically, such as security, can be understood and measured within a two-dimensional system. In this chapter we have tried to clarify how security and other attachment prototypes are situated within a two-dimensional space, how they can be assessed and studied psycho-metrically, and some important caveats about the difference between additive and nonadditive combinations.

Third, there are many self-report measures available to assess individual dif-ferences in adult attachment and it is not always clear how to choose a measure or to evaluate whether researchers have used optimal measures in light of their research questions. For most research purposes, we recommend the ECR (Bren-nan et al., 1998) or its modern variants (eg, the ECR-R or the ECR-S; Fraley et al., 2000; Wei et al., 2007). However, if researchers are interested in attach-ment in specific relational contexts (eg, parents, peers), contextualized mea-sures, such as the ECR-RS (Fraley et al., 2011a), might be preferable. Similarly, if one is interested in assessment of the momentary activation of attachment-relevant states, state measures, such as the SAAM (Gillath et al., 2011), are preferable. Finally, if one needs a more nuanced investigation of how different facets of avoidance, for example, might function across contexts, a measure that focuses on the facets of the two dimensions would be preferable (eg, Karantzas et al., 2010).

Chapter 6

How Stable Are Attachment Styles in Adulthood?

One of the key themes of attachment theory is that people's attachment styles—their typical ways of thinking, feeling, and behaving in close relationships—are relatively stable across time. Indeed, the continuity of attachment styles is what enables theorists to explain a variety of psychologically interesting phenomena, including the tendency for people to recreate maladaptive relationship patterns. But the theory also emphasizes the plasticity of attachment styles. In order for working models to reflect people's relationships experiences, they must be capable of being modified and revised in light of ongoing experiences. Indeed, part of what motivates much of the clinical interest in attachment theory is the assumption that attachment styles can change in adulthood (see chapter: What Are the Implications of Attachment Processes for Psychopathology and Therapy?). If people cannot change, there is little reason to invest in therapy or interventions that might promote security.

The purpose of this chapter is to review what is known about stability and change in attachment styles in adulthood. We begin by reviewing some of Bowlby's ideas concerning stability and change. One of the ideas that Bowlby emphasized was that the processes giving rise to stability and change were often features of the same system. Thus, rather than viewing stability and change as mutually exclusive outcomes of these processes, he viewed them as forces that coexist within dynamic systems. Using these ideas as a general framework, we review research on mechanisms that promote continuity as well as mechanisms that promote change. We then turn to the empirical literature that has attempted to quantify the degree of stability that exists in attachment styles. We also address some of the debates that have ensued over the years about stability and change. We review what is known about the ways in which attachment styles vary across different phases of the adult life course. Finally, we attempt to highlight some of the questions that remain and suggest ways in which researchers can answer those in the future.

We begin by noting that there are many ways to conceptualize and measure continuity in individual differences research (see Caspi & Roberts, 2001, for a review). One of the most crucial distinctions is between what is called rank-order stability and mean-level stability. *Rank-order stability* is concerned with

Adult Attachment. http://dx.doi.org/10.1016/B978-0-12-420020-3.00006-2

the ordering of individual differences across time. For example, if we were to assess attachment styles in a sample of individuals at the beginning of the year and then reassess the same sample a year later, we might wish to know whether the people who were highly secure at Time 1 are also the people who are highly secure at Time 2. We could index this quantitatively using a test–retest correlation. If everyone maintained their standing relative to others, then the test–retest correlation would be 1.00. If, however, some of the people who were highly secure at Time 1 are not so secure at Time 2 and others who were insecure at Time 1 are now relatively secure at Time 2, then the correlation would be closer to 0.00. Rank-order stability is one of the most commonly used ways to measure stability in attachment research.

An alternative way to conceptualize and measure stability is mean-level stability. Mean-level stability is concerned with the extent to which the average level of a variable changes across time. If the sample described earlier, for example, had an average score of 5.23 on a 1- to 7-point scale of security at both assessment waves, we would conclude that there was no mean-level change across time. To the extent to which those means are different, however, we may conclude that there are forces leading people to increase (or decrease) in security systematically across time.

Importantly, mean-level and rank-order stability are conceptually and statistically independent (Caspi & Roberts, 2001). It is possible, for example, for the average level of security to remain constant across time, despite there being zero stability in the rank ordering of individuals. This could happen if everyone who is highly secure at Time 1 happens to be highly insecure at Time 2 and vice versa. Similarly, it is possible for mean levels of security to increase (or decrease) across time, even if the rank ordering of individuals is perfectly preserved (ie, test–retest $r = 1.00$). As a result, researchers often address questions about rank-order and mean-level stability separately. This does not mean, however, that the answers to one question are irrelevant for the other; it simply means that one cannot logically conclude that, just because people become less anxious in their attachment patterns across time (eg, Chopik, Edelstein, & Fraley, 2013), the rank ordering of individual differences is changing too. It is quite possible that the same kinds of factors that give rise to mean-level changes in some circumstances also give rise to instability in the rank ordering of individual differences.

With that as context, in this chapter we review research that is primarily concerned with rank-order stability. Specifically, we will focus on processes (eg, breakups) that are assumed to lead to change in attachment at the individual level and, as a consequence, disrupt the rank ordering of individual differences. Near the end of the chapter we will also discuss mean-level changes in attachment, with a focus specifically on how attachment changes as a function of age. We should also note that continuity and change are two sides of the same coin. Although some processes may specifically facilitate continuity in attachment whereas others may facilitate change (see later), the outcomes of both processes are indexed in the same way (eg, with test–retest correlations). Thus, rank-order coefficients quantify *both* stability and change. The larger those coefficients are, the more stable people are; the closer to zero those coefficients are, the less stable people are.

WHAT DID BOWLBY SAY ABOUT STABILITY AND CHANGE? METAPHORS FOR DYNAMIC PROCESSES

Many of Bowlby's ideas about stability and change in attachment organization were inspired by C. H. Waddington's (1967) discussion of cell development (see Fraley & Brumbaugh, 2004, for an in-depth discussion). Waddington was an esteemed developmental embryologist in Bowlby's time who was trying to understand how a cell may maintain a specific developmental trajectory in the face of varying environmental forces. Waddington and others had observed that, once a cell begins to assume specific functions (eg, it will become part of the visual system), minor changes to the cell's environment are unlikely to alter the cell's developmental trajectory. That is, despite attempts to disrupt the cell's growth, the cell continues as if it has a specific goal in mind. Although a cell has the potential to assume many different functions early in its development, once a specific trajectory has been established, Waddington argued that the trajectory becomes *canalized* or *buffered*, making it increasingly unlikely that the cell will deviate from that developmental course.

To illustrate this process more concretely, Waddington compared cell development to the behavior of a marble rolling down a hill. In Waddington's analogy, the marble represents a cell and the various troughs at the end of the landscape represent alternative developmental functions that the cell can assume. Waddington considered the specific shape of the landscape to be controlled by the complex interactions among numerous genes, and, as such, he referred to it as the *epigenetic landscape* (Fig. 6.1). Once the marble begins its descent, it settles into one of several pathways defined by the valley floors of the landscape. A slight nudge may push the marble away from its course, but the marble will eventually return to the trajectory previously established. As the marble continues along the basin of the specific valley, it becomes increasingly unlikely that external forces will cause it to jump from one valley to the next. Certain features of the marble, such as its momentum, help to keep the marble moving along the existing pathway, and certain features of the landscape itself, such as the steepness and curvature of the valleys, serve to buffer the marble against forces that might disrupt its trajectory.

Waddington's illustration was highly influential in Bowlby's thinking about stability and change in attachment organization. Bowlby noted, for example, that understanding the behavior of the marble in Waddington's example required understanding not only the mechanics of the marble itself, but

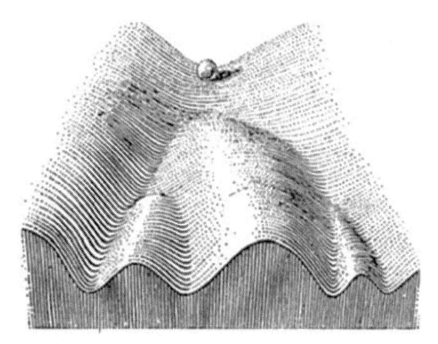

FIGURE 6.1 Waddington's epigenetic landscape.

also the environment in which it was situated. Some of the valleys in the hill are much steeper than others and, as a result, are much more likely to steer the marble toward a specific outcome. In the case of human development, Bowlby suggested that certain features of the individual's interpersonal environment can sustain the individual's developmental trajectory. For example, when the individual's family context is stable, he or she is unlikely to experience interactions that challenge his or her representations of the world. The powerful nature of this dynamic was emphasized by Bowlby's (1973) observation that children and adults typically have the same parents, same community, and same broad culture for long periods of time. When the environment is stable, an individual is unlikely to be confronted with experiences that are inconsistent with existing expectations—a point to which we return later in this chapter.

Bowlby also noted that certain properties of the marble itself—its momentum, direction, and speed, for example—also determine its trajectory. In the case of attachment dynamics, Bowlby also called attention to a number of individual-level or psychodynamic processes that may promote continuity. Bowlby observed that people often select environments that are consistent with their preexisting working models. For example, an individual who is relatively secure is more likely, than one who is insecure, to be accepting of others and to interact with them in ways that will help build and establish trust. Moreover, Bowlby argued that basic social-cognitive processes lead individuals to assimilate new information into existing knowledge structures rather than to build new representations to accommodate for discrepancies.[1]

Despite the many forces that promote stability, there are many forces that promote change. In Waddington's metaphor, for example, although a marble is likely to return to the trajectory previously established when it is nudged in one direction or another, a sizable push can knock it into a new valley—especially early in the developmental process. As a consequence, not only does the marble change direction temporarily, its long-term trajectory can be changed as well. Bowlby recognized that there are experiences that people have that have the potential to knock them out of equilibrium, so to speak. The loss of a spouse, for example, can often lead people to question fundamental assumptions they hold about the world (Bowlby, 1980; Fraley & Shaver, 2015), all of which have some bearing on how safe they feel in the world and how responsive they believe people will be to their needs.

One of the important features of the epigenetic landscape metaphor was that it provided Bowlby with a unified framework in which to understand both continuity and change. The framework captured his intuition that, once certain dynamic processes were set in motion, they would be naturally self-sustaining. Indeed, we will discuss some research below on some of the social-cognitive mechanisms that lead working models to reinforce themselves. But the metaphor also provides a framework for understanding how change can occur despite the self-sustaining nature of the system. Specifically, by nudging the marble with enough force or when the marble is at an unstable location in the landscape (eg, near the cusp of a valley), it is possible to modify the marble's trajectory. Indeed, there is a growing body of research that we review below which suggests that certain life events may be capable of creating shifts in people's attachment styles. In the sections that follow we discuss in more depth some of the research on continuity and change in adult attachment styles.

WHAT LEADS TO STABILITY IN ADULT ATTACHMENT STYLES?

According to Bowlby, there are many factors that can facilitate continuity in attachment styles across time. In the sections that follow we discuss two broad mechanisms of stability: those that concern intrapsychic processes and

---

1. Many of these ideas are commonplace in modern personality and developmental research and theory. For example, Scarr and McCartney (1983), in their classic paper on niche picking, argued that one mechanism that promotes stability involves the way in which people select and construct environments that are compatible with their preexisting, genetically influenced dispositions. Modern research on adult personality development (eg, Caspi & Roberts, 2001; Specht et al., 2014) also emphasizes the ways in which continuity can be maintained through the processes of evocative transactions (ie, other people interact with the individual in ways that sustain his or her dispositions), reactive transactions (ie, people interpreting their environment in ways that are compatible with or biased towards the assumptions they already hold), and proactive transactions (eg, selection effects, such as people choosing social contexts, occupations, or partners that reinforce existing dispositions).

those that concern the structure of the environment. Importantly, each of these mechanisms is thought to be self-sustaining in the way entailed by the epigenetic landscape metaphor. That is, once these processes are set in motion, they have the potential to feed back onto themselves, further sustaining continuity in attachment patterns.

Intrapsychic Processes

Research suggests that the working models people hold may play a role in shaping the ways in which people interpret and understand their interpersonal experiences. The consequence of which is that people can create self-fulfilling prophecies by interpreting the behavior of others in ways that reinforce the assumptions they already have about close relationships.

Attributional Processes and Confirmation Bias

Imagine, for example, that you are at a party with your partner. After mingling a bit and having a few drinks, you notice that your partner is no longer by your side. You wander around a bit, refresh your drink, and, eventually, find your partner in another room. Your partner is talking to someone you do not recognize and is smiling and playfully laughing. How does this make you feel? What do you think their intentions are?

Collins (1996) conducted a study in which people were asked to imagine a variety of scenarios like the one above—situations in which the behavior of a loved one was potentially ambiguous—the behavior could be harmless or could represent a threat to the relationship. Although each participant read identical scenarios, the way participants reacted to the scenarios differed dramatically. Some people believed that their partner was trying to make them feel jealous; other people wrote the event off as it was nothing out of the ordinary. Importantly, Collins (1996) found that how people responded—the attributions they made about their partner's behavior—was a function of their attachment styles. People who were relatively insecure, for example, were more likely than those who were secure to construe the partner's ambiguous behavior as a threat to the relationship.

Collins' research shows, that even when different people are exposed to the same information, the way they interpret that information is biased by their working models. Thus, what people "see" and what they experience tends to reinforce rather than challenge the assumptions they already hold about the world. This dynamic provides one potential mechanism of stability. That is, it is difficult for people to modify their assumptions about the availability and responsiveness of other people in their lives if they are predisposed to view the behavior of others as negligent or insensitive. Vicary and Fraley (2007) expanded on this theme by studying the decisions people made over the course of a narrative about a hypothetical relationship. Specifically, they adopted the format of a popular book series from the 1970s and 1980s, the *Choose Your Own Adventure* series. In these books, readers assume the role of the protagonist in the story and, at various crucial moments in the narrative, the reader must decide between two or more options (eg, enter the dark cave or turn back and head for safety). Depending on the decision the reader makes, he or she flips ahead in the book to different parts of the story. As a consequence, different choices lead to different narratives, with new choices and different outcomes.

Vicary and Fraley adopted this format to examine the way in which people navigate imaginary relationships. They asked people to imagine themselves in a relationship with a person who behaved in ways that could be ambiguous at times. Participants made 20 choices at various points in the story, choices that had the potential to be beneficial for the relationship (eg, telling your partner that you understand the issues he or she is confiding in you) or destructive (eg, telling your partner that he or she is overreacting). Vicary and Fraley found that, overall, people with insecure attachment styles tended to make poorer choices than people with secure attachment styles (see also Gillath & Shaver, 2007). Although most participants gradually came to make better choices over the course of the interactive story, the rate at which insecure people did so was slower than that for secure people. Stated differently, not only were insecure people biased to transform a potentially ambiguous situation into a negative one, they had a tendency to persist with those detrimental choices, making it difficult for them to recover and steer their interpersonal relations in a more constructive direction.

Zhang and Hazan (2002) argued that confirmation biases can come into play in the kind of information people seek out when evaluating other persons. These authors used a person perception paradigm to investigate the way in which working models may bias how people weigh information about others. Participants were provided with a description of a person (either a classmate or a romantic partner) and were asked to judge how many times the person would have to behave in a way that was inconsistent with the trait in question (eg, considerate) for the participant to be convinced that he or she does not possess that trait. They also asked people how many times the person would have to behave in a way that was consistent with certain traits (eg, trustworthy) to conclude that the person did, in fact, possess that trait. They found that people who were highly avoidant required more evidence to make positive judgments (eg, that the person was considerate or trustworthy) and more evidence to reject a negative judgment (eg, that the person was lazy or rude). These findings suggest that the quantity of behavioral evidence that people use to inform their judgments about others is shaped by their working models. Specifically, people with avoidant attachment styles require a great deal of positive exemplars to disconfirm assumptions about a person's potential negative attributes and require very few negative exemplars to confirm the negative impressions they already hold.

Transference Processes

As people forge new relationships, they sometimes learn that they have recreated the same kinds of relationship dynamics that characterized their previous relationships. Social-cognitive psychologists have attempted to explain this process through the idea of transference (eg, Andersen & Cole, 1990; Andersen, Glassman, Chen, & Cole, 1995). *Transference* is defined as the process by which existing mental representations of significant others are activated and applied to make sense of new social interactions. When interacting with a new person, one observes a number of important cues, such as whether the person is a smoker, the color of his or her hair, whether the person is outgoing or shy, and so on. The presence of these cues has the potential to activate mental representations of other people who possess similar attributes. As a result, representations of significant others have the potential to color the way we perceive new individuals and, in some cases, "go beyond the information given" when attempting to make inferences about the new person.

In a prototypical transference study, people visit the lab and provide information about significant others from their lives. Then, in a separate and "unrelated" study weeks later, people may interact with a real or hypothetical individual. For participants in the experimental condition, the new person is designed to have certain features that are similar (but not necessarily identical) to those of the person's significant other. For example, if people described the significant other as a poet, the new person may be described as a writer. In a yoked control group, different people learn about the new person, but, for them, the individual does not have features that resemble a significant other from their past. After learning about the new person, all participants are then asked to perform a new task. They may be asked, for example, to write down as much as they can remember about the new person they read about. The outcome of interest in such a study is whether people "remember" things about the new person that were not actually present, but were true, in fact, of the person's significant other.

Brumbaugh and Fraley (2006) used this paradigm to study the ways in which mental representations of significant others may guide the way in which individuals relate to novel people. Specifically, in the first session, participants were asked to nominate a significant other from their past and provide a number of facts about the person, including the person's traits, interests, and habits. Then, 2 weeks later in an unrelated study, people came to the lab to view and evaluate personal ads on a website. In the experimental condition, the ads were constructed to contain a few features that were similar to those of the person's significant other. Participants in the yoked control condition saw the same ad, but it was not based on their significant other. After viewing the ads, participants rated how secure or insecure they thought they would feel in a relationship with the person.

Brumbaugh and Fraley found that people who were insecure with their significant other were also more likely to feel insecure when imagining what it would be like to be dating the person described in the ad. This was true regardless of whether the ad contained information that was similar to that of the significant other. Stated differently, people who were insecure in past relationships were likely to feel insecure with respect to a new potential partner. But, beyond that general association, Brumbaugh and Fraley (2006) found that this effect was magnified when the ad was designed to resemble the subject's significant other. That is, subtly activating the significant other representation led people to relate to the person described in the personal ad in a way that was congruent with preexisting patterns of attachment.

One of the noteworthy findings in the Brumbaugh and Fraley study was that, although people were more likely to feel insecure about the people described in the personal ads if an insecure significant other representation had been primed, they nonetheless expressed a greater interest in dating the person described in the ad. Thus, it appears that, at least in some cases, a feeling of familiarity can trump an assessment of security when deciding whether a potential partner is a desirable option.

Selection and Attraction Processes

Chappell and Davis (1998) proposed the attachment-security hypothesis; the idea that, when given a choice between partners who are potentially secure and partners who are potentially insecure, most people will choose the secure partner as more desirable. According to Chappell and Davis, this is expected because the attachment behavioral system is designed to seek cues that others are responsive and available; attributes that are more typical of secure than insecure partners. One consequence of this attraction process is that insecure people may seek out potentially secure partners when developing new relationships. Indeed, in their early research Chappell and Davis found that, when people were given a choice between hypothetical partners who varied in their attachment security, people tended to choose the secure-seeming partner over those who were designed to be insecure.

Despite the tendency for most people to find secure prospects more attractive, not everyone ends up in relationship with a secure individual (we review some of this work in more depth in chapter: What Are the Effects of Context on Attachment?). Part of the explanation is likely due to market forces: there are not enough secure people to go around. But part of the explanation may also have to do with the ways in which insecurities play out in relationship contexts. Namely, highly anxious people, for example, might be viewed as bad relationship partners, making secure–insecure pairings relatively unstable (eg, Pietromonaco & Carnelley, 1994). Moreover, insecure people may drive secure partners away in dating contexts. In a striking demonstration of this process, McClure and Lydon (2014) studied people in a speed-dating paradigm and found that individuals who were more anxious with respect to attachment were more likely to come across in undesirable ways, expressing greater verbal disfluencies and interpersonal awkwardness. These interpersonal behaviors, in turn, have the potential to undermine the formation of intimate relationships, potentially reinforcing the insecurities that highly anxious people already have.

Although both highly secure and insecure people tend to prefer partners who are secure, people tend to end up with others who are similar to them with respect to attachment (Holmes & Johnson, 2009). People who are relatively anxious, for example, tend to be paired with others who are relatively anxious. Thus, it seems that something takes place in the development of romantic relationships that leads insecure people to be with others who are insecure. It is unclear whether couples who are discordant with respect to attachment styles are more likely to breakup early in the relationship formation process or whether, in the process of mutually influencing one another, partners become more alike in the way they think, feel, and behave with respect to attachment-related concerns (see further for more on this possibility).

Environmental and Relational Processes

The processes we have discussed up to this point emphasize what takes place within the individual—social-cognitive mechanisms that lead people to see what they expect and to recreate interpersonal patterns with which they are familiar. But another source of stability emerges from the structure of the person's interpersonal world and the way in which the person shapes it and the way it shapes him or her. For example, if two people are in a relationship, they are in a position to mutually influence one another. Thus, not only is one person interpreting the behavior of the other in a way that is consistent with his or her own working models, but the partner is also doing the same. The consequence of this is that the couple is essentially engaged in a dyadic process in which they are reinforcing one another's attachment patterns; they function like atoms that are orbiting around one another in a dynamically stable pattern.

Hudson, Fraley, Brumbaugh, and Vicary (2014) examined this process in a longitudinal study of couples who were followed five times over the course of a year. Specifically, these researchers examined the way in which each individual in the couple, related to the other (ie, partner-specific attachment styles; see chapter: What Are Attachment Working Models?) and studied the way in which those attachment styles changed jointly across time. They found that, in general, people did not show a strong tendency to systematically increase or decrease in attachment anxiety or avoidance across the year. But people's attachment styles did vary across time; the same person, for example, was more secure on some occasions than others. Importantly, these person-specific deviations tended to be correlated within couples. That is, on occasions on which a person was feeling more insecure than usual, his or her partner was also likely to feel more insecure than he or she would typically feel (see also Davila, Karney, & Bradbury, 1999). Thus, the idiosyncratic changes that people experienced tended to be shared with, and in some cases, possibly even influenced by, the partner (see Sbarra & Hazan, 2008, for an in-depth discussion of these kinds of processes). This suggests that one source of stability in adult attachment styles stems from dyadic processes. Simply being in a close relationship with another person creates a system of mutual influence that leads people to converge to some degree in their attachment styles and reinforce that pattern of relating. Thus, if a relatively secure person begins to drift in a more insecure direction, the other partner may pull him or her back.

WHAT LEADS TO CHANGE IN ADULT ATTACHMENT STYLES?

According to Bowlby (1973), people tend to assimilate ongoing experiences into the working models that they already have. Thus, when a partner behaves in a way that is slightly at odds with one's existing expectations, one is more likely to perceive the interaction as being consistent rather than inconsistent with one's expectations (Collins, 1996). But Bowlby (1973) also argued that working models are responsive to ongoing relational experiences. Thus, if one's experiences sufficiently challenge one's existing expectations, those experiences have the potential to lead to changes in attachment organization (Fraley, 2002).

What kinds of factors lead to change in adult attachment styles? In the sections below we review some of the events and experiences that have received the most attention in the attachment literature. This review is not meant to be exhaustive, or to imply that the absence of certain factors (eg, the loss of a loved one) from the review implies that such factors may not be relevant to understanding change. We should also note that, in many cases, these factors represent the flip-side of processes that may facilitate stability. For example, to the extent to which relationship breakups may lead to instability in attachment style, the persistence of a committed relationship represents a factor that promotes continuity in attachment.

Major Life Transitions

A large body of research has investigated the implications of major life transitions, such as the transition to parenthood (eg, Simpson, Rholes, Campbell, Tran, & Wilson, 2003) or the transition to college (Lopez & Gormley, 2002), for understanding attachment dynamics. Although work in this area has been broad—examining a variety of issues beyond questions of stability and change—the work is clearly relevant to basic questions about change, such as whether people undergoing major transitions are more or less likely to exhibit stability in their attachment styles.

Why the focus on major life transitions? Simpson and colleagues argue that lawful change is most likely to occur when individuals face a stressful, life-altering event (Simpson, Rholes, Campbell, & Wilson, 2003). The reason for this is that such events expose people to new information and experiences that create opportunities for one's core assumptions to be challenged. Moreover, such experiences may lead people to reflect upon or reevaluate the assumptions they hold about themselves, their partners, and their relationships. In the sections below we discuss two major life transitions—parenthood and breakups—that have been studied extensively in the attachment literature.

Parenthood

The transition to parenthood is one major life transition that has received a lot of attention in adult attachment research. Having a child can be a stressful experience, one that has the potential to tax people's interpersonal resources considerably. Moreover, the birth of a child has the potential to rekindle significant attachment-related experiences from the expecting parent's past, leading the individual to reflect upon his or her own developmental experiences and to consider ways in which one may wish to parent differently. Becoming a parent has the potential to lead to other social-structural changes as one begins to socialize with other parents with same-age children and interact with local educational communities and teachers. Parenting can also be stressful for couples as they find themselves with less time for adult activities that they may have enjoyed previously (eg, dining out, theater) and potentially struggling with the negotiation of child care responsibilities.

Feeney, Alexander, Noller, and Hohaus (2003) examined the association between adult attachment styles and depression during the transition to parenthood. Specifically, they assessed 76 couples who completed surveys during the second trimester of pregnancy, and 6 weeks and 6 months after childbirth. Importantly, Feeney and colleagues also studied an age-matched control sample of 74 childless couples, thereby allowing them to draw comparisons between attachment processes for couples who were and who were not undergoing the transition to parenthood. Feeney and colleagues found that attachment-related anxiety was less stable for wives undergoing the transition (test–retest correlation of approximately 0.54) than for other participants (test–retest of approximately 0.72). (In addition, attachment anxiety predicted increases in new mothers' depressive symptoms across time. Women who were more insecure preterm, in other words, were more likely to experience symptoms of depression after the birth of their children.)

Simpson et al. (2003a) examined a sample of approximately 100 couples both 6 weeks before and 6 months after childbirth. Importantly, they found that, on average, attachment styles did not change from pre- to postbirth. Thus, the transition to parenthood per se did not lead people to become more (or less) secure. However, there were individual differences in the extent to which women sought support from their spouses in the prenatal assessment. They found that women became more anxious with respect to attachment if they entered into parenthood perceiving less support from their spouses and more spousal anger. Moreover, women who entered parenthood seeking less spousal support became more avoidant in their attachment across the transition. Thus, although the transition to parenthood did not lead to mean-level changes in attachment security across time, the way in which people navigated the transition was consistent with—and potentially sustained—their attachment styles.

Breakups

Another significant life transition is relationship dissolution. The breakup of a romantic relationship has the potential to lead to substantial disruption in attachment processes (Sbarra & Hazan, 2008). For example, if an exclusive relationship ends because one of the individuals has been unfaithful, this experience is likely to shatter the sense of trust that exists between partners. This may have implications for the extent to which the person feels that he or she can open up to or depend on others and, potentially, may make it more challenging for the person to fully trust his or her next partner.

A few empirical studies have examined the potential impact of relationship dissolution on attachment styles. In one of the classic studies on this topic, Kirkpatrick and Hazan (1994) followed a sample of individuals over a 4-year period. They found that changes in relationship status were associated with changes in attachment. Specifically, of the participants who were involved in a romantic relationship at the initial assessment, 90% of secure individuals who did not experience a breakup were secure 4 years later whereas approximately 50% of those who experienced a breakup remained secure. These findings suggest that relationship dissolution has the potential to undermine the sense of security that people feel in close relationships.

Ruvolo, Fabin, and Ruvolo (2001) examined a sample of 301 dating couples longitudinally and found that women became less secure after a breakup. They also found that people were likely to become more secure across time if they were involved with the same partner over the course of the longitudinal study. Scharfe and Cole (2006) examined stability and change in attachment among a sample of university students who were graduating. They found that relationship status partially moderated the stability of attachment, such that the test–retest stability of attachment was lower among those who changed their status compared to those who did not (ie, those who stayed single or stayed coupled).

In summary, it appears that the loss of a romantic partner has the potential to undermine people's security. To be clear, however, these associations are relatively weak. This is probably because most of the research to date has not been able to carefully evaluate whether the relationship was ending for reasons that were agreeable to both individuals. In addition, breakups themselves are not always discrete events; they represent a seemingly arbitrarily timed transition in a relationship that is already unsatisfying or not mutually rewarding. Thus, any change that has taken place in attachment styles is likely to have occurred before the breakup itself took place. Finally, not all breakups are as tumultuous as we sometimes assume in our culture. The end of a dissatisfying relationship can be a positive event for some people and, as a result, may not challenge their working models in ways that facilitate dramatic change. Thus, although research suggests that breakups facilitate attachment change, we would not want to assume that the effects are dramatic.

War-Related Trauma

Mikulincer, Ein-Dor, Solomon, and Shaver (2011) assessed the 17-year trajectories of attachment orientations in two groups of Israeli veterans from the 1974 Yom Kippur war. One group was comprised of ex-prisoners of war and the other was a comparison group of veterans who had not been held captive. Both groups of veterans completed measures of adult attachment styles at 18, 30, and 35 years after the war, along with a variety of other measures, including PTSD symptoms. Mikulincer and colleagues found that, overall, exprisoners of war were less secure than those in the comparison group and that, while the comparison group generally became more secure across time, exprisoners of war became more insecure across time. They also found that the experience of PTSD at each assessment heightened feelings of insecurity at that time point, beyond the potential effects of other variables.

These findings are important for at least two reasons. First, they reveal that specific events have the potential to lead to long-term changes in attachment style. Second, not only were these veterans less secure than others 18 years after the war, they were on a *trajectory* toward greater insecurity across time. Thus, the experience of being a prisoner of war led not only to shifts in security, but shifts in the developmental time course of security. In Mikulincer's words, this traumatic experience had a "long-term pathogenic effect."

Relationship Conflict and Support

According to attachment theory, the security that a person experiences at any one moment is derived from the knowledge that others are available and accessible. As a result, people should be more likely to feel secure in their relationships on occasions in which they perceive their partner as being supportive and responsive. Similarly, they should also feel insecure on occasions when their partners are not supportive—occasions when they perceive conflict, excessive distance, or a lack of mutual understanding and respect.

There are now a number of intensive longitudinal studies, which suggest that fluctuations in security hinge on the state of interpersonal relationships. For example, Holman, Galbraith, Timmons, Steed, and Tobler (2009) assessed the extent to which individuals perceived threats to the availability of their parents and their romantic partners. Specifically, they assessed the extent to which people felt that their attachment figures were accessible, responsive, and openly communicative. Holman and colleagues found that people who perceived greater threats to the availability of their attachment figures were less likely to be secure 1 year later.

Green, Furrer, and McAllister (2011) examined stability and change in attachment style in a sample of 181 low-income mothers. The mothers were assessed across three waves, starting shortly after the birth of their children. Green and colleagues found that increases in social support led to decreases in attachment-related anxiety. And, although decreases in anxiety did not lead to prospective increases in social support, decreases in attachment-related avoidance did.

La Guardia, Ryan, Couchman, and Deci (2000) examined attachment security in a 30-day daily diary study. On days in which people felt that their basic needs for autonomy, competence, and relatedness were met, they experienced greater attachment security. (And, when those needs were not met, they felt more insecure relative to their average.)

Chow, Ruhl, and Buhrmester (2014) examined a sample of approximately 300 adolescents from 6th to 12th grade. They found that attachment-related avoidance prospectively predicted friendship exclusion. In turn, friendship exclusion prospectively related to avoidant attachment. One of the valuable features of this study is that it demonstrates that there may be bidirectional influences between attachment security and relational experiences in adolescent friendships. That is, it seems that not only do friendship experiences have the potential to change attachment, attachment has the potential to shape friendship experiences.

The Meaning of Life Events

In their review of the literature on change, Davila and Sargent (2003) noted that many studies failed to provide convincing evidence that specific life events were related to change in attachment. They suggested that one reason why it has been so challenging for researchers to demonstrate consistently that specific life events, such as relationship breakup, might be associated with changes in attachment style is that these events do not have the same meaning for everyone. Some people who end a relationship, for example, may be relinquishing ties to someone who was making them miserable. Others, in contrast, may be truly heartbroken and the experiences of the breakup may prompt them to revise their working models of close relationships. According to Davila and Sargent it is necessary to understand the way specific life events are construed in order to know their implications for attachment change.

To address this issue, Davila and Sargent (2003) studied a sample of approximately 150 students who were asked to complete measures of their attachment style every day for 56 days. In addition, students were asked to indicate whether specific life events (eg, taking an exam, having a fight with a partner) had occurred each day. Importantly, Davila and Sargent asked people to indicate the extent to which each event that had occurred was indicative of an interpersonal loss as indicated, for example, by ratings of the extent to which the event led to a loss in emotional support, friendship, or trust. Thus, in addition to having information about whether or not specific events had taken place, Davila and Sargent also had information on that event's meaning to the participant.

Davila and Sargent found that, in general, the kinds of events most people would construe as negative did, in fact, predict decreases in security across time. When Davila and Sargent also included the meaning of those events in their analyses, however, the predictive value of the events themselves was weakened considerably. Instead, the meaning of the events was what was most predictive of attachment-related change. Specifically, on days on which people experienced events that they construed as being interpersonal losses, they were more likely to experience increases in attachment-related anxiety. Importantly, Davila and Sargent also assessed academic-related losses and stressors and found that those were not related to changes in attachment. Instead, change in attachment style was associated uniquely with changes in interpersonal rather than academic experiences.

Zhang (2009) conducted a follow-up study in which 30 individuals completed measures of daily events twice a week for 4 weeks. Zhang specifically targeted the occurrence of relatively mundane events (rather than low base-rate events, such as breakups) that might be relevant to relationship functioning. Zhang found that when people experience negative daily events, they tend to experience increases in attachment-related anxiety relative to their own baseline. Moreover, when people were asked to rate the implications of these events for interpersonal loss, the extent to which the events were loss-related further contributed to change.

Stable Vulnerability Factors

Davila and colleagues have also advanced the idea that some individuals are more inclined to experience changes in their attachment orientation than others due to stable vulnerability factors. Specifically, individuals who have a history of depression and psychopathology—in their family or personally—are going to have an identity that is less stable than that of others. As a result, they are less likely to have a consistent attachment style across time. Davila, Burge, and Hammen (1997) assessed attachment styles in 155 women several times over the course of a 2-year longitudinal study. They quantified change in a few ways, such as the standard deviation in a person's attachment scores across time. People with high deviation scores experienced more change than those with smaller deviation scores. Davila and colleagues found that those who experienced more change were also likely to report a history of psychopathology and personality disturbance.

Therapy

There have been a wide variety of interventions inspired by attachment theory over the past 20 years (see chapter: What Are the Implications of Attachment Processes for Psychopathology and Therapy? for an in-depth discussion of these issues). Although the objective of these interventions varies (eg, to improve marital function and communication), a reasonable question to ask is whether they lead to changes in people's attachment styles. Taylor, Rietzschel, Danquah, and Berry (2015) reviewed the research literature on this issue, examining both studies that used self-reports and interview-based methods for assessing attachment. They found that, overall, attachment security tends to increase following therapy. Specifically, attachment-related anxiety tends to decrease, but the findings were less clear on whether avoidance also changed. Moreover, the findings seemed to be largely consistent across different methods of assessing attachment (eg, interviews, self-reports) and different patient and therapy variants (eg, therapeutic approaches, settings, and patient groups).

HOW STABLE ARE ATTACHMENT STYLES IN ADULTHOOD?

The research reviewed up to this point indicates that there is evidence for mechanisms that promote stability as well as mechanisms that facilitate change. But how do these different processes stack up? Do the various forces promoting continuity overshadow those promoting change? Do these two kinds of processes balance one another out?

One of the long-standing debates in the study of adult attachment concerns the stability of attachment styles. As Baldwin and Fehr (1995) observed, one reason attachment theory was appealing to many psychologists was that it suggested that attachment styles were trait-like or dispositional variables. That is, it was assumed that a person could be characterized as having a single attachment style and that this attachment style captured the person's patterns of behavior and emotion across both time and circumstance. Baldwin and Fehr (1995) were two of the first researchers to call this assumption into question empirically. They surveyed the literature and found that, in fact, approximately 30% of people tend to report a different attachment style when surveyed on more than one occasion. Thus, if a person reported having an avoidant attachment style at, say, the beginning of the semester, there was a 30% chance that the same person would report a different attachment style a few weeks later. This degree of instability is clearly problematic if one assumes that attachment styles should be relatively trait-like across time.

Baldwin and colleagues also observed that, when people are asked to think of relationships in which they felt relatively secure, avoidant, or anxious, most people are able to do so. That is, the same person can call to mind relationships in which he or she felt secure as well as relationships in which he or she felt insecure. This indicates that a single attachment style does not capture all of the important relationships that a person has. Some people, for example, may be relatively secure in their relationships with their mothers, but less secure in their relationships with their fathers. Moreover, Baldwin and colleagues showed that it is possible to manipulate the attachment style that people report simply by having them bring to mind different kinds of interpersonal experiences (see chapter: What can Social Cognition and Priming Tell us About Attachment?). Thus, it is possible, at least momentarily, to make someone who would otherwise report being secure report being insecure simply by making certain experiences from their past more salient.

As an alternative to the dispositional view, Baldwin and Fehr (1995) advanced a social-cognitive model of attachment styles. Specifically, they argued that most people have working models that are consistent with multiple attachment styles, but that some of those models are more available and accessible than other ones (see chapter: What Are Attachment Working Models?). Thus, someone who self-reports being secure in his or her relationship may do so not because he or she has a secure disposition, but because secure working models are more likely to be accessible to him or her at the moment of assessment.

Can Some of the Observed Instability be Understood as Measurement Error?

Baldwin and Fehr (1995) concluded that the measurement of attachment, while not being perfect, was good enough and was unlikely to explain the high degree of instability that they had reported. Other researchers challenged this claim, however. Most of the work Baldwin and Fehr (1995) summarized was based on categorical models of attachment (see chapter: How Are Individual Differences in Attachment Measured?). Fraley and Waller (1998) argued that, if attachment styles are not truly categorical, then a substantial amount of instability will exist simply due to cases that are near the threshold. Specifically, if the majority of people are in the middle of the two-dimensional space, minor movements in that latent two-dimensional space will lead to dramatically different attachment classifications, making a secure person at one point in time seem preoccupied at another point in time. Indeed, Fraley and Waller (1998) demonstrated that, in a simple two-dimensional situation in which the variables are normally distributed and there is no true change in attachment, the imprecision of categorical systems will nonetheless lead to observations of 30% of people "changing" their attachment styles across time. Thus, on the basis of measurement error alone, it is possible to explain why approximately 30% of people report different attachment styles across time when categorical assessments are used.

Scharfe and Bartholomew (1994) were the first team to attempt to estimate the continuity of attachment style using methods that (a) did not rely exclusively on categorical assessments and (b) were designed to factor out random measurement error as much as possible. Using latent variable modeling methods, they found that the estimated continuity of attachment over an 8-month period was equivalent to a test–retest correlation of approximately 0.80. Sibley, Fischer, and Liu (2005) found a similar result over a period of 3 weeks. Specifically, about 85% of the variance in attachment measures was shared across measurement occasions (equivalent to a test–retest correlation of approximately 0.92).

What do these recent findings mean? First, they suggest that, for the most part, attachment styles, when measured continuously and over intervals ranging from a few weeks to a few months, are highly stable in adulthood. Although there is clearly some change taking place (see our review in previous section), one could become reasonably wealthy by betting that people who are highly secure today will also be highly secure months from now. Second, these findings suggest that one cannot easily conclude that attachment is not a "general disposition or trait" (Baldwin & Fehr, 1995, p. 247) on the basis of lack of stability when the measurements themselves are highly imprecise. When better measures are used and measurement imprecision is taken into consideration, estimates of stability increase.

What Does it Mean to say that Something is a General Disposition or Trait? Trait-State Models of Adult Attachment

One of the potential complications underlying debates about continuity and change is that dispositional and social-cognitive perspectives are sometimes treated as if they are mutually exclusive. Namely, many scholars assume that, if something is a trait, it does not require a social-cognitive explanation (eg, Costa & McCrae, 1994). And, conversely, that if something has a social-cognitive explanation, then it is not a trait or disposition (eg, Baldwin & Fehr, 1995; Cervone & Shoda, 1999; Reynolds & Branscombe, 2014).

These stances, however, do not consider the possibility that attachment can have both trait-like and state-like properties. Take room temperature as an example. At any one moment in time a room has a measurable ambient temperature; it may feel too cool, too warm, or just right. However, that temperature can easily change if, for example, the window is opened or if a heater is turned on. In such cases, the temperature of the room now might be quite different from the temperature 60 min ago. Nonetheless, many people would acknowledge that rooms tend to have dispositional qualities with respect to temperature. We complain about some rooms being too drafty, others being too hot, whereas other rooms tend to not attract our notice at all. Due to a combination of factors (eg, quality of the insulation, the efficiency of the heater, number of exterior walls, height from the ground), the typical temperature of various rooms tends to be relatively consistent and predictable. This predictability does not imply that the temperature of a room cannot change suddenly and dramatically. Nor does the ease with which the temperature can be adjusted imply that there are not relatively stable differences between rooms across time.

In short, something as familiar as room temperature can be easily construed as having state- and trait-like properties. The same is the case for attachment. Fraley and colleagues have argued that, in theory, attachment styles can be viewed as being trait-like *and* state-like (Fraley, 2002; Fraley & Roberts, 2005). That is, it should be possible for attachment styles to reflect on-going experiences in the way conceptualized by Baldwin and Fehr (1995). If one has an argument with one's romantic partner, for example, that conflict is likely to undermine the sense that one feels understood and accepted by that person. This might not make a highly secure person swing all the way to the depths of insecurity, but it is likely to produce some degree of change. But Fraley and colleagues also argued that the change is likely to be state-like or temporary. Unless the conflict persists, the person will gradually revert to his or her prior levels of security. To refer back to Waddington's metaphor, a small perturbation is unlikely to affect the long-term trajectory of the marble as it rolls down a hill. But that does not mean that the perturbation is unimportant or inconsequential.

These ideas can be formally modeled using variations of trait-state models (Fraley, 2002; Fraley & Roberts, 2005; Kenny & Zautra, 2001). According to one such variation, which Fraley (2002) refers to as a *prototype model* (see also chapter: How Do Individual Differences in Attachment Develop?), a person's attachment security at any one point in time is a function of a stable value of security (ie, a trait-level), previous levels of security (ie, an autoregressive component), and state-like factors that might lead to deviations in security (eg, responsive or conflictual interactions with an attachment figure that may lead to changes in security). These various components are illustrated in Fig. 6.2. One of the valuable features of using a formal model is that one can modify its parameters and study the consequences of those modifications for the predicted test–retest correlations. Experimenting with the parameters of the trait-state model reveals a few important things. First, the model predicts that the overall degree of stability, expressed as a test–retest correlation, observed between attachment measured across two time points can be large or small—even if there is a stable, trait-like source of variance in attachment styles. This is an important observation because it is often assumed that low stability is incompatible with trait models (eg, Baldwin & Fehr, 1995). And, similarly, it is sometimes assumed that high levels of stability

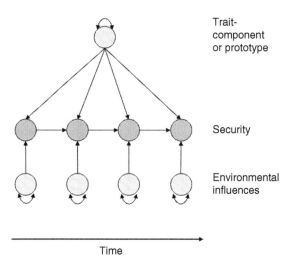

FIGURE 6.2 **The prototype model of adult attachment, a trait-state model of continuity and change.** The model assumes that variation in security at different assessment waves is a function of (1) a stable trait component, (2) autoregressive processes (ie, security at any point in time t is a function of itself at $t - 1$), and (3) environmental influences.

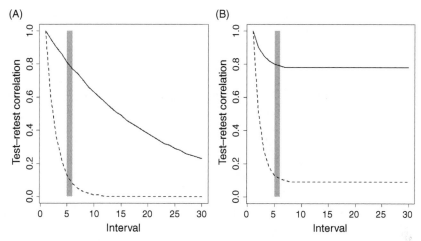

FIGURE 6.3   Test–retest correlations for security as predicted under different parameter values by a trait-state model. (A) Illustrates predicted correlations for a state-only model under various assumptions. As highlighted by the gray bar, the test–retest correlations over a 5-week interval can be as high (eg, 0.80) or low (eg, 0.10) depending on the specific parameter values assumed. (B) Illustrates predicted correlations for a trait-state model under various assumptions. As highlighted by the gray bar, the test–retest correlations over a 5-week interval can be as high (eg, 0.80) or low (eg, 0.10) depending on the specific parameter values assumed. Overall, these figures reveal that the magnitude of a test–retest correlation across an arbitrary test–retest interval can be high or low in models that assume stable traits/dispositions as well as in models that do not. But they also reveal that the patterns of those associations across time are distinctive. A state-only model predicts decaying test–retest stabilities across increasing intervals; a trait-state model implies that those associations will approach a nonzero value in the limit.

are incompatible with state models. When trait-like assumptions are formalized, however, it can be shown that a trait model can account for low or high levels of stability (Fraley, 2002; Fraley & Roberts, 2005).

Fig. 6.3 illustrates this finding more clearly. The left-hand panel illustrates the way in which the test–retest correlations between two measurements of attachment style vary across increasing test–retest intervals. Fig. 6.3A illustrates the expected test–retest correlations under the assumptions of a model that is a pure state model (ie, the trait variance is set to 0). Notice that the model is capable of predicting both low and high test–retest correlations across a 5-week test–retest interval, depending on some of the parameters of the model. The upper curve in Fig. 6.3A, for example, shows an example in which the test–retest correlation over 5 weeks is as high as 0.80; the lower curve shows an example in which the test–retest correlation over the same period of time is 0.10. Fig. 6.3B illustrates the expected test–retest correlations under the assumptions of a model that assumes both trait-like and state-like processes. Notice that this model is also capable of predicting both low and high test–retest correlations across a 5-week test–retest interval depending on the parameters in the model. Thus, even when there is a stable trait giving rise to security, it is possible for the test–retest correlation to be quite small. In short, although it is obviously useful to know the magnitude of stability that exists between any two time points, this information is not useful for determining whether attachment is trait-like (ie, dispositional) or not.

Does this mean that empirical data cannot be used to examine the extent to which individual differences can be understood as resulting from trait-like and state-like processes? Not necessarily. The second implication that follows from this model is that the way to distinguish trait-state models from nontrait models (eg, strict contextual or social-cognitive models) lies in the *patterns* (not the magnitude) they predict in test–retest correlations across time. This can be seen by comparing the curves illustrated in the two panels of Fig. 6.3. Although trait models are not precise enough to suggest whether stability will be high or low in an absolute sense (see earlier section), trait models do make a risky prediction, namely, that the degree of stability, whether high or low, will not get increasingly smaller across increasing assessment intervals (Fig. 6.3B). At some point the test–retest stability will stabilize at a nonzero value. This suggests that it is possible to forecast what people will be like in the future with the same degree of precision over 20 weeks as 10 weeks. In contrast, a state-only model predicts that the stability of individual differences will get smaller and smaller as the interval between assessments increases, approaching zero in the limit (Fig. 6.3A). This does not mean that there is *no* stability across assessment waves. But it does imply that one's ability to predict individual differences in the future will become less accurate the further into the future the prediction is made. The association between measurements of security across 2 months might be quite high, depending on the parameter values in question. But the correlation between assessments of security across 2 years will be smaller (see the solid curve in Fig. 6.3A).

The third implication revealed by these simulations is that there is an asymmetry in stability when one is moving forward versus backward in time (Fig. 6.4).

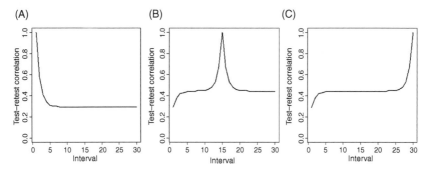

FIGURE 6.4 The predicted (under hypothetical parameter values) test–retest correlations between measures of security at wave 1 and each subsequent wave (A), wave 15 and all waves prior to and following it (B), and wave 30 and each previous wave (C) under the assumptions of a trait-state or prototype model. These graphs illustrate the asymmetry in predictions about stability that can emerge when moving forward through time versus looking backward through time.

Stated in a way that sounds less like the premise of a science fiction novel: The model predicts that the overall amount of stability observed among *adults* over a constant time period (eg, 1 year) will be higher than the amount of stability observed among *children* over the same time period. As a result, it is easier to know where someone is going than to know where they have been.

One can see this more clearly by examining the middle panel of Fig. 6.4. This figure illustrates the expected test–retest correlations between security measured at wave 15 and all the assessments that precede or follow it. Notice that the predicted test–retest correlation between wave 15 and wave 1 is lower ($r = 0.29$) than the predicted test–retest correlation between wave 15 and wave 30 ($r = 0.44$). The implications of this point are profound because it indicates that, although it might be challenging to accurately infer whether a secure adult was also secure as a child, it is a comparatively safe bet to infer that a secure adult will continue to be secure in the future. This particular prediction dovetails nicely with Bowlby's use of Waddington's metaphor for canalization. Essentially the model implies that, as time progresses, people become increasingly entrenched in the ways in which they relate to others. The consequence is that they exhibit greater stability later in life than they do early on. A model that does not posit a role for trait/dispositional factors does not make this prediction.

We should note that this latter prediction regarding asymmetry is not restricted to childhood versus adulthood in practice. Formally, the prediction emerges because in the initial phases of the process, security is a function of the latent trait, but later in the process it is both a direct *and* indirect function of the latent trait. The consequence of this is that the asymmetry can emerge in any system in which there is a plausible "starting point," such as in the developmental case where children are born into families or when a couple begins dating. In other words, canalization processes emerge naturally within this model and apply to any situation where there is a natural beginning to the dynamic process.

It is difficult to test the various predictions of the prototype model without assessing attachment styles across multiple waves; the traditional two-wave, test–retest design cannot speak to the issues. Fortunately, there are datasets available now that enable these various predictions to be evaluated. Fraley, Vicary, Brumbaugh, and Roisman (2011) reported on data from two samples that were designed to evaluate trait-state models of attachment. The first sample was assessed once a day for 30 days. The second sample was assessed once a week for up to a year. Importantly, attachment was assessed in a contextual fashion (see chapter: How Are Individual Differences in Attachment Measured?). That is, attachment was assessed in relation to people's parents and their romantic partners separately.

One of the important findings in this research was that the data were more consistent with a trait-state model than a model that did not assume a trait-like source of variance (ie, a pure contextual or social-cognitive model). Thus, although people clearly changed their attachment styles across time, those changes did not accumulate. As a result, the degree of instability observed did

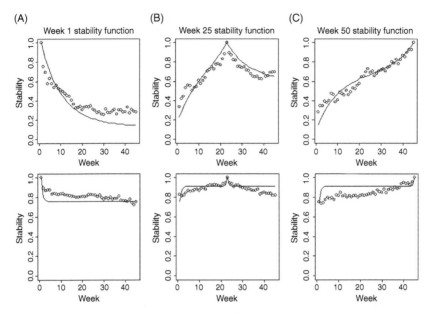

FIGURE 6.5 Empirical test–retest correlations between measures of security at wave 1 and each subsequent wave (A), wave 25 and all waves prior to and following it (B), and wave 50 and each previous wave (C) from Fraley et al. (2011b). The top row shows the data for partner-specific avoidance; the bottom row shows the data for avoidance with mother.

not get lower and lower as the delay between assessments increased. To illustrate, the results for attachment-related avoidance, measured in the context of the relationship to romantic partners, are illustrated in the top row of Fig. 6.5. As can be seen, although the test–retest stability initially gets lower as the test–retest interval increases, it eventually levels off around a value of approximately 0.35 and stays there. As a result, the degree of stability observed over 20 weeks is comparable to that observed over 40 weeks. The second row illustrates the observed correlations for attachment-avoidance with respect to people's relationships with their mothers. Again, the associations tend to exhibit stabilizing properties; the test–retest correlation between initial measurements of avoidance and avoidance measured 20 weeks later is comparable to that between initial avoidance and avoidance measured 40 weeks later. Taken together, these findings provide strong evidence that there is something dispositional about attachment styles, something that remains invariant despite short-term fluctuations in security.

The second and third panels in the first row of Fig. 6.5 highlight the asymmetry in continuity across time. Namely, the test–retest correlation between partner-avoidance measured in week 23 and week 13 (a 10-week delay) was lower than the correlation between partner-avoidance in week 23 and week 33 (also a 10-week delay). This is compatible with the canalization effects emphasized by Bowlby (1973) and implied by the trait-state model.

Does the Stability of Attachment Vary Across Relationship Types?

In chapter: What Are Attachment Working Models?, we highlighted the idea that attachment styles can vary in their degree of specificity. That is, theoretically, people have general attachment styles, but they also have unique patterns of attachment that characterize the way they relate to specific people in their lives, such as their parents or their romantic partners. Empirical research indicates that attachment styles may be more stable in some contexts than in others.

In the Fraley et al. (2011b) studies people's attachment styles toward their parents and their romantic partners were assessed separately. When people were evaluating their attachments to their parents (mother and father, separately), the test–retest stability of attachment was over 0.80 (see the second row of Fig. 6.5). When people were evaluating their attachments to their romantic partners, however, the overall association was lower, closer to 0.60, on average (see the first row of Fig. 6.5). Although the patterns of correlations in both cases were consistent with a trait-state model, the overall level of stability was lower in romantic contexts than in parental contexts.

Why might there be more stability in parental than in romantic relationships? We believe Bowlby's ideas on canalization may be helpful for explaining these findings. The relationships adults have had with their parents have existed for decades. As a result, it seems likely that adults have settled into a robust pattern of interacting with their parents. Adults are no longer trying to gauge whether their parents are available, supportive, and responsive; they *know* whether their parents are relatively available and responsive. In addition to this, most adults are unlikely to interact with their parents on a daily basis. As a consequence, there are fewer opportunities for parental interactions that might lead to changes in the way in which one conceptualizes the parental relationship. These dynamics, of course, could change as people's parents' age and adult children become increasingly concerned about managing care for their aging parents.

In contrast, romantic relationships, by necessity, are often more nascent than the relationships people have with their parents. Not only are adults more likely to interact with their partners more than their parents, but also those relationships are still forming. Thus, as new events take place (eg, marriage, parenthood), there are multiple opportunities for those interaction patterns to shift around in subtle ways.

Although we believe the different patterns of stability observed in parental and romantic relationships are consistent with Bowlby's ideas concerning canalization, we should note that the research to date provides, at best, an indirect test of the key ideas. What would be ideal is an evaluation of trait-state models in the context of romantic relationships as they develop. The model implies that stability should be higher in long-term relationships than in short-term relationships. But evaluating this prediction in a truly compelling way would require examining the stability of attachment in young relationships as they develop across time.

DO ADULT ATTACHMENT STYLES CHANGE ACROSS THE LIFESPAN? NORMATIVE SHIFTS IN ATTACHMENT

Up to this point, our discussion of continuity and change has largely concerned the stability of individual differences: whether people who are relatively secure at one point in time are also likely to be relatively secure at another point in time. This is often referred to as "rank-order stability" in the personality literature because the primary concern is whether the relative ordering of people is the same across time. Another important form of stability, however, concerns mean-level or absolute stability. This is relevant to understanding whether, on average, people tend to increase (or decrease) in security across time. These two forms of stability are conceptually and mathematically independent of one another because people could preserve their rank ordering perfectly across two time points even if everyone became more secure, on average. And, similarly, even if the average levels of security were the same across two time points, if the people who were most secure at time 1 became the least secure at time 2 (and vice versa), mean-level stability could be perfect despite rank-order stability being zero.

One of the largest studies to examine mean-level stability and change in adult attachment was published by Chopik et al. (2013). They examined age differences in attachment style using a cross-sectional design in a sample of over 23,000 individuals ranging in age from 18 to 70. Attachment was assessed using the ECR-R, a self-report measure that focuses on romantic attachment, but not on specific romantic partners. Chopik and colleagues found that older individuals tended to have lower levels of attachment-related anxiety than younger individuals. One potential explanation for this finding is that, as people get older, they may have fewer reasons to be concerned with the availability and responsiveness of others. Chopik and colleagues also found that older individuals tended to be slightly more avoidant than younger individuals. A similar finding was reported by Magai et al. (2001). In a community sample of approximately 800 North Americans (average age of 74), they found that the average scores for avoidance were higher than they typically are in younger samples. Magai et al. (2001) attribute this finding to the long-term impact of economic hardship on families earlier in the century.

Hudson, Fraley, and Chopik (2015) conducted a similar analysis in a separate sample, but focused on attachment in specific relational contexts. That is, they assessed people's general attachment orientation in addition to how people related specifically to their parents, their romantic partners, and their best friends. They found that people generally became less anxious with respect to attachment across time. That is, younger adults had higher anxiety scores than older adults. In contrast, there were few age differences in avoidance. For the most part, global avoidance tends to be relatively stable across age groups. The patterns of age-related differences varied across specific relational contexts, however. Younger people, for example, were generally more anxious in romantic and friend relationships than older people. But the reverse was true in parental relationships. In parental relationships, younger people were less anxious than older people in their relationships with their parents. Why might this be the case? One possibility is that, as people's parents' age, people become less confident in the availability and responsiveness of their parents, potentially heightening the sense of anxiety people feel in their relationships with their parents.

In both peer (romantic and friendship relationships) and parental relationships, people seemed to become more avoidant across time. That is, older people were more avoidant toward their partners, friends, and parents than younger adults. The authors speculate that one reason for this shift is that role norms for adults typically emphasize a greater need for autonomy and independence as people make the transition from young to middle adulthood. It is also possible that the increase in avoidance in romantic relationships mirrors shifts in marital satisfaction that are commonly observed in long-term marriages. It is important to note that global avoidance, however, did not show systematic, replicable age differences across time. This suggests that, as a general rule, people do not become more avoidant across time, but the dynamics of specific relationships may create a press for greater degrees of independence with age. The obvious limitation of these studies is that they are based on cross-sectional data. To fully understand how attachment tends to change as a function of the life course, one needs to study people longitudinally as they develop.

SUMMARY AND FUTURE RESEARCH DIRECTIONS

Some of the fundamental questions in the study of attachment concern the stability of individual differences in attachment style: How stable are individual differences in attachment? What processes promote continuity and change? How does stability vary across relationship contexts and across different phases of the adult lifespan? We believe there are few broad conclusions that can be reached based on existing research. First, attachment styles appear to function in both trait-like and state-like ways. Although attachment styles tend to reflect variation in people's ongoing interpersonal experiences, underlying that variation are relatively stable dispositions—something that appears to undergird variation across time.

A second theme is that people's developmental trajectories appear to become increasingly canalized across time. Holding the time-interval constant, the test–retest stability in attachment observed early in romantic relationships is lower than the test–retest stability observed later. Moreover, people's representations of their parental relationships—relationships that are more established—are more stable than their representations of their romantic relationships. Taken together, these kinds of findings suggest that, in the early phases of a relationship (whether it be an infant–parent relationship or a fledgling romantic relationship), people construct working models of that relationship based on their relational experiences. But, as the relationship progresses, those patterns of interaction begin to stabilize and working models begin to consolidate to some extent. The consequence is that people's sense of security or insecurity in a relationship is more resistant to change later than early in relationship development (Fraley & Brumbaugh, 2004).

A third theme is that people's working models, despite functioning as dispositional variables in adulthood, can and do change. On occasions in which people experience interpersonal losses, for example, they are more likely to feel insecure than they are on other occasions (Davila & Sargent, 2003). Certain developmental experiences, such as a history of family or personal psychopathology, have the potential to heighten the instability of working models, making people more likely to change, but not always nudging them in a specific direction consistently (Davila et al., 1997). Moreover, above and beyond changes in the rank ordering of individual differences, cross-sectional research suggests that people tend to become less anxious across time in their romantic relationships (see also chapter: What Are the Effects of Context on Attachment?).

Despite the progress that has been made in understanding stability and change in attachment, we still have a lot of work to do to more fully understand the dynamics of stability and change. One of the gaps in our current knowledge is that we do not have a strong handle on how specific experiences impact attachment because we tend to know very little about what people are like before certain events or transitions take place in their lives. Take loss as an example. There is a large literature on how losing a loved one can disrupt psychological functioning (Parkes & Weiss, 1983), and many scholars have been interested in the question of whether attachment style, for example, predisposes people to experience chronic or disordered forms of grief (Fraley & Bonanno, 2004). But much of the research that examines the association between attachment and adaptation to loss has been forced to assess bereaved people's attachment styles *after* the loss has taken place. As a consequence, it is difficult to know whether people are responding in ways—adaptive or maladaptive—that are predictable from their preloss attachment orientation and how and if that orientation is affected by the loss itself.

One solution to this kind of problem is to assess attachment styles across multiple occasions before major life events take place. This would enable researchers to characterize the person's prototypical trajectory of attachment (ie, the extent to which the person's pattern is state-like and trait-like, whether he or she is increasing in anxiety over time and the rate at which he or she does so, and the amount of variability the person exhibits across time) before specific events take place and to examine the ways in which specific events alter or disrupt that trajectory.

A second gap in the existing literature involves understanding whether certain experiences have short- or long-term consequences for attachment orientation. At first glance, this would seem like a relatively simple problem to solve. All a researcher would need to do, presumably, is examine the consequences of a specific event (eg, a breakup, the death of a loved one) in a long-term follow-up study. But as Fraley, Roisman, and Haltigan (2013) observed, these kinds of designs do not enable one to determine whether a specific event had enduring or transient consequences for the outcome in question. Imagine, for example, that a research team finds that the association between psychotherapy and attachment security assessed 6 months later is 0.30. Most researchers would conclude on the basis of those data that therapy has long-term benefits for security. But what if the team were to continue their assessments and learn that the association between treatment and security is 0.10 after 8 months, and 0.00 after 12 months? That would lead to a dramatically different conclusion about the efficacy of therapy than if we observed, instead, that the association between treatment and security was 0.30 after 6, 8, and 12 months. What are needed in future research are multiple measurements of the construct across time so one can detect whether the changes are persistent and sustained or whether they are getting smaller as the time between the event and the outcome increases.

Chapter 7

What Can Social Cognition and Priming Tell Us About Attachment?

One of the important themes of attachment theory and research is that people hold working models of themselves and their relationships and that those representations play a pervasive role in shaping people's interpersonal experiences (see chapter: What Are Attachment Working Models?). Because individual differences in attachment are based on cognitive structures—working models—and their functioning, these differences can be studied using experimental methods used to study similar cognitive structures (like schemas and scripts). To achieve this, scholars have turned to research conducted in social cognition and more specifically priming (Bargh, Schwader, Hailey, Dyer, & Boothby, 2012) and applied these methods to the context of attachment. Recent years have seen an exponential increase in attachment-related priming papers (for reviews see Gillath, Karantzas, & Karantzas, 2016; Gillath, Selcuk, & Shaver, 2008; Mikulincer & Shaver, 2007b). The current chapter serves as an introduction to the topic by defining key concepts, providing background into attachment-related priming, and reviewing the effects of priming, its limitations, and implications.

Priming is defined as the activation of a particular mental representation or association in one's memory. Frequently, priming is conceptualized and tested by its effects on a succeeding action or task—the effects of an event or action on subsequent associated responses (eg, Tulving, 1983) or on the activation of stored knowledge (Higgins & Eitam, 2014). The priming process is thought to increase sensitivity to particular stimuli. Often exposure to one stimulus facilitates (creates a mental readiness for) the processing of a following stimulus (Bargh & Chartrand, 2000). For example, in a lexical decision task (deciding whether letter strings are proper English words or not), exposure to the word chair (prime) makes the identification of the letter string "table" (target) easier and faster as compared with exposure to the word "phone." Priming can occur following a conscious or an unconscious exposure to a cue (supraliminal vs. subliminal priming) and can operate at a presemantic level (ie, before a meaning is inferred; Tulving & Schacter, 1990). The effects of priming can range from cognitive and affective responses to behavioral changes (Mikulincer & Shaver, 2007b).

Adult Attachment. http://dx.doi.org/10.1016/B978-0-12-420020-3.00007-4

The effects of priming, such as the facilitation observed in the lexical decision task described earlier, are thought to occur due to the spreading of activation from one concept (or node) in an individual's memory to another (Anderson & Bower, 1973; Srull, 1981). Constructs are thought to be associated with each other in human memory (Meyer & Schvaneveldt, 1971). When people are exposed to one construct all the other constructs associated with it are primed or preactivated due to the spreading of activation from that related concept. This makes the other constructs more cognitively accessible and available to be used in succeeding tasks (Bruner, 1957; Higgins & King, 1981). Metaphorically, priming is like the gunpowder placed in the pan of a firearm to ignite a charge; it starts an action or a chain reaction.

Typically priming is thought to occur when a target is closely followed by a semantically related prime. But priming can also occur when two concepts are related in other ways (eg, they share affective content or are conceptually similar). Moreover, the effects of priming are not necessarily constrained to the controlled settings of the laboratory, but can also take place outside the lab. For example, Charles-Sire, Guéguen, Pascual, and Meineri (2012) showed that exposure to words like "loving" (as compared with the word "donating") on solicitors' t-shirts increased blood donations during an on-campus blood donation drive. Moreover, priming manipulations have the potential to persist for longer periods of time than is typically observed in brief lab studies (eg, Gillath et al., 2008b; Silverman & Weinberger, 1985).

PRIMING IN CLOSE RELATIONSHIPS

Priming methods have become increasingly common in the study of close relationships (eg, Baldwin, Keelan, Fehr, Enns, & Koh-Rangarajoo, 1996; Banse, 2003). Priming methods allow researchers to overcome some of the limitations of other research methods (eg, observational assessments, self-reports, and interviews), such as social desirability bias, positive self-presentations bias, and the inability to access people's unconscious processes or mentalization abilities (their ability to understand the mental state of oneself or others). For example, with self-report measures the only information captured is that which is consciously accessible to the person reporting it, and that which can be expressed verbally (Schwartz, 1999). Priming is thought to bypass some of these limitations, by assessing automatic and less controlled cognitive processing, which is thought to be less affected by self-presentation biases and social desirability. The use of priming is also not as expensive as conducting interviews, and not as susceptible to demand characteristics or experimenter biases as other manipulations; simply because people often do not know what is expected from them, or what the goal of the study is. Priming is also relatively quick and easy to set up, score, and analyze, as we describe below.

Taking advantage of these benefits, researchers (eg, Baldwin, 1992; Baldwin, Fehr, Keedian, Seidel, & Thomson, 1993; Baldwin et al., 1996) have used priming techniques to study central constructs within close relationships, such as people's relational schemas. *Relational schemas* are knowledge structures, which include representations of oneself and of one's close relationships, or more broadly, one's social world. Relationship experiences and interactions are stored in these representations as they were observed, interpreted, and encoded by the individual. Once stored, these representations can be activated in the laboratory using priming methods, allowing researchers to study the activation and functioning of these relational schemas. Of interest to the current chapter are the attachment-related relational schemas known as working models (see chapter: What Are Attachment Working Models?).

Researchers often use priming to study the influence of context or the activation of a certain state of mind (Bargh & Chartrand, 2000; Cesario, 2014; Molden, 2014). In the attachment literature, priming is used to activate people's internalized working models. That is, researchers activate a certain attachment-related state of mind, making people temporarily feel more securely, anxiously, or avoidantly attached. Once activated, researchers can examine the outcomes of this activation as well as the outcomes of this activation's interaction with people's chronic attachment style. Using priming allows researchers to study the unique effects of each variable (the prime, one's level of anxiety or avoidance, etc.), and the issues related to directionality and causality of attachment processes in relatively controlled settings.

WHAT'S BEING PRIMED? ATTACHMENT-RELATED SCHEMAS

As mentioned in chapter: What Are Attachment Working Models?, interactions with primary caregivers, or as Bowlby (1969/1982) termed them *attachment figures*, are consolidated over time into *internal working models* (eg, Bretherton & Munholland, 1999). These models represent the *self* and *others*. These models or mental representations, which can be positive or negative in nature, are incorporated within long-term memory along with particular emotions, motives, goals, and behaviors which, collectively, form a person's *attachment style* (eg, Gillath et al., 2006; Mikulincer & Shaver, 2007ba).

The formation of an attachment style is thought to rely on learning processes such as conditioning (Mikulincer & Shaver, 2007a). As such, interactions with attachment figures that provide safety and support in times of need reinforce associations in long-term memory between turning to these figures for support, having one's insecurity and distress reduced, and his or her sense of security restored. Eventually, merely calling a supportive attachment figure to mind becomes a source of solace and acts as a mental resource to buffer life stressors and strains (Canterberry & Gillath, 2012; Mikulincer & Shaver, 2004). In the laboratory, attachment-related mental representations can be artificially activated, via priming, making people's sense of security more accessible and potentially affecting their cognitions and behaviors.

As we described earlier in the book (chapters: What Is an Attachment Relationship? and How Do Individual Differences in Attachment Develop?), repeated encounters with sensitive and responsive attachment figures are likely to result in the formation of a secure attachment style (see DeWolff & van IJzendoorn, 1997, for a metaanalysis), whereas interactions with inconsistent, insensitive, and unresponsive attachment figures are likely to result in the development of an insecure attachment style (Ainsworth, Blehar, Waters, & Wall, 1978). As a result of unsupportive experiences with attachment figures, people with an insecure attachment style develop negative representations of their relationships, relationship partners, and in some cases themselves.

According to Baldwin et al. (1993, 1996) most people experience different relational interactions, situations, and relationship histories, which can make them feel secure, anxious, or avoidant. Hence, everyone should have mental representations of secure and insecure experiences available in long-term memory; memories that can be activated in the laboratory. In other words, researchers can prime a sense of attachment security, anxiety, or avoidance among study participants due to their preexisting models.

Hundreds of studies to date have shown that attachment style is a reliable predictor of various outcomes. For example, attachment security predicts relationship satisfaction and longevity, well-being, adaptive forms of coping with stress, and successful regulation of affect (Cassidy & Shaver, 2008; Obegi & Berant, 2010; Wallin, 2007). Such findings demonstrate the benefits of having a secure attachment style. Thus, it may be worthwhile to discover ways in which a person could become more secure with respect to attachment (see Mikulincer & Shaver, 2007b; and Steele & Steele, 2008, for comprehensive reviews). Indeed various researchers have used security priming to increase prorelational and prosocial behavior, positive mood, tolerance of outgroup members, and reduce symptoms of psychopathology (eg, Carnelley, Otway, & Rowe, 2015).

HOW DO YOU ALTER PEOPLE'S SENSE OF SECURITY IN THE SHORT TERM IN THE LABORATORY?

Several methods have been used to create short-term changes in people's sense of attachment security in the laboratory (see reviews by Gillath et al., 2008b; Mikulincer & Shaver, 2007b). These methods involve: (1) exposing people (subliminally/unconsciously or supraliminally/consciously) to security-related words (eg, love, hug, affection, support) or the names of security-providing attachment figures via different tasks (eg, a cross word puzzle); (2) exposing people (subliminally or supraliminally) to pictures representing attachment security (eg, a mother hugging a child); and (3) asking participants to recall memories of being loved and supported by attachment figures, or asking people to imagine such scenarios or relationships. These priming procedures have been shown to influence such diverse variables as mood (Mikulincer et al., 2001a), attitudes toward novel stimuli (Mikulincer, Hirschberger, Nachmias, & Gillath, 2001), reactions to out-group members (Mikulincer & Shaver, 2001), death anxiety (Gillath & Hart, 2010), aggression (Mikulincer & Shaver, 2007a), and compassion and altruism (Gillath, Shaver, & Mikulincer, 2005; Mikulincer, Shaver, Gillath & Nitzberg, 2005). Moreover, security priming has been shown to decrease mental health symptomatology (Carnelley, Otway, & Rowe, 2015; Mikulincer, Shaver, & Horesh, 2006).

DO PRIMING EFFECTS LAST? THE LONG-TERM EFFECTS OF SECURITY PRIMING

In cognitive priming experiments, it has generally been found that the effects of priming one of two associated words and thus increasing the speed of identifying the other word ("semantic priming") last only a few seconds (eg, Becker, Moscovitch, Behrmann, & Joordens, 1997; Joordens & Becker, 1997). However, there are exceptions to this finding. For example, Srull and Wyer (1980) when using personality trait concepts as primes (eg, "hostile" and "kind") found effects on participants' judgments of a target person 24 h after the study. Dasgupta and Greenwald (2001) primed study participants with pictures of admired black or disliked white individuals and found that it weakened implicit prowhite attitudes measured 24 h after the priming session. Lowery, Eisenberger, Hardin, and Sinclair (2007) subliminally primed participants with intelligence-related words and found that it improved their test performance in an actual midterm examination one to four days after the priming session. Going beyond a few days, Cave (1997) demonstrated that the effects of semantic priming could be detected between 6 and 48 weeks after the priming procedure took place. Finally, Mitchell (2006) reported that people who saw pictures for only 1–3 s in a study could identify fragments of these pictures 17 years later.

One factor that seems to contribute to long-lasting priming effects is the number of times people are exposed to the prime. Brown, Jones, and Mitchell (1996), for example, found that as the number of exposures to the prime (repetitions) increased, the effects of the prime became stronger and longer-lasting. Similarly, Salasoo, Shiffrin, and Feustel (1985) found that accuracy of identification a year after priming was affected by the number of repetitions of the prime stimuli.

Based on Bowlby's (1973) conceptualization that repeated interactions with an attachment figure not only alter attachment-system functioning in the short term but also affect the consolidation of working models in the long term, Gillath et al. (2008b) suggested that repeated security priming will have long-lasting effects on people's attitudes and behaviors. A few empirical studies provide support for the ideas regarding the lasting effects of security priming. Sohlberg and Birgegard (2003) subliminally primed participants with either the phrase "Mommy and I are one" (MIO; Silverman, 1983), designed to create a sense of closeness to—or merger with—an attachment figure, or "People are walking" (PAW), a control prime. They found that 7–10 days after the priming manipulation the MIO group showed stronger correlations than the PAW group. Specifically, self–mother similarity was more strongly related to secure attachment and to low depressive symptoms, whereas fear of intimacy was more strongly associated with anxious or avoidant attachment in the MIO group.

In two more recent studies, Dandeneau, Baldwin, Baccus, Sakellaropoulo, and Pruessner (2007) demonstrated the effects of a task that might be interpreted as a security priming procedure. The task was learning to find an accepting/loving/smiling face out of an array of negative expressions. The researchers examined the effects of engaging in the task on reactivity to naturally occurring stressors. Although participants in the experimental and control groups did not differ in baseline exam stress, those in the experimental group experienced significantly less stress by the end of the fifth day of priming. And the effects of priming persisted even after the students took their final exams at school. In a second field study, telemarketers completed the same task for five consecutive days. Dependent variables included cortisol levels (assessed from saliva), sales data, and supervisor ratings. Participants in the experimental group had higher self-esteem, decreased self-reported stress, lower cortisol levels, improved sales performance, and higher ratings by supervisors compared with control participants.

Carnelley and Rowe (2007) found similar results following repeated security priming. Specifically, participants primed with security had more positive expectations of relationship partners' behavior and more positive self-views. Further, for both expectations of relationships partners' behavior and self-views, the increase showed a linear trend across priming sessions. No significant increase was observed in the control group for either expectations of relationships partners' behavior or self-views. Repeated security priming also decreased attachment anxiety: Participants in the experimental group reported lower levels of attachment anxiety, whereas no such change occurred in the control group. However, there was no such effect on avoidant attachment, perhaps because avoidant individuals attempt to actively block or deactivate the effects of the security prime, as part of their use of deactivating strategies (Mikulincer & Shaver, 2007b). Finally, neither trait attachment anxiety nor trait avoidant attachment moderated the effects of security priming.

Gillath et al. (2008b) reported a study where they tested whether repeated security priming might result in benefits that persist for one week after priming. Specifically, these authors tested the effects of repeated subliminal security priming on mood, and on the functioning of the caregiving and exploration systems. Changes in caregiving were operationalized as a change in willingness to show compassion to others, and changes in exploration as better performance on a creativity task. There were a few differences between the Carenelley and Rowe study and the Gillath et al. study. First, whereas Carnelley and Rowe (2007) used a supraliminal priming technique, Gillath and colleagues used subliminal technique. Second, Carnelley and Rowe exposed participants to either a security or a control prime each day for a total of 3 days, whereas Gillath and colleagues exposed participants to a security or a control prime three times a week for 3 weeks. Third, the time period between the final priming session and assessment of the dependent variables was 2 days in the Carnelley and Rowe study and 1 week in the Gillath study. Nevertheless the results of the two studies are in line with one another.

Gillath et al. (2008b) found that participants in the experimental condition had higher self-esteem and higher positive mood scores at the end of the study as compared with participants in the control group, even though the two groups were not different at baseline. Participants in the experimental group also reported higher compassion toward others by the end, and there was a trend in the expected direction for creativity. Overall, the evidence to date provides initial support for the idea that security priming has long-term effects; however further research is needed to fully understand these effects and their underlying mechanisms.

WHAT IS THE RELATIONSHIP BETWEEN ATTACHMENT PRIMING AND ATTACHMENT STYLE?

The effects of security priming remain statistically significant, even when one controls for factors such as dispositional neuroticism, positive affect, and self-esteem (eg, Mikulincer, Hirschberger, Nachmias, & Gillath, 2001). But what happens when one controls for the effects of dispositional attachment style? In many of the studies conducted to date, security priming procedures (Mikulincer & Shaver, 2007b) are not moderated by attachment style (ie, trait attachment anxiety and avoidance). Rather, the priming procedures yield beneficial effects on study participants regardless of their dispositional attachment style. For example, in one study conducted by Gillath and Shaver (2007) people were asked to select how they would respond to various relational scenarios, many of which included negative acts by their partner (eg, their partner betraying them, revealing a secret, embarrassing them). At first people were asked to select among different behaviors that represent secure, anxious, or avoidant responses to the act. In this first stage of the study, people's attachment style was found to predict which option they were likely to select (eg, anxious people were likely to select an anxious response). In the second stage of the study, participants were primed with a security or insecurity prime first, and then completed the questionnaire including the hypothetical scenarios for a second time. Priming people with a security prime caused them to react in a secure manner to threatening relationship scenarios, regardless of their dispositional attachment style. By-and-large the responses chosen after exposure to security priming were secure and pro-social in nature.

Although in many studies the effects of security priming occur regardless of one's dispositional style, some studies have shown that security priming sometimes interacts with people's dispositional styles. In one such study, participants were asked to recall an incident when a close relationship partner hurt their feelings (Shaver, Mikulincer, Lavy, & Cassidy, 2009). After recalling this event, participants were primed with a security or a control prime, and then asked to rate their current feelings. Security priming had a different effect on people as a function of their attachment styles. Among anxiously attached individuals the prime reduced the tendency to exaggerate and augment hurt feelings, leading to a decrease in reported hurt feelings. Conversely, among avoidantly attached individuals security priming decreased the tendency to defensively deny hurt feelings or to react aggressively rather than minimize the experience of being hurt. That is, increasing people's sense of security lowered avoidant individuals' defensive tendencies (see also Arndt, Schimel, Greenberg, & Pyszczynski, 2002), leading to an increase in reported hurt feelings.

A different set of studies focusing on breakup strategies (Collins & Gillath, 2012) provides further support for the moderation by attachment style. Participants were asked to select which breakup strategy best fits their typical response to relationship dissolution (eg, the degree to which they use compassionate or direct breakup strategies). In one study, people's attachment styles were found to predict which strategies they selected (eg, people high on avoidance chose less direct breakup strategies and those high on anxiety chose strategies to keep the option of getting back together open). Participants were then primed with either a security or a neutral control prime. Prime type (security/neutral) interacted with people's attachment style, such that those high on avoidance were less likely to choose the less direct strategies, and those high on anxiety were less likely to select the "keep open" strategies after exposure to the security prime.

The fact that in some studies security priming interacts with chronic attachment style, but not in others, raises questions. For example, is there a moderator that influences whether or not such an interaction takes place? Is it an issue of statistical power, prime strength [some procedures (eg, subliminal vs. supraliminal) or stimuli (eg, words vs. pictures) might be more efficient at increasing security], or some other factor? Can these studies be replicated? Are the findings valid and do they have meaningful real world implications? These questions are in line with recent concerns regarding priming findings and the inability to replicate them (eg, Harris, Coburn, Rohrer, & Pashler, 2013; Waroquier, Marchiori, Klein, & Cleeremans, 2009). Various researchers have tried and failed to replicate "classic" priming studies, concluding that these findings are at best unreliable (Donnellan, Lucas, & Cesario, 2015; Doyen, Klein, Pichon, & Cleeremans, 2012; LeBel & Campbell, 2013). In light of the concerns regarding attachment priming, further investigation into the reliability of priming effects is necessary.

CAN WE TRUST ATTACHMENT PRIMING EFFECTS? USING META-ANALYSIS

To deal with these concerns Gillath et al. (2016) conducted a metaanalysis of the studies related to security priming and its benefits. Examining published and unpublished research papers and doctoral theses between the years 1981 and 2013, they identified a total of 92 studies that examined the effects of security priming (most studies were conducted in the late 1990s and beyond, after Baldwin et al. (1996) introduced the idea of multiple attachment models and their temporary activation). Just over 91% of studies reported an effect for security priming, with approximately 65% of studies employing supraliminal priming methods, while the remainder of studies employed subliminal methods. Across all these studies, investigating the effects of security priming revealed an average effect size of ($r = 0.28$, $p < 0.01$).

Thus, it appears that security priming has detectable effects on various outcomes. Metaanalyses, however, cannot solve all the problems that have been levelled against priming research. There are at least two issues that should be considered more carefully in the future. First, given the bias in the field against publishing null findings, the odds of getting a paper written and ultimately accepted are substantially higher if the priming effect worked than if it did not. Thus, the metaanalytic effect size probably better summarizes the average effect in studies in which the priming "worked" than in a random sample of studies that employed priming. Second, given the small sample sizes often used in this kind of research, the effects that are statistically significant are likely to be overestimates of the true effect. We hope future research will strive to solve these challenges and the perplexing questions that still remain unanswered in security priming research.

WHAT PHYSIOLOGICAL/NEURAL MECHANISMS UNDERLIE SECURITY PRIMING?

Although ample research documents the effects of attachment security, relatively little is known about the physiological mechanisms and neural pathways by which security priming results in these effects. To address this gap in the literature, Canterberry and Gillath (2013) conducted an fMRI study examining the neural mechanisms that underlie enhanced attachment security. Canterberry and Gillath's findings indicate that security enhancement involves cognitive, affective, and behavioral aspects or processes (see more details in chapter: What can Neuroscience, Genetics, and Physiology Tell us About Attachment?). These findings support the conceptualization of attachment security as part of a behavioral system with multiple components (affective, cognitive, and behavioral). These components are thought to act together as a resource—allowing the person to calm down, focus on the task at hand, and not be distracted by anxieties and concerns. These resources could facilitate the functioning of other behavioral systems—if one does not have to cope with anxieties, he or she can focus on behaviors such as exploration or providing care for others. Thus, the findings based on brain activation are in line with the idea that attachment security allows a person to relax, boosts the person's self-esteem and positive affect, and buffers distress and anxiety (affective component). Specifically, the activation in prefrontal areas is in line with the idea that internalized working models are being primed, which provides the person examples of how to deal with stressors, schemas of secure base scenarios, and caregiving provision (cognitive). Brain activation in areas related to motivation and motor functioning supports the proposition that security priming provides motivation to act or strengthen behavioral tendencies.

Further support for the idea that attachment security can act as a resource comes from another recent study that focused on the association between security and glucose. Glucose serves as a vital resource for our metabolism and brain functioning (eg, Gailliot et al., 2007). In the study by Gillath, Pressman, Stetler, and Moskovitz (2016) participants were assigned either to a security priming or a control priming condition. Following the priming procedure participants' glucose levels (assessed via saliva samples) were measured. If indeed, security acts as a resource, one would expect an increase in glucose to occur following the security priming. As expected, security priming resulted in higher glucose levels compared to exposure to a control prime. These findings suggest that security priming not only results in affective and cognitive changes (eg, mood and attention), but also physiological changes, and specifically, the enhancement of physiological resources such as blood-level glucose. It is more than likely that the various cognitive, affective, behavioral, and neurophysiological changes that have been linked to security priming co-occur. If this is the case, then it may be posited that the effects of security priming are multilevel in nature and involve various physiological and psychological pathways.

CONCLUDING REMARKS

This chapter reviews research on the importance of security priming and its outcomes. Security priming seems to increase people's sense of attachment security, and, at least temporarily, make them feel, think, and behave like securely attached people. The findings further suggest that security priming procedures do not simply create a semantic connection between a positive stimulus and a resulting positive affect, but actually result in a multitude of outcomes that resemble the correlates of attachment security (eg, prosocial and prorelational tendencies). The effects of security priming have been found even when researchers controlled for positive affect, and self-esteem, suggesting that there is more to security priming than mood enhancement, or boosts to self-esteem.

Although the findings reviewed above add to our understanding of security priming, they also raise concerns and there are still open questions, such as: How do state security (primed) and trait security differ? How long can the effects of security priming last? What changes seem to occur in people as a result of security priming? Future research using a multilevel multimethod approach to the study of security priming is needed to answer these questions and improve our understanding of the underlying mechanisms and processes that underpin attachment security.

Chapter 8

What Is the Attachment Behavioral System? And, How Is It Linked to Other Behavioral Systems?

One of Bowlby's (1982) aims was to explain phenomena of psychodynamic interest without referencing psychic energy and drives. He found his solution, in part, in the ideas of ethologists who were studying motivated, organized behavior and, in part, control systems theory. Up until that point in time, control systems theory was being applied by engineers and early artificial intelligence scholars to model complex intelligent behavior by linking together the operations of multiple unintelligent subsystems (for a similar approach see Beckes, IJzerman, & Tops, 2014). Drawing on the principles governing control systems, Bowlby realized that the concept of a *behavioral system* could provide an elegant way to explain normative and nonnormative psychological functioning. Unbeknownst to Bowlby, his behavioral systems concept became one of his main contributions to the field of psychology. In particular, the "behavioral system" has provided important insights into the study of close relationships, personality, social development, and motivational processes. Here we describe the concept of a behavioral system, review the literature about the various behavioral systems Bowlby and his followers examined, and offer some directions for future research.

WHAT IS A BEHAVIORAL SYSTEM?

Bowlby (1969/1982) suggested that people's behavior is guided by a set of innate *behavioral systems*[1]. Through evolution these systems were shaped to increase the likelihood of an organism's survival and reproductive success. These species-universal neural programs or mechanisms, guide the choice, activation, and

▶

---

1. The concept of unique behavioral systems each organizing a specific type of behavior and working together (or against each other) in guiding human behavior, is similar to the concept of modularity (eg, Fodor, 2005; Pinker, 2005). That said, modules tend to focus on general information-processing mechanisms [Pinker (1997): "modules should be defined by the specific operations they perform on the information they receive"]; whereas behavioral systems focus on behaviors (but do

Adult Attachment. http://dx.doi.org/10.1016/B978-0-12-420020-3.00008-6

termination of behavioral sequences in a way that serves a specific function, such as the forming of an attachment bond, seeking out affiliations, or providing care to a person in need. This takes place in a goal-corrected manner—that is—specific features of strategic behaviors can be altered to fit particular environments or social situations (eg, insecure behaviors may fit better a dangerous environment, so when exposed to signs of danger, people may exhibit more insecure behaviors).

WHAT ARE THE FEATURES OF A BEHAVIORAL SYSTEM?

As summarized by Mikulincer and Shaver (2003) behavioral systems have six central features: (1) a specific biological function that increases the likelihood of an individual's survival or reproductive success; (2) a set of activating triggers; (3) a repertoire of interchangeable responses. These responses include the primary and secondary strategies people use to attain a particular goal state; (4) a specific set-goal—the change in the person–environment relationship that terminates system activation; (5) a range of cognitive operations that guide the system's functioning; and (6) associations with other behavioral systems. We describe each of these features in the following sections.

The Biological Function of the Attachment System

Although all behavioral systems share the ultimate goal of guiding behavior in a way that would increase survival and reproduction, each system has a unique function that separates it from the other systems. The function of the attachment system is to guide the individual to maintain proximity to a stronger, wiser caregiver (attachment figure). The adaptive value of the system is relatively easy to appreciate in infancy given that human infants are born immature, without the ability to feed or protect themselves. The function of attachment in adulthood, however, is subject to debate (see Lee Kirkpatrick's work and chapter: What Is an Attachment Relationship?).

The Triggers That Activate the Attachment System

Triggers are the perceived threats and dangers that could compromise a person's survival. The presence of these triggers leads an individual to engage in specific behaviors or responses and pursue the system's goals. These triggers can be external/environmental cues, or internal cues—thoughts, emotions, worries, and

▶ ──────────────────────────────

have an information-processing component). Furthermore, the features that characterize modules and behavioral systems are different [compare the list Fodor (1983) provided—domain specificity, encapsulation, mandatory operation (automaticity), inaccessibility to consciousness, speed, shallow outputs, fixed neural localization, and characteristic breakdown patterns, with the list we bring in the chapter]. So, the two different intellectual traditions converge on the same idea, but emphasize different parts of it. We hope that by highlighting this similarity between modularity and behavioral systems we might help people familiar with, say, modularity, to better appreciate the attachment perspective.

alike. For example, a stranger in one's vicinity can act as such a trigger (as is the case in the strange situation; Ainsworth, Blehar, Waters, & Wall, 1978).

The Repertoire of Interchangeable Responses

Like other behavioral systems, the attachment system is thought to be organized around a primary strategy. In the case of attachment, this primary strategy is regaining (or maintaining) proximity to a stronger and wiser close other. The responses associated with the primary strategy include behaviors such as crying, smiling, and reaching out to security-providing figures. This repertoire of behaviors or behavioral tendencies is activated automatically when people are exposed to relevant triggers that signal danger (eg, a loud noise or a stranger approaching). The behaviors are deactivated or terminated by cues signaling goal attainment—a sense of security. If the primary strategy does not work, people may try using secondary strategies, such as hyperactivating or deactivating the attachment system (Mikulincer & Shaver, 2003).

The Set Point for the Attachment System

The set point of the system is thought to be a sense of security (what is sometimes called felt security; Sroufe & Waters, 1977a). Once security is threatened or its level decreases below the set-point, the system is activated and people are motivated to try and return the system to "baseline." To accomplish this they engage in behaviors that lead to a change in the person–environment relationship (eg, reach out to an attachment figure). Once that change is achieved—the set point is reached—the system's activation is terminated.

The Cognitive Operations of the Attachment System

The attachment system operates in a complex goal-corrected manner. For this operation to occur, people need to process, monitor, and appraise their interactions with attachment figures. Based on the monitoring of one's environment, people adjust their behavior. Over time, these interactions and whatever modifications are made to the system are stored as mental representations and become a part of the system's programming or guidelines. Thus, if a caregiver or a partner is being insensitive and rejecting, the system will come to represent him or her, and close others more generally, as being unavailable and in turn tendencies to approach others under stressful circumstances are deactivated. These representations are what Bowlby termed internal working models of self and others (see chapter: What Are Attachment Working Models?) and they can be positive or negative in valence.

Associations With Other Behavioral Systems

Whereas each behavioral system has its own function, triggers, and responses, the systems do not work in isolation. Instead, the systems are thought to interact with each other and jointly affect people's behavior. This interaction can take different forms as we review later in this chapter.

HOW CAN WE EXAMINE THE CONCEPT OF A BEHAVIORAL SYSTEM?

One approach researchers have adopted to examine the dynamics of behavioral systems is by exposing people to potential activating triggers of the system, and testing the outcomes of the system's activation. For example, Mikulincer, Gillath, and Shaver (2002) showed that exposure to threat prime words—such as *separation* and *death*—led to increased accessibility of names of attachment figures. This increase was specific to attachment figures (these effects were not found with the names of close others who were not security-providing attachment figures) and was replicated across different tasks (lexical decision and stroop) in three different experiments.

Simpson, Rholes, and Nelligan (1992) examined the activation of the attachment system by putting couples in anxiety-provoking or stressful situations in the laboratory. Independent observers then evaluated each partner's behavior, revealing that in such situations people tend to make efforts to seek and give emotional support (no comparison or control condition was used in this study).

Fraley and Shaver (1998) took the investigation regarding the activation of the attachment system outside the laboratory. They argued that one way to study attachment behavior naturalistically in adult romantic relationships is by observing couples separating from one another in a context similar to that of the strange situation. To do so, they examined the behavior of couples who were separating from one another at a large metropolitan airport. There are at least two reasons why this is a useful context in which to study adult attachment dynamics. First, when couples are separating from one another for an extended period of time, attachment-related concerns may be raised. People may worry about whether their partner will make it to their destination safely. Some of them may even wonder whether their partner will want to return. Second, airports provide a public context (ie, a place where people's behavior is seen by others and hence can be observed by researchers) in which people exhibit private behavior (that they otherwise might only exhibit in private settings).

The study was conducted before 9/11 when airports in the United States allowed anyone to enter the gate area, whether they were ticketed passengers or not. Fraley and Shaver (1998) coded the behavior of each individual in a relationship as they waited in the gate area for their planes. Importantly, some of the couples in the study were in fact separating (one person was leaving and the other was staying behind), but approximately half of the couples were not; they were flying together. The observers, however, were not aware of the flying together versus separating status before boarding time. Fraley and Shaver reported that many of the observed behaviors were indicative of attachment.

For example, couple members would often hold hands and maintain proximity to one another. When the separation was imminent, they would often express sadness and seek comfort from one another. Couples also showed resistance to the separation by refusing to let go of a partner's hand as he or she left to board the plane.

Couples exhibited not only attachment-related behaviors, but caregiving and sex behaviors too. For example, one person often patted the other on the back as a way of providing comfort and support. And, on the sexual end, comforting embraces occasionally transformed into intimate kisses and light fondling. Importantly, Fraley and Shaver (1998) found that all three kinds of behaviors (ie, attachment, caregiving, and sex) were more pronounced among couples who ended up separating from one another than couples who were flying together. The implication of this finding is that, in adulthood, physical separations have the potential to activate not only attachment-related behavior, but caregiving and sexual behavior too.

Researchers have studied other behavioral systems using similar kinds of methods. For example, Gillath, Mikulincer, Birnbaum, and Shaver (2008) activated the sex behavioral system by exposing people to sex-related cues (eg, pictures of naked opposite sex members). They found that subliminal activation of the sex system resulted in increased: (1) willingness to self-disclose, (2) accessibility of intimacy-related thoughts, (3) willingness to make sacrifices for one's partner, and (4) preference for using positive conflict-resolution strategies. All four outcomes represent initiation and maintenance, which are thought to be two of the goals of the sex system (the main function of the sex system is to facilitate reproduction, more than once; initiation and maintenance increase the likelihood of reproduction happening—by finding a sex partner, initiating a relationship, and staying with him or her). The studies reviewed above demonstrate the effects of exposure to relevant triggers on a behavioral system. Next, we review the interplay between behavioral systems and describe how this interplay changes when one system is activated.

WHAT HAPPENS WHEN ONE BEHAVIORAL SYSTEM "MEETS" ANOTHER?

Human behavior is complex, and is often guided by more than one behavioral system. Hinde (1982), Bowlby (1982), and others (eg, Cicchetti & Serafica, 1981; Shaver & Hazan, 1987) have suggested that rather than studying one system at a time researchers should study the dynamic interplay between different systems. Researchers have used different ways to study this interplay, but in this chapter we focus on two approaches. One examines the interplay as a developmental process—development of a species, development of a new close relationship, or the development of an individual—from the beginning of his/her life through to the end or as Bowlby (1979) put it "from the cradle to the grave" (p. 127). Another way of studying the interplay is by examining the effects of the levels of one behavioral system—either chronic levels, or state levels due to activation—on other behavioral systems. For example, one can examine the effects of being securely or insecurely attached on caregiving or exploration tendencies and behaviors.

WHAT CAN DEVELOPMENT TEACH US ABOUT THE INTERPLAY BETWEEN BEHAVIORAL SYSTEMS?

Evolution

Studying the evolution of a species can shed light on when, why, and how behavioral systems evolved. In turn, this understanding can provide insights into the links and the interplay between behavioral systems, such as, whether particular conditions result in the prioritized activation of systems. That is, are there situations in which the activation of one system is likely to take priority over another? Eastwick and Finkel (2012) examined the evolution of the sex and attachment behavioral systems and put forward predictions regarding the interaction between these systems. They predicted that the attachment system, which presumably evolved later in evolution than the sex system, will have the ability to mute or refocus adaptations of the sex system to ensure the maintenance of adult pair bonding (eg, attachment would reduce the likelihood that people act based on their attraction to an alternative potential mate when they are already in a relationship). Examining their prediction they found that among women who were strongly attached to their partners, conception probability (assessed as ovulatory cycle phase) positively predicted reports of intimate physical contact and sexual motives regarding intimacy. Conversely, among unbonded women, these same associations were negative. The results held even when controlling for attachment anxiety and avoidance, relationship satisfaction, relationship commitment, and partner physical attractiveness. These findings, using the timeline of hominid evolution (ie, phylogeny), support the idea that behavioral systems do not function independently. As shown in this study, the attachment system has the potential to modify the functioning of other behavioral systems, including the sex system. More broadly it suggests that behavioral systems can either "cooperate" or "compete" with each other when guiding human behavior (we will elaborate on this idea later).

Shifting to attachment and caregiving, Fraley, Marks, and Brumbaugh (2005) used phylogenetic analysis of data across multiple mammalian species to examine the evolution of specific behaviors. They found that pair-bonded species (the authors' way of operationalizing the presence of adult romantic attachment across species) were more likely to have fathers who played a direct role in child rearing than were nonpairing species. They also found that species in which offspring were more developmentally immature were more likely to exhibit pair bonding (see chapter: What Is an Attachment Relationship?). Based on their analysis Fraley et al. concluded that the link between paternal care and adult attachment (or pair bonding) is likely to be a functional one (ie, due to convergent evolution—coping with the same environmental pressures). In contrast, the link between neoteny and adult attachment is likely due to homology (ie, shared ancestry—the reason these traits come together is because they evolved together in the same ancestor). Because pair bonding emerged after paternal care in mammalian evolution, Fraley and colleagues have speculated that the presence of paternal care sets the stage for pair bonding. Fathers who played a greater role in child care, which increased the survivability of offspring, were more likely to be around not just the child, but also the mother. This, in turn, increased the probability of pair bonding. Together, these lines of work show that attachment takes precedence over sex, and caregiving facilitates the development of adult attachment.

Development of a Close Relationship

A different approach to studying development involves examining the interplay between behavioral systems in the context of forging a close relationship. According to Hazan and Shaver (1994) and Zeifman and Hazan (2008), three behavioral systems—attachment, sex, and caregiving—facilitate the formation and maintenance of pair bonding. In theorizing about the development of romantic love, Hazan and Shaver (1994) suggested that sexual interest serves as the initial force that brings adults together. Later on, they claimed, the attachment and caregiving systems come into play and facilitate the development and maintenance of the relationship (Fig. 8.1 depicts hypothetical trajectories).

Gillath et al. (2008a) provided support for the role of sex in the initiation of pair bonding, by demonstrating that exposure to sexual cues or triggers (ie, pictures of naked opposite sex members) results in the activation of relational goals (such as initiating or maintaining a romantic relationship). Thus, participants exposed to sexual images demonstrated behavioral tendencies that facilitate the initiation (self-disclosure and intimacy) and maintenance (willingness to sacrifice for one's partner, and positive strategies to resolve conflicts) of a romantic relationship. This is not to say that adult pair bonding must develop from sex or sexual interest. Some relationships may evolve out of a friendship, while other relationships may result from an alternative set of processes or circumstances (such as in the case of an arranged marriage). Regardless of how adult pair bonding comes to be, studying its development can teach us a lot about the interplay between behavioral systems.

Once a romantic relationship has been established, behavioral systems "take turns" in guiding each partner's behavior. For example, romantic partners tend to switch between the roles of caregiver and care recipient. When one partner is threatened or stressed, and his or her attachment system is activated, he or she assumes the role of care recipient. Seeking help is likely to be guided by the attachment system. The other partner, in response, is likely to assume the role of a caregiver, and thus, his or her caregiving system is activated and guides

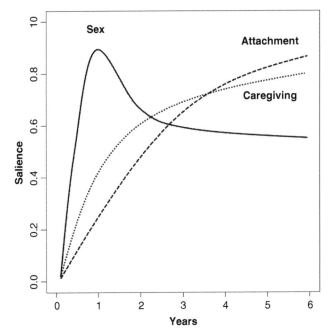

FIGURE 8.1 Developmental course of the three components of romantic love. *(Adapted from Hazan and Shaver (1994).)*

his or her behavior (interestingly, whether or not the partner will provide help is guided not only by his or her caregiving system, but also by his/her attachment system—see further). So within couple interactions, the caregiving system of one partner is activated by their reactions to distress signals from the other partner—signals that are generated by the partner's activation of his or her attachment system.

According to Bowlby (1969/1982), each partner in a romantic relationship can be, and usually is, the target of all three systems (attachment, caregiving, and sex) for the other partner. That is, at different times in the relationship, a partner can be the attachment figure (attachment system), the care provider (caregiving system), or the object of sexual attraction (sex system) for his or her partner. This makes for the possibility that the systems can operate at the same time, and either facilitate or interfere with the achievement of each system's goals. Regarding goal facilitation, Davis, Shaver, and Vernon, (2004) have found that some people engage in sexual behavior—a response related to the sex system—to comfort or care for their partner—a behavior associated with their caregiving system. Other people have sex to feel more secure—a behavior related with the attachment system. Both of these examples could be interpreted as motives or behaviors associated with the sex system that facilitate the fulfillment of goals and functions related to the other systems.

Regarding interference with goal attainment, situations may arise when the motivations or acts associated with one system are at odds or compete with the motivations or acts of another system. For example, when a couple is facing a danger, each partner's attachment system is likely to become activated, guiding him or her to avoid the danger by running away or looking for an attachment figure. At the same time, seeing one's partner in potential danger is likely to activate the caregiving system, motivating each partner to stick around and provide care for his or her partner. Thus, the motivations generated by the two systems "compete" with each other, and the actual behavior is likely to be based on which system generates stronger activation. This is in line with the work of Eastwick and Finkel (2012) described previously, who claimed that the attachment system overrides the sex system to facilitate relationship maintenance.

Development of an Individual

A third approach involves the study of an individual's development. Both the evolutionary perspective and the perspective focusing on relationship development suggest that the sex system precedes the caregiving and attachment systems developmentally. Conversely, examining the development of the individual shows that attachment is the first system to emerge, guiding infants' behavior from a very early age. Attachment behaviors are observable among infants who are a few months old, and attachment style can be evaluated in infants as young as 9 months of age. Developing at a later point in the individual's lifespan, the caregiving system is thought to guide behavior at a very young age. Infants as young as 1 year old show concern for others (Davidov, Zahn-Waxler, Roth-Hanania, & Knafo, 2013), and preschoolers actually exhibit caring behavior (Kestenbaum, Farber, & Sroufe, 1989). Sexual behavior is thought to emerge last in an individual's development, emerging during the onset of puberty.

This is not to say that the systems are not innate. Rather, these three systems exist from birth, but differ in when they start guiding behavior. Furthermore, a distinction should be made here between behavior and *organized* behavior. Whereas young children may exhibit certain behaviors related to a behavioral system it is unclear whether this represents behavior organized to achieve the set goal of the given system or not. For example, Bowlby reports that infants do engage in sexual behavior, such as pelvic thrusts; however, the behavior is not organized in a way that enables it to lead to predictable outcomes related to sexual functioning. Likewise, when "care" for certain objects or people is exhibited by children, it is unclear whether this is organized caregiving behavior or merely behavior that is indicative of the system. That is, although the behavior may represent a caring response, this behavior might not be indicative of the operation of the caregiving behavioral system per se.

HOW DO THE LEVELS OF ONE BEHAVIORAL SYSTEM AFFECT OTHER SYSTEMS?

A different approach to study the interplay between the behavioral systems is to take a cross-sectional perspective, where researchers investigate how the levels of one system (eg, security or insecurity) affect the functioning of another system (eg, the tendency to explore one's environment). According to Bowlby (1982), high levels of attachment insecurity and the activation of the attachment system are likely to interfere with the functioning of other behavioral systems. Conversely, the sense of security or having a secure base (in the form of an accessible attachment figure) can support or facilitate the functioning of other systems. Ainsworth et al. (1978) demonstrated this in their *strange situation* laboratory procedure. In this procedure, children explored a new unfamiliar environment when they felt secure (ie, the exploration system was activated), but ceased to explore or avoided exploration (deactivation of the exploration system) when they felt insecure and were preoccupied by the whereabouts of their attachment figure. Numerous studies have been carried out throughout the years, highlighting the associations between attachment style, or levels of attachment (in)security, and the functioning of other behavioral systems (eg, Gillath, Shaver, & Mikulincer, 2005b).

Below we review some of the work that has been conducted on the interplay between the attachment system and other behavioral systems (eg, caregiving, sex, exploration, affiliation). A significant proportion of the research investigating the interactions between the attachment system and other systems has focused on the caregiving system, largely due to the early work of Shaver, Hazan, and Bradshaw (1988) and others. Therefore we commence by focusing on the caregiving system. After describing the characteristics of the caregiving system we discuss research regarding the interactions between this system and the attachment system.

WHAT IS THE CAREGIVING SYSTEM?

The *caregiving system* is activated when another being (human or otherwise) experiences suffering or is in need of care and protection (Canterberry & Gillath, 2012; Gillath et al., 2005b). Thus, the caregiving system can be seen as complementary to the attachment system in that it motivates individuals to offer assistance, comfort, and support in response to the cues generated by another person's distress (Canterberry & Gillath, 2012; Karantzas & Simpson, 2015).

Mikulincer and Shaver (2009) suggested that studying the activation of a behavioral system can improve the understanding of how individual differences are associated with the functioning of the system. For example, with regard to attachment, people high on attachment anxiety tend to hyperactivate their attachment system—they are more vigilant to cues in the environment and are more likely to turn to their attachment figures for help. Conversely, people high on avoidant attachment tend to deactivate their attachment system, disregard cues or threats in the environment, and are less likely to turn to their attachment figure (compulsive self-reliance) even when they feel threatened or stressed. Further, Mikulincer and Shaver have suggested that individual differences in the caregiving system can also be conceptualized as patterns of hyperactivation or deactivation of the system. Across various studies, they have demonstrated that hyperactivation or deactivation of the caregiving system is associated with problems in the regulation of emotions, impulses, and goal-directed actions and puts a person at risk for emotional problems and maladjustment (eg, being less helpful or showing less care and more distress in various caregiving contexts). We discuss the outcomes of co-occurring system activation in detail in the following section.

Although caregiving and attachment are separate behavioral systems, and each system affects behavior in a unique way, the two systems have been proposed by Bowlby (1969/1982) to also interact in shaping people's behavior (see also, George & Solomon 2008; Mikulincer & Shaver, 2009). We (Canterberry & Gillath, 2012; Gillath et al., 2005b) and others (eg, Feeney & Collins, 2001) have argued that while there is a natural tendency to provide care to dependent or needy others, the interplay between the two systems can result in caregiving tendencies being overridden or suppressed by attachment insecurity (Kunce & Shaver, 1994). Thus, a person's attachment style (ie, secure or insecure) or state attachment (sense of security or insecurity) is thought to influence the interplay between the two behavioral systems, and the outcomes of this interplay (eg, providing help or not).

The interplay between the two systems is even more complicated as caregiving (mainly in childhood) is likely to affect the development of attachment style. Thus, sensitive, supportive caring by one's primary caregivers is likely to result in a secure attachment, which can facilitate an individual's ability to provide sensitive, supportive caregiving later in life. Conversely, insensitive, unsupportive caring is likely to result in an insecure attachment style, which is known to be associated with poor caregiving in adulthood. This suggests a developmental link between attachment and caregiving (eg, Kestenbaum et al., 1989).

The degree of sensitive and responsive care that an individual experiences in childhood and adulthood not only influences the development of one's attachment style, but is theorized to also shape one's caregiving style (Kunce & Shaver, 1994). Experiencing responsive and sensitive parenting promotes a secure attachment style and provides good models of how to deliver effective caregiving. As a result, individuals develop a pattern of behavior that reflects sensitive and responsive caregiving—attending to others' needs through the provision of support and maintenance of proximity, cooperating with the care-recipient in ways that effectively deal with threats and challenges, and providing help in a nonsmothering or noncompulsive manner. On the other hand, experiencing inept and inconsistent parenting promotes an insecure attachment style and impedes the development of models of effective caregiving. As a result, individuals develop a pattern of behavior that reflects a highly insensitive approach to caregiving—providing help in either a distant and cold manner, or a highly controlling and intrusive manner

(Collins & Feeney, 2000; Kunce & Shaver, 1994). Specifically, being securely attached facilitates a caregiving style characterized by high proximity, sensitivity, and responsiveness; being avoidant facilitates a more controlling and distant approach to caregiving coupled with low proximity and sensitivity; and finally being anxiously attached facilitates a compulsive, intrusive caregiving style that is inconsistent and that lacks sensitivity and responsiveness.

WHAT HAPPENS WHEN BOTH SYSTEMS ARE ACTIVATED?

Previously we described a situation where the attachment and caregiving systems motivate people to behave in two potentially opposing ways—a self-focused manner versus an other-focused manner (ie, either save oneself or save/care for another). In this section we elaborate on the outcomes that can ensue when both the attachment and caregiving systems are activated. One outcome is that people may ignore the distress of others and continue to focus on their own worries. This is likely to be the case for insecure individuals whose self-focused worries and concerns can disrupt caregiving behaviors.

An alternative outcome is that people may shift their focus away from their own anxieties and concerns to address the distress of others through the provision of care and support (for a similar idea see Batson, Fultz, & Schoenrade, 1987). However, what determines if the interplay between the two systems results in a reaction of self-focused concern (an act of nonprosociality) or an other-oriented response (provision of help/care—an act of prosociality)?

One determinant relates to whether a person has the necessary mental resources available to attend compassionately to other people who are in need of help (Mikulincer & Shaver, 2004). As mentioned earlier, work by Gillath et al. (2005b) and others suggests that attachment security can be conceptualized as a mental resource that is available for individuals when they are faced with demanding situations. In particular, secure individuals are thought to possess various mental resources (eg, attention and energy) as well as the flexibility to direct these resources toward the functioning of other behavioral systems such as the caregiving system. Secure people are also thought to be able to regulate their own emotions, which could otherwise generate personal distress, cognitive and emotional strain, and depletion of mental resources (eg, Batson et al., 1987; Finkel & Campbell, 2001; Fredrickson, 2001).

Thus, attachment security allows a person to perceive others not only as a source of safety and support, but also as people who might themselves be in need of help. This sense of security allows people to temporarily overcome their own anxieties and forgo their needs in order to attend to the plight of others. Finally, mental representations associated with attachment security are thought to provide a model for helping behavior that secure individuals can implement. That is, remembering how one was assisted in the past, or how a caregiver behaved in the past, can provide procedural knowledge and guidelines on how to deal with a situation when help is needed.

In contrast to securely attached individuals, insecure individuals may fail to notice people in need, or may lack the mental resources necessary to provide sensitive and effective care to others even if they do notice a need (Gillath et al., 2005b; Mikulincer, Shaver, Gillath, & Nitzberg, 2005). Even when noticing others in need, and possessing some resources to provide support (eg, time, money, energy), insecure people appear to lack the mental models or experience on which to base their provision of help (Mikulincer & Shaver, 2004). Lack of models and experience may render the help of insecure individuals unfit or inappropriate—they may be too controlling, insensitive, or intrusive. Thus, insecure individuals not only lack the sense of security to buffer the negative feelings evoked by the threatening situation, but they also lack the procedural knowledge about how to respond, and the mental resources (such as cognitive flexibility) to mobilize an effective and coordinated caregiving response. Therefore, individuals who are insecurely attached are less likely to provide help compared to secure individuals. Specifically, avoidant individuals are more likely to distance themselves from caregiving situations, whereas anxious individuals are more likely to become overwhelmed and render ineffective caregiving.

WHAT EMPIRICAL EVIDENCE EXISTS FOR THE INTERPLAY BETWEEN THE CAREGIVING AND ATTACHMENT SYSTEMS?

The association between attachment style and caregiving has been demonstrated across different situations involving prosocial behavior and relationship contexts. For example, secure individuals have been found to endorse more prosocial values such as benevolence and universalism, engage in more volunteering activities and spend more time doing so, exhibit generosity, and report altruistic reasons for volunteering as compared to people scoring high on attachment avoidance or anxiety (eg, Gillath et al., 2005b). Moreover, research by Gillath and colleagues on attachment, caregiving, and volunteerism has replicated the associations just outlined across different cultures (similar results were obtained in the United States, the Netherlands, and Israel).

Similar findings regarding attachment and prosociality have been found in other contexts. For instance, high-school students high on attachment anxiety or avoidance were perceived by peers as less supportive than their secure classmates, and were less likely than secure students to engage in reciprocally supportive relationships (Priel, Mitrany, & Shahar, 1998). Within the context of family caregiving, researchers have found that attachment anxiety and avoidance are negatively associated with adult children's current care of older parents (Carpenter, 2001; Crispi, Schiaffino, & Berman, 1997; Karantzas, 2012; Karantzas et al., 2010; Karantzas, Evans, & Foddy, 2010). Relatedly, lower scores on the anxiety and avoidance dimensions (ie, secure attachment) were found to predict adult children's future care plans for older relatives, suggesting that secure adults are care-oriented even before care is explicitly called for (Sörensen, Webster, & Roggman, 2002; see also Karantzas, 2012; Karantzas et al., 2010).

As attachment security has been repeatedly associated with numerous positive caregiving-related outcomes, orienting people toward a secure attachment style or enhancing their sense of security is likely to result in increased caregiving and helping behavior, and less caregiver-related strain. Thus, fostering attachment security and effective functioning of the caregiving system can enhance people's prosocial tendencies and behaviors. We next review the literature on the enhancement of attachment security and its effects on outcomes related to caregiving and prosociality more broadly.

WHAT HAPPENS WHEN SECURITY IS ENHANCED?

Enhancing one's sense of security has been found to increase other-oriented prosocial tendencies and behaviors (see chapter: What can Social Cognition and Priming Tell us About Attachment?). For example, Mikulincer et al. (2001a), and Mikulincer et al. (2003) showed that exposing people to attachment security primes (eg, attachment-security-related words, such as *love*, *hug*, and *secure*) led participants to endorse more self-transcendence values (universalism and benevolence) and report higher willingness to behave more empathically toward people in need (eg, spend more time and money on helping a girl who lost her parents). Moreover, participants who were exposed to a security prime actually exhibited a greater willingness to take the place of a fellow participant who could not complete various aversive tasks, as compared with participants in the control condition (Mikulincer et al., 2005). For example, Mikulincer et al. (2005) exposed people in the laboratory to either attachment-security-related prime or a control prime. Following exposure to the prime, participants were instructed to watch another study participant (via a monitor), who was supposedly in the next room, engaging in a series of increasingly aversive tasks (eg, watching gory pictures, placing one's hand in a bucket of ice water, petting a tarantula).

The participant engaging in the aversive tasks was in fact a study confederate. Halfway through the aversive tasks, the confederate exclaims that she cannot continue. At that point in time, the experiment is stopped, and the participant watching the clip is asked to complete a few questionnaires, tapping into, among other things, his or her willingness to help the confederate by volunteering to take over from where the confederate left off. After completing the questionnaires the participant is given the option to go into the other room and help by actually taking the "other participant's" place. Once this option was given to the participant the study concluded. Mikulincer et al. found that 70% of the people primed with security were willing to help—this was significantly more than the people in the control condition (less than 30%).

Experimentally increasing people's sense of attachment security (even in people with an insecure attachment) has also been found to increase compassionate responses to the suffering of others (Mikulincer et al., 2005). People high on attachment avoidance typically have less empathic reactions to others' suffering, including being less willing to help a distressed person. However, when exposed to a security prime, avoidantly attached people tend to be more prosocial, compassionate, and helping; thus their behavioral responses appear similar to their secure counterparts (eg, Mikulincer et al., 2005). Anxiously attached people are more likely to have an emotional reaction to a person in need. That is, they do not ignore or downplay the event, but rather experience negative affect, a response termed by Batson as *personal distress* (Batson et al., 1987). The negative emotions accompanied by a sense of being overwhelmed by these emotions make anxious people focus inward. Thus, while they may want to help others (in order to stop experiencing negative emotions) they often cannot, because they are overwhelmed by their own distress. This, in turn, leaves anxious individuals in a state where they are not more (or less) likely to provide help. However, when exposed to a security prime anxiously attached people, much like avoidant individuals, show increased levels of caregiving (for similar findings see Mikulincer et al., 2001a, 2003). These findings provide evidence for a possible causal link between attachment security and the tendency to care, such that enhancing one's sense of attachment security increases a person's tendency to be more compassionate and behave in a more prosocial manner.

WHAT ABOUT SEX?

Numerous studies have focused on another interplay between two behavioral systems—attachment and sex (eg, Shaver & Mikulincer, 2012). The function of the *sex system* is to pass the genes from one generation to another via intercourse with an appropriate partner (eg, Buss & Kenrick, 1998). The system is activated by a variety of cues, including being in the presence of an attractive potential mate. The system's responses include approaching such a partner (initiating a relationship/interaction), getting an erection or experiencing vaginal wetness, pelvic thrusting, engaging in sexual activity, and experiencing enjoyable sex (ie, increases in positive mood and approach motivation). For example, Gillath et al., 2008a exposed people to either sex-related words or sexual images (pictures of naked opposite sex members) and then measured their willingness to self-disclose and the accessibility of intimacy-related words. Gillath and colleagues found that participants demonstrated increases across both outcomes following exposure to a sexual prime. These outcomes are thought to be related to initiating new relationships (ie, the propensity to self-disclose and to thinking about intimacy), suggesting that when the sex system is activated, people are more inclined/open to initiate new sexual relations.

In many of the studies focusing on attachment and sex, an association was found between attachment security and higher sexual satisfaction, attentiveness to a partner's sexual needs, openness to experience within the sexual domain (and in general), and a preference for engaging in sex within the boundaries of long-term committed relationships as opposed to short-term relationships (Gillath & Schachner, 2006). Insecure attachment, conversely, was found to be associated with less sexual satisfaction and pleasure, and with sex as means to obtain other nonsex-related goals, such as status, prestige, and enhanced self-esteem. Insecure people are less likely to have sex, less likely to enjoy it, and more likely to feel coerced to do it (Brassard, Shaver, & Lussier, 2007; Karantzas et al., 2016). Avoidant individuals tend to have more uncommitted and nonemotional or distant sex, and have the tendency to poach others' relationship partner. Anxiously attached individuals have an ambivalent approach to sex, and use it as means to gain love, reassurance, and closeness as well as to prevent rejection (eg, Davis, Shaver, & Vernon, 2004). Overall, anxiously attached people seem to conflate sex with love, which may reflect a fusion (or confusion) of the attachment and the sex behavioral systems.

Although there are plenty of studies about attachment and sex, there is relatively less systematic research targeting directly the sex behavioral system and its interplay with attachment (eg, Shaver & Mikulincer, 2012). Birnbaum and Gillath (2006) and Gillath et al. (2008a) have attempted to address these gaps by examining the activation and functioning of the sex system. Specifically they theorized that the system has three main subgoals: initiation (of new sexual relationships), maintenance (of existing relationships), and enjoyment (experiencing sex as fun and harboring a desire to approach a partner for sex). Initiation is meant to generate new relationships or opportunities to have sex. Maintenance is meant to sustain existing relationships so people can have multiple opportunities to engage in sex and thereby increase (1) the probability of fertilization and (2) the likelihood that a couple will stay together and tend to their progeny, which can increase the survival chances of the offspring. Enjoyment is meant to motivate people to continue to engage in sex, and again, increase the chances of fertilization.

Gillath et al. (2008a) and Gillath and Collins (2016) showed that, when the sex system was activated (subliminally or supraliminally), people exhibited tendencies or behaviors in line with the pursuit of the suggested subgoals. For example, in a series of studies, Gillath et al. exposed people to images of naked members of the opposite sex or control images (eg, pictures of the same individuals dressed) and then assessed their willingness to make sacrifices for one's partner, or to use positive conflict-resolution strategies. People exposed to sexual images reported higher willingness to sacrifice and a higher tendency to use positive conflict-resolution strategies than people exposed to the control images. These findings support the idea that when the sex system is activated people are motivated to maintain their romantic relationship.

As with the caregiving system, researchers have examined the interactions between the sex system and the attachment system, and how priming people with attachment security or insecurity cues affects their sexual responses. For example, Gillath and Schachner (2006) reported that priming people with attachment security cues lowered their preference for short-term sexual strategies (such as engaging in a one night stand), and increased their preference for long-term strategies (looking for a long-term partner, or dating the "right" partner). Conversely, priming people with insecurity cues increased people's preferences for short-term strategies, especially among men (Gillath, Landau, Selcuk, & Goldenberg, 2011).

We cannot finish the review about the interplay between attachment and sex without referring, if briefly, to the evolutionary perspective advocated by Lee Kirkpatrick (2005). Kirkpatrick suggested that attachment in adulthood is very different from attachment in childhood. In childhood the function of the system is protection, in adulthood it is similar to that of the sex system—reproduction. Furthermore, adult attachment styles represent, according to Kirkpatrick, one's preference for long- or short-term sexual strategies. In other words, Kirkpatrick suggests that the two systems (attachment and sex) do not simply interact with each other in adulthood, but rather are two manifestations of the same phenomenon.

Another view that has emerged from evolutionary psychology is expressed in the work guided by Life History Theory (see Del Giudice, Gangestad, & Kaplan, 2015; Gillath et al. 2011 for a review). Researchers adopting this view suggest that both attachment style and sexual strategies are shaped by the environment in which people grow up. For example, growing up in a poor and dangerous neighborhood is likely to result in the development of an insecure attachment style and a preference for short-term sexual strategies. These evolutionary-based theories offer an opportunity to broaden the research on the interplay between attachment and sex and challenge existing assumptions about how these behavioral systems are related.

ARE THERE OTHER BEHAVIORAL SYSTEMS AND IF SO, WHAT ABOUT THEIR INTERPLAY?

Whereas Shaver and colleagues (Shaver & Hazan, 1988; Shaver et al., 1988) focused their research on adult pair bonding or romantic love to three behavioral systems (attachment, caregiving, and sex), more and more research has been carried out on other behavioral systems (eg, exploration, affiliation, anger/dominance). It is not clear exactly how many systems exist; people have different opinions on what should be considered as a behavioral system. For example, Leedom (2014) suggested that there are four behavioral systems, each aligned with a different class of social reward. These behavioral systems are the attachment, caregiving, dominance, and sex systems. Each of these systems organizes humans' processing of social information and the coordination of responses. In addition to the systems just noted, it has been suggested by some that behavioral systems extend beyond the social realm and can include systems associated with domains such as the physical functioning of an individual. For example, Leedom (2014) and Schaller and Duncan (2007) propose the existence of physical systems such as the feeding system and the immune behavioral system. Does this mean that anything can be described as a behavioral system?

According to Hinde (2005), the behavioral systems framework can be used broadly to describe various behaviors. The framework conceptualizes "the motivation and control of a group of behavior patterns that are closely and more or less causally (and often also functionally) related to each other" (Hinde et al.,

2005, p. 6). As long as the behavior is goal-directed and the characteristics of the "system" meet the qualifications outlined previously (see also Leedom, 2014 for additional conditions) then it is possible for any number of organized behavioral patterns to constitute a behavioral system. In the current chapter, however, we only focus on the systems that have been studied with regards to attachment.

The Exploration Behavioral System

The research regarding the links between attachment and other behavioral systems such as the exploration, affiliation, and anger systems, especially among adults, is quite sparse. For example, a handful of studies have examined the links between attachment and exploration in adults. The goal of the *exploration behavioral system* is to curiously explore and learn about the environment. Ainsworth et al. (1978) based the strange situation task—used to classify infants into attachment styles—on the interplay between the attachment and the exploration systems. Ainsworth's assumption was that secure infants tend to explore their environment, whereas infants who feel insecure do not. However, neither she nor other researchers that followed investigated the exploration system among adults. The first researchers to address this limitation were Green and Campbell (2000). They found that both attachment anxiety and avoidance were negatively correlated with willingness to explore the environment. Green and Campbell found similar results for different types of exploration, namely, social exploration (eg, I would like the chance to meet strangers), intellectual exploration (eg, I would like to go to a modern art museum), and environmental exploration (eg, If I had the time and money, I would like to travel overseas this summer). They also found that people who were primed with security were more open to exploration.

Elliot and Reis (2003) found similar results. Their work focused on integrating the exploration system as discussed within attachment theory with R. W. White's (1959) concept of effectance motivation (also known as competence motivation or mastery). Elliot and Reis also integrated the constructs of motives and goals as part of their research given their central importance in the achievement motivation literature. Then they reported four studies in which attachment security was found to be associated with achievement motivations (positively with need for achievement and negatively with fear of failure), and goals (positively associated with mastery-approach goals, and negatively with mastery-avoidance and performance-avoidance goals). Attachment insecurity was associated with a low need for achievement and a high fear of failure. Insecurity was also positively associated with mastery-avoidance and performance-avoidance goals, and negatively associated with approach-personal goals and mastery-approach goals.

Insecurity was also found to be associated with lower trait curiosity (Mikulincer, 1997), lower creativity following induction of positive affect (Mikulincer & Sheffi, 2000), and lower cognitive openness and higher dogmatic thinking

(Mikulincer, 1997). Coy, Green, and Davis (2012) showed that attachment style affected duration and enjoyment of exploration, such that insecurity was associated with shorter duration and less enjoyment. Gillath et al. (2008b) found that the contextual activation of security via repeated security priming was also associated with exploration in the form of people's creativity. Specifically, Gillath and colleagues reported that individuals that were repeatedly primed with security demonstrated higher creativity as compared with a control group. Focusing on exploration, but its interplay with caregiving rather than attachment, Feeney (2004) showed that responsive (nonintrusive) caregiving by a relationship partner in response to an individual's goal strivings and explorations, resulted in greater happiness, self-esteem, and perceived likelihood of achieving specific goals by the target individual.

The Affiliation Behavioral System

Another behavioral system thought to be related to attachment is the *affiliation behavioral system* (Gillath & Karantzas, 2015; Weiss, 1998). The affiliation system is thought to promote survival by motivating people to socialize with others. Being sociable protects humans and nonhumans from predators, increases the likelihood of finding mates, and enhances people's abilities to collect food, build shelter, and explore the environment (Cassidy, 2008; Mikulincer & Selinger, 2001). According to Weiss (1998) the affiliation system fulfills various social functions, including: (1) companionship and friendship; (2) development of knowledge and skills; (3) intellectual and social stimulation; (4) engagement in diverse social activities such as play; and (5) development of alliances to defend against protagonists or outgroup members. Mikulincer and Selinger (2001) argued that the affiliation system is activated when a person is in a good mood and there is no immediate source of stress; however, Mikulincer and Selinger did not mention a specific trigger, and did not provide any information regarding when people are likely to initiate new relationships. For example, are they more likely to initiate a new friendship when they are having a good time with someone, or when they feel lonely and in need of company?

When describing the interplay between the attachment and the affiliation behavioral systems, Bowlby (1982) coined the concept "attachment-affiliation balance." Affiliation behavior is enacted during periods when an individual is in a state of felt security, which means the attachment system is in a state of deactivation. However, when an individual experiences distress or threat and the attachment system is activated, affiliation behaviors (in a similar fashion to behaviors guided by other behavioral systems such as the caregiving; eg, Gillath et al., 2005b) are inhibited. Insecurity is thought to interfere with and even inhibit affiliation activities. Insecure individuals are self-focused, preoccupied with their relationship concerns or have difficulties trusting one's partner— characteristics that can be disruptive for affiliation behaviors (Mikulincer

& Selinger, 2001). Conversely, attachment security fosters engagement in affiliation behaviors—perceiving others not only as a source of security, but also as meeting nonattachment needs such as companionship and other social or instrumental needs.

Gillath and Karantzas (2015) have recently suggested that the interplay between the attachment and affiliation systems can be successfully examined via the prism of social networks in at least two different ways. First, attachment figures are thought to be a part of one's attachment network (ties that fulfill people's needs for love, comfort, and security, see chapter: What Is an Attachment Relationship?), which in turn is a part of people's general network (Dunbar & Spoors, 1995; Sutcliffe, Dunbar, Binder, & Arrow, 2012). Gillath and Karantzas suggested that members of one's general social network can gradually become members of the attachment network (or become attachment figures), as people learn to trust each other and the closeness between them increases. This is especially likely to happen during life transitions, when people may lose contact with their old ties or become separated from their existing attachment figures.

A different way that attachment and networks are linked is similar to the interaction we describe above between levels of (in)security and the functioning of other behavioral systems. Specifically, attachment style may predict the perception and management of social networks. To examine this proposition, Gillath and Karantzas (2015) conducted a study in which they asked participants to complete various self-report measures on social networks. Participants first listed anywhere between 10 and 30 people with whom they shared an acquaintance and who were thus part of their social network. They were then asked to rate their closeness to each person as well as their perceptions of the closeness between all pairs of network members. Measures were also administered to assess the extent that network members fulfilled various attachment and affiliative functions as well as the frequency with which network members interacted with one another. These assessments allowed Gillath and Karantzas to compute a series of social network indices. These indices included network density (the extent to which network members were known to one another), tie strength (the closeness experienced between network members), and multiplexity (the number of social functions that network members fulfill). Participants also completed a self-report measure of attachment.

Gillath and Karantzas found that attachment anxiety was negatively correlated with network density and tie strength. These findings suggest that anxiously attached individuals' perceptions of network ties share similarities with their appraisals of their romantic relationships—thus anxious people perceive the ties between themselves and network members as lacking closeness. Attachment avoidance was not associated with closeness or density, but rather it was negatively associated with multiplexity. Gillath and Karantzas suggested that the concerns about trust that avoidant individuals harbor as part of their dyadic relationships may apply broadly to their connections with social network members. That is, rather than trusting one or a few close others to fulfill all their attachment and affiliative functions, they use a large number of close others—each fulfilling only one or a limited amount of functions, which results in low multiplexity. Avoidance was also associated with initiating fewer new ties, and dissolving a greater number of existing ties. Overall, these findings suggest that insecurity hinders the functioning of the affiliation behavioral system.

The Power Behavioral System

The *power behavioral system* is another system likely to interact with the attachment system. According to Shaver, Segev, and Mikulincer (2011) the goal of the system is to gain or control materials and social resources in a world of competitors or thwarters. The triggers of the system include (1) attempts by others to acquire one's valuable psychological or physical resources and (2) efforts by others to constrain one's access to such resources. Once the system is activated, it motivates people to engage in behaviors aimed at protecting or restoring resources and regaining a sense of control or influence. This motivation manifests in behaviors such as asserting dominance, expressing confidence in one's strengths, deterring others from competing for or exerting control over one's resources, and verbally or physically attacking (or threatening to attack) others (eg, Gilbert, 2000).

While there is no research explicitly investigating the associations between the attachment and power behavioral systems, some insights regarding the interplay between these systems can be gleaned from research investigating associations between attachment and anger. For example, in a study by Diamond and Hicks (2005), attachment anxiety was found to be positively associated with outbursts of anger, aggression, and violence. People high on anxiety reported more anger and had lower vagal tone (a physiological indicator of the downregulation of negative emotions) during and after anger-provoking tasks. These findings suggest that individuals high on attachment anxiety exhibit hyperactivation of the power system, reflected in intense anger that is difficult to subdue. Simpson, Rholes, and Phillips (1996) found a similar association between anxiety and anger, among dating couples who discussed an unresolved problem in their relationship. Attachment anxiety has also been found to be a predictor of domestic violence, antisocial behavior (such as delinquency and criminality), and intergroup aggression (see Mikulincer & Shaver, 2007a, for a review).

Similar associations have been reported between avoidant attachment and variables thought to index the hyperactivation of the power system (Simpson et al., 1996). For instance, avoidant individuals have been found to express hostility toward others, but also to perceive others as hostile (Mikulincer, 1998a,b).

The Health Behavioral System and the Morality Behavioral System

Two other potential behavioral systems for which we provide a cursory note are the *health behavioral system* and the *morality behavioral system*. With regard to health, the system's goal is to promote health and reduce health risks such as exposure to diseases and pathogens (see Schaller & Park, 2011). There are many studies about attachment style and health. These studies generally demonstrate a positive correlation between attachment insecurity and symptom reporting, lower health-care utilization, and restriction of daily living activities (eg, Feeney, 2000; Kidd & Sheffield, 2005; Sakaluk & Gillath, 2016). Furthermore, attachment insecurity has been shown in numerous studies to be associated with poor well-being and psychopathology (eg, Dozier, Stovall-McClough, & Albus, 2008, see chapter: What Are the Implications of Attachment Processes for Psychopathology and Therapy?). In other words, attachment insecurity may hamper or hinder the functioning of the health system.

With regard to morality, the system's goal seems to be in between those of the caregiving and the health behavioral systems, promoting authenticity, honesty, and morality (eg, van IJzendoorn, 1997). A few researchers have shown that attachment security is positively associated with moral reasoning and authenticity whereas insecurity is negatively associated with these constructs. For example, Cole (2001) found that insecure attachment was associated with dishonesty, and similarly, Lopez and Rice (2006) found that both attachment anxiety and avoidance were inversely related to unwillingness to engage in or accept deceptive and inaccurate self and partner representations. Gillath, Sesko, Shaver, and Chun (2010) showed that priming people with security reduces their propensity to lie and increases their authenticity.

Readers may wonder how many behavioral systems are out there and whether anything and everything can be considered a behavioral system. For example, does JavaScript programming qualify as a behavioral system? Do people's sleep-wake cycles reflect another kind of behavioral system? The list of potential behavioral systems can go on and on. Likewise, readers may wonder what we as a field gain by describing findings regarding attachment and other behaviors, like aggression, in terms of the interactions between behavioral systems (eg, attachment and power). Readers may also wonder why we touched on the interplay of attachment and anger/power, for example, rather than the interplay between attachment and other emotions. Starting with the last question first, in this chapter we only covered findings from studies in which researchers had explicitly acknowledged and defined that their investigation involved understanding the functioning of a behavioral system. There might be other behavioral systems we have not covered in this chapter, like for example a nutrition behavioral system (Wilkinson, Rowe, Bishop, & Brunstrom, 2010); however there is not enough work currently to allow a fuller discussion of such systems here. Therefore, we do not know, and perhaps may never know, how many behavioral systems (or modules) are in existence (some scholars write about hundreds; Schmitt & Pilcher, 2004). As for the question "Can anything be described as a behavioral system?"—the short answer is "no," the long answer however is "it is complicated." Any set of behaviors (ie, not one behavior) that were shaped over the course of evolutionary history, and are organized around the six criteria described earlier in this chapter (eg, having a function, triggers, responses, goals), can qualify as a behavioral system. However, readers must keep in mind that a behavioral system has to be species universal, functional (ie, contribute to the organism's survival and reproduction), innate, and motivate goal-corrected behavior. These criteria limit the possibilities of what constitutes a behavioral system. Further research is needed before more specific conclusions can be drawn. We next summarize the work we have reviewed throughout the chapter and suggest ways it can be applied to other systems in the future.

IMPLICATIONS AND CONCLUSIONS

The current chapter reviewed the different behavioral systems and their interplay (mainly with regard to the attachment system). Overall there are many similarities in the ways the different behavioral systems interact with the attachment system. Bowlby (1982) suggested that attachment security is a basis for the development and functioning of other behavioral systems. Bowlby further suggested that the operation of different behavioral systems is connected by excitatory or inhibitory links, such that activation of one system can activate or deactivate other systems. As reviewed in this chapter, various scholars have conducted studies that support Bowlby's claims regarding the interplay between behavioral systems. Although we focused on attachment, other systems interact as well. For example, a new potential mate, which triggers the sex system, may also activate the exploration system, resulting in exploration of interests and desires, which may further facilitate the formation of a sexual relationship (Mikulincer & Shaver, 2009).

Multiple systems can lead to the same or a similar behavioral outcome. Thus, a behavior such as moving physically closer to another person can be motivated by the attachment system—if, for example, the intent is to obtain support, comfort, or relief from threats and stressors. However, it can be also motivated by the sex system—if the intent is to increase the likelihood of sexual intercourse. In other words, we may describe and study each system separately, but in real life the systems are much more entwined—and it is often hard to know what certain behaviors mean because of the multicausal nature of things.

It is also important to note that the functioning of behavioral systems yields both visible outcomes in the form of physical acts (eg, seeking out protection and care) and invisible outcomes such as the subjective feelings that are associated with physical acts (eg, experiencing felt security after seeking out protection). So even when a system is activated, a person may not show overt changes. This does not mean that changes are not taking place on a cognitive or affective level. Furthermore, some of these changes may be long term, so for example, activation of the caregiving system in the long run may affect the attachment system by making people more secure (Gillath et al., 2008b).

In summary, the behavioral systems model is a comprehensive model of personality, motivation, and social behavior, which considers both individual differences and the impact of the environment (relationship partners, characteristics of the social situation, etc.) on one's behavior. By conceptualizing behavior in terms of goals and the social-cognitive regulation of goal-directed behavior, Bowlby (1982) laid the foundation for a behavioral systems approach to the study of human relationships, and potentially a comprehensive theory of motivation.

Chapter 9

What Are the Effects
of Context on Attachment?

"The great strength of attachment theory in guiding research is that it focuses on a basic system of behavior—the attachment system—that is biologically rooted and thus species-characteristic. This implies a search for basic processes of functioning universal in human nature, despite differences attributable to genetic constitution, cultural influences, and individual experience."

~ Ainsworth, 1991, p. 33

The aforementioned quote by Mary Ainsworth emphasizes the idea that the attachment system is assumed to be biologically based and active in all humans. And although some researchers have followed Ainsworth's lead and focused on the normative aspects of attachment, there is an emerging sense that the way attachment is expressed can, in fact, vary in interesting ways across contexts. Thus, while humans may have evolved a behavioral system that functions similarly from person to person, Bowlby's emphasis on the dynamic nature of internal working models (see chapter: What Are Attachment Working Models?) makes it clear that context is likely to play an important role in shaping individual differences in attachment.

In this chapter we review a number of contextual factors that have been studied in attachment research. Before delving into a review of the literature it is important to note that our goal in this chapter is not to review all the contexts that have been studied. Rather, our focus is on specific contexts that have either received significant attention in the literature or have important implications for our understanding of adult attachment. In particular, we focus on gender, culture, age, relationship status and length, and one of the most widely studied contexts in adult attachment, romantic relationships. In chapters: How Stable Are Attachment Styles in Adulthood? and To What are the Implications of Attachment Processes for Psychopathology and Therapy?, we also address other important contextual factors, such as the experience of traumatic events, mental health concerns, and stressful life events.

Adult Attachment. http://dx.doi.org/10.1016/B978-0-12-420020-3.00009-8

ARE THERE SEX DIFFERENCES IN ADULT ATTACHMENT?

The question of whether adult attachment differs as a function of sex is one that has been considered extensively over the years. Interest in this issue has emerged due to research in psychology more broadly (social psychology, personality, developmental, and evolutionary psychology) that has found sex differences between men and women in the way they think and act in relationships (eg, Dunbar & Machin, 2014). This research suggests that men are more emotionally guarded than women, and women are more invested in their relationships than men. Because people who are avoidantly attached are also less invested in their relationships compared to those who are secure, it is possible that attachment styles could reflect sex-based biological differences or gender norms rather than attachment-related experiences in particular.

Until recently, attachment researchers have largely been of the view that there are no reliable differences between the sexes when it comes to adult attachment (eg, Beckes & Simpson, 2009; Penke, 2009). Indeed, Bowlby (1969/1982) did not make any claims regarding sex differences in the normative and non-normative functioning of the attachment system. Studies investigating sex differences in attachment anxiety and avoidance either find no differences (eg, Conradi, Gerlsma, van Duijn, & de Jonge, 2006; Donnellan, Burt, Levendosky, & Klump; 2008; Wei, Russell, Mallinckrodt, & Zakalik, 2004) or differences appear small to moderate (ie, effect sizes usually range in magnitude between $d = 0.01$ and $d = 0.40$; eg, Lopez, 2001; Rogers, Bidwell, & Wilson, 2005).

However, scholars such as Del Giudice (2009a,b) and Kirkpatrick (1998) have suggested that attachment in adulthood may be manifestations of mating strategies known to differ between the sexes. As a way of formalizing these suggestions, Del Giudice (2009a,b) proposed a model based on life history theory (Belsky, Steinberg, & Draper, 1991) and sexual selection that makes predictions regarding sex differences in adult attachment. This model has received considerable attention in recent years (eg, Del Giudice & Belsky, 2010; Ein-Dor, Mikulincer, Doron, & Shaver, 2010; Hoeve et al., 2012). A central premise of Del Giudice's model is that sex differences in attachment should only be expected amongst insecurely attached individuals. Specifically, Del Giudice suggests that harsh and unpredictable environments lead people to adopt a fast life strategy, a strategy that involves greater risk-taking and faster sexual maturation in order to accelerate the opportunities for reproduction in an uncertain environment. As part of this life strategy, individuals typically reach sexual maturation sooner, engage in sex earlier, and engage in more uncommitted and casual sex compared to individuals exposed to stable and predictable environments (Belsky et al., 1991).

According to Del Giudice (2011; see also Jackson & Kirkpatrick, 2007) a fast life strategy is characterized by a short-term relationship orientation (ie, engagement in uncommitted and casual sexual encounters), and is thought to reflect a strategy more commonly used by men and people high on attachment avoidance. In contrast, because women are generally the primary caregivers of offspring, a fast life strategy in women not only includes some of the characteristics already described (ie, short-term relationship orientation, uncommitted sexual encounters), but also entails eliciting the attention of mates to assist with parenting. Thus for women, a fast life strategy shares similarities with attachment anxiety in that women become more preoccupied with their relationship partners. Del Giudice (2011) notes however that under extremely stressful and dangerous contexts, in which parental investment may not result in the successful survival of progeny, insecurely attached women would also default to a strategy resembling attachment avoidance.

In the context of stable and nonharsh environments, few if any gender differences are expected because the reproductive strategies of men and women should converge with both sexes demonstrating high parental investment and a long-term orientation toward romantic relationships. This life strategy (also known as a slow life strategy) is thought to resemble attachment security (Del Giudice, 2009a, 2011).

Del Giudice (2011) makes an important point about his model: on average, sex differences in adult attachment should be small, as approximately two-thirds of people demonstrate attachment security (eg, van IJzendoorn & Bakermans-Kranenburg, 1996), and thus are likely to develop in safe, supportive, and predictable environments. However, sizable sex differences in adult attachment should emerge when data are analyzed as a function of contexts indicative of high environmental stress.

To test these predictions, Del Giudice (2011) conducted a meta-analysis that included 100 studies investigating sex differences in adult romantic attachment. The average effect sizes for sex differences in adult attachment were weak ($d = -0.04$ for attachment anxiety, and $d = 0.02$ for attachment avoidance). However, substantial variability was found in these effect sizes as a function of geographic regions. For example, in some regions that were deemed harsh or unpredictable (eg, the Middle East and parts of Europe) the sex differences were larger (eg, ds = 0.28 to 0.34) than in more stable and predictable regions (eg, North America; ds = 0.10). Across unstable regions, men demonstrated higher attachment avoidance compared to females, whereas females demonstrated higher attachment anxiety than males. According to Del Giudice (2011), the findings of the meta-analysis provided support for his life-history take on sex differences in adult attachment. Recently, Del Giudice (2016) has found further support for his model, demonstrating that sex differences appear even more pronounced when attachment is analyzed at the facet level (ie, decomposing attachment style into more fine-grained factors such as self-reliance, discomfort with closeness, preoccupation, and alike) rather than at the broad level of attachment anxiety and avoidance. In summary, Del Giudice's findings suggest that small but reliable sex differences exist in attachment style, but only in contexts indicative of environmental harshness or unpredictability. In these environments, insecure men are characterized by greater attachment avoidance whereas insecure women are characterized by greater attachment anxiety.

Other researchers have interpreted observed sex differences in attachment from a social-developmental perspective rather than from an evolutionary standpoint. In particular, some suggest that sex differences in attachment insecurity may be a product of gender stereotypes (eg, Eagly & Steffen, 1984; Feeney & Noller, 1996; Karantzas et al., 2016). For example, males high in attachment avoidance demonstrate exaggerated features of the masculine gender role such that they are overly self-reliant and minimize the display of emotion or react with little emotion within the context of relationships. In contrast, females high in attachment anxiety display exaggerated features of the feminine gender role such that they are overly emotionally available, and place great emphasis on intimacy. Some theorists contend that gender differences may vary as a function of culture. In which case, these differences will be larger in cultures that more readily endorse masculine and feminine stereotypes. While this may indeed be the case, social-developmental accounts of gender differences in attachment say little about whether the harshness and unpredictability that may be associated with particular cultures or regions around the world play a role in determining sex differences. Given these competing explanations, future work into sex differences in attachment should attempt to test whether evolutionary or social-developmental accounts are better equipped to explain such differences.

In a related line of work, researchers have investigated whether the associations between attachment insecurity and various outcomes, such as partner support, sexual coercion, and communication are related to sex differences. Generally, no consistent sex differences are found for associations between adult attachment style and relationship outcomes (eg, Donovan & Emmers-Sommer, 2012; Karantzas, Feeney, Goncalves, & McCabe, 2014; Karantzas et al., 2016). For example, in a study of heterosexual couples, Karantzas et al. (2014) found no sex differences in actor effects linking attachment anxiety and avoidance with partner support and trust. In contrast, in a meta-analysis examining the association between adult attachment style and sexual coercion, Karantzas et al. (2015c) found that attachment avoidance in men was associated with the perpetration of sexual coercion, while no such association was found for women.

Summary

Del Giudice's meta-analytic work suggests that, although sex differences are small and not easy to detect in individual studies, there are sex differences in adult attachment styles. Namely, men are more likely to demonstrate attachment insecurity in the form of attachment avoidance while women demonstrate insecurity in the form of attachment anxiety. Evolutionary perspectives that incorporate life history theory and sexual strategies may be especially important in understanding sex differences in attachment. Del Giudice (2011) suggests that the sex-neutral assumptions about adult attachment require revision to acknowledge variation in attachment as a function of sex. Although this is a reasonable conclusion based on the existing literature, van IJzendoorn and colleagues (eg, Bakermans-Kranenburg & van IJzendoorn, 2009; van IJzendoorn & Bak-ermans-Kranenburg, 2010) claim that there is too much inconsistency in the findings to draw any firm conclusions regarding sex differences. So the most appropriate way forward may be to take a conservative approach to claims re-garding sex differences in adult attachment. Namely, differences may well exist but they are likely to be pretty small at best.

ARE THERE CULTURAL DIFFERENCES IN ADULT ATTACHMENT?

According to Bowlby (1969/1982) the attachment system is an evolved behav-ioral system that governs the development and maintenance of the bond between an individual and his or her primary caregiver. Thus, all humans, regardless of cultural context, have the ability to form attachment bonds. However, research-ers have been interested in determining whether individual differences in adult attachment differ across cultures (eg, Schmitt et al., 2004). The premise behind this research is that cultural differences including, but not limited to, parenting practices, the expression of emotion, and the collectivist or individualist nature of cultures may influence the degree to which individual differences in adult attachment are expressed. Differences as a function of culture may then have important implications for how broad contextual factors impact the way in which individual differences in attachment develop and are maintained.

To date, considerable attempts have been made to understand the role of culture in the study of attachment. When it comes to the relative distributions of attachment styles in different cultures, some studies find no differences where-as other studies demonstrate clear cultural variability. For instance, a study by Doherty, Hatfield, Thompson, and Choo (1994) did not find significant differ-ences in the distribution of attachment styles across cultures (ie, European-Americans, Japanese-Americans, Chinese-Americans, and Pacific Islanders). Doherty and colleagues found that across cultures, over 60% of individuals were classified as secure, approximately 25% were classified as avoidant, and 8% were classified as anxious. Meta-analytic studies (that focused on AAI as-sessments of attachment) have found similar distributions in attachment styles across cultures (eg, van IJzendoorn & Bakermans-Kranenburg, 1996, 2010).

Schmitt and colleagues (Schmitt, 2008, 2011; Schmitt et al., 2004) con-ducted one of the most comprehensive studies of culture and attachment and found cultural variability in adult attachment. Specifically, Schmitt and col-leagues studied over 17,000 individuals across 62 cultures from 11 regions around the world. They found that secure attachment was the most prevalent adult attachment style in 79% of cultures. However, preoccupied attachment was more prevalent in East Asian countries compared to other regions (Schmitt et al., 2004; Schmitt, 2011). Dismissive attachment was more prevalent in coun-tries located in Africa and Southeast Asia (Schmitt et al., 2004; Schmitt, 2008).

Other studies have reported cross-cultural differences in adult attachment. A number of these studies have focused on comparing African-American, Asian, and

Hispanic cultures with Caucasian or European-American cultures. For example, there are a number of studies that find African-Americans rate higher on attachment avoidance than European Americans (eg, Lopez, Melendez, & Rice, 2000; Magai et al., 2001; Wei et al., 2004). Other studies suggest that people in some Asian cultures, such as Japan and Korea, report higher attachment anxiety than people in Western cultures (eg, You & Malley-Morrison, 2000). For example, Agishtein and Brumbaugh (2013) found that individuals who identified themselves as Asian rated significantly higher on attachment anxiety compared with other ethnicities (eg, Asian-Indian, African-American, Caucasian, and Hispanic), while no ethnic differences emerged in terms of attachment avoidance. Interestingly, greater identification with one's culture was negatively associated with both attachment anxiety and attachment avoidance. However, other studies conducted on Asian cultures report different findings. For instance, Kim and Zane (2004) found that individuals of Korean descent reported higher attachment avoidance than people of European backgrounds. In relation to people of Hispanic background, Wei et al. (2004) found Hispanic-Americans to be higher on attachment anxiety compared to Caucasians, while Lopez et al. (2000) found differences in attachment avoidance but not in attachment anxiety between the two cultural groups.

In a related line of work, Mak, Bond, Simpson, and Rholes (2010) and You et al. (2015) examined the extent to which cultural differences moderated the direct and indirect effects of attachment anxiety and avoidance on depression. Across these studies, partner support, relationship satisfaction (Mak et al., 2010), and relational conflict (You et al., 2015) were examined as mediators of the direct associations between attachment and depressive symptoms. Analyses revealed that partner support and relational conflict mediated the link between attachment avoidance and depressive symptoms to a greater extent in the Hong Kong-Chinese sample relative to the sample from the United States.

Some scholars (eg, Agishtein & Brumbaugh, 2013) have suggested that the differences found between cultures reflect variation in different socio-developmental factors. For example, African-Americans tend to respond more punitively to emotional expression than Caucasians (Montague, Magai, Consedine, & Gillespie, 2003). This, in turn, may contribute to higher levels of avoidance, and to the variability in attachment avoidance between cultures. Similarly, differences in attachment anxiety between Eastern and Western cultures may reflect variation in individualism versus collectivism (ie, the extent to which cultural norms emphasize the goals of the individual above the goals of groups versus cultures where the goals of groups are prioritized above the goals of a given individual). The highly interdependent nature of collectivist cultures may place a greater emphasis on seeking the approval of others and maintaining vigilant monitoring of their relationships with others than is the case in individualist cultures (Markus & Kitayama, 1991). To this end, attachment avoidance may be viewed as more problematic in collectivist cultures as it explicitly violates cultural norms of investing in and tending to one's relationships (Mak et al., 2010; You et al., 2015).

Schmitt and colleagues (eg, Schmitt, 2008, 2011; Schmitt, 2005) suggest that differences in attachment avoidance (ie, dismissing attachment) across cultures may be best explained through life history theory and sexual mating strategies. Drawing on the work of Belsky et al. (1991), Schmitt (2005) suggest that attachment avoidance, and a focus on short-term mating strategies, are likely adaptations to harsh/high-stress environments. In support of this explanation, Schmitt et al. (2004) found that regions of high stress (characterized by low Gross Domestic Product output, lower life expectancy, higher incidence of infectious disease, lower adult literacy, and political freedom) had a higher proportion of individuals with a dismissing attachment style. These ideas are similar to the explanations proposed by Del Giudice (2009a, 2011) regarding sex differences.

Discrepant findings across studies investigating the same culture require a different explanation, however. Oftentimes, discrepancies may reflect sampling differences between studies. For example, some studies of Asian cultures, such as Japan or Korea, are conducted with residents who still live in Japan or Korea. In contrast, other studies include participants whose ethnic background is Japanese or Korean, but who reside in a Western society such as the United States. Potentially the different findings in studies on similar culture groups are due to the different origins of the samples.

Summary

The findings relating to culture and adult attachment suggest that cultural differences are not always found. Explanations for why cultural differences exist are largely speculative. That is, researchers make assumptions about why culture may moderate individual differences in adult attachment but these assumptions are rarely operationalized and tested as part of studies. Studies that test these assumptions are likely to significantly advance our understanding as to the precise mechanisms by which culture influences adult attachment.

ARE THERE AGE DIFFERENCES IN ADULT ATTACHMENT?

Bowlby believed that attachment was relevant across the lifespan. And although researchers have studied attachment in samples of various ages (eg, children, young adults), only recently have researchers begun to explore the way in which attachment styles might vary across age periods. This kind of research is important because it can help us understand whether attachment plays out differently at various stages of the lifespan. It may be that age differences reflect the impact of important developmental tasks and transitions that tap into attachment-related processes and experiences such as the transition to marriage or parenthood, or dealing with the loss of a spouse after illness during old age (Chopik & Edelstein, 2014; Karantzas, Feeney & Wilkinson, 2010; Magai, 2008).

Over the last two decades, a small but nonetheless important body of research has built up to address the question of age differences in attachment during different stages of adulthood (eg, Antonucci, Akiyma, & Takahashi, 2004; Diehl, Elnick, Bourbeau, & Labouvie-Vief, 1998; Karantzas et al., 2010). Using either interview or self-report measures of attachment, studies suggest that individuals in middle to late adulthood report higher attachment avoidance (or dismissing attachment) compared to young adults and youth (Kafetsios & Sideridis, 2006; Magai, Hunziker, Mesias, & Culver, 2000; Magai et al., 2001; Mickelson, Kessler, & Shaver, 1997; Segal, Needham, & Coolidge, 2009; Webster, 1997; Wensauer & Grossmann, 1995). In contrast young adults report significantly higher attachment anxiety (or preoccupied attachment) compared to adults in the middle or later stages of life (Kafetsios & Sideridis, 2006; Magai et al., 2001; Mickelson et al., 1997; Segal et al., 2009). Some studies find no age differences in adult attachment (eg, Consedine & Magai, 2003; Montague et al., 2003; Noftle & Shaver, 2006). Like with sex and culture, it is unclear whether inconsistencies reflect differences in methodology and measurement of attachment (ie, categorical versus self-report assessments), differences in sample sizes across studies (see Van Assche et al., 2013), or the actual lack of age-related differences.

In an attempt to address the limitations and inconsistencies of past research, Chopik, Edelstein, and Fraley (2013) conducted a large-scale study ($N > 86,000$) investigating age differences in adult attachment. In line with a number of previous studies, young adults tended to score significantly higher on attachment anxiety compared with middle and older adults. Attachment avoidance was found to be higher in middle adults and lower in both young adults and older adults (though the differences between age groups for avoidance were smaller compared to the age differences for attachment anxiety). Chopik and Edelstein (2014) replicated these age group findings using a similarly large sample ($N > 90,000$). Furthermore, they found little difference in these findings across cultures, suggesting the trends observed as a function of age appear to be universal.

Research into age differences in adult attachment is largely based on cross-sectional findings, with little by way of longitudinal research to systematically investigate age groups across time. However, existing longitudinal studies provide findings consistent with those emerging from cross-sectional studies. For example, in a 6-year longitudinal study, Zhang and Labouvie-Vief (2004) found that while attachment demonstrated a high degree of average stability over this period, older adults compared to younger adults became either more avoidant or secure and less anxious over time. Likewise, in a 25-year longitudinal study of women, Klohnen and John (1998) found attachment anxiety to decrease as individuals aged.

The evidence to date suggests that there are modest but consistent differences in adult attachment as a function of age. This raises the question of why age differences exist. A number of explanations have been proposed. Chopik et al. (2013) and Karantzas and colleagues (Karantzas & Cole, 2011; Karantzas et al., 2010) suggest that age differences in attachment may reflect normative age-related developmental imperatives. That is, it may be developmentally appropriate, even functional, for levels of attachment anxiety and avoidance to spike and attenuate at different ages. Having a slightly heightened level of anxiety during young adulthood may serve to assist with emotional bonding during the development of new romantic relationships. In fact, the forming of long-term adult relationships is regarded as a novel but key developmental task for young adults according to major lifespan developmental theories (eg, Erikson, 1968; Havighurst, 1972; Levinson, 1986). Therefore, the uncertainty regarding how romantic relationships should be navigated is likely to manifest in some trepidation and ambivalence for young adults. As individuals become more mature and experienced in navigating romantic relationships, attachment anxiety may attenuate, that is, people become more secure in themselves, their relationships, and their skills and abilities to manage relationships.

In relation to attachment avoidance, Chopik et al. (2013) suggest that higher levels of avoidance in middle adulthood relative to young adulthood may be indicative of developmental processes associated with individuation. While individuation begins in young adulthood, it may be that it is consolidated and manifested in middle adulthood (eg, Buhl, 2008). Alternatively, Magai and colleagues (eg, Fiori, Consedine, & Magai, 2009; Magai, 2008; Magai et al., 2001) propose that increases in attachment avoidance as a function of age may reflect person by environment interactions. Specifically, socio-historical factors (such as the Great Depression and the World Wars) may have meant that older generations have experienced significant life adversity and interpersonal losses. These difficult life circumstances may have given primacy to self-reliance and the need to develop a sense of stoicism. These personal responses to harsh contexts may manifest in the form of attachment avoidance. While Magai and colleagues frame their explanation in socio-historical terms, this explanation resonates with the life history perspectives proposed by Del Giudice (2011) and Schmitt (2005) in their discussion of sex and cultural differences. That is, environments characterized by greater harshness and unpredictability may bias individuals to demonstrate greater attachment avoidance during middle adulthood and possibly beyond.

Summary

Evidence suggests that age has a small to moderate but consistent association with individual differences in adult attachment. Specifically, attachment anxiety appears to peak in young adulthood while attachment avoidance seems most pronounced during middle adulthood. We reviewed a number of the proposed explanations for these age differences in adult attachment. The explanations put forward by attachment researchers largely focus on normative age-related processes or on the role of socio-historical factors. We further contend that socio-historical explanations share much in common with life history perspectives. Thus, it appears that development, historical, and evolutionary perspectives may provide important insights into future research examining age-related differences in adult attachment.

WHAT IS THE ROLE OF RELATIONSHIP STATUS AND RELATIONSHIP LENGTH IN ADULT ATTACHMENT?

There exists a significant body of research demonstrating that people who are in a romantic relationship experience a greater number of physical and mental health benefits than people who are single (eg, deVaus, 2002; Holt-Lunstad, Birmingham, & Jones, 2008; Uecker, 2012). Various relationship theorists contend that the benefits associated with being in a romantic relationship tap into humans' innate needs for social affiliation, love, and comfort (eg, Baumeister & Leary, 1995; MacDonald & Leary, 2005). The research outlined in chapter: What Is an Attachment Relationship? suggests that romantic partners assume the role of the primary attachment figure in adulthood, and are relied upon to fulfill various attachment functions (eg, Doherty & Feeney, 2004; Pitman & Scharfe, 2010). It thus stands to reason that relationship status (eg, single, dating, cohabiting, married) and relationship length may be important factors that influence individual differences in adult attachment.

Attempts specifically aimed at investigating the role of relationship status and relationship length in romantic adult attachment are few and far between. However, in recent years, there has been increasing interest in understanding how relationship involvement (either the type of relationship people are in [eg, cohabiting, married], or the time spent together) moderates adult attachment. The research conducted to date demonstrates some consistency in the moderating role of relationship status, but little by way of consistency in terms of relationship length.

Relationship Status

A number of studies have found that people in romantic relationships report lower attachment anxiety and attachment avoidance compared to people who are not in a relationship (eg, Edelstein & Gillath, 2008). In a study of Polish young adults, Adamczyk and Bookwala (2013) found that partnered individuals demonstrated significantly lower attachment anxiety than single individuals. A similar finding was reported by Brown and Trevethan (2010) who found that single gay men reported greater attachment insecurity (higher levels of attachment anxiety and avoidance) compared to gay men that had been previously married. The cross-cultural work of Schmitt and colleagues (Schmitt, 2011; Schmitt et al., 2004) demonstrated that a higher proportion of secure attachment was found amongst partnered individuals (steady dating, cohabiting, engaged, married) compared to individuals who were single or dating multiple people (eg, Schachner, Shaver, & Gillath, 2008). When studying over 86,000 individuals, Chopik et al. (2013) found that partnered individuals demonstrated lower attachment anxiety and attachment avoidance compared with single individuals. Furthermore, these findings were largely consistent across different age groups ranging from young adults to older adults.

Longitudinal studies that have examined the effects of relationship status have found status to moderate attachment security over time. For example, in a study of newlyweds, Davila, Karney, and Bradbury (1999) found attachment security increased over a 2-year period as couples transitioned into married life. Tarabulsy et al. (2012) found that, over a 1-year period, individuals who remained single demonstrated greater preoccupied attachment than partnered individuals. These effects held even when controlling for the experience of different life events, personal adjustment, and socioeconomic status (SES).

However, studies also exist that have found no differences in adult attachment as a function of relationship status. For example, Schachner, Shaver, and Gillath (2008) found no differences in attachment anxiety and avoidance between long-term singles and those who were in a relationship. Likewise, Mickelson et al. (1997) found no difference in the attachment classifications of individuals who were married compared to those who were never married.

Like with, sex, culture, and age, relationship status was also found to moderate the associations between attachment style and relational outcomes. For example, Kafetsios, Andriopoulos, and Papachiou (2014) found that individuals in a romantic relationship who were also high on attachment avoidance demonstrated lower accuracy in decoding facial expressions of positive affect compared to those who were not in a relationship. According to Kafetsios et al., being in a relationship may trigger avoidant individuals' defensive strategies. As a result, avoidant individuals are likely to ignore positive affirming and affiliative signals from romantic partners, a point echoed by Edelstein and Gillath (2008). Young and Acitelli (1998) found that relationship status moderated the association between individuals' positive appraisals of partners and attachment style. Specifically, married men high on attachment anxiety perceived their partners less positively than married men that were securely or avoidantly attached. Furthermore, securely attached married women appraised their partners more positively than insecurely attached married women. No such differences were found for unmarried men and women.

Relationship Length

The findings for relationship length appear to be far less consistent compared to those for relationship status. For instance, Henderson, Bartholomew, and Dutton (1997) found that in abused women, relationship length was negatively associated with preoccupied attachment and positively associated with fearful attachment. In a prospective dyadic study, Duemmler and Kobak (2001) found relationship length was positively associated with attachment security in dating couples. In a prospective study of couples, Kirkpatrick and Davis (1994) found that relationship duration did not impact the stability of attachment style in couple members.

In a field study, Fraley and Shaver (1998) observed the attachment behaviors of couples in an airport in which partners were either separating from one another or flying together. That is, the study focused on behaviors indicative of attachment system functioning rather than individual differences in attachment style. Findings revealed that attachment behavior (eg, proximity maintenance and proximity seeking, resistance, sadness) was negatively associated with relationship length. That is, couples that had been together longer demonstrated less attachment behavior when separating. Fraley and Shaver suggested that this finding may indicate that couples with a longer relationship history may perceive short periods of separation as unlikely to threaten the longevity of the relationship.

There are a number of studies that however find relationship length does not moderate attachment processes (eg, Collins, Ford, Guichard, & Allard, 2006; MacIntosh, Reissing, & Andruff, 2010). For example, in a study of couple functioning, Karantzas et al. (2014) found that relationship length did not moderate the strength of the direct and indirect associations between attachment anxiety and avoidance and relationship factors such as trust, social support, intimacy, conflict-centered communication, and relationship satisfaction.

In an attempt to reconcile the extent to which relationship length moderates the associations between attachment style and relationship outcomes, Hadden, Smith, and Webster (2014) conducted a meta-analysis of 57 studies examining the impact of relationship duration on the links between adult attachment and relationship satisfaction and commitment. The findings demonstrated that as relationship duration increased, the negative associations between attachment anxiety and avoidance and relationship satisfaction strengthened. No such findings were observed in relation to commitment, with the authors citing a lack of statistical power to find moderation effects.

Summary

Research on relationship status generally suggests that being in a more committed relationship is associated with greater attachment security and attenuates the effects of attachment insecurity on relationship processes and outcomes. In contrast, the effect of relationship length demonstrates a somewhat inconsistent picture, enhancing attachment security in some studies (eg, Duemmler & Kobak, 2001) while yielding little to no effects or negative effects in other studies (eg, Hadden et al., 2014; Karantzas et al., 2014).

So, why would relationship status appear to demonstrate consistent and facilitative effects when it comes to adult attachment? A relationship status that reflects greater involvement and commitment may be characteristic of a relationship context in which partners can more readily develop common relationship goals and fulfill one another's socio-emotional needs. Therefore, the inherent properties associated with more involved relationships may enhance attachment security and relationship functioning in couples. However, this explanation assumes that relationship status has some causal influence over attachment processes. We acknowledge that it is just as plausible that relationship partners' attachment styles may propel couples into a particular relationship status. That is, couples that report a more secure attachment may be more inclined to pursue either a steady dating, cohabiting, or marital relationship compared to insecurely attached couples.

HOW DO INDIVIDUAL DIFFERENCES IN ATTACHMENT MANIFEST IN DIFFERENT RELATIONSHIP STAGES?

Up until this point in the chapter we have focused on how particular contexts may influence individual differences in adult attachment. In the remainder of this chapter, we switch tack somewhat and approach the topic of context from a different angle. Here we focus on how attachment styles are associated with various relationship processes across three different relationship phases. These phases represent the life cycle of romantic relationships, their formation, maintenance, and dissolution. We regard each of these phases as contexts unto themselves, milieus that individuals must navigate when forming lasting relationships with romantic partners.

In outlining a case for how attachment theory can be used as a framework for understanding romantic relationships, Hazan and Shaver (1994) noted (in part) that attachment dynamics can be best understood across these three stages of the relationship life-cycle. Indeed the study of attachment dynamics during the formation, maintenance, and dissolution of romantic relationships provides important insights into the reasons behind individuals' cognitive-affective and behavioral responses within their most intimate of adult relations.

Relationship Formation

The attachment system is likely to be highly active in the early stages of a relationship because people are likely to experience trepidation and uncertainty about how the relationship will progress. Thus, it is assumed that individual differences in attachment style are associated with the extent to which an individual seeks proximity and closeness to the dating partner as well as engages in flirtatious behavior with a potential romantic partner.

Shaver and Mikulincer (2006) suggest that securely attached individuals feel more comfortable seeking proximity and engaging in flirting behavior with a romantic partner during the early stages of a relationship compared with insecure individuals. Shaver and Mikulincer contend that this flirtatious approach is underpinned by securely attached individuals' positive working models of self and others and their propensity to cope with novel situations in an optimistic and constructive manner. Moreover, securely attached individuals tend to report more positive interactions in the initial phase of a relationship than individuals that are insecurely attached (Duemmler & Kobak, 2001; Shaver & Mikulincer, 2006). These positive interactions, coupled with their positive working models of themselves and others, mean that securely attached individuals hold optimistic views about the longevity of relationships from early on (eg, Creasey & Jarvis, 2009). Furthermore, securely attached individuals present themselves in an authentic manner, reducing the need or desire to engage in self-presentation tactics designed to inflate one's self-image in the eyes of one's partner (Gillath, Sesko, Shaver, & Chun, 2010; Mikulincer & Shaver, 2007a). Securely attached individuals tend to self-disclose in the early stages of a relationship; however, the self-disclosure is generally in proportion to the degree of partner self-disclosure (eg, Bradford, Feeney, & Campbell, 2002; Keelan, Dion, & Dion, 1998; Mikulincer & Nachshon, 1991).

In contrast, the behaviors of anxiously attached individuals can make relationship interactions early in the relationship seem tense and distressing which can reduce partner interest and may precipitate early breakup (McClure & Lydon, 2014; Shaver & Mikulincer, 2006). Thought to be underpinned by anxious individuals' hyperactivating behavioral strategies, and the desire to solicit sympathy and compassion, anxious individuals can often be perceived as overly needy, weak, or helpless, thus compromising the longevity of one's relationship. When it comes to self-disclosure, anxiously attached individuals tend to engage in frequent and indiscriminate disclosure early in a relationship, perhaps in an attempt to foster intimacy and a connection with one's romantic partner. However, Reis and Shaver (1988) propose that intimacy is a dyadic process in which the disclosure by one partner needs to be met with a sensitive response by the other. In the case of attachment anxiety, anxious individuals focus on their own self-disclosure, leaves little by way of cognitive and affective resources to attend sensitively to the disclosure of a romantic partner. Thus intimacy is likely to suffer as a function of anxious individuals' high and indiscriminate self-disclosure. In addition to issues of self-disclosure, anxiously attached individuals can exaggerate or spend considerable time worrying over real or imagined instances of partner rejection (eg, Besser & Priel, 2009; Downey & Feldman, 1996). To this end, anxiously attached individuals can experience the stage of relationship initiation/formation as one filled with greater tension, distress, and worry compared to individuals who are securely attached (McClure & Lydon, 2014).

That being said, research by Brumbaugh and Fraley (2010) suggests that anxious individuals are particularly good at portraying a very positive persona in the very early stages of a romantic relationship. According to Fraley and Brumbaugh, individuals high in attachment anxiety may have a degree of awareness regarding some of their more negative characteristics. To avoid making a poor first impression, anxious individuals attempt to conceal their negative characteristics when meeting a potential mate. By reaching out to a potential romantic partner and eliciting conversation, anxious individuals increase the likelihood of coming across as interesting and friendly. Likewise, Eastwick and Finkel (2008) found that in fledgling relationships, experiencing attachment anxiety toward a potential partner was found to have a facilitative effect. Specifically, partner-specific attachment anxiety was found to motivate individuals to engage in greater proximity seeking, supportive behavior, and to experience passionate love.

The behaviors of individuals high on attachment avoidance can appear reject-ing and emotionally detached from one's partner during the initial stages of a re-lationship, minimizing the chances for a fledging romance to evolve into a more committed relationship. Thought to be underpinned by deactivating behavioral strategies, avoidant individuals tend also to overexaggerate their strengths. Some contend that this is an attempt by avoidant individuals to inflate their self-image in the eyes of their partner, even at the risk of diminishing a partner's own worth, value, or contributions to the relationship (eg, Gabriel, Carvallo, Dean, Tippin, & Renaud, 2005; Lopez, 2001). Such self-presentation early in a relationship is thought to help avoidant individuals maintain a sense of self-reliance while keep-ing emotional distance from one's partner (eg, Mikulincer et al., 1998; Pietromo-naco & Barrett, 1997). As a case in point, Fraley, Davis, and Shaver (1998) found that attachment avoidance was negatively associated with behaviors signaling intimacy and closeness such as holding hands, mutual gazing, and cuddling. Given their approach to romantic relationships, avoidant individuals appear to engage in little if any self-disclosure in the early stages of a relationship (eg, Mikulincer & Nachshon, 1991). Furthermore, avoidant individuals often place a premium on keeping the relationship purely sexual (Mikulincer & Shaver, 2012). Specifically, individuals high in attachment avoidance endorse engaging in ca-sual sexual relationships and seek out short-term sexual encounters to avoid the emotional involvement associated with long-term relationships (eg, Brennan & Shaver, 1995; Feeney, Noller, & Patty, 1993; Schachner & Shaver, 2004).

Despite the negative portrayal of avoidant individuals with respect to their attitudes and behaviors during relationship formation, Brumbaugh and Fraley (2010) found that avoidant individuals tend to use humor and physical touch as two dating strategies during relationship initiation. According to Fraley and Brumbaugh, the use of humor to build rapport enhances a partner's positive mood, and thereby, promotes a partner's positive evaluation of the avoidantly attached individual. The use of touch on the other hand is surprising given that numerous studies have found that attachment avoidance is associated with a discomfort with emotional closeness (eg, Collins & Read, 1990; Karantzas et al., 2010). Fraley and Brumbaugh suggest that while this may be the case in established relationships, avoidant individuals may not have an aversion to getting close to a new relationship partner or, physical touch is used as a way to circumvent emotional closeness but to establish a relationship nonetheless.

Research has also examined whether adult attachment is associated with mate selection and the qualities desired in a romantic partner (eg, Chappell & Davis, 1998; Mikulincer & Arad, 1999; Surra, Gray, Boettcher, Cottle, & West, 2006). Research has examined three tenable hypotheses regarding the associa-tion between attachment style and partner selection.

The first hypothesis, termed the attachment-security hypothesis (eg, Chappell & Davis, 1998; Kholnen & Luo, 2003), suggests that irrespective of a person's attachment style, all individuals are drawn to securely attached partners. Implicit in this hypothesis is that despite a person's attachment style, all individuals will value partners who are characterized as caring and trustworthy.

The second hypothesis is termed the similarity hypothesis (eg, Frazier, Byer, Fischer, Wright, & DeBord, 1996) and is drawn from the broader literature on attraction (eg, Byrne, 1971). This hypothesis suggests that individuals are likely to prefer romantic partners that exhibit similar characteristics to themselves, and thus will be attracted to a person with an attachment style similar to their own.

The third hypothesis, again drawn from the literature on attraction, is the complementarity hypothesis (eg, Brennan & Shaver, 1995; Kirkpatrick & Davis, 1994; Surra et al., 2006). This hypothesis suggests that people value and prefer partners that exhibit characteristics, beliefs, and attitudes which complement those of their own. According to Holmes and Johnson (2009) the implication of this hypothesis is that individuals high in attachment anxiety would prefer partners who are high on attachment avoidance and vice-versa. While the complementary hypothesis seems paradoxical, self-consistency theory (Snyder & Swann, 1978; Swann, 1983; Swann & Read, 1981) suggests that the desire to maintain a predictable social reality motivates individuals to interact with others who fit with their existing knowledge structures and facilitates the maintenance of a stable self-image. Holmes and Johnson (2009) contend that in relation to anxious individuals, partnering with an avoidant person would substantiate anxious individuals' negative expectation of others as distant in relationships. Holmes and Johnson also suggest that in contrast, an avoidant individual who partners with an anxious person would confirm the avoidant individual's negative expectations of romantic partners as excessively dependent and clingy (Holmes & Johnson, 2009).

Before discussing the evidence regarding these alternative hypotheses, we believe it is important to highlight some theoretical inconsistencies that relate to Holmes and Johnson's (2009) description of the complementarity hypothesis as it relates to adult attachment. When discussing the primary dimensions underlying attachment styles (ie, attachment anxiety and attachment avoidance), the "complement" to high attachment anxiety or avoidance is low attachment anxiety or avoidance and not the high end of the alternative dimension. Put another way, the complement of high attachment anxiety is low attachment anxiety and not high attachment avoidance. Likewise, the complement of high attachment avoidance is low attachment avoidance and not high attachment anxiety. Thus, we consider the description of the complementarity hypothesis provided by Holmes and Johnson as one that does not reflect an accurate interpretation of this hypothesis according to the dimensional conceptualization of adult attachment.

Studies examining these competing hypotheses have found considerable support for the security hypothesis (eg, Chappell & Davis, 1998; Collins, Cooper, Albino, & Allard, 2002; Pietromonaco & Carnelley, 1994). A series of correlational and experimental studies on attraction and mate selection suggest that individuals who encompass the qualities of a securely attached individual are generally favored as partners irrespective of participants' own attachment style (eg, Chappell & Davis, 1998; Klohnen & Luo, 2003; Pietromonaco & Carnelley, 1994). According to Latty-Mann and Davis (1996), the tendency to be attracted to and aspire for a securely attached individual reflects the fact that secure partners offer the best chance for developing positive and enduring couple relationships. This is largely because secure partners are skilled at responding to a partner's needs and engage in pro-relationship behaviors that include the fostering of intimacy, effective communication, and commitment (see section on relationship maintenance). Moreover, given that the attachment needs of individuals are to feel loved, comforted, and secure, it stands to reason that secure individuals are preferred as ideal partners by many individuals irrespective of their own attachment style.

While people generally prefer secure romantic partners, there is some support for the similarity hypothesis (Baldwin, Keelan, Fehr, Enns, & Koh-Rangarajoo, 1996; Frazier, Byer, Fischer, Wright, & DeBord, 1996; Le Poire, Shepard, & Duggan, 1999). For example, in a study of couples Frazier and colleagues (1996, Study 1) found that individuals were attracted to and more likely to be dating a romantic partner that had a similar attachment style. In an experimental study, Baldwin et al. (1996, Study 3) found that individuals that were primed with either a secure, anxious, or avoidant attachment relationship reported increased attraction to a potential partner with a similar attachment style.

According to Holmes and Johnson (2009) support also exists for the complementarity hypothesis. Support for this hypothesis has been purportedly found in a series of correlational and prospective studies involving romantic couples (eg, Collins et al., 2002; Kirkpatrick & Davis, 1994; Simpson, 1990). For example, in a longitudinal study of couples, Kirkpatrick and Davis (1994) found no evidence of romantic relationships comprising anxious–anxious or avoidant–avoidant pairings of men and women; rather, anxious–avoidant pairings were found amongst a large proportion of couples. More recently, Strauss et al. (2012) found that individuals high on attachment anxiety reported perceiving their partner as having characteristics representative of attachment avoidance, while individuals high on attachment avoidance reported partners as exhibiting features akin to attachment anxiety. We again stress that we do not regard these studies as providing evidence for the complementarity hypothesis. For the complementarity hypothesis to be supported, the findings would need to reflect that individuals high on attachment anxiety would prefer a partner low on attachment anxiety; likewise an individual high on attachment avoidance would prefer a partner low on this dimension.

Summary

The findings provide solid support for the security hypothesis. Irrespective of a person's attachment style, a secure relationship partner is deemed an attractive mate with whom one can develop a relationship. Support also exists for the similarity hypothesis, and that similarity may play a role when seeking out a potential partner or in the very early stages of relationship formation. It may also be that one seeks out a partner who is similar in the absence of having access to a potential mate who exhibits attachment security. That is, in the absence of security, familiarity may be the next best option. Finally support for the complementarity hypothesis is somewhat mixed, if not because of the findings, then because some researchers have inappropriately assumed that the complement of attachment anxiety is attachment avoidance. All that we can say is that in some instances, people do partner with individuals that have a different attachment style to their own. However, the reasons for this are largely unknown.

Relationship Maintenance

One of the most widely studied associations in romantic relationships is the link between adult attachment style and relationship satisfaction. However, over the last two decades, researchers have attempted to understand aspects of relationship functioning that help to explain why securely attached individuals maintain loving and satisfying relationships, while insecurely attached individuals maintain relationships that are largely turbulent and unsatisfying. In the sections that follow, we review research on the direct association between adult attachment and relationship satisfaction. We then turn our focus to discuss some of the most widely investigated mechanisms that can help us understand how individual differences in adult attachment lead to successful—and unsuccessful—relationship functioning.

Attachment Style and Relationship Satisfaction

When it comes to relationship satisfaction, studies consistently find that securely attached individuals report romantic relationships as satisfying (eg, Collins & Read, 1990; Hazan & Shaver, 1987; Simpson, 1990). In particular, secure individuals report their relationships as loving, as involving passion, commitment, and intimacy, as well as selfless acts to meet the needs of a romantic partner (eg, Heaven, Da Silva, Carey, & Holen, 2004; Hendrick & Hendrick, 1989; Levy & Davis, 1988). Secure individuals also demonstrate the capacity to balance being emotionally close to a romantic partner with being independent. Conversely, insecurely attached individuals tend to report significantly less satisfaction with their romantic relationships compared to securely attached individuals (eg, Collins & Read, 1990; Feeney & Noller, 1990). Specifically, individuals high in attachment avoidance describe their romantic relationships as encompassing more game playing, lacking intimacy, and low on passion and commitment (eg, Brennan & Shaver, 1995; Levy & Davis, 1988). Anxiously attached individuals report their romantic relationships as encompassing possessiveness, a sense of neediness, and frequent jealousy (eg, Feeney & Noller, 1990; Fricker & Moore, 2002). Individuals high in attachment anxiety also desire passion, commitment, and intimacy, but report their relationships as falling short of these desires, which can lead to heightened dissatisfaction and conflict (eg, Collins & Read, 1990; Feeney & Noller, 1990).

Having established the direct associations between attachment style, relationship satisfaction, and people's experiences of romantic relationships, attachment researchers have attempted to understand these associations further by investigating whether various relationship processes act as explanatory mechanisms (or mediators). Specifically, we focus on three broad mechanisms: (1) cognitive mechanisms such as goals and beliefs, (2) behavioral responses (specifically conflict patterns, responding positively toward one's partner, reactions to a partner's negative behavior, and partner support), and (3) relationship trust. Although researchers have focused on many more mechanisms, we highlight these three broad mechanisms in particular because they: (1) have strong theoretical connections with attachment, (2) represent many of the mechanisms that have generated attention in relationships research, and (3) have been studied the most by attachment researchers.

Relationship Maintenance Mechanisms

Goals and Beliefs

Securely attached individuals endorse goals of intimacy and closeness and maintain optimistic beliefs about relationship partners (eg, Hazan & Shaver, 1987; Simpson, 1990). As outlined in chapter: What Are Attachment Working Models?, these relationship-promotion goals and optimistic beliefs about partners are based on secure individuals' positive attachment working models (Mikulincer & Arad, 1999; Rowe & Carnelley, 2005; You & Malley-Morrison, 2000; Whiffen, 2005). Furthermore, these positive goals and beliefs have been found to enhance securely attached individuals' commitment toward long-term relationships (eg, Dandurand, Bouaziz, & Lafontaine, 2013).

Avoidantly attached individuals tend to harbor goals that emphasize emotional distance and hold relationship beliefs that place little value or priority on relationship maintenance (Gillath et al., 2006; Locke, 2008). These goals and beliefs inhibit avoidantly attached individuals from committing, or attending, to their relationships (eg, Feeney, 2008). Rather their goals and beliefs help to maintain their avoidant ways in romantic relationships. Anxiously attached individuals, on the other hand, tend to maintain negative beliefs about relationship partners and their relationship goals reflect an ambivalent approach-avoidance orientation. Specifically, anxiously attached individuals have been found to subscribe to relationship goals with an emphasis on minimizing distance from one's partner as well as avoiding emotional closeness (eg, Dandurand et al., 2013; Gillath et al., 2006; Locke, 2008).

Conflict Patterns

The strategies that people use to handle conflict have received much attention in relationship research, especially in reference to adult attachment (Feeney, Noller, & Hanrahan, 1994; Keelan et al., 1998; Noller, 2012). Securely attached people demonstrate highly constructive ways of dealing with conflict involving attempts to compromise, openly listen to their partner's perspective, and endeavor to deal with problems in a solution-focused manner (Feeney et al., 1994; Simpson, Rholes, & Nelligan, 1992, 2002). Conversely, attachment anxiety has been found to be positively associated with having more dominating and manipulating partners who demonstrate an inability to compromise during conflicts. Attachment avoidance has been found to be associated with less negotiation and increased conflict withdrawal (eg, Feeney, 1994, 1998). The different use of conflict patterns by individuals with different attachment styles has been found to differentially influence the maintenance of romantic relationships. Specifically, in a series of longitudinal studies, patterns associated with insecure attachment such as manipulation, demand, and withdrawal have been found to reduce relationship quality and operate as a risk factor for relationship breakdown (eg, Feeney et al., 1994). The constructive conflict patterns associated with attachment security have on the other hand been found to buffer against such breakdown and facilitate the effective problem-solving of relationship issues (eg, Feeney et al., 1994; Simpson et al., 1992, 2002).

Reactions to Negative Partner Behavior

Aside from focusing on conflict patterns, research has also investigated the extent to which adult attachment style is associated with people's general reactions to a partner's negative behavior. Research has generally found that securely attached individuals respond with anger and frustration to a partner's negative behavior; however, this response is often controlled and the affective tone does not reflect hostility, vengeance, or hatred toward the partner (eg, Kachadourian, Fincham, & Davila, 2004; Mikulincer, 1998a; Mikulincer & Shaver, 2008). Moreover, secure individuals demonstrate the capacity to forgive a relationship partner and help to facilitate apology by openly accepting and acknowledging a partner's remorse, which can increase relationship stability and maintenance (eg, Feeney & Fitzgerald, 2011).

In contrast, attachment anxiety is associated with an uncontrolled negative emotional response often characterized by hostility and anger (Jang, Smith, & Levine, 2002; Mikulincer, 1998). Of note, this angry and hostile response can be directed either at the relationship partner or toward oneself (chastising the self for having put their faith in the partner only to experience being let down, eg, Collins, 1996; Mikulincer, 1998a; Rholes et al., 1995). These hostile and negative responses have been found to hamper relationship repair and heighten the experience of adjustment problems (eg, Feeney, 2004, 2005).

Attachment avoidance is associated with a negative emotional response to a partner's negative behavior. However, the response tends to be a dissociative hostile response. That is, the partner acts in a hostile manner, but the hostility is not always directed at the partner during the negative episode, rather the hostility may manifest sometime after the interaction (Collins, 1996; Mikulincer, 1998b; Rholes et al., 1995). This dissociative response is thought to occur as a function of avoidant individuals' use of deactivating strategies in which attempts are made to suppress negative affect. Furthermore, individuals high on attachment avoidance perceive partners as lacking remorse for their negative behavior and that the relationship has deteriorated; these perceptions only increase conflict and hamper relationship repair (eg, Feeney, 2004; Kachadourian et al., 2004; Mikulincer, Shaver, & Slav, 2006).

Expression of Positivity Toward a Romantic Partner

Securely attached individuals demonstrate greater respect, admiration, and gratitude toward their relationship partners than insecure individuals (eg, Frei & Shaver, 2002; Mikulincer & Shaver, 2003). Individuals high in attachment anxiety tend to respond to their partner with a mixture of gratitude and love; however, this response is often accompanied by expressions of inferiority about themselves or concerns about their partner or relationship generally (Mikulincer & Shaver, 2003). Individuals high in attachment avoidance on the other hand tend to express little gratitude or appreciation toward their partner, even in instances when the romantic partner has behaved in a positive and thoughtful manner (eg, Mikulincer et al., 2006).

Social Support

The support that is provided and received between relationship partners has been widely studied as an important dyadic process for the maintenance of a romantic relationship (eg, Cutrona, 2012). Individual differences in attachment have been studied at length in relation to the provision and the seeking of social support. When it comes to providing support to one's partner, attachment insecurity is generally negatively associated whereas attachment security is positively associated with the provision of sensitive and responsive partner support (Collins & Feeney, 2000; Feeney & Hohaus, 2001; Simpson, Rholes, & Phillips, 1996, 2002). More specifically, avoidantly attached individuals appear to be less empathic and provide partner support in a manner that is both distant and controlling (eg, Kunce & Shaver, 1994; Feeney & Collins, 2001; Simpson et al., 2011). In contrast, anxiously attached individuals provide support to one's partner in a very smothering and interfering manner (eg, Kunce & Shaver, 1994; Feeney & Collins, 2001). Securely attached individuals demonstrate empathy and care for their partner and respond in a manner that makes the partner feel supported, while maintaining his or her autonomy (eg, Feeney & Hohaus, 2001; Simpson et al., 2002).

Anxiously attached individuals tend to demonstrate an ambivalent pattern of support seeking. On some occasions they engage in excessive reassurance seeking, a pattern of support elicitation that can be viewed as demanding and intrusive by relationship partners (eg, Feeney, 2008; Shaver, Schachner, & Mikulincer, 2005). Yet, on other occasions, when they expect their neediness to be met with rejection, they are less likely to openly express their needs for support (eg, Feeney, 2008). Avoidantly attached individuals are generally reluctant to seek support as partners are perceived as rejecting and incapable of providing a safe haven and secure base (eg, Collins & Feeney, 2000; Feeney, 2004; Simpson et al., 1992, 2002). On the rare occasions when support is elicited, it is generally instrumental support that is sought rather than emotional support (eg, Karantzas & Cole, 2011; Simpson et al., 1992, 2002). Securely attached individuals feel comfortable depending on relationship partners and perceive them as sensitive and responsive to one's needs (eg, Ognibene & Collins, 1998; Simpson et al., 2002; Simpson, Collins, Tran, & Haydon, 2007). As a result, securely attached individuals seek support from romantic partners and generally report being satisfied with the support received. These positive support-seeking interactions have been found to predict relationship maintenance behaviors (eg, Feeney & Hohaus, 2001; Reiter & Gee, 2008).

Relationship Trust

Another important aspect of relationship maintenance processes is that of relationship trust. Trust is also fundamentally tied to issues pertaining to adult attachment. Some argue that issues of trust underpin attachment insecurity, with individuals high in attachment anxiety and avoidance having experienced relationships with romantic partners who are unreliable or inconsistent in responding to an individual's needs (eg, Feeney & Collins, 2001; Simpson et al., 2003). It is important to note that according to Bartholomew and Horowitz's (1991) prototypic model of attachment (reviewed in chapter: How Are Individual Differences in Attachment Measured?), while individuals high on attachment avoidance (referred to as dismissing within their framework) are assumed to hold negative views of others, thus it is implied that relationship partners may be viewed as distrusting. However, individuals high in attachment anxiety (termed preoccupied within the prototypic model) are thought to have positive views of others. Thus one could assume that anxiously attached individuals may have few, if any, concerns regarding relationship trust. However, as we outline in chapter: How Are Individual Differences in Attachment Measured?, research finds to the contrary when it comes to attachment anxiety, with anxious individuals holding quite negative perceptions of partners (eg, Collins, 1996; Simpson et al., 1996). Similarly, research on trust demonstrates that when it comes to attachment both anxious and avoidant individuals perceive relationship partners as untrusting (eg, Karantzas et al., 2014). This distrust of others is thought to be rooted in insecure individuals' concerns regarding the reliability and responsiveness of close others, which includes their relationship partners (Feeney, 2008; Karantzas et al., 2014; Mikulincer, 1998a). However, avoidant and anxious individuals differ in their reactions to trust violations by romantic partners.

In particular, the response of avoidantly attached individuals to trust violations is to dismiss the importance of relationship trust and to increase emotional distance from one's partner (Mikulincer, 1998a). This response is regarded as a self-protective response to minimize or short-circuit the experience of emotional hurt, a strategy underpinned by attachment deactivation strategies (Feeney, 2008; Mikulincer & Shaver, 2007a). In contrast, the response of anxiously attached individuals to trust violations is one of strong negative affect coupled with rumination over the violation(s) (Mikulincer, 1998a). This response is thought to reflect attachment hyperactivation strategies (Mikulincer & Shaver, 2007). As such, not only do anxiously attached individuals respond with negative affect and rumination, but they maintain a hypervigilance for trust violations by one's partner (Mikulincer, 1998). Securely attached individuals tend to trust relationship partners and are quick to remember instances that provide evidence for trusting one's partner (Mikulincer, 1998a). The trusting nature of securely attached individuals is thought to be underpinned by their positive working model of others and a bank of positive past relationship experiences (Pietromonaco & Barrett, 2000).

As a way of developing a more integrative account of how relationship maintenance processes are associated with adult attachment Karantzas et al. (2014) recently developed an attachment theory-based model of relationship functioning. As part of this model Karantzas and colleagues targeted relationship maintenance factors that had been examined separately as mediators of the association between attachment style and relationship quality. Based on previous research, Karantzas et al. hypothesized that trust, partner support, communication, and intimacy would mediate the association between attachment anxiety and avoidance and relationship satisfaction in romantic couples. Of note, evidence was found to support a series of hypothesized mediation paths such that trust and intimacy were found to mediate the associations between attachment anxiety and avoidance and relationship satisfaction. Likewise, partner support was also found to mediate the association between attachment and relationship satisfaction through intimacy. Finally, communication also figured as a mediator such that women's attachment anxiety and avoidance were negatively associated with trust, and in turn communication, which was further associated with their partner's relationship satisfaction. In particular, the results suggest that attachment style is indirectly, rather than directly, associated with relationship satisfaction through a series of proximal relationship maintenance factors, that is, factors that reflect dyadic processes that signal the ebb and flow of couple interactions.

Summary

Securely attached individuals tend to report romantic relationships as satisfying and this is likely due to their optimistic goals and beliefs in which intimacy and closeness are valued. Furthermore, secure individuals deal with conflict in highly constructive ways as well as having ability to inhibit destructive responses to a partner's negative behavior. Not only do they inhibit destructive tendencies, but secure individuals demonstrate positivity toward their partners by exhibiting admiration and respect. They also are skilled at providing support to a relationship partner that meets their needs in a way that doesn't compromise the partner's sense of autonomy. On the flip-side, secure individuals are comfortable with seeking support from romantic partners and are highly trusting of relationship partners.

Insecurely attached individuals report relationships as lacking satisfaction, but the pathways linking attachment insecurity to relationship dissatisfaction seem to differ in part for individuals high on either attachment avoidance or attachment anxiety. In relation to goals and beliefs, individuals high in attachment avoidance place a premium on emotional distance and have little by way of goals regarding relationship maintenance. Their conflict patterns reflect withdrawal from one's partner with little by way of negotiation. This distant pattern of responding is also reflected in avoidant individuals' reactions to negative behavior by one's partner. In these instances, individuals high in attachment avoidance demonstrate a displaced hostility, but also demonstrated little gratitude and appreciation in situations where a romantic partner behaves in a considerate or caring way. In terms of the provision of support, avoidant individuals respond in a distant and controlling manner, while seeking little support from a romantic partner, even in times of need. Individuals high on attachment avoidance are largely untrusting of relationship partners and when trust violations occur within a romantic relationship, these individuals dismiss the importance of trust and seek distance from relationship partners.

In contrast, individuals high in attachment anxiety demonstrate a different profile across these various relationship process variables. In relation to goals and beliefs, they desire reducing the distance between themselves and one's partner but at the same time have worries and concerns about emotional closeness. Anxious individuals also demonstrate conflict patterns that reflect criticism and the expression of a high degree of negative affect; a response that is not dissimilar to their reactions to a partner's negative behavior, a reaction that is often hostile and angry. Individuals high on attachment anxiety also demonstrate ambivalence in their attempts to respond to a partner in a positive way, a response that conflates gratitude and love with inferiority issues and worries about the relationship. With regards to social support, they exhibit a highly compulsive and smothering approach to providing support while demonstrating ambivalence in seeking support. Finally, anxious individuals are sensitive to trust violations, and thus, respond with strong negative affect to relationship transgressions.

Relationship Dissolution

In his trilogy on attachment theory, Bowlby (1980) devoted the final volume to the topic of loss and reactions to bereavement. While this volume placed emphasis on loss from the perspective of the child (and especially the loss of one's mother), Bowlby devoted a sizable part of the book to discussing relationship loss in adulthood, namely the loss of one's spouse. Since then, research on loss in romantic relationships has broadened to not only include loss in the form of the death of one's romantic partner, but also people's reactions to the dissolution of a romantic relationship.

Research has generally found that insecure individuals (especially those high on attachment avoidance) are more likely to experience relationship dissolution compared to securely attached individuals. This finding has been replicated across correlational and longitudinal studies (eg, Davis et al., 2004; Feeney & Noller, 1992; Pistole, 1995). Research suggests that securely attached people (compared to people who are insecurely attached) have a less negative emotional response to relationship dissolution (Pistole, 1995), assign less blame to the expartner for the breakup, are more likely to turn to friends and family for support in coping with the breakup, and report a greater willingness to recommence dating post breakup (eg, Davis et al., 2004; Madey & Jilek, 2012).

As part of a daily diary study designed to understand the processes that explain the differential outcomes of relationship dissolution for securely and insecurely attached individuals, Sbarra (2006) found that acceptance of relationship termination mediated the association between attachment security and recovery from negative affect post breakup (sadness and anger). In contrast, attachment anxiety was inversely associated with recovery from negative affect after relationship dissolution.

Other studies also find that anxiously attached individuals experience heightened affect following breakup and obsess more over one's expartner. For example, a number of studies report that anxiously attached individuals report greater surprise and upset as a result of relationship dissolution, greater preoccupation with the loss, and heightened attempts to reestablish the relationship compared to securely attached individuals (eg, Barbara & Dion, 2000; Davis, Shaver, & Vernon, 2003; Feeney & Noller, 1992). Furthermore, anxious individuals have been found to direct angry and vengeful behavior toward an expartner, as well as engage in unwanted pursuit of one's expartner (eg, Davis, Shaver, & Vernon, 2003; Dutton & Winstead, 2006). Post breakup responses of anxiously attached individuals are thought to reflect their heightened rejection sensitivity and separation anxiety (Mikulincer & Shaver, 2007). In relation to attachment avoidance, findings suggest that avoidant individuals report little by way of distress postseparation, nor do they engage in proximity-seeking attempts to reconnect with one's expartner (eg, Davis et al., 2004). Collins and Gillath (2012) suggest that the findings pertaining to attachment avoidance and relationship dissolution align with avoidant individuals' tendencies to avoid situations that may involve confrontations with one's partner and the experience of emotional discomfort.

In the only study to investigate the association between attachment style and strategies used when ending a relationship, Collins and Gillath (2012) found that attachment avoidance was associated with the use of less direct breakup strategies. In contrast, attachment anxiety was associated with the use of strategies designed to facilitate getting back together with one's expartner. Indirect strategies were associated with the experience of greater distress post breakup. Furthermore, Collins and Gillath found that security priming attenuated the associations between attachment insecurity and breakup strategies.

Summary

Research suggests that individuals who are securely attached are generally more accepting of relationship dissolution and deal with dissolution in a constructive way by turning to others for support. They also do not place emphasis on assigning blame and are willing to recommence dating post breakup. On the other hand, attachment insecurity is associated with negative behavioral and affective reactions to breakup. Attachment anxiety is often associated with partner obsession and pursuit-like behavior post dissolution, and heightened negative affect. Attachment avoidance has been found to be consistently associated with relationship dissolution. Individuals high on attachment avoidance seem to engage in indirect strategies for ending relationships and do not make attempts to reconnect with expartners. While some studies suggest that attachment avoidance is not associated with postdissolution distress (eg, Davis et al., 2004), other studies find avoidance to be indirectly associated with distress as a function of the use of indirect breakup strategies (Collins & Gillath, 2012). Thus, the approach to relationship dissolution may be particularly important as to whether avoidant individuals experience negative affect post relationship dissolution.

CHAPTER SUMMARY

In this chapter we reviewed research on a discrete but important set of contextual factors pertaining to adult attachment. We specifically focused on the contexts of gender, culture, age, relationship status and length. We also reviewed literature examining the associations between adult attachment and various relationship processes tied to the formation, maintenance, and dissolution of romantic relationships. We centered on relationship processes because relationship functioning reflects a within-couple context in which to consider adult attachment. Our review of the literature suggests that not all contexts affect adult attachment in the same way. However, research into the associations between relationship processes and adult attachment has provided important and largely consistent insights into how individual differences in adult attachment influence people's navigation of their romantic relationships through three broad mechanisms, namely: (1) cognitive mechanisms (goals and beliefs), (2) behavioral responses (conflict patterns, responding positively toward one's partner, reactions to a partner's negative behavior, and partner support), and (3) relationship trust.

Chapter 10

What Can Neuroscience, Genetics, and Physiology Tell Us About Attachment?

In the current chapter we review the literature on relationship neuroscience (Beckes & Coan, 2013; Cozolino, 2006) and its implications for attachment. Relationship neuroscience, similar to social neuroscience, brings together social and biological approaches to improve the understanding of the neurobiological basis of interpersonal behavior (Wilson, 1998). In this chapter, we describe leading principles and ideas relevant to attachment, as well as tools and methods from the natural sciences that have been incorporated into social science research and more specifically attachment. We finish the chapter by proposing some new and promising directions for future research.[1]

WHAT IS NEUROSCIENCE?

Neuroscience is an interdisciplinary area, which builds and interacts with other fields such as psychology, computer science, psychoneuroimmunology, neuroendocrinology, and genetics, to study the structure, development, and functioning of the nervous system and the brain. It involves a diverse set of techniques, such as brain imaging and genetic mapping, and draws on different sources of information, such as animal models and computer simulations. All of these tools

---

1. Some concerns have been raised regarding some of the findings revealed in social/cognitive/affective neuroscience. The most salient example of this is the Vul, Harris, Winkielman, and Pashler (2009) paper on exaggerated correlations in fMRI, other examples are the so-called "dead salmon" study (Bennett, Baird, Miller, & Wolford, 2010), recent work by Button et al. (2013) on the low power of imaging studies, and the concerns over the false positive rate in candidate gene studies (Duncan & Keller, 2011). That said, and as suggested by Farah (2014), it is important to distinguish between specific criticisms of particular applications or specific studies and wholesale criticisms of the entire enterprise of functional neuroimaging or social neuroscience. None of the criticisms in the studies mentioned earlier constitute reasons to reject or even drastically curtail the use of neuroimaging to understand social-personality psychology in general or relationships and attachment specifically. Rather, they should remind the reader that neuroimaging, and neuroscience more generally, like other scientific methods, is subject to various specific errors that the self-correcting process of science continues to address (see Lieberman & Cunningham, 2009; Poldrack, 2012, and others for similar claims).

Adult Attachment. http://dx.doi.org/10.1016/B978-0-12-420020-3.00010-4

can be used to improve the understanding of the role that anatomy, physiology, biochemistry, and the molecular biology of nerves and nerve tissue play in human behavior and experience in general and attachment dynamics in particular. We refer to these approaches as "neuroscience" for simplicity, but to be clear, we will focus in the chapter on a wide gamut of physiological indexes, as well as genetics, endocrinology, and immunology.

WHY NEUROSCIENCE?

What can blood flow to specific brain regions, electrical activity along the scalp, levels of chemicals in a synapse or the bloodstream, or the structure of one's double helix, tell us about abstract concepts such as love, relationship security, and attachment? Judging by the recent upsurge in research focusing on the microlevel analysis of attachment, the answer is—a lot. Employing the knowledge base and methods developed within cognitive psychology, neuroscience, psychophysiology, genetics, endocrinology, and immunology, researchers provide a new and exciting set of answers to fundamental questions related to attachment theory and research. Questions such as: "How do attachment bonds develop?", "Why do people have a specific attachment style?", "What is attachment security?," and "Is attachment an emotion or a motivation?" are being revisited with renewed interest. These questions are now being tackled from new angles, focusing on the neural systems and processes that underlie attachment. Neuroscience can provide a lens on these issues that other methods cannot.

NEUROSCIENCE IN THE SERVICE OF ATTACHMENT

The majority of research on attachment has dealt with macrolevel processes (Levinger, 1994). Research and analysis at the macrolevel focus on the associations or effects that environment, context, and experience (eg, dyad, family, society, culture) can have on attachment processes and outcomes. For example, research from a macro perspective may tackle questions such as "How does growing up in a poor, dangerous neighborhood predict one's attachment style?" (Del Giudice, 2009a, and chapter: What Are the Effects of Context on Attachment?). Conversely, research and analysis at the microlevel focus on the associations that neurons, hormones, genes, neurotransmitters, and so on, have with attachment processes and outcomes. For example, researchers taking the micro level perspective may ask, "How does hippocampus size or brain activation within the hippocampus correlate with people's attachment style scores?" To more fully understand attachment and its underlying mechanisms, one must look beyond (or below) macrolevel processes and effects, and into microlevel processes and effects (Levinger, 1994).

To investigate the microlevel of attachment, researchers have relied on the knowledge base and methods developed within cognitive psychology (to study processes such as attention, memory, control, and inhibition, to name but a few), psychophysiology (including animal models), and social/affective/

developmental neuroscience. One of the central questions in attachment neuroscience is whether attachment processes and constructs (such as bonds, style, and figures) are based on a unique neural system (parallel to the theoretical notion of the attachment behavioral system) or a combination of other systems, such as thought control and emotion-regulation. A related question is whether attachment is one system/mechanism or a set of modules/systems. For example, there might be one system underlying insecurity and a different one underlying security. To answer these questions, researchers have used a diverse set of methods and techniques ranging from brain activation to levels of oxytocin in one's blood or saliva.

WHAT ARE THE TOOLS, METHODS, AND TECHNIQUES USED TO STUDY THE NEUROSCIENCE OF ATTACHMENT?

There are different ways to study brain functioning, including functional magnetic resonance imaging (fMRI), electroencephalography (EEG), near infrared spectroscopy (NIRS), positron emission tomography (PET), computerized tomography (CT)/computerized axial tomography (CAT), and transcranial magnetic stimulation (TMS). To date, researchers have mainly used fMRI and EEG to study the neural mechanisms underlying attachment (eg, Canterberry & Gillath, 2012; Zhang, Li, & Zhou, 2008). Both of these noninvasive methods allow researchers to assess brain activation. fMRI relies on the fact that cerebral blood flow and neuronal activation are coupled. When a brain area is in use, blood flow to-and-from that region increases. These changes can be captured using an fMRI scanner. EEG is a method to record electrical activity (ionic current within the neurons) of the brain, as measured along the scalp. fMRI is thought to provide better spatial resolution of brain activity, whereas EEG provides better temporal resolution.

Before delving into specific questions regarding the neuroscience of attachment an extensive mapping of brain regions and processes involved in attachment needs to occur. This type of research will help to identify which brain regions or neural systems/processes are particularly relevant to the study of attachment. Based on such mapping, researchers can understand how general processes, such as consolidation of memories, or shifts of attention, take place and clarify their contribution to attachment. For example, understanding how people form new social ties and which brain processes are involved, can potentially help us better understand how people form attachment bonds (as well as affiliation bonds). Once this understanding is achieved, researchers can search for ways to change or improve bonding (eg, Johnson, 2002; Perry, 2001). For instance, by using drugs or other chemical interventions researchers may be able to affect people's brains in a way that enables people to feel more secure. Knowing which brain regions or processes are active during certain attachment-related behaviors can also allow researchers to compare people with different attachment styles, thereby facilitating a better understanding of the neuroscientific bases of the differences between such individuals. Next we provide a few examples of research that has focused on central topics in the attachment literature and have used neuroscientific methods.

WHAT HAS ALREADY BEEN DONE? EXAMPLES OF ATTACHMENT NEUROSCIENCE

fMRI

As reviewed in depth in chapter: What Are Attachment Working Models? Bowlby (1969/1982) coined the term internal working models (IWMs) to capture the different attachment-related mental representations that people have. According to Bowlby, IWMs allow people to understand the past, act in the present, and plan/prepare for the future (eg, Brumbaugh & Fraley, 2006). This conceptualization suggests that attachment includes a top-down regulation process that modulates people's emotions, thoughts, and behaviors (top-down is a cognitive process where existing knowledge affects the perception and processing of incoming new knowledge. This is in contrast to bottom-up processing in which perception and processing of new information serve to build knowledge). Despite ample work on IWMs (eg, Bretherton & Munholland, 2008), our understanding of them is still far from complete. For example, it is still unclear what mechanisms allow the formation of IWMs and their updating over time. Likewise it is unclear how the top-down cognitive process involved in IWMs differs from general top-down processes—that is, do working models function just like schemas and similar cognitive structures, or is there a unique mechanism only for IWMs? The use of neuroimaging can help provide a novel approach to answer these questions that may help us better understand how IWMs function.

In one of the first studies to examine the neural correlates of attachment style, Gillath and colleagues (Gillath, Bunge, Shaver, Wendelken, & Mikulincer, 2005) used fMRI to scan 20 women and found that the regulation of attachment-related thoughts was associated with activation in the prefrontal cortex (PFC)—an area involved in various cognitive processes that are not necessarily related to attachment (eg, Miller & Cohen, 2001). Specifically, Gillath and his colleagues found that when women were trying to stop thinking about rejection and separation from a romantic partner, there was greater brain activation in areas associated with attention, conflict-monitoring, and working memory [ie, the medial PFC, the anterior cingulate cortex (ACC), and the dorsolateral PFC; see also Anderson et al., 2004; Fig. 10.1]. These patterns of activation are similar to those identified when people suppress nonattachment-related thoughts, suggesting that IWMs and their associated top-down regulatory mechanisms are manifestations of general regulatory processes used to cope with attachment-related material (for a fuller discussion, see Gillath, Giesbrecht, & Shaver, 2009).

Neuroimaging studies not only shed light on general attachment processes, they also allow these processes to be studied across people with different attachment styles. For example, in the same study discussed earlier, Gillath and

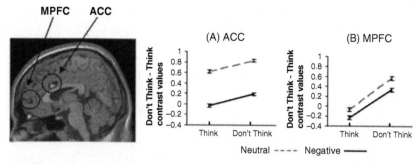

FIGURE 10.1   Neural correlates of thought suppression.

his colleagues found that, although most participants exhibited activation in the medial PFC and ACC when suppressing attachment-related thoughts (which is similar to the activation pattern viewed when suppressing other general thoughts, such as thoughts of white bears), avoidantly attached people showed a different pattern of activation. Whereas less avoidant people deactivated various brain regions when suppressing attachment-related thoughts such as the subgenual cingulate cortex (SCC; known to be associated with the regulation of emotion; Anderson et al., 2004; Drevets, 2000), avoidantly attached people did not. Gillath and his colleagues interpreted this lack of deactivation as related to the constant suppression that highly avoidant people engage in—suppression of emotions and relationship-related thoughts. This suppression (of emotions and attachment-related thoughts) is potentially being done in a way that involves brain activation in the same areas that other people, low on avoidance, deactivated during the task.

Neuroimaging methods have also provided insight into another central component of attachment theory: the formation of attachment bonds and identification of attachment figures (see chapter: What Is an Attachment Relationship?). Specifically, two brain areas appear to be involved in these processes—the amygdala and hippocampus (eg, Gillath et al., 2005a). The attachment system is activated when people feel threatened. When the system is activated, people look for help and for someone who can provide safety and security, such as an attachment figure. For this to occur, people need to quickly process information, identify the risk and a potential solution (enlisting help or support), and learn to associate a specific person with this solution.

The amygdala underlies many of these processes. Activation in the amygdala is associated with processing of emotional or salient material, paying attention to novel stimuli, and the consolidation of new memories through tagging (ie, labeling something as important or meaningful; see Phelps & LeDoux, 2005). For example, when a child experiences stress and then receives help, these events are likely to be associated with heightened activation in the amygdala. The amygdala is thought to tag such events as meaningful and the people who provided help as important, making recall of these people more likely in the future

(Lemche et al., 2006). Lemche et al., 2006 demonstrated that when people were exposed to cues of insecurity, the amygdala was indeed active—presumably as people processed the risk and retrieved images to help them cope. Other studies have identified neighboring brain regions, such as the anterior temporal pole (ATP)—known to be associated with emotion perception and response—to be activated when people are exposed to attachment-insecurity-related cues. This activation is thought to represent the recollection of attachment-related memories (eg, Gillath et al., 2005a; Vrticka & Vuilleumier, 2012).

Retrieval of images or scenarios is thought to take place in the hippocampus, which is also involved in creating associations between internal states (eg, feeling secure or distressed) and cues in the environment (eg, having a caregiver around; Kennedy & Shapiro, 2004), and with the consolidation of memories. Together, the amygdala, ATP, and hippocampus appear to allow the formation of an association between close others and meaningful events and experiences, which contributes to the perception of these others as attachment figures (eg, Buchheim et al., 2006; Lemche et al., 2006; Vrticka, Andersson, Grandjean, Sander, & Vuilleumier, 2008).

We suggest that the attachment system relies on such general abilities to generate lifelong associations regarding the roles of others in one's life (eg, provide love and care) and to tag specific people who are more important than others as attachment figures. By better understanding the mechanisms involved in the conditioning and processing of emotional information in the amygdala, the ATP, and the hippocampus, we might be able to help people form better attachment bonds and potentially help those who have issues creating such bonds (eg, Romanian orphans; Chisholm, 1998). For example, knowing that the amygdala and other brain regions are active during bond formation, it might be possible to help people form bonds by manipulating their brain chemistry (Hurlemann et al., 2010) or stimulating their brain using methods such as transcranial magnetic stimulation (Camprodon et al., 2015) or deep brain stimulation (Bewernick et al., 2010).

A third example of how neuroscience sheds light on attachment involves emotion regulation. People with different attachment styles cope differently and exhibit different emotion-regulation strategies (eg, suppression vs. enhancement). For example, anxiously attached people tend to be highly emotional and overwhelmed by their emotions, whereas avoidantly attached people have a weaker emotional reaction to distressing information (eg, Nash, Prentice, Hirsh, McGregor, & Inzlicht, 2013). A number of explanations have been suggested for these behaviors, but it remains unclear why anxiously attached people manifest emotions so intensely. Is it due to higher sensitivity to environmental cues? Lower ability to control emotions? Or both? Using neuroimaging, Gillath et al. (2005a) have found that when people are asked to suppress their negative thoughts and emotions during an emotion-regulation task, anxiously attached people exhibit lower activation in the orbitofrontal cortex (OFC). The OFC is associated with emotion regulation skills—the lower activation found in anxiously attached people could be interpreted as lesser engagement of this brain area among anxiously attached people. This, in turn, suggests that the extreme emotional reactions of anxiously attached people are at least in part due to their lack of ability to regulate emotions (Gillath et al., 2005a; Warren et al., 2010).

A final example to the contribution of neuroimaging involves attachment security priming. Whereas most of the research on attachment in general, and attachment neuroscience in particular, has focused on attachment styles (anxiety and avoidance), less is known about the enhancement of attachment security and especially its underlying neural mechanisms. To address this gap, Canterberry and Gillath (2012) exposed people to attachment security-related primes or control primes and examined the activation of various brain regions. Behavioral studies have provided ample evidence that the enhancement of attachment security has a host of beneficial outcomes for personal and relational well-being (see Gillath et al., 2008b; Mikulincer & Shaver, 2007a, for reviews). Canterberry and Gillath suggested that the benefits associated with security are the result of cognitive, affective, and behavioral processes. Indeed, they found that security priming led to distributed, cooccurring activation in brain areas reflective of cognitive, affective, and behavioral processes (eg, the PFC, parahippocampus, and temporal and parietal gyri). These patterns of activation related to security priming were moderated by attachment styles. For example, avoidance was associated with activation in areas related to encoding and retrieval (parahippocampal gyrus), suggesting that avoidantly attached people were making increased memory retrieval attempts, perhaps reflecting a difficulty in accessing secure working models.

These findings, although consistent with the existing attachment literature, go beyond behavioral findings to show that all three components (cognitive, affective, and behavioral) operate simultaneously. Thus, security seems to act as a mental resource derived from multiple sources that facilitates prorelational and prosocial tendencies. Furthermore, the findings provide support for the idea that security priming is not merely a shift in the cognitive accessibility of security-related concepts. Rather, it seems to activate a system of emotions, cognitions, and behaviors (or behavioral tendencies) that contribute to growth and well-being (see also Eisenberger et al., 2011; Karremans, Heslenfeld, van Dillen, & Van Lange, 2011).

These are only a few examples within the rapidly growing literature on brain regions and mechanisms involved in bonding and attachment processes (see also Coan, 2008). These studies reveal that there are additional regions involved in attachment processes, such as the nucleus accumbens (eg, Aron et al., 2005), the ACC (dorsal ACC; eg, DeWall et al., 2012; Warren et al., 2010, and rostral ACC; Eisenberger & Lieberman, 2004), the dorsolateral PFC (eg, Gillath et al., 2005a; Warren et al., 2010), and the insula (eg, DeWall et al., 2012). These areas are thought to be involved in emotions related to attachment and bonding, such as love and desire (reward) or rejection and fear (punishment), and their regulation. Knowing which brain regions are involved in each of these processes and how they work together can improve the design of attachment-related interventions. For example, one reason that anxiously attached people show lower activation in the OFC when trying to suppress thoughts may be that they have fewer/more specific neurotransmitters and receptors in the OFC. If this is the case, neurotransmitters could be modulated with chemical or pharmaceutical interventions. This, in turn, could potentially assist anxiously attached people to cope better with emotions and feel less insecure.

EEG

Another way to study the neural correlates of attachment is via EEG, which unlike fMRI, provides high temporal resolution. In EEG studies participants are often exposed to various events or cues and their event-related potential (ERPs) components are monitored. These components often have labels, such as P3 or N1, which represent whether the signal has a negative (N) or positive (P) polarity; and the number represents the latency in hundreds of milliseconds from the event (eg, P300 or in its short form P3 represents a positive signal that manifests approximately 300 ms after an event). ERPs are caused by cognitive processes that involve memory, expectation, attention, and other changes in mental states. Correlating attachment style with the amplitudes of ERP components can help us understand the timing with which various cognitive processes unfold for people who vary in attachment style.

For example, Zhang et al. (2008) examined people's brain activity following exposure to facial expressions. They found that as people were exposed to facial expressions, attachment style was associated with differences in ERP components (N1, N2, P2, and N4). These differences suggest that attachment styles are associated with both early automatic encoding as well as late elaborative retrieval of emotional content. Specifically, avoidant participants showed a less negative N1 compared to anxious and secure participants. N1 is thought to represent level of attention to cues (Hillyard, Teder-Sälejärvi, & Münte, 1998). Based on these results one might conclude that avoidant individuals devote less attention to emotional stimuli than secure or anxious people.

In a similar manner, Dan and Raz (2012) found differences on C1 and P1 mean amplitudes at occipital and posterior-parietal channels in response to angry faces versus neutral faces, but only among people high on avoidance (C1, or Component 1, can be either positive or negative; it is the first visual ERP component, which peaks between 50 and 100 ms). The processing biases toward angry faces (in the P1 component) and toward neutral faces (in the C1 component) among avoidant people suggest that only avoidant participants have the capacity to identify cues at such early stages of information processing, which allows them to rapidly apply their deactivating strategies (also see Niedenthal, Brauer, Robin, & Innes-Ker, 2002).

Focusing on anxious individuals, Zayas and colleagues (Zayas, Shoda, Mischel, Osterhout, & Takahashi, 2009) and Zilber, Goldstein, and Mikulincer

(2007) demonstrated attachment anxiety to be associated with later ERP components, such as N4 (reflecting the amount of semantic processing elicited by a stimulus) and late positive potential (LPP; an index of the emotional salience of a stimulus). For example, Zayas et al. found that when exposing participants to attachment-related cues, rejection-related words (eg, dismissing) elicited greater N4 amplitudes than acceptance-related words (eg, supporting) among women high on anxiety and low on avoidance. People tend to process more when the stimulus is unexpected or has a greater personal significance. Zayas and her colleagues concluded that anxiously attached women perceive rejection cues as more personally significant, posing greater threat to the self, and requiring more processing.

Laterality

A different way electrophysiology can help us understand attachment dynamics is by providing information on where in the brain activation takes place, and specifically in which side—what scholars refer to as brain laterality. For example, using EEG, Dawson et al. (2001) found that insecurely attached infants, as compared with secure ones, exhibited reduced left frontal brain activity. Whereas left frontal brain activity is often associated with positive emotions and approach tendencies (Hellige, 1993), reduced activity in the left frontal brain is associated with depression. Dawson and colleagues suggested that the reduced left frontal brain activity they found among insecure infants represents a greater tendency to use withdrawal-type emotion regulation strategies (turning away from the external environment) and a failure to use appropriate approach regulation strategies (eg, approaching an attachment figure when stressed). These findings that tie attachment insecurity with laterality, suggest more broadly that attachment insecurity is associated with alterations in infants' psychophysiological responses.

In a similar vein, Cohen and Shaver (2004), using a divided visual field task, found that avoidantly attached adults, as compared with nonavoidants, made more errors when judging positive attachment-related words presented to the right hemisphere (which is often involved in the processing of negative emotions; eg, Ahern & Schwartz, 1985). The findings further support the idea that people's attachment history and attachment style—levels of avoidance—are correlated with the way they represent and process attachment-related information. Cohen and Shaver suggested that because avoidantly attached people have less experience with positive attachment-related information, they are more likely to make more errors, especially in the hemisphere that has less to do with processing of positive information.

Brain Volume

In addition to looking at brain activation, either per region (fMRI), at a specific time-point (ERPs), or per hemisphere (in laterality studies), researchers have

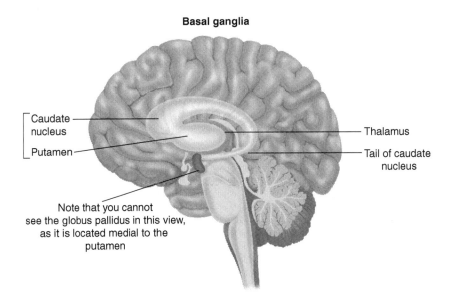

Basal ganglia

Caudate nucleus

Putamen

Thalamus

Tail of caudate nucleus

Note that you cannot see the globus pallidus in this view, as it is located medial to the putamen

FIGURE 10.2   Depiction of the basal ganglia.

also investigated brain structure or volume. For instance, Quirin et al., 2010 found that attachment insecurity was associated with a smaller hippocampal cell density. This finding is compatible with a neurotoxic model of stress-induced cell reduction in the hippocampus. According to this model, unresponsive and insensitive caregiving promotes insecure attachment and simultaneously induces high stress for long periods of time. In turn, chronic high stress and high levels of cortisol (stress-related hormone) result in smaller hippocampus size. Benetti et al. (2010) found similar results, such that attachment anxiety was associated with a decrease in gray matter in the ATP. Activations in this area and the adjacent hippocampus were associated with greater attachment anxiety by Gillath et al. (2005a), providing convergent validity for the relevance of these brain areas (hippocampus and ATP) for attachment anxiety.

Tharner et al. (2011) also examined brain volume. However, they did so using a longitudinal rather than a cross-sectional design. Utilizing ultrasound imaging, they assessed infants' brain volume when they were 6 weeks old, followed them until they were 14 months old, and then used the strange situation (see Ainsworth, Blehar, Waters, & Wal, 1978) to assess individual differences in attachment. They found that infants who had a larger gangliothalamic ovoid, which is comprised of the basal ganglia (including the caudate, putamen, nucleus accumbens; Fig. 10.2) and the thalamus, were at a lower risk of developing attachment disorganization—regardless of their general brain development/maturity. The basal ganglia are thought to connect higher cortical regions, such as the PFC, with lower motor areas, and are believed to be involved in voluntary motor action and learning (eg, Redgrave, Prescott, & Gurney, 1999). To achieve the set goals of the attachment system (proximity to caregiver and a sense of safety/security), specific behaviors such as crawling, reaching out, and crying must take place. The inability to select and execute such goal-directed attachment behaviors is a salient characteristic of people with insecure or disorganized attachment (Main & Solomon, 1990). Smaller volume of the basal ganglia structures may contribute to this inability and, in turn, to the development of disorganized attachment. Tharner and colleagues suggest that either intrauterine influences (eg, stress) or genetics (eg, a dopamine receptor gene, DRD4) may underlie the subcortical volume differences they identified in their study.

Together, the findings described earlier emphasize the importance of investigating brain volume either on its own or in conjunction with other methods (eg, brain functioning and genetics) to fully understand how attachment functions and develops over time. The existing findings suggest that attachment styles are associated with differences in brain volume, and that smaller volume in specific areas is related to disorganized (basal ganglia) or anxious attachment (hippocampus and ATP). More research is needed to understand how these structural differences come to be, and to what extent individual differences in brain volume are shaped by environmental cues. As suggested by Tharner et al. (2011), structural differences are likely to be the outcomes of both genes and environmental cues; however, no study to date has examined this.

Physiological Correlates

Physiological indices such as heart rate, blood pressure, skin conductance, and glucocorticoid levels can shed further light on the neuroscience of attachment (eg, Powers, Pietromonaco, Gunlicks, & Sayer, 2006; see Diamond & Fagundes, 2010, for a review). For example, Quirin et al. (2010) have made claims, based on their findings of brain volume differences regarding the association between attachment insecurity and the hypothalamic–pituitary–adrenocortical (HPA) axis system. These claims have received ample support from studies using physiological markers (eg, heart rate, blood pressure), which have repeatedly found associations between attachment insecurity and stronger physiological reaction (eg, higher HPA activity as an index of stress), especially following relational stressors (eg, Powers et al., 2006).

These findings, which demonstrate regulation failures or deficits among insecurely attached people, can be explained based on the decreased volume or increased activity in specific brain areas. To tie these bodies of research together, studies that combine neural and physiological indexes should be carried out. Such studies will allow scholars to tie the relatively new and sometimes unclear neural findings, with the broad knowledge base on human physiology, and the literature about attachment in a comprehensive explanatory model. As suggested by Tharner et al. (2011), an additional step will be to integrate neural and physiological findings with genetics.

GENES, NEUROTRANSMITTERS, AND HORMONES

There are different ways to utilize the knowledge about genes, neurotransmitters, and hormones to investigate attachment. First, researchers can use *behavioral* or *molecular genetic* methods to estimate the contribution of genetic and environmental factors to attachment style. *Behavioral genetic* methods partition the variation among individuals into genetic and environmental components (shared vs. unique environment). A common way to do so is by examining differences among identical twins (who share 100% of their genetic material) and fraternal twins (who share an average of 50% of their genetic material). Conversely, *molecular genetic* methods focus on the structure and function of genes at the molecular level. A common research methodology is to examine associations of a given trait or behavior and various *polymorphisms.*[2] These polymorphisms are often on genes that regulate either the release, reuptake, or degradation of hormones and neurotransmitters or the density of receptors of these hormones and neurotransmitters in the brain. With regard to attachment, scholars can examine the contribution of unique and shared environment and genetics to the development of a specific attachment style, or examine the correlations between attachment style or attachment behavior and specific polymorphisms.

Second, researchers can examine the correlation between the *blood or saliva levels* of neurotransmitters or hormones and people's attachment-related behaviors or style (eg, Edelstein, Stanton, Henderson, & Sanders, 2010). For example, one can measure levels of cortisol in the blood, or oxytocin in the blood or saliva, and correlate these with people's attachment style. Finally, going back to brain structure and functioning discussed earlier, researchers can use the distribution of receptors for neurotransmitters such as dopamine, oxytocin, and vasopressin in the brain to identify brain regions most likely to be associated with attachment processes and outcomes. For example, the nucleus accumbens, which is rich in neurotransmitter receptors related to dopamine, plays a role in various processes associated with attachment and bonding (eg, Young & Wang, 2004). We briefly provide a few examples of research focusing on behavioral and molecular genetics below.

Behavioral Genetics

Early studies using *behavioral genetics* found little consistent evidence for heredity or genetic influence, and more support for shared environment influence on infant attachment (eg, O'Connor & Croft, 2001). More recently, researchers focusing on adults have started to provide evidence to support the influence of genetics on attachment styles. For example, Crawford et al. (2007) found that 40% of the variance in adult attachment anxiety was accounted for by genetic

---

2. Polymorphisms can be homozygous (having identical alleles at corresponding chromosomal loci) or heterozygous (having dissimilar alleles).

influences, and Donnellan and colleagues (Donnellan, Burt, Levendosky, & Klump, 2008) found that additive genetic effects accounted for 45% of the variability in attachment anxiety and 39% of the variability in avoidance. These findings suggest that part of the variation in adult attachment styles can be accounted for by genetic differences among individuals. Similar findings were obtained recently with regard to adolescents (Fearon, Shmueli-Goetz, Viding, Fonagy, & Plomin, 2014).

Molecular Genetics

Turning to *molecular genetics*, the three main genetic candidates that scholars have been studying with regard to attachment are dopamine, serotonin, and oxytocin (but see Troisi et al., 2012, for findings on μ-opioid). Dopamine is involved in the motivation/reward system and in goal-related behavior (eg, Berridge, 2007) as well as in social and relational behaviors (eg, Schneier et al., 2000). Gillath et al. (2008c) found that attachment anxiety was associated with polymorphisms of dopamine (DRD2), and Lakatos and colleagues (Lakatos et al., 2002) found an association between dopamine (DRD4, the 7-repeat allele) and the likelihood of disorganized attachment. Bakermans-Kranenburg and van IJzendoorn (2011) highlight the interactions of dopamine (receptor DRD2, DRD4, and transporter DAT) with environmental conditions to affect attachment outcomes. For example, children who have less efficient dopamine-related genes do worse in poor environments (eg, insensitive parenting) than those without "genetic risk," and they are more likely to be insecurely attached, with a particular predisposition toward disorganized attachment. However, children who have these genes also profited more from nurturing environmental conditions, such as high parental involvement, enrichment programs, and alike.

Serotonin, the second gene candidate, is also known to be related with affect and affective disorders (eg, Gross et al., 2002) and social behavior (Raleigh, Brammer, & McGuire, 1983). In line with this research, serotonin was associated with greater attachment avoidance by Gillath et al. (2008c) and with greater anxiety by Salo, Jokela, Lehtimäki, and Keltikangas-Järvinen (2011) and Fraley, Roisman, Booth-LaForce, Owen, and Holland (2013). Both Salo et al. and Fraley et al. found that this association was moderated by environmental factors (defined as either maternal nurturance or maternal sensitivity). Caspers et al. (2009) found an association between the serotonin short 5-HTTLPR allele and increased risk for disorganized attachment. They interpreted this as being consistent with the role of serotonin in modulating the frontal-amygdala circuitry (see also Cicchetti, Rogosch, & Toth, 2011).

Oxytocin also plays a central role in social behavior and specifically in attachment. Costa et al. (2009) found associations between the GG genotype of OXTR single-nucleotide polymorphisms (SNPs; 6930G > A or 9073G > A) and attachment scores, such that it was negatively associated with "confidence" (an aspect of attachment security) and positively associated with "need for approval" (a facet of attachment anxiety) and "relationship as secondary" (a facet of attachment avoidance). In contrast, Chen and Johnson (2012) found (only among females) that those who had at least one copy of the A allele of OXTR rs2254298 reported greater attachment anxiety than females who had two copies of the G allele. However, neither Gillath et al. (2008c) nor Fraley et al. (2013b) found an association between attachment and oxytocin OXTR (see also Bakermans-Kranenburg & van IJzendoorn, 2014).

Together, these findings suggest that, rather than conceptualizing attachment style as a blank slate at birth (ie, people having an equal or similar potential to develop a secure or insecure attachment style based on their interactions and the environment), some people might be more predisposed than others to develop (in)secure attachment styles. In apprising the research reviewed in this chapter on neuroimaging, we suggest that specific polymorphisms may affect the development and functioning of specific brain areas, which in turn, are associated with certain attachment behaviors, and more broadly people's predispositions for specific attachment styles (Fig. 10.1).

Recently researchers have started to use experimental methods to study the links between neurotransmitters and attachment variables, with a focus on oxytocin. Researchers have done so by investigating the effects of intranasal oxytocin (compared with placebo), which is thought to bypass the blood brain barrier (Talegaonkar & Mishra, 2004), on attachment-related behaviors. For example, Bartz et al. (2010) found that oxytocin affected attachment cognitions (eg, remembering one's mother as being more caring and close), but that these effects were moderated by attachment styles. Thus, people low on attachment anxiety remembered their mothers as more close and caring after oxytocin induction (vs. placebo), whereas people high on attachment anxiety remembered their mothers as less caring and close after the same manipulation.

Similarly, while oxytocin induction increased the ease of imagining a secure-script scenario (someone else being deeply compassionate to the self), this was moderated by attachment styles, with insecure individuals having less positive experiences (had a harder time to imagine another person being deeply compassionate to them) after the induction (Rockliff et al., 2011). De Dreu (2012) also found that oxytocin interacted with attachment styles; however, it specifically interacted with avoidance. That is, among people who scored higher on avoidance, oxytocin reduced betrayal aversion, and increased trust and cooperation compared to the placebo group.

Animal Models

There is a long research tradition in using animal models to study bonding, attachment, and close relationships (eg, Carter et al., 2005) —a research tradition that we will only briefly touch upon. Animal models are a powerful method to study the social brain and the neurobiological mechanisms underlying social relationships, attachment included (eg, Bales, Maninger, & Hinde, 2012). For instance, oxytocin, which is thought to be a central player in human attachment and bonding, was first examined in animal models (see Carter et al., 2005; Insel & Young, 2001). Importantly attachment theory was partially developed on the basis of ethology (the science of animal behavior), which guided Bowlby's thinking regarding universal behavioral systems and bonding.

In studies using animal models, researchers use observational methods to identify bonding (social or pair-bonding) behaviors such as separation distress and soothing, or relationship/attachment styles. Animal models of attachment and pair bonding created by Michael Meaney and others are crucial in our understanding of the role that epigenetics and neural mechanisms play in these systems and behaviors (see Bagot et al., 2009; Bales et al., 2012; Carter et al., 2005; Lim & Young, 2006). Meaney's work demonstrated that parental behavior affects gene expression in the rat pup, which in turn affects the future parenting behavior of the pup when it reaches adulthood. The major advantages of this approach over work based on humans are the abilities to: (1) study intergenerational effects in much shorter timeframes and by moving pups from the care of their biological parents to genetically different rat caretakers; (2) use genetic or chemical manipulations that would be hard or impossible to use in humans; (3) inflict lesions; and (4) perform postmortem analysis. All of these methods are either impossible or more difficult to perform with humans. Utilizing these methods, animal models permit a better and deeper understanding of the structures, mechanisms, and functions involved in attachment processes and outcomes in ways that typically are not possible with human participants or with correlational research designs.

THEORETICAL MODELS

Although research in the domain of attachment neuroscience is relatively young, important findings have started to accumulate, and researchers have developed preliminary conceptual models to organize these findings. For example, Fonagy, Luyten, and Strathearn (2011) suggest a developmental, biobehavioral switch-model, not focused on attachment per se, but rather on the association between attachment with mentalization (ie, the ability to understand the mental state of oneself and others) and stress. The model is based on early work of Panksepp (1998) and Insel (eg, Insel & Young, 2001) on animals. The work links attachment bonds with substance dependence and opioids, suggesting that attachment bonds might be based on the same mechanisms as addictive disorders (Burkett & Young, 2012). These mechanisms involve two neural systems, which are the same systems that Fonagy and his colleagues focus on in their model: (1) the dopaminergic system (Ferris et al., 2005; Strathearn, Fonagy, Amico, & Montague, 2009), and (2) the oxytocinergic system (Bartels & Zeki, 2004; Champagne, Diorio, Sharma, & Meaney, 2001; Feldman, Weller, Zagoory-Sharon, & Levine, 2007). The dopaminergic system is associated with sensitivity to cues, and both the dopaminergic and oxytocinergic systems are associated with responding to social cues and with rewarding social and relational behaviors.

Tying their model to personality disorders, Fonagy et al. (2011) suggest that a complex set of interactions among environmental, biological, and psychosocial factors affect the two neural systems (dopaminergic, oxytocinergic), which in turn shape the attachment system, and more specifically its threshold of activation. These interactions also affect people's ability to differentiate the mental states of self and others. This, in turn, decreases the sensitivity to and susceptibility of being influenced from other people's mental states, reduces integration of cognitive and affective aspects of mentalization, and increases dysfunctions in stress-regulation systems. These, then, affect the ability of people to regulate their behavior. Together, the changes in threshold level and regulation or control can lead to the development of insecure or even disorganized attachment.

Fonagy et al.'s model focuses on attachment and its association with mental disorders. It draws a lot of its evidence from findings relevant to mothers' behaviors in response to their offspring, which are more closely related to the activation of the caregiving system than that of the attachment system (for similar models, see Atzil, Hendler, & Feldman, 2011; Galynker et al., 2012). Given this emphasis on the caregiving system, we turn next to Vrticka and Vuilleumier's (2012) model, which focuses less on mental disorders and the caregiving system, and more on the attachment behavioral system.

Vrticka and Vuilleumier (2012) suggest that individual differences in attachment styles correlate with various affective and cognitive processes, particularly in attachment-relevant or social contexts. Their model, on the influence of adult attachment on social processing [which incorporates Fonagy et al.'s (2011) model] involves two core networks: one network associated with affective evaluation processes (such as threat or reward and includes approach and avoidance components); and another network associated with cognitive control and mentalizing abilities (and includes emotion-regulation and mental state representation components). Their model is similar to the attachment model suggested by Pietromonaco and Barrett (2000) in terms of its affective and emotion-regulation components, and to more general models of social cognition and emotion processing (eg, Lieberman, 2007).

When describing the neuroscientific aspect of their model, Vrticka and Vuilleumier (2012) add the serotonergic and cortisol systems to the dopaminergic and oxytocinergic systems suggested by Fonagy et al. (2011). They discuss a set of specific brain regions for each network's component. *Approach* is associated with the ventral tegmental, hypothalamus, striatum, and ventral medial orbitofrontal cortex (OFC). *Avoidance* is associated with the amygdala, hippocampus, insula, anterior ACC, and ATP. *Emotion-regulation* is associated with the dorsolateral PFC and lateral OFC, and *mental state representation* is associated with the medial PFC, posterior cingulate cortex, precuneus, posterior superior temporal sulcus, temporoparietal junction, and anterior superior temporal gyrus.

Vrticka and Vuilleumier (2012) further suggest that there is a dynamic balance between the threat-sensitive system motivating social aversion and the attachment system that promotes a sense of safety via close relationships and approach behavior (MacDonald & MacDonald, 2011). According to this explanation, attachment bonds serve as social rewards in the approach system. Both approach and aversion are thought to be shaped by genes and the environment, and modulated by attachment avoidance and anxiety. Thus, people high on attachment avoidance are thought to have weaker brain activation in areas related to both the approach and the avoidance systems—in line with their use of deactivating strategies. Conversely people high on anxiety have higher brain activation, but mainly with regard to the aversion system, and the processing of negative social cues—in line with their use of hyperactivating strategies. People who are low on both dimensions are thought to also have weaker reactions as compared with anxiously attached individuals, but due to their effective regulation rather than their deactivation of the attachment system (for a similar model and findings, see Warren et al., 2010).

Coan (2010) proposed a different model, one that focuses on the regulatory role of the attachment system via overt behavior associated with emotional and social functioning. His model describes the neural systems involved in the formation and maintenance of adult attachment relationships and the way the brain supports attachment behaviors. Similar to Vrticka and Vuilleumier (2012), Coan (2010) builds on research done on the neural systems that support the experience of emotion, emotion-regulation, motivation, and social behavior. He also introduces the social baseline model of social affect regulation. The model integrates existing models of attachment with a neuroscientific principle—economy of action—in the management of metabolic resources devoted to emotional and social behavior. According to the model, adult attachment relationships conserve brain metabolic resources, especially those of the PFC.

Coan's (2010) model, which tries to bridge the gap between the broad animal literature on bonding and the extended work on human attachment behavior, depicts the attachment behavioral system as a higher-order construct. This construct includes basic behaviors, such as recognition and familiarity, proximity-seeking, separation distress, soothing behaviors, and maternal caregiving. Like Vrticka and Vuilleumier (2012) and Fonagy et al. (2011), Coan discusses the emotion and emotion-regulation systems used for attachment behaviors, the relevance of threat- and reward-related systems, and associations between attachment and cognitive processes, such as attention and memory. However, he adds an economic aspect above and beyond these other models. According to this aspect, attachment is tied to the brain's management of energy expenditure. Being together with other people, or feeling securely attached, "saves" brain energy. Interacting with others—the default of human existence according to Coan—is less effortful. Being with others allows people to spend fewer resources on activities such as threat detection and emotion-regulation. People can share or distribute the load of these activities via familiarity, interdependence, and interpersonal conditioning. Conversely, being alone is straining and costly—there is no one to share the burden with and no one who can provide energy or resources (Beckes & Coan, 2011). Attachment security is therefore conceptualized as a sign that less energy is needed, allowing people to save energy.

SUMMARY AND FUTURE DIRECTIONS

The three theoretical models reviewed earlier share a few things in common. They all discuss two aspects or systems underlying attachment styles, which broadly represent (1) threshold or sensitivity and (2) regulation. Furthermore, these models also incorporate automatic and controlled processes. This is in line with both nonneuroscientific models of attachment (eg, Pietromonaco & Barrett, 2000), and nonattachment-related models in neuroscience (eg, Lieberman, 2007). All three models reviewed also connect attachment with broader literatures, be it the temperament or personality literature, or the cognitive literature on affect regulation and thought control. The models use findings from these broader literatures to explain attachment-related processes, and identify brain systems or genes relevant to attachment. Finally, all the models highlight similar neurotransmitters (eg, dopamine, serotonin, and oxytocin) and their role in animal and human attachment [although this is less central in Coan's (2010) model].

There are a few things missing in the current models of attachment neuroscience. First, there is a need for an integrative explanation that describes how the various components reviewed earlier (eg, brain structure and function, genes, neurotransmitters) fit together to generate a comprehensive model of attachment. Second, existing neuroscientific models focus on the microlevel of attachment (intraindividual factors) without connecting it to the macrolevel (eg, context, culture). Third, most models (and the attachment literature more broadly) focus on explaining attachment insecurity, and less attention is given to the underlying mechanisms of attachment security. We suggest some new directions to fill these gaps later in the chapter.

A model of attachment neuroscience should integrate all the components reviewed earlier (and potentially others not reviewed here) into a comprehensive explanation that takes advantage of the unique contributions of each method or approach and integrates them into an overall picture. This idea is not unique to the neuroscience of attachment, and is related to data fusion and analytical approaches that deal with data fusion (Calhoun, Liu, & Adali, 2009). For example, in many recent studies, researchers collect multiple types of imaging data from the same participants (fMRI, ERPs, etc.). Each imaging method focuses on a limited domain (eg, near scalp electrical activity) and provides both common and unique information about the issues being studied. For instance, ERPs reveal the *when*, whereas fMRIs reveal the *where* of a phenomenon. Combining them in the same study with the same participants can provide a more complete picture than having them in separate studies using different samples and different designs.

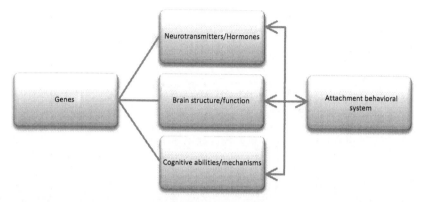

FIGURE 10.3   Attachment as the outcome of genes and brain structure and function. Genes include dopamine (DRD2, DRD4, DAT), serotonin (5HT), oxytocin (OXTR), and catechol-O-methyltransferase (COMT), among others. Brain structure/function includes volume, connectivity, and mechanisms in areas such as the hippocampus, amygdala, dACC, SCC, and OFC. Cognitive abilities and mechanisms include attention, emotion-regulation, thought control, self-regulation, working models, etc.

Statistical approaches such as independent component analysis (ICA) allow one to put these pieces (brain imaging, electrophysiology, genetics, etc.) together. Going beyond the mathematical or statistical level represented by ICA, there is also a need to provide a theoretical framework that connects all the informational dots. Gillath, Canterberry, and Collins (2012) have started this task (Fig. 10.3), connecting genetics, specific brain structure/volume and functioning, connectivity between the areas of activation, and attachment behaviors. For example, attachment anxiety is associated with polymorphisms of dopamine (fewer D2 receptors), decreased hippocampal volume, higher activation of the hippocampus, ATP, dorsal ACC (and a few other areas), lower activation of the OFC (and negative correlations between these activations), and higher sensitivity to attachment-related information. Conversely, avoidant attachment is associated with polymorphisms of serotonin (fewer 5HT receptors), increases in early brain waves (C1 and P1), higher activation in the dorsolateral PFC, and higher ability to suppress attachment-related cues. Future research should further test the associations among the components of the framework suggested by Gillath and colleagues, including different methodologies in the *same* study, and by adding more components (or pieces of the puzzle) as the evidence for their role accumulates.

Although neuroscience provides researchers with a preview of the microlevel of attachment, combining microlevel research with the macrolevel is necessary to better understand the attachment system (see Fig. 10.4, and Gillath et al., 2012). For instance, adopting a cultural perspective can allow researchers to grasp how the brain adapts to better fit with specific contexts or environmental demands (eg, Wilson, 2010). Understanding the functions of attachment in the culture-ready brain (Whitehead, 2010) can position attachment at

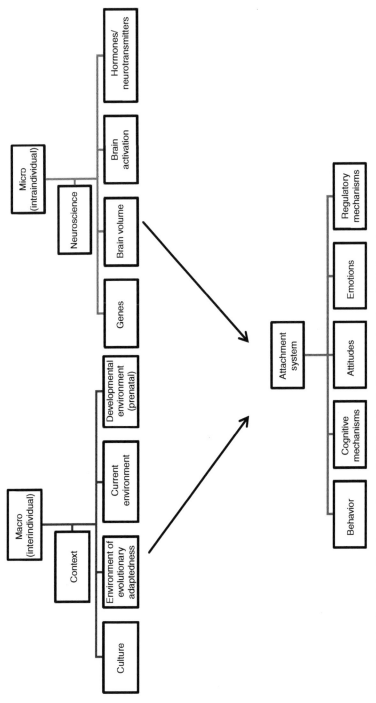

FIGURE 10.4   Combining the micro- and macrolevels to gain a better understanding of attachment.

the forefront of the new domain of cultural neuroscience (Chiao, 2010). Some preliminary work in this direction already exists. For example, Eisenberg et al. (2010) describe the role of D4 dopamine receptors in pair-bonding processes across different cultures/contexts, and Ray et al. (2010) describe differences in neural representations of self and other (specifically, the mother) as a function of a specific cultural context—interdependent self-construal.

Any model that seeks to explain the neuroscience of attachment should also deal with the construct of attachment security and its underlying mechanisms. As mentioned earlier, Canterberry and Gillath (2012) have conducted a study focusing on this aspect, showing that security involves affective (increased positive mood and relaxation), cognitive (increased self- and emotion regulation), and behavioral (prorelational and prosocial tendencies) components. In a different study, Gillath, Atchley, Imran, and El-Hodiri (2016a), using cognitive methods and ERPs, showed that priming attachment security increased the tendency to behave generously, and affected the reactions people had to their generosity being reciprocated or not. Examining feedback negativity (FN) and P3 ERP components, they found that security priming buffers emotional reactions to loss, especially among insecurely attached people, potentially making them focus on the importance of social cues (other people) rather than financial ones (possessions). In yet another study, exposing people to an attachment security prime resulted in increased glucose levels, supporting the idea that security provides resources to people, which in turn allows them to deal with stress and react more efficiently and flexibly to threats (Gillath, Pressman, Stetler, & Moskovitz, 2016). This extends Coan's (2010) model, showing that security not only helps to save energy, but actually provides energy, that could potentially help a person to cope better with the threats that activate the attachment system.

While providing initial information on security, these studies do not deal with the relations between security and insecurity. Currently, for example, it is unclear whether the two represent two different systems (similar to approach and avoidance systems or to threat-oriented vs. growth-oriented systems), or two sides/poles of the same system/dimension (see Fig. 10.5). More work is needed to answer questions such as "What happens when people are exposed to an insecurity prime?" We know that the attachment system is activated (Mikulincer, Gillath, & Shaver, 2002), and that people seek proximity to attachment figures to regain security, but what is the end result of this process with regard to the system? Is it "returning to baseline" (its zero or default state)? Or, because security is achieved or regained, are people reaching a state that is "above" baseline, which is closer to how they would feel (or what they would have experienced) when primed with a security prime? Using neuroscience techniques and comparing activation when security versus insecurity is primed can help answer these important questions. Based on our own findings, it seems that security priming brings people into a higher state of growth or flow (Csikszentmihalyi, 2014), which are associated with different brain mechanisms compared with insecurity.

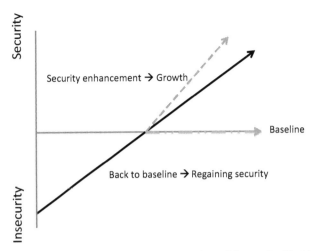

FIGURE 10.5   The relations between attachment security and insecurity. The black line represents a continuum from insecurity to security; the *dash-dotted line* (*green* in the web version) and *dash line* (*blue* in the web version) represents two alternatives: one is that security can only be increased up to the baseline, the other that security can be elevated beyond that to some growth or flow state, but both of them suggest a nonlinear move/growth/trend from insecurity to security.

Another question has to do with state versus trait differences in attachment (eg, Gillath, Hart, Noftle, Stockdale, 2009). For example, what happens when a dispositionally insecure person is primed with security? Or primed repeatedly over time? Do temporary changes in state attachment accumulate to yield some kind of change in trait attachment over time? And if so, how do these changes reflect in brain structure and functioning or gene expression? These issues should be tested and integrated into the suggested framework of attachment, while keeping other models of attachment in mind [eg, how does security fit into models depicting attachment (and love) as an addiction; Burkett & Young, 2012].

In summary, the domain of human attachment neuroscience, although young, is mushrooming and continuously contributing to our understanding of attachment. Although adult attachment has been studied for almost 30 years, and attachment in general has been studied for more than 50 years, there is still much to learn and many questions remain open. Neuroscience is an essential approach to finding answers for these questions. In this chapter, we have reviewed some of the key findings obtained using various methods of neuroscience, have described some of the models suggested to explain the neuroscience of attachment, and have provided a few directions for future investigations. Despite all we have covered in this chapter, this is merely the tip of the iceberg when it comes to understanding attachment neuroscience. Finally, modern psychology is increasingly interested in understanding the relationship between psychological outcomes and brain function and structure. Both neuroscience and relationship science stand to benefit from this relatively new, yet successful integration represented here in the neuroscience of attachment.

Chapter 11

What are the Implications of Attachment Processes for Psychopathology and Therapy?

Bowlby developed attachment theory as a way of understanding how problems or disruptions in infant–mother attachment relationships shape personality development in childhood and beyond. Although Bowlby's early work was inspired by children who had been separated from their primary caregivers, he believed that attachment was important throughout the lifespan. In particular, he suggested that disruptions in childhood, resulting in the development of insecure attachment, can forecast adjustment issues and mental health problems well into adulthood (Bowlby, 1988). According to attachment researchers, attachment insecurity can act as a stressor that heightens psychological distress by compromising emotion regulation and heightening interpersonal difficulties (eg, Crawford et al., 2006). As such, attachment theory provides a useful framework for understanding the underpinnings, development, and sequelae of psychopathology and mental health, and in guiding therapy. Although our focus in the chapter is on adult mental health, we should note that much work has been done on related issues in the infant–parent literature. Interested readers should consult Bakermans-Kranenburg, van IJzendoorn, and Juffer (2003), Berlin, Ziv, Amaya-Jackson, and Greenberg (2005), and Groh, Roisman, van IJzendoorn, Bakermans-Kranenburg, and Fearon (2012) for examples.

In this chapter we provide an overview of the research examining the associations between adult attachment and mental health problems. In particular we review whether attachment insecurity functions as a risk factor for mental health concerns, and whether attachment security functions to buffer mental health problems. This is followed by a discussion of the pathways most widely cited as linking attachment insecurities to mental health problems. We then turn our attention to understanding the implications of attachment theory for therapy and practice. In doing so, we outline some of the broad therapeutic strategies advocated by therapists working in the area of adult attachment. We examine studies investigating the efficacy of therapy in bringing about change in adult attachment and review two evidence-based attachment therapies (Attachment-Focused Group Therapy and Emotionally Focused Therapy) for working with adults.

Adult Attachment. http://dx.doi.org/10.1016/B978-0-12-420020-3.00011-6

IS ATTACHMENT INSECURITY A RISK FACTOR FOR MENTAL HEALTH PROBLEMS?

The short answer to this question is yes. There are hundreds of studies investigating associations between adult attachment styles and numerous mental health problems and psychopathologies, including substance abuse, conduct disorders, suicidality, and pathological grief. Nonetheless, there are four particular categories of mental health problems that have received considerable attention in the attachment literature, largely because these mental health issues involve problems with distress regulation and interpersonal functioning. These categories of mental health problems include: (1) affective disorders, (2) posttraumatic stress disorder (PTSD), (3) eating disorders, and (4) personality disorders.

Affective Disorders

When it comes to affective disorders, the most widely researched disorders are depression and anxiety (eg, Selcuk & Gillath, 2009). To date there are over 100 studies in adult attachment that have investigated depression and anxiety using either community or clinical samples (eg, Eng, Heimberg, Hart, Schneier, & Liebowitz, 2001; Feeney, Alexander, Noller, & Hohaus, 2003; Wei, Vogel, Ku, & Zakalik, 2005). Bowlby noted either separation from a parent due to death or an inability to form a secure attachment with one's primary caregiver early in life, promotes the development of pessimistic and hopeless attitudes and beliefs of the self and the world. Bowlby (1973) also suggested that attachment insecurity could contribute to experiencing general anxiety because inconsistent or rejecting attachment figures hinder people's ability to achieve felt security. Thus, people are left experiencing chronic distress and uncertainty regarding how safe it is to explore their social worlds.

Research into the associations between adult attachment and depression and anxiety suggests that attachment anxiety (including preoccupied attachment) demonstrates very consistent associations with these affective disorders. Studies find that the higher an individual's attachment anxiety [measured using either self-report or interview assessments (eg, adult attachment interview, AAI)], the higher their symptoms for depression and anxiety (eg, Bifulco et al., 2004; Cassidy, Lichtenstein-Phelps, Sibrava, Thomas, & Borkovec, 2009; Gamble & Roberts, 2005; Oliver & Whiffen, 2003).

Attachment avoidance on the other hand may not necessarily be associated with affective disorders. While some debate exists regarding this assumption, various attachment scholars have proposed that attachment avoidance may be unrelated to negative mental health outcomes (eg, Fraley & Bonanno, 2004; Fraley & Shaver, 1999) such as depression and anxiety. It may be that avoidant individuals' excessive self-reliance and use of cognitive and behavioral deactivating strategies inoculate them from experiencing psychopathology. Thus, speculation that attachment avoidance is associated with mental health problems may actually reflect an assumption about fearful avoidance (individuals high on attachment avoidance and anxiety). That is, attachment anxiety rather than attachment avoidance is the driver behind the associations between fearful avoidance and mental health outcomes.

In support of this notion, the associations between attachment avoidance are far less consistent. Some studies find a positive association between attachment avoidance and depression and anxiety, while other studies find either negative associations or no associations between attachment avoidance and these disorders. And in line with the argument summarized earlier, the picture becomes clearer when examining associations in studies where attachment avoidance is separated into fearful-avoidance and dismissing-avoidance. In these studies, fearful-avoidance is more consistently associated with depression and anxiety compared with dismissing-avoidance (eg, Irons, Gilbert, Baldwin, Baccus, & Palmer, 2006; Murphy & Bates, 1997; Reis & Grenyer, 2004). Thus, it may well be the anxiety dimension of attachment insecurity that is more central to the experience of these affective disorders.

However, the inconsistencies found between attachment avoidance and depression and anxiety may not only be explained by decoupling dismissive-avoidance from fearful-avoidance, but by separating out the different symptoms of depression and anxiety. As a case in point, some studies that have unpacked depressive symptomology have found that attachment avoidance is positively associated with depression, but only with depressive symptoms related to achievement (self-criticism, self-punishment, and perfectionism, eg, Batgos & Leadbeater, 1994; Davila, 2001; Murphy & Bates, 1997; Zuroff & Fitzpatrick, 1995) and depressive symptoms associated with bipolar or schizoaffective depressive disorders (eg, Fonagy et al., 1996). In contrast, attachment avoidance appears not to be as consistently associated with depressive symptoms pertaining to agency and relatedness (lack of autonomy, overdependence, neediness, eg, Fonagy et al., 1996). Rather, these depressive symptoms are associated with attachment anxiety (Crawford et al., 2006; Fonagy et al., 1996).

Research has also been conducted with a focus on specific forms of depression and anxiety that are contextually bound, such as depression and anxiety experienced after the birth of a child. In these studies, a diathesis-stress approach has been adopted in which attachment insecurity is framed as a vulnerability factor (ie, diathesis) that when coupled with a challenging, negative, or stressful environment (ie, stress) may yield psychological difficulties (eg, Simpson, Rholes, Campbell, & Wilson, 2003). Across these studies, attachment anxiety in women has been shown to be positively associated with postnatal depression (and anxiety) anywhere between 3 months and 2 years postpartum (eg, Behringer, Reiner, & Spangler, 2011; Condon, Corkindale, Boyce & Gamble, 2013; Feeney et al., 2003; Simpson et al., 2003a,b).

Furthermore, in a number of studies investigating the transition to parenthood, the association between attachment anxiety and depression is moderated by such factors as perceptions of partner support and the experience of anger (eg, Simpson et al., 2003a,b). For instance, anxiously attached mothers that perceive adequate support from their partners report less postnatal depressive symptomatology than anxiously attached mothers that perceive partner support as inadequate (eg, Simpson et al., 2003a,b; Simpson, Rholes, & Shallcross, 2012). Other studies have found that the association between attachment anxiety and generalized anxiety is heightened during the transition to parenthood as a function of paternal work-life spillage and difficulties with childcare arrangements (eg, Trillingsgaard, Elklit, Shevlin, & Maimburg, 2011). When it comes to attachment avoidance however, other than Besser, Priel, and Wiznitzer (2002), hardly any studies have found links between this dimension of insecurity and postnatal depression and anxiety. That is, attachment avoidance appears to have little to do with the experience of postnatal depression and general anxiety.

There is also some research to suggest that people who are high on both attachment anxiety and avoidance [ie, fearful-avoidance in Bartholomew & Horowitz's (1991) terms] experience quite severe depression and anxiety symptoms (Carnelley, Pietromonaco, & Jaffe, 1994, Study 2; DiFilippo & Overholser, 2002; Marganska, Gallagher, & Miranda, 2013; Reis & Grenyer, 2004, Study 1). That is, scoring high on both insecurity dimensions appears to exacerbate the symptoms of depression and anxiety.

In relation to attachment security (ie, people scoring low on dimensions of attachment anxiety/avoidance, or rating as secure using typological self-report or interview assessments) findings generally suggest that attachment security is negatively associated with depression and anxiety across community and clinical samples (eg, Kenny, Lomax, Brabeck, & Fife, 1998; Wautier & Blume, 2004). That is, attachment security appears to act as a buffer against experiencing affective disorders such as depression and anxiety.

Trauma Symptoms and Posttraumatic Stress Disorder

There are close to 150 studies examining the association between attachment in adults and PTSD or trauma symptoms more broadly. Research into this area has exploded in recent times, with approximately 40% of studies published in the last 5 years (eg, Fowler, Allen, Oldham, & Frueh, 2013; Sandberg, 2010). The majority of these studies are cross-sectional in nature (ie, attachment style and trauma symptoms are assessed contemporaneously). However, some longitudinal studies do exist and speak to the directionality of the association between adult attachment and trauma (eg, Fraley, Fazzari, Bonanno, & Dekel, 2006; Mikulincer, Ein-Dor, Solomon, & Shaver, 2011; Solomon, Dekel, & Mikulincer, 2008). The interest in investigating the associations between adult attachment and trauma reflects widely held assumptions regarding the interplay between the experiences of trauma and attachment system dynamics. That is, traumatic events by their very nature compromise a person's felt security, and thus, traumatic events can activate the attachment behavioral system.

Given the theoretical link between attachment behavioral system activation and the experience of trauma, Mikulincer and colleagues (Mikulincer &

Shaver, 2007a,b; Mikulincer, Shaver, & Solomon, 2015) suggest that individual differences in attachment system functioning are likely to yield consistent associations with trauma symptoms, and in particular, PTSD. In fact, Mikulincer and colleagues provided some of the first evidence linking attachment to PTSD symptoms (eg, Mikulincer, Florian, & Weller, 1993; Mikulincer, Horesh, Eilati, & Kotler, 1999). In studies focusing on war time and related contexts (ie, the Gulf War, Iraq–US war, and war captivity) Mikulincer and colleagues found cross-sectional and longitudinal evidence that attachment insecurity is positively associated with symptoms of PTSD (eg, Mikulincer et al., 2011; Mikulincer et al., 1999; Mikulincer, Solomon, Shaver, & Ein-Dor, 2014). By and large, this research has found that attachment anxiety is positively associated with the two broad types of trauma symptoms that characterize PTSD: *intrusion* (the experience of unwanted and uncontrollable thoughts, images, emotions, and nightmares related to the traumatic event); and *avoidance* (numbing, denial of the significance and consequences of the traumatic event, and behavioral inhibition). Attachment avoidance tends to be positively associated with the experience of severe avoidance trauma symptoms, although no consistent relationships are found with intrusion symptoms.

Studies of trauma in other contexts and samples, such as interpersonal violence, sexual abuse, and terrorist attacks (eg, Alexander et al., 1998; Muller & Lemieux, 2000; Muller, Sicoli, & Lemieux, 2000; Roche, Runtz, & Hunter, 1999; Sandberg, 2010), recruits in military training (Neria et al., 2001), prisoners of war (eg, Zakin, Solomon, & Neria, 2003), war veterans (eg, Ghafoori, Hierholzer, Howsepian, & Boardman, 2008), Holocaust survivors (Cohen, Dekel, & Solomon, 2002), survivors of terrorist attacks (eg, Besser, Neria, & Haynes, 2009; Fraley et al., 2006), and victims of interpersonal violence (eg, Scott & Babcock, 2010), find similar associations.

However, there are a handful of studies that have found no association between attachment insecurity and PTSD. Interestingly the studies that have found associations have primarily used self-report measures of attachment, while studies that find no associations appear to have primarily used interview assessments such as the AAI (eg, Kanninen, Punamaki, & Qouta, 2003; Nye et al., 2008). These inconsistencies may thus reflect methodological and measurement differences between the types of individual differences in attachment captured by self-report and interview assessments. The self-report measures largely tap into conscious cognitive-affective and behavioral responses, whereas the interview assessments (such as the AAI) focus on the coherence of discourse concerning early attachment experiences. Given that PTSD symptoms reflect cognitive-affective and behavioral responses to traumatic events, it may be that assessments of attachment that target individual differences along the same lines (ie, cognitions, emotions, and behaviors) more directly map onto the experience of trauma symptoms.

In contrast to attachment insecurity, studies focusing on attachment security (whether it be via dimensional or categorical assessments of attachment style) generally find negative associations with posttraumatic symptoms (eg, Dekel, Solomon, Ginzburg, & Neria, 2004; Mikulincer et al., 1999; Zakin et al., 2003). However, the association between attachment security and posttraumatic symptoms appears to be less consistent in trauma situations that are of a highly interpersonal nature. For instance, Palestinian political prisoners classified as securely attached exposed to physical torture demonstrated significantly less severe PTSD symptomatology compared to prisoners classified as insecurely attached (Kanninen et al., 2003). However, no differences in trauma symptoms were found between securely and insecurely attached prisoners when the torture involved interpersonal cruelty. A study of college students found that for those that experienced interpersonal trauma in the form of child sexual abuse, attachment security demonstrated inconsistent findings with trauma symptoms. Specifically, attachment security was found to attenuate symptoms of agitation, but not symptoms of dysphoria (Aspelmeier, Elliott, & Smith, 2007). Mikulincer and Shaver (2007) suggest that while attachment security may buffer against the experience of trauma symptoms in noninterpersonal events, traumatic interpersonal events may compromise the positive working model of securely attached individuals to the extent that it weakens the protective properties of this attachment style.

Based on the existing longitudinal research the links between adult attachment and trauma seem reciprocal. In some studies, attachment style is found to predict the subsequent experience of trauma symptoms at a later time point, while in other studies, trauma symptoms, such as those associated with PTSD, seem to predict changes in a person's experience of attachment insecurity (eg, Mikulincer et al., 2011). For example, Fraley et al. (2006) found that for survivors of the World Trade Center terrorist attacks, attachment anxiety and avoidance were positively associated with the experience of trauma symptoms and depression 11 months after reporting on their adult attachment. In a diary study of Israeli citizens' psychological reactions to the US–Iraq 2003 war, Mikulincer, Shaver, and Horesh (2006) found that over a 21- day period, attachment insecurity (assessed prior to the commencement of the war) predicted the day-to-day experience of trauma symptoms during the war.

In a study demonstrating the inverse association, Solomon et al. (2008) found that compared to a control group of non-POW war veterans, POW war veterans experienced increases in attachment insecurity. While the non-POW veterans demonstrated some reductions in levels of attachment anxiety and avoidance over a 12- year period, ex-POWs demonstrated increases in both attachment anxiety and avoidance. In particular, ex-POWs showed an increase in attachment avoidance was three times the rate of attachment anxiety. Moreover, PTSD severity was a better predictor of increases in attachment insecurity over time than ex-POWs' baseline assessments of attachment insecurity. In a follow-up study of this sample, Mikulincer et al. (2011) found similar associations when controls and ex-POWs were assessed 5 years later. In this subsequent study, the severity of PTSD symptoms was again associated with increases in attachment insecurity. Thus it appears, at least within the context of a traumatic event such as war captivity, that enduring trauma symptoms or PTSD either increase attachment insecurity or wear away at attachment security.

Experimental studies however suggest that contextual manipulations of attachment security in the form of security priming appear to yield shifts in people's experience of trauma symptoms. For instance, in the same diary study that found dispositional attachment insecurity to increase day-to-day trauma symptoms, Mikulincer et al. (2006) found that priming security in individuals on a given day was negatively associated with severity of intrusion and avoidance trauma symptoms reported the following day. Further, security priming moderated the link between dispositional attachment anxiety and trauma symptoms, such that this association was attenuated, especially for the experience of intrusion symptoms. However, no moderation effects were found between attachment avoidance and avoidance trauma symptoms. Similarly, in another study Mikulincer et al. (2006) found that security priming reduced Israeli civilians' cognitive accessibility of trauma-related thoughts and again moderated the link between attachment anxiety and people's reaction time towards trauma-related thoughts. However, security priming was found not to moderate the association between cognitive accessibility of trauma thoughts and attachment avoidance. Mikulincer and Shaver (2007) explained these findings by suggesting that avoidant individuals' deactivating strategies do not respond to security priming of actual or symbolic supportive attachment figures. That is, when it comes to people's implicit trauma-related vulnerabilities, attachment avoidance may short-circuit the effects of security priming, such that these vulnerabilities remain active even when comforting attachment representations are available.

Eating Disorders

Over 100 studies have investigated the links between adult attachment and eating disorders across clinical and community samples. Some of these studies have focused exclusively on eating disorders while others have investigated symptoms of disordered eating more broadly (eg, Cole-Detke & Kobak, 1996; Dakanalis et al., 2014; Suldo & Sandberg, 2000). Across all the studies conducted in the area of eating disorders and symptoms (largely with female samples), the focus has ranged from anorexia nervosa (AN) and bulimia nervosa (BN) (eg, Cole-Detke & Kobak, 1996; Evans & Wertheim, 2005; Orzolek-Kronner, 2002), to binge eating (both symptoms and binge eating disorder), emotional eating (eg, Taube-Schiff et al., 2015), and body dissatisfaction more generally (eg, Cash, Theriault, & Annis, 2004; Troisi et al., 2006).

Within clinical samples, research on attachment style and eating disorders has consistently demonstrated that women who experience disordered eating report more attachment insecurities than women who do not experience eating pathology (Gutzwiller, Oliver, & Katz, 2003; Kenny & Hart, 1992; Orzolek-Kronner, 2002). For example, Chassler (1997) compared women who were diagnosed with either AN or BN to a nonmatched control group of women without an eating disorder. Findings revealed that women with AN or BN scored higher on insecure attachment (either attachment anxiety or avoidance) and lower on secure attachment compared to the control group—a finding consistent with those reported by Kenny and Hart (1992) and Orzolek-Kronner (2002). A more recent study by Illing, Tasca, Balfour, and Bissada (2010) found that women seeking treatment for an eating disorder scored significantly higher on attachment insecurity (ie, attachment anxiety and/or avoidance) compared to a comparison group of noneating disordered women. Similar findings emerge in studies using community samples. Generally, attachment insecurity has been found to be positively associated with the severity of eating disorder symptoms and increased concern about body shape and weight (eg, Brennan & Shaver, 1995; Evans & Wertheim, 1998, 2005; Tasca et al., 2006a,b).

Whilst a consistent link seems to exist between attachment insecurity and eating pathology, it is not entirely clear whether eating pathology is differentially associated with anxiety and avoidance. Some researchers (eg, Cole-Detke & Kobak, 1996) argue that disordered eating behaviors represent deactivating strategies used by avoidantly attached individuals, which serve to suppress and divert attention from real or imagined attachment-related distress (ie, feeling rejected). Individuals exert control over food consumption and body weight to compensate for the helplessness and vulnerability they feel pertaining to interpersonal relationships.

Other researchers (eg, Orzolek-Kronner, 2002) argue that disordered eating behaviors represent hyperactivating strategies used by anxiously attached individuals, to either gain or maintain attention, love, and approval from attachment-figures. More specifically, Orzolek-Kronner suggests that for anxiously attached individuals, eating disorders may manifest as means to perpetuate a thin, child-like body to delay the onset of adulthood and, therefore, maintain a dependency on attachment figures (see also Bruch, 1973; Masterson, 1977; Palazzoli, 1978).

In light of these views, Mikulincer and Shaver (2007) conclude that both avoidant and anxious attachment-related behaviors and cognitions may contribute to eating disorders depending on a person's preexisting tendencies to deactivate or hyperactive the attachment system. Therefore, individuals high on attachment anxiety or attachment avoidance may both develop disordered eating behavior; however, the pathways that lead to disordered eating may differ as a function of individuals' attachment style.

Given that attachment theory can be framed as a broad theory of distress and emotion regulation, recent research has attempted to delineate the pathways that link attachment style to disordered eating through various coping and affect regulation strategies. For instance, Tasca et al. (2009), in a sample of women seeking treatment for an eating disorder, found that attachment had direct effects on disordered eating, as well as indirect effects through affect regulation strategies. Specifically, Tasca et al. found that attachment avoidance was found to be associated with disordered eating symptoms indirectly through emotional deactivation—an affect regulation strategy that aligns with the deactivation tendencies of avoidant individuals. In contrast, attachment anxiety was indirectly associated with disordered eating symptoms through emotional reactivity—a strategy consisting of emotional flooding, emotional lability, and hypersensitivity.

Studies have also examined the association between attachment and dietary restraint as another factor that may impact on eating disorders and associated symptomatology. The research conducted in this area suggests that dietary restraint is more likely to be associated with attachment avoidance (Candelori & Ciocca, 1998; Turner, Bryant-Waugh, & Peveler, 2009). According to Mikulincer and Shaver (2007), these findings may represent the "suppressive, need-denying nature of deactivating strategies" (p. 394) that underpin attachment avoidance. Furthermore, dietary restraint may be used as a deactivating strategy by avoidant individuals such that it maintains their evaluation of the self in terms of personal achievements and accomplishments rather than in terms of their relationships with others (Feeney et al., 1994). Researchers (Fitzgibbon, Sánchez-Johnsen, & Martinovich., 2003; Heatherton & Baumeister, 1991) propose that, by focusing attention on body shape and one's ability to control dietary intake, an individual may also avoid focusing on aversive emotions, such as those associated with current and past relationships that consistently fail to meet one's attachment needs. It may be argued that dietary restraint is used by avoidant individuals as a means of suppressing or minimizing the experience of negative emotions related to past hurtful relationship experiences.

There are also a handful of studies that have investigated the links between adult attachment and binge eating (eg, Pace, Cacioppo, & Schimmenti, 2012; Tasca et al., 2006a,b). Across these studies attachment insecurity is again found to be positively associated with binge eating (eg, Pace et al., 2012). However, studies seem to more readily find associations between attachment anxiety and binge eating than attachment avoidance (eg, Pace et al., 2012; Suldo & Sandberg, 2000). Research has attempted to uncover the factors that may explain the associations between attachment insecurity and binge eating. These studies have found that issues of body disturbance, negative affectivity, perfectionistic tendencies, and difficulties in regulating emotions, mediate the associations between attachment anxiety and attachment avoidance and binge eating (Boone, 2013; Han & Pistole, 2014; Shakory et al., 2015).

Finally, recent research by Karantzas, Karantzas, and McCormack (2015c) has investigated the extent that food is perceived to fulfill attachment functions for people that experience symptoms of binge eating. The premise behind this research is that for people who binge eat, their preoccupation with, and consumption of, food may be a consequence of turning to food to fulfill needs for comfort and security that may not be effectively fulfilled by significant others. To this end, common expressions, such as "comfort eating" (Roth, 1992), may have strong ties to attachment processes. Karantzas and colleagues found that 46% of people who reported moderate to severe binge eating symptomatology ranked food in the top two of their attachment hierarchy for the attachment function of safe haven, 31% for the attachment function of secure base, and

20% for proximity seeking. In contrast, only 18% of participants reporting no to low binge eating symptoms ranked food in the top two rankings of their attachment hierarchy for both safe haven and secure base. Only 9% reported food in the top two rankings for the attachment function of proximity seeking.

Karantzas and colleagues also found that people reporting moderate to severe binge eating symptoms reported significantly higher attachment anxiety and avoidance compared to people classified as reflecting no to low binge eating symptoms. The findings suggest that binge eating may not only be associated with individual differences in attachment insecurity, but binging may reflect attempts to use food to fulfill attachment needs that may be inadequately addressed by significant others.

Personality Disorders

There are over 200 studies examining the links between attachment insecurity and various personality disorders. A common characteristic of most personality disorders is an unremitting difficulty with social relationships (Widiger & Frances, 1985). Lyddon and Sherry (2001) noted that difficulties in interpersonal behavior contributed 45% of the variance in personality diagnoses. Therefore, the application of attachment theory has been deemed a useful framework to understand personality disorders. From an attachment theory perspective, personality disorders can be framed in terms of the cognitive, affective, and behavioral problems associated with attachment insecurity (Bartholomew, Kwong, & Hart, 2001; Lyddon & Sherry, 2001; Meyer & Pilkonis, 2005). Specifically, attachment insecurity is associated with difficulties in regulating emotions, developing a positive and stable sense of self, effectively navigating key developmental tasks, and difficulties in establishing meaningful relationships. The personal and interpersonal problems associated with attachment insecurity are suggested by Mikulincer and Shaver (2007) to either reflect characteristics of personality disorders or heighten the risk for personality disorders.

Findings to date generally support the notion that attachment insecurity is positively associated with personality disorders (eg, Agrawal, Gunderson, Holmes, & Lyons-Ruth, 2004; Fossati et al., 2003a,b; van IJzendoorn et al., 1997). However, as has been the case with many of the other mental health issues reviewed in the chapter, the associations between attachment insecurity and personality disorders are somewhat varied when examined in terms of attachment anxiety and avoidance and the classes of symptoms associated with various personality disorders (Bartholomew et al., 2001; Brennan, Clark, & Shaver, 1998; Meyer & Pilkonis, 2005).

Specifically, attachment anxiety is associated with dependent personality disorder, which includes symptoms such as worries and concerns about being alone or being independent, self-deprecation, and excessive reliance on others (Bornstein, 1992; Brennan et al., 1998; Fossati et al., 2003b; Hardy & Barkham, 1994). Attachment anxiety is also positively associated with histrionic personality disorder that entails symptoms such as a desperate desire for attention, approval, and reassurance and excessive emotionality (Bartholomew et al., 2001; Brennan et al., 1998; Fossati et al., 2003b; Hardy & Barkham, 1994). Finally, attachment anxiety is related to borderline personality disorder (BPD) for which key symptoms include self-defeatist thoughts and behaviors and fluctuating emotions (Bartholomew et al., 2001) as well as other features of BPD, including experiences of emptiness, loneliness, low self-worth, intense and volatile relationships, an unstable sense of self, and outbursts characterized by rage and anger (American Psychiatric Association, 2013).

Studies utilizing both self-report and interviews to assess attachment generally find positive links between attachment anxiety and BPD in both clinical and community samples (eg, Barone, 2003; Fonagy et al., 1996; Rosenstein & Horowitz, 1996). In studies that have investigated the prevalence of attachment insecurity in BPD, it was shown that between 44% and 100% of BPD patients are classified as anxiously attached [or reflect a preoccupied state of mind (classified using the AAI), eg, Fonagy et al., 1996]. Other studies have shown BPD patients to be classified as high on attachment anxiety, but this is often coupled with attachment avoidance, and they are thus regarded as fearfully attached in self-report measures, or classified as unresolved (according to studies using the AAI, eg, Barone, 2003; Fonagy et al., 1996; Sack, Sperling, Fagen, & Foelsch, 1996). These studies underscore the association between attachment anxiety and BPD.

Both attachment anxiety and avoidance appear to be positively associated with the manifestations of avoidant personality disorder too (Brennan et al., 1998; Fossati et al., 2003b; Hardy & Barkham, 1994; Meyer, Pilkonis, & Beevers, 2004; Sheldon & West, 1990; West, Rose, & Sheldon-Keller, 1994). This makes theoretical sense given that individuals that experience this disorder can be characterized as longing for emotional closeness and intimacy coupled with fears of being rejected (Millon & Davis, 1996). However, an important point made by Bartholomew et al. (2001) is that avoidant personality disorder is manifested across many and varied social situations whereas fearful avoidance is essentially expressed in the context of close relationships. The point being that avoidant personality disorder and fearful avoidance should not be conceived as one-and-the-same.

While attachment anxiety seems to be an important dimension (either independent of, or coupled with, attachment avoidance) in predicting personality disorders, attachment avoidance appears to be uniquely associated with schizoid personality disorder (Brennan et al., 1998; West et al., 1994). According to Bartholomew et al. (2001), this disorder reflects an extreme case of attachment system deactivation, characteristic of highly dismissive people. Thus, the behavioral characteristics of dismissive avoidance align closely with the symptoms associated with schizoid personality disorder, namely, little interest in social relationships and sexual experiences with another person, an indifference to praise or criticism, emotional coldness, or flattened affect (American Psychiatric Association, 2013).

Summary

In reviewing some of the most widely studied mental health issues that have been researched within the context of adult attachment, it becomes clear that attachment insecurity is a vulnerability factor for a broad array of mental health problems. What is also apparent is that the two attachment dimensions have different associations with different disorders. Attachment anxiety is more consistently associated with affective disorders and particular personality disorders (eg, histrionic personality disorders, dependent personality disorder). In contrast, attachment avoidance is more commonly associated with schizoid personality disorder. Disorders that are more difficult to treat seem to be associated with both attachment dimensions (eg, borderline personality disorder and avoidant personality disorder). Thus, the attachment dynamics associated with these hard-to-treat disorders reflects a disorganized pattern involving both behavioral system hyperactivation and deactivation.

WHAT ARE THE FACTORS LINKING ADULT ATTACHMENT TO MENTAL HEALTH PROBLEMS?

According to attachment theory, the linkage between attachment insecurities and mental health problems is mediated by several important factors (Mikulincer & Shaver, 2012). These factors can be distilled into three broad categories: self-representations, emotion regulation, and problems in interpersonal relations. Fundamental to attachment insecurity and mental health issues are negative cognitions that individuals hold about themselves. Therefore, self-representations can be regarded as a key explanatory mechanism of the association between adult attachment and mental health problems.

Emotion regulation reflects another mechanism that plays a central role in both adult attachment and mental health problems. As a theory of distress regulation, attachment theory provides insights into the way individuals use security-based strategies or strategies associated with attachment insecurity such as hyperactivation and deactivation to modulate the experience of affect. Difficulties in the regulation of emotions are a common issue associated with many mental problems, the most obvious being affective disorders.

Finally, problems with interpersonal relations are fundamental to the experience of attachment insecurity and many mental health issues. In terms of attachment, individuals characterized by attachment insecurity report many and varied difficulties in developing and sustaining positive interpersonal relationships. Likewise, a number of mental health problems such as BPD or avoidant personality disorder include difficulties in relating to others and forming close, loving, and satisfying relationships. Therefore, problems with interpersonal relations may help in developing an understanding of how attachment insecurities feed into mental health issues. In the sections that follow, we provide a brief review of the research associated with each of these factors.

Self-Representations

Insecurely attached and securely attached individuals tend to differ on two dimensions with regard to their self-representations, and these differences play an important role in explaining their divergent experience with regards to mental health problems. The two dimensions are the valence of the representations and their coherence (a clear and connected understanding of oneself). First, as described in chapter: What Are Attachment Working Models?, insecure individuals hold negative self-perceptions (eg, Corcoran & Mallinckrodt, 2000; Mikulincer, 1995; Pietromonaco & Carnelley, 1994; Pietromonaco & Barrett, 1997; Strodl & Noller, 2003). It is these negative self-representations, manifested in beliefs, attitudes, and feelings of hopelessness, neediness, incompetence, and self-criticism, which contribute to mental health problems—especially affective disorders, eating disorders, and trauma symptomatology (eg, Batgos & Leadbeater, 1994; Davila, 2001; Mikulincer et al., 1993; Orzolek-Kronner, 2002). That is, these negative evaluations of the self give rise to cognitive distortions about one's competence, worthiness for love and attention, concerns regarding safety, and ability to relate to other people. These distortions can be so pervasive and chronic that they manifest as clinical or subclinical symptoms, and thus, mental health problems ensue.

Second, insecurely attached individuals' self-representations appear to be more labile and lack cohesion compared to those of securely attached individuals (eg, Davila & Cobb, 2003; Stalker & Davies, 1998; Steiner-Pappalardo & Gurung, 2002). Lack of coherence compromises one's ability to make sense of life stressors and challenges, appropriately manage stressors and life events, and understand one's reasons for dealing with matters in a given way (Antonovsky, 1987). Therefore, this lack of coherence in self-representation is likely to contribute to the experience of various personality disorders and severe psychological outcomes of trauma such as PTSD (eg, Fonagy et al., 1996; Mikulincer et al., 2015).

Emotion Regulation

Emotion regulation is linked with the functioning of the attachment system. In fact, some regard attachment theory as a theory of distress regulation and regard the attachment behavioral system as a distress regulatory system calibrated for regulating threats and punishment in close relationships (eg, Karantzas, Kamboroupoulos, & Ure, 2015b). Once the system is activated, individuals seek security and comfort from their attachment figures. The provision of sensitive and responsive caregiving by attachment figures helps an individual regulate his or her emotions and foster their abilities and competencies in a manner that develops their constructive coping strategies to regulate distress (Cassidy, 1994; Karantzas et al., 2015a; Mikulincer & Shaver, 2007a,b). Conversely, inept, inconsistent, or neglectful caregiving during times of distress is thought to result in emotion-focused coping strategies that either intensify emotional responses (ie, hyperactivation, as in the case of attachment anxiety) or suppress emotional responses (ie, deactivation, as in the case of attachment avoidance, Cassidy, 1994; Karantzas et al., 2015a; Mikulincer & Shaver, 2007a,b).

People high in attachment anxiety engage in regulation and coping strategies such as venting and rumination that intensify the experience of negative affect. In turn, these affective experiences and emotion regulation strategies have been found to be associated with affective disorder symptomatology as well as eating disorders, both of which relate to difficulties in regulating emotions (eg, Tasca et al., 2009; Wei et al., 2005). In contrast, people high in attachment avoidance tend to experience shallow affect (eg, Mikulincer, 1998b; Mikulincer & Orbach, 1995). Their shallow affective experience is thought to be the result of their tendency to either suppress the experience of affect (especially negative affect) or to short-circuit the processing of uncomfortable emotions (Mikulincer & Shaver, 2007a,b). Research to date supports these assumptions, with attachment avoidance found to be positively associated with emotion regulation strategies geared towards the suppression of negative affect (eg, Bartholomew et al., 2001; Wei et al., 2005). However, under conditions of high cognitive or emotional strain, the attempts to suppress emotions appear to break down for people high on attachment avoidance (eg, Mikulincer, Gillath, & Shaver, 2002; Mikulincer et al., 2004). The result of this faltering in defensive regulation strategies is the experience of heightened negative affect. These findings speak to the fragility of the affect regulation strategies of individuals who experience attachment avoidance. The findings across the studies reviewed suggest that different emotion regulation pathways contribute to secure and insecure individuals' experience of mental health issues.

Problems in Interpersonal Relations

In chapter: What Are the Effects of Context on Attachment?, we reviewed a number of interpersonal problems associated with attachment insecurity. In short, attachment anxiety is associated with excessive support seeking from relationship partners, a dissatisfaction with support received, excessive self-disclosure, the use of destructive conflict strategies, vigilance to violations of trust, heightened concerns regarding partner commitment, and lower relationship satisfaction (eg, Gillath & Shaver, 2007; Holland, Fraley, & Roisman, 2012; Karantzas et al., 2014; Simpson, Rholes, & Phillips, 1996). Attachment avoidance has been negatively associated with perceptions of partner trust and support, the desire for relationship intimacy, and relationship satisfaction (eg, Karantzas et al, 2014; Simpson et al., 1996).

Thus, attachment insecurity represents an aspect of individual differences that reduces people's abilities to develop and sustain high-functioning and rewarding interpersonal relationships. The difficulties experienced as part of relationships can act as a stressor that heightens psychological distress and threatens a person's emotional well-being (eg, Pincus & Ansell, 2003). Rather than relationships functioning to soothe the distress and worries associated with the pressures of the external world, interpersonal difficulties short-circuit the protective function of relationships. That is, the relationships themselves become another stressor that feeds into the mental health problems experienced by an individual.

For people who experience mental health problems such as personality disorders, interpersonal difficulties reflect variations in people's tendencies regarding dominance within relationships and a desire for affiliation (eg, Pincus & Ansell, 2003; Pincus & Wiggins, 1990). The dominance dimension ranges from dominance through to submissiveness, while the affiliation dimension ranges from cold and detached through to self-sacrificing (eg, Pincus & Ansell, 2003; Pincus & Wiggins, 1990). Both dimensions of interpersonal functioning are thought to tie in with the primary dimensions of attachment insecurity, such that individual differences in attachment insecurity yield different linear combinations of interpersonal functioning (eg, Haggerty, Hilsenroth, & Vala-Stewart, 2009; Horowitz, Rosenberg, & Bartholomew, 1993; Kobak & Sceery, 1988). For instance, research suggests that individuals high on attachment avoidance demonstrate a highly dominant and hostile approach to interpersonal functioning, while individuals high in attachment anxiety demonstrate interpersonal functioning that is more reflective of a submissive orientation that can be of a hostile or nonhostile nature (eg, Haggerty et al., 2009; Horowitz et al., 1993; Kobak & Sceery, 1988). Thus, difficulties with interpersonal functioning can be thought of as a manifestation of attachment insecurities. When these interpersonal issues are highly problematic or chronic, they contribute to the experience of personality disorders.

CAN KNOWLEDGE ABOUT ATTACHMENT INSECURITY AND MENTAL HEALTH BE USED TO FACILITATE THERAPY?

Approaching therapy from an attachment theory perspective can provide practitioners with important insights in helping clients work through attachment issues and mental health problems. First, understanding the attachment style of a client can inform both the therapist and the client about how therapy should be tailored to meet the socio-emotional needs of the client (eg, Clulow, 2001; Obegi & Berant, 2009; Wallin, 2007). Second, the attachment functions of secure base and safe haven provide practitioners with a "therapeutic blueprint" on how to balance the provision of encouragement, support, and comfort towards clients when exploring challenging and uncomfortable issues during therapy. That is, creating a therapeutic environment in which people feel safe and are acknowledged for their strengths and capabilities empowers the client to tackle difficult issues in a more open and confident manner. Third, understanding the characteristics of secure attachment can help therapists model security-enhancing relationships with clients. Security-enhancing interactions between a client and therapist can then help clients revise their working models of attachment in a manner that can reduce attachment insecurity.

According to Bowlby (1969/1982, 1988), therapeutic work requires the therapist to develop an understanding of the life experiences and pathways that have influenced the development of a person's attachment style. This understanding can help the therapist shape the work undertaken with the client to revise insecure mental representations, and thus bring about change in a person's attachment style. While chapter: How Stable Are Attachment Styles in Adulthood? reviews and discusses some of the theory and research relating to change in attachment styles, we expand on this discussion here to specifically focus on the ways in which therapeutic interventions may lead to changes in attachment organization.

Davila and Cobb (Cobb & Davila, 2009; Davila & Cobb, 2004) discuss various theoretical models of attachment style change that emphasize the role of working models as a mechanism for bringing about change. Two models that are relevant to our discussion are the life-stress model and the social-cognitive model. Each model sheds light on different aspects of therapeutic work.

The life-stress model posits that stressful life events disrupt people's socioemotional worlds, and with it, relationships with significant others. Davila et al. suggest that at the heart of therapeutic work is unpacking and reframing of the cognitive and emotional experiences of clients. To this end, treatment is often targeted at assisting individuals to either develop new meanings or new insights regarding the life stress experienced. These new insights and interpretations can be used to augment or reframe aspects of people's internal working models of attachment. However, it is important for therapists to keep in mind that, for insecurely attached individuals, entering therapy may itself be deemed a stressful life event (Davila & Cobb, 2004). Thus, not only must the therapist work on the cognitive and affective reframing of past or recurrent stressful life events, but they must also cultivate a therapeutic relationship (ie, working alliance, Horvath & Greenberg, 1989) that is appraised by the client as nonstressful. Such an environment provides a safe and encouraging context to deal with issues of attachment insecurity.

According to the social-cognitive model, individuals may hold multiple attachment representations of different attachment relationships in addition to more global/general mental representations (see also chapter: What Are Attachment Working Models?). Davila and Cobb (2004) claim that this affords the opportunity in treatment to explore clients' more secure working models to guide behavior and interpretations as a way of strengthening those models or making them more salient and frequently activated. Frequent activation of these secure models may induce more lasting change by making the secure models more chronically salient. As a related point, security priming (covered in chapter: What Can Social Cognition and Priming Tell Us About Attachment?) is geared towards this goal, to make secure models more salient in the minds of individuals (eg, Carnelley, Otway, & Rowe, 2015).

Like Davila and Cobb, Bowlby (1988) placed a strong emphasis on the importance of attending to working models in therapy as a way to modify a person's insecure attachment mental representations. Specifically, Bowlby (1988) discussed five therapeutic tasks that contribute to the revision of insecure working models and the achievement of positive therapeutic outcomes: (1) the therapist provides a secure base and safe haven for the client to engage with challenging and difficult issues; (2) the therapist helps the client explore and understand how they relate to other people as a function of their attachment goals, perceptions, expectations, and fears; (3) an examination of the client–therapist relationship as the client is likely to project and transfer their self-destructive modes of relating to close others onto the therapeutic relationship; (4) the therapist helps the client to reflect on how their working models are rooted in childhood experiences with primary attachment figures; and (5) the therapist assists the client to recognize that although their working models may have been adaptive in the past, they are no longer functional.

While Bowlby's five therapeutic tasks provide a detailed and programmatic framework for how to approach psychotherapy related to attachment issues, there is little research that has investigated the efficacy of Bowlby's therapeutic model. For instance, Parish and Eagle (2003) found that clients viewed their therapist as a security-providing figure and perceived their therapist as being stronger, wiser, and more available and sensitive than their primary attachment figures. Furthermore, Parish and Eagle found positive associations between clients' reports of the therapist as security-enhancing and the extent and frequency of therapy as well as the quality of the therapist–client relationship. However, clients' attachment avoidance was negatively associated with reports of the therapist as a security-enhancing figure. In other studies investigating the therapist's security-promoting characteristics and therapeutic outcomes, similar results are found, such that those clients who perceived their therapist as a security-enhancing figure reported greater exploration of personal issues during counseling (eg, Goodwin, Holmes, Cochrane, & Mason, 2003; Litman-Ovadia, 2004).

HOW CAN ATTACHMENT THEORY INFORM US ABOUT THE KIND OF DIFFICULTIES INSECURE PEOPLE MAY HAVE IN RELATION TO THERAPY?

Attachment theory has been applied to a wide variety of existing therapeutic approaches, such as psychodynamic, cognitive-behavioral, and dialectic-behavioral therapies. As mentioned previously, one insight that attachment theory has to offer to the therapist is a priori knowledge about the kinds of difficulties clients may possess in relation to therapeutic work. Cobb and Davila (2009) note that insecurely attached individuals hold relatively rigid views of themselves and others and engage in cognitions and behaviors to confirm their existing attitudes, beliefs, expectations, and behavioral strategies. These rigid views help insecure individuals defend or uphold their self-image. Coupled with their behavioral tendencies, insecure individuals perpetuate self-fulfilling prophecies regarding interpersonal relationships that further feed into their inflexibility regarding cognitions and behavior.

Cobb and Davila (2009) further note that an inherent difficulty in targeting cognition in therapy is that internal working models often operate on an unconscious and automatic level. Thus, it is difficult for clients to reflect and appraise the content of their thoughts and attitudes, let alone make considered judgments about the adaptiveness or maladaptiveness of these working models in different contexts. If therapy is perceived by insecurely attached individuals as a stressful or threatening context, then it is likely that clients' cognitive and behavioral reactions to therapy will reflect the hyperactivating and deactivating strategies characteristic of attachment anxiety and attachment avoidance respectively. Thus, therapists need to be aware that an insecurely attached client's presentation during therapy may well reflect the manifestation of attachment system dysregulation.

Finally, Cobb and Davila (2009) point out that while the ultimate goal of therapy may be to shift clients from harboring an insecure attachment style to a secure attachment style, the reality of therapeutic work may be such that the best a therapist can do with some clients is to help them become less insecure. This final point is an important and sobering consideration for therapists working with insecurely attached clients, especially those who demonstrate very high attachment anxiety and/or attachment avoidance. This does not mean that change via therapy is impossible. Rather, therapists should consider what attachment theory provides in the form of strategies to overcome these difficulties (eg, Berant, 2009; Wallin, 2007).

HOW CAN ATTACHMENT THEORY INFORM US ABOUT DEALING WITH AVOIDANTLY ATTACHED CLIENTS?

According to Berant (2009), therapists need to be mindful that challenging avoidant individuals or having them confront their vulnerabilities can activate defensive reactions that are in line with their attachment deactivation strategies. From a cognitive standpoint, a therapeutic approach that challenges avoidant individuals threatens their self-perceptions regarding excessive self-reliance and exaggerated views of being capable and independent. Berant suggests that in the early stages of therapy it may be worthwhile to sidestep issues that highlight inadequacies or issues that require deep reflection. This approach is likely to reduce resistance and can assist with establishing rapport in the early stages of therapy. However, this does not mean that avoidant individuals should not be challenged in therapy; rather it is more about using one's therapeutic expertise and observational skills to know when is an opportune time to challenge an avoidant person or ask them to engage in deep reflection.

On the one hand, creating a security-enhancing environment in therapy is likely to reduce avoidant individuals' tendencies to engage in defensive reactions against the therapist. As already reviewed, there exists some evidence to suggest that if a therapist is viewed as a security-enhancing figure, then clients are more likely to engage in exploration during therapy. However, attempts to make an avoidant client more secure, or to make the client see the therapist as a security-providing figure are less likely to succeed with avoidant clients (Levy, Ellison, Scott, & Bernecker, 2011; Taylor, Rietzschel, Danquah, & Berry, 2015). To date, some studies suggest that avoidant clients are less likely to seek out help and are inclined to reject a practitioner's attempts at providing comfort and support during therapy (eg, Dozier, 1990; Korfmacher, Adam, Ogawa, & Egeland, 1997).

So where does that leave therapists working with avoidantly attached clients? Research shows that when avoidant individuals become cognitively overloaded or stressed, their defensive strategies become compromised (eg, Mikulincer, Dolev, & Shaver, 2004). In these instances, the cognitive responses of avoidant individuals resemble those of anxiously attached individuals. This research suggests that avoidant individuals have the same underlying attachment concerns as anxiously attached people but have developed defense mechanisms to minimize dealing with these worries. Accordingly, Berant (2009) suggests that the best time to engage in some reflective work with clients or to challenge the client is when therapists sense that an avoidant person's defenses are lowered (eg, when they appear less resistant or when they open up slightly during therapy).

Wallin (2007) points out that some degree of confrontation may be in order when working with avoidant individuals. From a therapeutic perspective, the confrontation is viewed as functional in that its purpose is to give the avoidant individual insight into the subjective experience of the therapist. That is, the avoidant individual is provided with an explicit account of an interaction between the client and therapist from the therapist's perspective that challenges the avoidant individual's response or behavior towards the therapist. By engaging in such confrontation the avoidant individual can also be exposed to how the therapist was feeling during or post the interaction. The purpose of this approach is to alert the avoidant individual to their behavior and how it impacts the therapist. Such explicit confrontation may be required given that avoidant individuals tend to experience shallow affect (eg, Mikulincer, 1998b; Mikulincer & Florian, 1998) and have a poor ability to perspective-take (eg, Corcoran & Mallinckrodt, 2000). According to Wallin (2007), avoidant individuals are likely to be surprised in learning that they are behaving in a manner that makes the therapist feel uncomfortable, inadequate, or hurt.

While confrontation may be one approach that can be used with avoidantly attached clients on occasions, Wallin (2007) also suggests that framing therapeutic activities in terms of empowering the individual—giving them tools to deal with things themselves—may be a way to get "buy-in" from avoidant clients. This type of approach may well be a path of least resistance in therapy as it aligns with avoidant individuals' views of the self as independent and self-reliant. However, therapists need to temper the extent to which the approach they undertake feeds into avoidant individuals' perceptions of self-reliance, as this is one of the characteristics that make avoidant individuals devalue relationships and minimize disclosure.

Irrespective of the strategies used in working with avoidantly attached individuals, Berant (2009) and Wallin (2007) highlight that therapists need to be prepared to be devalued by the clients or that the client is dismissive of therapy. These reactions by avoidantly attached individuals may be strategies to bolster their sense of self-reliance and minimize investment in the therapeutic relationship—strategies that Berant and Wallin suggest are reflective of avoidant individuals' worries regarding the ending of the therapeutic relationship in the future.

HOW CAN ATTACHMENT THEORY INFORM US ABOUT DEALING WITH ANXIOUSLY ATTACHED CLIENTS?

Berant (2009) suggests that therapists should target the anxiously attached client's sense of self-competence and value as an individual. To this end, therapy should center on the reassurance of a client's worth, and on encouraging anxiously attached individuals to deal with relational issues in a more independent, agentic, and constructive way. Another emphasis should be on enhancing a client's coping and emotion regulation strategies. For this to happen effectively, Berant notes that the therapist needs to "provide adequate scaffolding and suggestions to help the anxious client find new strengths and better methods of handling thoughts and feelings" (p. 186). However, Berant notes that therapy with anxiously attached clients can be "slow going" (p. 186) due to their excessive need for approval and validation. Nevertheless, this type of therapeutic approach is designed to assist revision of a client's model of self and to reduce his or her reliance on attachment hyperactivation strategies.

Wallin (2007) suggests that the therapeutic relationship should provide emotional availability and unconditional acceptance. The idea behind creating such a therapeutic relationship is to diminish the notion that a response can only be obtained if an anxious person amplifies affect and a sense of helplessness, thus rendering the hyperactivating strategy increasingly unnecessary. As a way of dampening the hyperactivating tendencies of anxiously attached individuals, Wallin also suggests that integrating mindfulness and meditation-based strategies can help to reduce physical arousal and quiet the mind. Furthermore, the implementation of these therapeutic strategies can help an anxious client to notice sensations and emotions as well as to connect with uncomfortable internal states—capacities and skills that are generally not part of the default repertoire associated with hyperactivation strategies. As such, it can be useful to begin sessions with a brief meditation or relaxation.

Wallin (2007) also highlights that early on in therapy, anxious people can appear eager for change and prepared to commit to therapeutic work. However, this eagerness may be an attempt to gain the approval of the therapist rather than a genuine commitment to change. Accordingly, what appears like a client ready for change, may quickly turn into one who presents a sense of helplessness, need for validation, and resistance to empowerment. Therapists need to be mindful that, for anxiously attached individuals, working on attachment insecurities runs the risk of not having to rely on people as much, including the therapist. This possible reality can be very confronting for anxiously attached individuals, especially if it becomes clear that getting better involves terminating the therapeutic relationship. Given the intense neediness of individuals high on attachment anxiety, Wallin (2007) recommends that it is important that therapists set clear boundaries with such clients to protect both parties from becoming too enmeshed and to guard against negative countertransference—an outcome of the therapeutic relationship that would make it difficult for the therapist to provide empathy.

CAN THERAPY HELP INSECURE CLIENTS?

Despite the theoretical writings and strategies that have been advocated for use in therapy when working with people who experience attachment insecurity (eg, Berant, 2009; Wallin, 2007), there is relatively little rigorous scientific research on the ability of therapy to bring about change in adult attachment. The research that has been conducted to date suggests that therapy can have an impact on enhancing clients' attachment security and reducing attachment anxiety. However, it appears that attachment avoidance is far more resistant to change initiated through therapy.

In a randomized controlled trial investigating the effects of integrative couple behavior therapy and cognitive behavior therapy on changes in attachment style, Benson, Sevier, and Christensen (2013) found that therapy yielded no direct changes to couple members' attachment style over time. However, an indirect effect was found such that increases in marital satisfaction as a function of therapy were associated with increases in attachment security and decreases in attachment anxiety. Again, no changes were found in relation to attachment avoidance.

In reviewing group therapy work amongst people experiencing binge eating symptomatology, Marmarosh and Tasca (2013) suggest that group interpersonal therapy yields significant reductions in both attachment anxiety and group avoidance from pretreatment to 12 weeks posttreatment. A study by Maxwell, Tasca, Ritchie, Balfour, and Bissada (2014) demonstrated a similar finding, but this time effects were found for up to 1 year posttreatment.

In a metaanalytic study also involving 14 studies, Levy et al. (2011) found that across various therapeutic contexts and therapeutic approaches, attachment anxiety showed a reduction posttherapy ($d = -0.46$) while attachment security demonstrated an increase ($d = 0.37$). Levy and colleagues found no significant association between therapy and posttherapy changes in attachment avoidance. Likewise, a recent systematic review by Taylor et al. (2015) located 14 published studies that specifically investigated changes in adult attachment style (measured using self-report measures or interview assessments) as a result of therapy. The systematic review suggested that therapy was associated with increases in attachment security, decreases in attachment anxiety, but little change in attachment avoidance. These findings seem to be consistent irrespective of the patient group, therapeutic approach, therapy setting, and research methodology employed as part of each study. While the consistency of the effects is impressive, many of these studies were characterized by small sample sizes, while a number of the studies suffered from confounds and possible selection bias of study participants. All in all about 79% of the studies reviewed were deemed to be of weak methodological quality using standardized indicators of quality assessment (such as The Effective Public Health Practice Project tool; Thomas, Ciliska, Dobbins, & Micucci, 2004).

These findings make it clear that far more clinically based research is required to develop greater confidence regarding the efficacy of therapy in bringing about change in people's attachment styles. This needs to be a key area of focus for future applied research into attachment theory.

HOW CAN ATTACHMENT THEORY INFORM THE DEVELOPMENT OF THERAPEUTIC INTERVENTIONS?

Numerous publications have been written on "attachment-based psychotherapy" or "attachment psychotherapy" (eg, Berry & Danquah, 2015; Clulow, 2001; Brisch, 2012). Whereas many of these publications discuss how attachment can inform therapy, only a few propose a therapeutic model or therapeutic protocol that can be regarded as an "attachment therapy" per se. Some attachment therapies target children or adolescents and their parents (the most common being: Parent–Child Interaction Therapy, McNeil & Hembree-Kigin, 2010; The Circle of Security, Hoffman, Marvin, Cooper, & Powell, 2006; Attachment-Based Family Therapy, Diamond et al., 2010; and Attachment Narrative Therapy, Dallos, 2006; Dallos & Vetere, 2009, 2010). While not the focus of this volume, many parent–child-focused therapies target enhancing the sensitivity and responsiveness of parents. By and large, therapies that address parenting behavior generally yield improvements in child behavior (eg, reductions in externalizing problems) and some yield changes in the attachment styles of children as well as parents (for a review see Bakermans-Kranenburg et al., 2003).

In contrast to therapies used with parents and their children, there exists little by way of evidence-based therapeutic protocols that target adults. Therefore, our review of this literature is limited to two therapeutic approaches: Attachment-Focused Group Therapy (Kilmann, 1996) and Emotionally Focused Therapy (Johnson, 2004).

Attachment-Focused Group Therapy

Kilmann (1996) developed a manualized attachment-focused (AF) group intervention that attempts to foster greater awareness of attachment issues in clients, thereby providing a platform to engage in therapeutic work within a group context to promote positive and satisfying current or future romantic relationships. Given the focus on attachment, AF has an extensive focus on identifying and resolving the attachment issues of each group member coupled with segments on developing healthy beliefs and skills for navigating relationships. AF includes three sequential segments: (1) dysfunctional relationship beliefs and expectations, (2) attachment issues influencing partner choices and relationship styles, and (3) relationship strategies.

The relationship beliefs segment includes an introduction into the rationale for the program to enhance participant motivation and involvement. Participants and group facilitators share background about themselves including information about families and dating experiences. Participants are then supported in developing a rational belief system about romantic relationships. The participants then form small groups and work through material related to commonly held unrealistic relationship beliefs regarding relationships. Using Socratic reasoning, the group facilitators challenge any unrealistic beliefs held by the participants. The "attachment issues" segment is focused on familial factors that may contribute to the development of a person's attachment style and their decision-making and choices regarding romantic partners. During this segment of the group therapy, group facilitators use cognitive restructuring methods to help group members identify and express disappointments and emotions such as anger and they are encouraged to resolve their negative affect as they relate to their relationship experiences. Group members also discuss their dating successes and failures along with the attachment-related emotions associated with these successes and failures. Participants are encouraged to resolve these feelings and related experiences. The relationship strategies segment provides participants with helpful guidelines and strategies to navigate relationships more successfully. Two published studies by Kilmann and colleagues have investigated the efficacy of this therapy. Kilmann et al., 1999 tested the AF group intervention on 13 women with attachment avoidance and compared this group against a nonintervention control group. At 6-month follow-up, AF participants reported improved and more positive interpersonal styles, enhanced satisfaction with family relationships, and a reduction in adherence to dysfunctional relationship beliefs compared to the control group. Furthermore, participants reported reduced fearful attachment and increased attachment security and reported more positive relationship experiences than the control group. However, as noted by Brennan (1999), given the small sample size of this study, the study was likely to be significantly underpowered.

In another study, Kilmann, Urbaniak, and Parnell (2006) randomly assigned college students with insecure adult attachment patterns into either an AF group intervention, a manualized relationship skills (RS) intervention group, or a no-intervention control group. At 6 months postintervention, the AF and RS groups reported reduced adherence to dysfunctional relationship beliefs and an increased ability to control anger compared to the control group. The AF intervention group also demonstrated higher self-esteem, decreased angry reaction, and increased control of anger. At 15–18 months postintervention, participants in the AF and RS group interventions reported enhanced self-awareness and positive relationship expectations and experiences, while participants in the control group demonstrated no changes over time.

Emotionally Focused Therapy

Emotionally Focused Couple Therapy (EFT, Johnson, 2004) is largely under-pinned by an attachment theory framework and is aimed at addressing people's needs for safety and security. Attending to these fundamental attachment needs as part of therapy creates a more secure attachment relationship between ro-mantic partners. EFT focuses on the regulation and processing of affect, gearing therapeutic work towards healing attachment injuries (emotional hurts that have compromised the attachment bond between relationship partners).

In dealing with attachment injuries in session, the therapist's role parallels that of a security-promoting figure (Johnson, 2009). The therapist acts as a se-cure base and safe haven thereby supporting couples to explore painful issues that have compromised the couple's attachment relationship in the past. As part of EFT, experiential, intrapsychic, and systemic factors that shape harmful and recursive interaction patterns in couples are targeted and addressed (Johnson, 2004). The therapist uses techniques such as constant validation, empathic re-flection, and evocative questioning to elicit an understanding of the role that these factors play in their relationship.

Therapeutic work within EFT involves nine steps separated into three stages.

Stage one is an assessment of the couple's destructive interaction pattern (eg, demand-withdrawal communication), and therapeutic work is aimed at de-escalating this destructive behavior. The therapist works on helping the couple to step out of their destructive patterns and view these patterns as the couple's joint enemy. In stage two, the therapist works on restructuring the couple's bond to yield positive interaction patterns. These patterns involve mutual emotional accessibility and responsiveness in which withdrawn partners become emotion-ally reengaged and criticism and blame are softened. According to Johnson and Rheem (2012) this restructuring of the relationship allows both partners to have their attachment needs met, while also assuaging their partners' distress, fears, worries, concerns, or vulnerabilities. Johnson and Rheem suggest that this alternative relationship environment (brought about as a function of therapy) constitutes what Bowlby (1969/1982) termed effective dependency, where each partner can offer the other a safe haven and a secure base.

In stage three, the therapist helps the couple work on consolidating their revised perceptions of their relationships. The couple generates a coherent nar-rative of their descent into distress and their ascent into a relationship charac-terized by love, comfort, and safety. As the couple develops their narrative, the therapist encourages them to acknowledge that problems that were once deemed threatening and distressing (and likely activated the attachment system) are now perceived as manageable and solvable, and hence can and should be addressed.

During therapy, the therapist uses empathic reflection, constant validation, and evocative questioning to help increase relationship partners' awareness and clarity about given problems or issues. The therapist also heightens the clients' experience through the use of images and replays, and subtle reinterpretations of language.

The therapist also reflects patterns of interaction between relationship partners and reframes interactions and responses in terms of attachment theory; for example, framing withdrawal as a response to rejection rather than as a response of indifference or apathy towards the complaining partner.

Currently there are about 30 empirical studies investigating various outcomes, including the effectiveness of EFT (eg, Dalgleish et al., 2015; Dalton, Greenman, Classen, & Johnson, 2013). Regardless of study design or the sample size of studies (some are randomized controlled trials and some are single case studies), the outcomes of EFT are largely consistent. Couples who go through EFT generally report enhanced relationship functioning, reductions in relationship-related depression and anxiety, resolution of attachment injuries, improved adjustment to chronic illness, and reduced trauma symptomatology (eg, Dalgleish et al., 2014; Dessaulles, Johnson, & Denton, 2003; Halchuk, Makinen, & Johnson, 2010). For instance, Halchuk, Makinen, and Johnson found that couples that sought EFT for marital distress reported improvements in trust, forgiveness, and couple adjustment, and reductions in the severity of attachment injuries. These improvements were sustained 3 years postintervention. In another study, Soltani, Shairi, Roshan, and Rahimi (2014) found that infertile couples demonstrated reductions in depression, anxiety, and stress symptoms once they were administered EFT.

Summary

Many therapists use attachment theory to inform their therapeutic practice in working with people experiencing mental health problems or attachment insecurities. Despite this, there is little by way of evidence-based manualized therapeutic approaches for working with adults that are based on attachment theory. In fact, only two therapeutic interventions explicitly target adults, "Attachment-Focused Group Therapy" (Kilmann, 1996) and "EFT" (Johnson, 2004). While both therapeutic interventions have received empirical support, the evidence for Kilmann's approach is limited to three studies. Thus, significantly more work is required to determine the efficacy of this therapeutic approach. EFT on the other hand has been evaluated as part of a large number of studies, and shows promising results in terms of mental health outcomes and in helping couples strengthen their romantic relationships.

CHAPTER SUMMARY

Attachment insecurities appear to be a risk factor for a wide variety of mental health problems. In the chapter we reviewed four of the most widely studied mental health problems that have been linked to adult attachment: affective disorders, posttraumatic stress disorder and trauma symptoms, eating disorders, and personality disorders. Our overview suggests that attachment insecurity heightens people's tendencies to experience mental health problems. It also suggests that there are three major factors explaining the link between attachment insecurity and mental health problems. Importantly, these factors provide avenues for mental health professionals to undertake therapeutic work with insecurely attached clients. The pathways highlight that intervention strategies may be most effective if they target cognitive and affective aspects of attachment insecurities while also attending to the interpersonal difficulties that people may have in relating to others.

In the chapter, we also provided an overview of the associations between attachment theory and therapeutic strategies and interventions. Interestingly, there exists little by way of research investigating the extent to which therapy can assist with shifting people's attachment style. This is clearly an area in need of further research if we are to develop therapeutic models that attenuate attachment insecurity, and for that matter, foster attachment security. We outlined two therapies that are heavily grounded in attachment theory for working with adults. In particular, EFT seems to be an effective therapeutic approach that is supported by numerous empirical studies. Irrespective of whether a therapeutic approach reflects a systematized protocol or a more nuanced method, what is clear is that attachment theory is a framework of wide appeal for therapists and is likely to provide further therapeutic insights in the future.

Epilogue

Thousands of articles, chapters, and books have been written on the topic of attachment. The book you just finished reading highlights some major questions that researchers, practitioners, and students of attachment have raised over the years, and summarizes the answers to those questions. Nevertheless, there are still many open questions for people to investigate. In the Epilogue we highlight some of these questions.

WHAT ARE SOME OPEN QUESTIONS IN ADULT ATTACHMENT?

Can Attachment Styles be Explained Away by Basic Personality Traits?

Some scholars have wondered how attachment styles relate to other kinds of personality constructs that are studied in social-personality psychology, such as the personality dimensions highlighted by the Big Five framework (ie, Extraversion, Agreeableness, Conscientiousness, Neuroticism, and Openness).

There are different perspectives in personality psychology on what the Big Five dimensions represent. For some scholars, the five factor framework is a descriptive taxonomy—a means to locate a variety of individual differences constructs within a common descriptive space (eg, John, Naumann, & Soto, 2008). The Big Five framework has been extraordinarily valuable for this purpose. One of the Big Five factors, Neuroticism, tends to correlate 0.40–0.50 with attachment anxiety (Noftle & Shaver, 2006). This suggests that attachment anxiety may be usefully construed as belonging to a family of traits that are relevant for understanding negative affective experiences. Attachment avoidance is more difficult to locate within the Big Five space, but most researchers report small to moderate negative correlations between avoidance and Conscientiousness and Extraversion (Noftle & Shaver, 2006). In short, if modern personality taxonomies are used as maps to locate a variety of descriptors in multidimensional space, then it seems appropriate to locate attachment anxiety near Neuroticism and to conceptualize avoidance as a vector that cuts through several of the traits.

Noftle and Shaver (2006) observed that attachment and personality dimensions tend to uniquely predict various outcomes, despite their overlap. For example, in predicting variation in relationship quality, the attachment dimensions were capable of explaining variance above and beyond that explained by the Big Five personality traits. The reverse analysis (starting with the attachment dimensions and adding the Big Five) did not improve prediction. This kind of

Adult Attachment. http://dx.doi.org/10.1016/B978-0-12-420020-3.00012-8
267

finding is commonly reported in the literature. Specifically, when general traits are statistically controlled, the attachment dimensions continue to predict outcomes of interest in theoretically anticipated ways (eg, Gillath, Bunge, Shaver, Wendelken, & Mikulincer, 2005).

For some scholars, the five factor framework is not merely a taxonomy. According to Costa and McCrae (2008), the five factors represent the foundational dimensions of personality in adulthood. Costa and McCrae, for example, view the five factors as basic tendencies, grounded in genetic variation between persons, which give rise to other aspects of human functioning (eg, the self-concept, attitudes). Further, Costa and McCrae argue that the five factors are not affected by external influences, such as cultural norms, life experiences, and relationship processes.

Within the Costa and McCrae (2008) framework, it would not be appropriate to view attachment styles as facets of more general traits in a descriptive taxonomy. One reason for this is that basic traits are not influenced by relational contexts. But, as we have reviewed in this book, attachment styles manifest differently across contexts (chapter: What Are the Effects of Context on Attachment?) and change in light of interpersonal experiences (chapters: How Do Individual Differences in Attachment Develop? and How Stable Are Attachment Styles in Adulthood?). Within Costa and McCrae's framework, attachment styles might best be characterized as "characteristic adaptations": characteristics of persons that are shaped to some extent by basic tendencies (eg, personality traits), dynamic processes, and interpersonal experiences.

In summary, we believe it is useful to locate the attachment dimensions—and other individual differences constructs—within a common space. Doing so makes it easier to see where the various islands exist within the sea of personality variables. But we are reluctant to suggest that the individual differences studied by attachment researchers are simply alternative labels for personality traits that are already studied by Big Five trait psychologists. Not only are the associations between them far from perfect, but what is known about attachment styles to date seems incompatible with certain ways of conceptualizing personality traits.

Having said this, we also don't want to err on the side of emphasizing the uniqueness of attachment styles too much. Bowlby and Ainsworth viewed their efforts as an attempt to build a theory of personality development. Thus, in some respects, attachment theory can be viewed as a theory of personality, but one that emphasizes specific aspects of personality functioning rather than attempting to explain the full gamut of individual differences (see Fraley & Shaver, 2008). Given the increased interest in recent years in gene–environment transactions (eg, Briley, Harden, & Tucker-Drob, 2014) and epigenetics (Slavich & Cole, 2013), we believe that future research on personality development can be enhanced by integrating some of the themes traditionally emphasized in the personality trait tradition (eg, the heritable foundations of individual differences) with those emphasized in the study of attachment (eg, person–environment transactions, mental representation, and affective processes). In other words, attachment theory could prove to be a valuable foundation for investigating personality dynamics and not just attachment processes themselves.

ARE ATTACHMENT STYLES REALLY JUST MATING STRATEGIES?

Some scholars have proposed that what attachment scholars call "attachment styles" are really just manifestations of long- and short-term sexual mating strategies (eg, Kirkpatrick, 1998, see chapter: What Are the Effects of Context on Attachment?). Long-term mating strategies reflect strategies used to obtain a long-term mate, a partner for life, and indicate investment of resources in child rearing (eg, finding one's soulmate or other half). Short-term mating strategies, conversely, reflect strategies to obtain short-term access to a mate, and genetic variety (eg, a one night stand). Attachment security is thought to reflect long-term mating strategies; whereas attachment avoidance is thought to reflect short-term mating strategies.

Kirkpatrick made at least four points in his 1998 chapter in which he leveled a series of criticisms regarding the explanatory value of attachment in understanding romantic relationships. One is that love (or commitment) is sufficient to solve the problem of bringing mates together for the purposes of raising children. We don't need an extra construct—the attachment behavioral system—to solve that conceptual problem. Second, the notion that the "attachment system" is what is driving the kinds of dynamics we study in romantic relationships is mistaken. Adult romantic partners do not protect one another against predators in the way that attachment figures protect their offspring. Moreover, a lot of what seems like attachment behavior can just as easily be understood as a manifestation of caregiving. Third, although individual differences exist in how people think about and behave in close relationships, those differences are reflections of short- and long-term mating strategies, not "attachment" per se. For example, preference for closeness and intimacy—that might be perceived as attachment security—can be the outcome of the endorsement of long-term mating strategies. Finally, he argues that, while attachment theorists emphasize the role of relational experiences in shaping individual differences, this argument is also put forth by life history theorists who suggest that mating strategies are conditional upon the environmental context in which individuals are raised (see chapter: What Are the Effects of Context on Attachment?).

Although Kirkpatrick raises some valid points, some attachment researchers (eg, Zeifman & Hazan, 2008) have argued that these ideas represent a narrow view of both the attachment bond and of attachment styles. First, Zeifman and Hazan (2008) argue that attachment helps ensure that infants receive routine adequate care (food, warmth, shelter, etc.), so whereas protection from one's partner might be less important, staying with one's partner to take care of offspring is still important. Replacing the concept of the "attachment system" with love (or commitment) as Kirkpatrick suggests in his first point raises other problems. For example, the concept of love is rather limited in its scope and

270 Epilogue

lacks the developmental, evolutionary, and cognitive roots attachment has. The attachment behavioral system is indeed a powerful framework for understanding interpersonal processes as we have demonstrated throughout this book. So from a practical point, studying these processes using attachment presents advantages for researchers that love does not.

Second, while adults might not need the physical protection of their attachment figures and do not turn to their attachment figures for such protection, attachment behavior in adulthood is not dissimilar from the behavior of older children and adolescents (see chapter: What Is Attachment Theory?) who have internalized mental representations of their attachment figures. However, children, adolescents, and adults all need someone to serve as their secure base and safe haven. Adults still need to be able to draw on the support of others when in need of help or in distress, and still want to share their happiness and achievements. Furthermore, the fact that a behavior is not identical at different phases of development does not mean that the behavior serves different functions or that other behavioral systems are in play. Zeifman and Hazan (2008) use feeding behavior as an example of this argument—although it changes dramatically over the course of development—the basic function of feeding remains the same.

Third, while Life History Theory suggests that similar mechanisms shape sexual strategies and attachment style, it does not suggest that attachment style and sex strategies are the same modules. Rather some are directly related to sex and reproduction, whereas others are more about feelings of closeness, security, dependence, and trust. Based on these points, and research on the unique and interactive effects of the attachment and the sex systems, we tend to agree with Zeifman and Hazan (2008). A final point to consider is that the fact that adults are attached to god, pets, places, and alike suggests that there is more to attachment than sex.

SHOULD ATTACHMENT THEORY BE CONSIDERED A THEORY OF CLOSE RELATIONSHIPS?

One of the criticisms leveled against attachment theory is that the theory offers an inadequate account of relational processes. For instance, critics such as John Holmes (Holmes & Cameron, 2005) suggest that attachment theory places too much emphasis on the individual and not enough on relational phenomena at the level of the couple. He also notes that attachment theory does not provide an adequate account of the interdependent nature of relationships.

We agree with Holmes and colleagues that attachment theory is a theory of the individual. It has its origins in psychoanalytic theory, which was largely concerned with inner life, a theme that is reflected in our modern emphasis on internal working models and mental representation. It isn't a relational theory in the way that interdependence theory is. Nonetheless, it *is* a theory about how relationships shape our lives. So, it has the potential to be a useful framework for understanding close relationships.

Importantly, however, the theory is not limited to the study of individuals. In fact, hundreds of studies have investigated attachment processes at the dyadic level, thereby modelling the relative contribution of relationship partners' attachment styles to various dyadic processes, such as the seeking and provision of support and the use of conflict patterns in dealing with relationship issues (eg, Simpson, Rholes, & Phillips, 1996; Feeney, Noller, & Hanrahan, 1994). These dyadic studies of adult attachment have provided another layer of understanding regarding relationship processes and outcomes on top of the knowledge already garnered from studies that focus on the individual.

Attachment theory also provides a highly integrative and comprehensive account of relationship dynamics across all stages of romantic relationships (initiation, maintenance, and dissolution) and across the cognitive, affective, and behavioral domains of interpersonal processes. Furthermore, attachment theory provides a historical account for how individual differences in relationship functioning are rooted in past relationship experiences and guide interactions in both the present and future. Whereas other theories may provide quite comprehensive accounts of relationship processes, they tend to focus on the origins of these processes in one's current relationship. Such theories say little about how experiences pertaining to previous significant close relationships may carry over into current relationships, or how relationship dynamics are rooted in the interplay between evolved behavioral systems. Furthermore, theories such as interdependence theory say little about people's reactions to the dissolution of a romantic relationship. Attachment theory has the potential to address many, if not all, of these issues.

IS ATTACHMENT INSECURITY FUNCTIONAL?

Research demonstrates that attachment security is associated with mental-health-related outcomes such as buffering the effects of psychopathology; whereas attachment insecurity is associated with a wide array of negative outcomes including mental health problems. As a result of these findings, many people come to label attachment security as "good," "adaptive," or "beneficial." In contrast, attachment insecurity is often considered "bad," "maladaptive," or "problematic." However, by drawing on life history theory, scholars such as Belsky (1999), and more recently Del Giudice (2009a) and Ein-Dor, Mikulincer, Doron, and Shaver (2010) have suggested that insecurity can be seen as an adaptive strategy that yields benefits and positive outcomes in contexts that reflect harsh, unsafe, or unpredictable environments (eg, living in a dangerous inner-city neighborhood characterized by high crime, see chapter: What Is the Attachment Behavioral System? And, How Is It Linked to Other Behavioral Systems?). In fact, research using a life history framework provides evidence to support claims of the adaptive advantage of attachment insecurity (eg, Del Giudice, 2011). For example, Ein-Dor et al. (2010) suggests that under conditions of serious danger, anxious individuals' hypervigilance to threat may offer an adaptive advantage by alerting people to serious imminent hazards. In terms of attachment avoidance, the premium placed on self-reliance and self-preservation by avoidant individuals may assist in the detection of escape paths that they and others can use to avoid danger. Part of Ein-Dor's argument is that, although these insecure strategies may seem maladaptive at the individual level, in group and social contexts—contexts in which most people reside—they can be advantageous.

The flip-side to the question "Is attachment insecurity functional?" can be framed in terms of "Is attachment security dysfunctional?" In an attempt to answer this question, Gillath, Gregersen, Canterberry, and Schmitt (2014) recently studied whether too much attachment security might be maladaptive or result in negative outcomes (such as lower life satisfaction, lower success, and lower SES). Gillath et al. found no evidence to support this suggestion. On the one hand, the findings by Gillath and coworkers may suggest that even high levels of attachment security reflect an adaptive advantage for individuals. On the other hand, this study does not provide unequivocal evidence regarding the adaptiveness of security.

WHAT MIGHT UNDERLIE OR EXPLAIN ATTACHMENT SECURITY?

Although we have already provided some answers in the book to this question, one answer we didn't directly provide (partially because we do not have a unified opinion about its validity) is the possibility that two systems, rather than one behavioral system, govern attachment behavior. One system may govern attachment insecurity and a separate behavioral system may govern security. From this perspective, attachment insecurity might reflect an evolved behavioral system with hard-wired brain circuitry to manage potential threats (Tooby & Cosmides, 1990, 2006; Trower et al., 1990; Pinker, 1997). This circuitry or system has already been proposed and is referred to in the literature by various names including the defense system (Trower et al., 1990), the hazard-precaution system (Boyer & Lienard, 2006), and (interestingly enough) the security motivation system (Woody & Szechtman, 2011, 2013). This system, as described by Woody and Szechtman, is designed for dealing with environmental dangers and threats and involves three features. The first feature relates to the ability for the system to detect and process threat. The second feature relates to a motivational system designed to promote specific behaviors to achieve a set-goal. The third feature reflects the termination of behaviors once the set-goal is restored. The description of this defense system shares much in common with the way Bowlby describes the attachment behavioral system.

Conversely, attachment security may reflect a different behavioral system with hard-wired brain circuitry designed to handle needs related to personal growth and well-being (Reeve, 2015). This behavioral system would be attuned to the detection of stimuli reflecting positive rewards and opportunities for personal development. This type of a behavioral system shares parallels with behavioral models and concepts outlined in various realms of positive psychology such as Fredrickson's (2001) "broaden and build" model of positive emotions. In her model, Fredrickson suggests that being open to and experiencing positive emotions and rewards act as a foundation that helps broaden and enhance a person's physical, intellectual, and psychological capacities (for a related perspective, readers are referred to Csikszentmihalyi, 2014 on flow-state).

Framing attachment dynamics from a dual-systems perspective in which one system is sensitized towards threat stimuli (attachment insecurity) and another system is calibrated towards reward stimuli (attachment security) shares much in common with broad systems of approach and avoidance motivation (eg, McNaughton & Gray, 2000; Gable, 2006). From this standpoint, attachment insecurity may be considered a system of avoidance motivation and attachment security a system of approach motivation. Our discussion of dual systems within the context of attachment is one of speculation. It does however raise the possibility that the relationship between security and insecurity is more complex than we think and may merit future investigation.

FINAL WORDS

The questions we address in this Epilogue remain very much open, even if we tried to provide some answers (that we did not all agree on). But we would like to remind readers that the questions outlined in this Epilogue are just *examples* of *open* questions. This means that there are potentially many other open questions about attachment theory. Our goal in this book has been to provide readers with an overview of attachment theory and research. In doing so, we have addressed many of the most common and fundamental questions we get asked when teaching classes and giving talks on the topic of attachment theory. We hope that this book has left readers with a fervent desire to learn more about attachment and to pursue such open questions in their future research or clinical practice. To close our Epilogue, and for that matter this book, we draw on yet another quote from Johnny Cash. A quote about his primary attachment figure, his wife June Carter:

> *There's unconditional love there. You hear that phrase a lot but it's real with me and her. She loves me in spite of everything, in spite of myself. She has saved my life more than once. She's always been there with her love, and it has certainly made me forget the pain for a long time, many times. When it gets dark and everybody's gone home and the lights are turned off, it's just me and her.*

References

Adamczyk, K., & Bookwala, J. (2013). Adult attachment and single vs. partnered relationship status in Polish University Students. *Psychological Topics, 22,* 481–500.

Admoni, S. (2006). *Attachment security and eating disorders.* Unpublished doctoral dissertation, Bar-Ilan University, Ramat Gan, Israel.

Agishtein, P., & Brumbaugh, C. (2013). Cultural variation in adult attachment: the impact of ethnicity, collectivism, and country of origin. *Journal of Social, Evolutionary, and Cultural Psychology, 7,* 384.

Agrawal, H. R., Gunderson, J., Holmes, B. M., & Lyons-Ruth, K. (2004). Attachment studies with borderline patients: a review. *Harvard Review of Psychiatry, 12,* 94–104.

Ahern, G. L., & Schwartz, G. E. (1985). Differential lateralization for positive and negative emotion in the human brain: EEG spectral analysis. *Neuropsychologia, 23,* 745–755.

Ainsworth, M. D. S. (1967). *Infancy in Uganda: Infant care and the growth of love.* Baltimore, MD: Johns Hopkins University Press.

Ainsworth, M. S. (1989). Attachments beyond infancy. *American Psychologist, 44,* 709–716.

Ainsworth, M. D. S. (1991). Attachments and other affectional bonds across the life cycle. In C. Parkes, J. Stevenson-Hinde, & P. Marris (Eds.), *Attachment across the life cycle* (pp. 33–51). New York, NY: Routledge.

Ainsworth, M. D. S., Blehar, M., Waters, E., & Wall, S. (1978). *Patterns of attachment: A psychological study of the Strange Situation.* Hillsdale, NJ: Erlbaum.

Alexander, P. C., Anderson, C. L., Brand, B., Schaeffer, C. M., Grelling, B. Z., & Kretz, L. (1998). Adult attachment and long-term effects in survivors of incest. *Child Abuse and Neglect, 22,* 45–81.

Alexander, R., Feeney, J., Hohaus, L., & Noller, P. (2001). Attachment style and coping resources as predictors of coping strategies in the transition to parenthood. *Personal Relationships, 8,* 137–152.

American Psychiatric Association. (2013). *Diagnostic and statistical manual of mental disorders* (5th ed.). Washington, DC: Author.

Andersen, S. M., & Cole, S. W. (1990). "Do I know you?": the role of significant others in general social perception. *Journal of Personality and Social Psychology, 59,* 384–399.

Andersen, S. M., Glassman, N. S., Chen, S. C., & Cole, S. W. (1995). Transference in social perception: the role of chronic accessibility in significant-other representations. *Journal of Personality and Social Psychology, 69,* 41–56.

Anderson, J. R., & Bower, G. H. (1973). *Human associative memory.* Washington, DC: V. H. Winston & Sons.

Anderson, M. C., Ochsner, K. N., Kuhl, B., Cooper, J., Robertson, E., Gabrieli, S. W., ... & Gabrieli, J. D. (2004). Neural systems underlying the suppression of unwanted memories. *Science, 303,* 232–235.

Antonovsky, A. (1987). *Unravelling the mysteries of health.* San Francisco, CA: Jossey-Bass.

Antonucci, T., Akiyama, H., & Takahashi, K. (2004). Attachment and close relationships across the life span. *Attachment and Human Development, 6,* 353–370.

Adult Attachment. http://dx.doi.org/10.1016/B978-0-12-420020-3.00013-X

Arndt, J., Schimel, J., Greenberg, J., & Pyszczynaski, T. (2002). The intrinsic self and defensiveness: evidence that activating the intrinsic self reduces self-handicapping and conformity. *Personality and Social Psychology Bulletin, 28*, 671–683.

Aron, A., Fisher, H., Mashek, D. J., Strong, G., Li, H. F., & Brown, L. L. (2005). Reward, motivation, and emotion systems associated with early-stage intense romantic love. *Journal of Neurophysiology, 94*, 327–337.

Aspelmeier, J. E., Elliott, A. N., & Smith, C. H. (2007). Childhood sexual abuse, attachment, and trauma symptoms in college females: the moderating role of attachment. *Child Abuse & Neglect, 31*, 549–566.

Atzil, S., Hendler, T., & Feldman, R. (2011). Specifying the neurobiological basis of human attachment: brain, hormones, and behavior in synchronous and intrusive mothers. *Neuropsychopharmacology, 36*, 2603–2615.

Bachi, K. (2013). Application of attachment theory to equine-facilitated psychotherapy. *Journal of Contemporary Psychotherapy, 43*, 187–196.

Bagot, R. C., van Hasselt, F. N., Champagne, D. L., Meaney, M. J., Krugers, H. J., & Joëls, M. (2009). Maternal care determines rapid effects of stress mediators on synaptic plasticity in adult rat hippocampal dentate gyrus. *Neurobiology of Learning and Memory, 92*, 292–300.

Bakermans-Kranenburg, M. J., & van IJzendoorn, M. H. (2009). The first 10,000 adult attachment interviews: distributions of adult attachment representations in clinical and non-clinical groups. *Attachment & Human Development, 11*, 223–263.

Bakermans-Kranenburg, M. J., & van IJzendoorn, M. H. (2011). Differential susceptibility to rearing environment depending on dopamine-related genes: new evidence and a meta-analysis. *Development and Psychopathology, 23*, 39–52.

Bakermans-Kranenburg, M. J., & van IJzendoorn, M. H. (2014). A sociability gene? Meta-analysis of oxytocin receptor genotype effects in humans. *Psychiatric Genetics, 24*, 45–51.

Bakermans-Kranenburg, M. J., Van Ijzendoorn, M. H., & Juffer, F. (2003). Less is more: meta-analyses of sensitivity and attachment interventions in early childhood. *Psychological Bulletin, 129*, 195–215.

Baldwin, M. W. (1992). Relational schemas and the processing of social information. *Psychological Bulletin, 112*, 461.

Baldwin, M. W., & Fehr, B. (1995). On the instability of attachment style ratings. *Personal Relationships, 2*, 247–261.

Baldwin, M. W., Fehr, B., Keedian, E., Seidel, M., & Thomson, D. W. (1993). An exploration of the relational schemata underlying attachment styles: self-report and lexical decision approaches. *Personality and Social Psychology Bulletin, 19*, 746–754.

Baldwin, M. W., Keelan, J. P. R., Fehr, B., Enns, V., & Koh-Rangarajoo, E. (1996). Social cognitive conceptualization of attachment working models: availability and accessibility effects. *Journal of Personality and Social Psychology, 71*, 94–104.

Bales, K. L., Maninger, N., & Hinde, K. (2012). New directions in the neurobiology and physiology of paternal care. In G. Adams, & O. Gillath (Eds.), *Relationship science: Integrating evolutionary, neuroscience, and sociocultural approaches* (pp. 91–111). Washington, DC: American Psychological Association.

Banse, R. (2003). Beyond verbal self-report: priming methods in relationship research. In J. Musch, & K. C. Klauer (Eds.), *The psychology of evaluation. Affective processes in cognition and emotion* (pp. 245–274). Mahwah, NJ: Lawrence Erlbaum Associates, Inc.

Barbara, A. M., & Dion, K. L. (2000). Breaking up is hard to do, especially for strongly "preoccupied" lovers. *Journal of Personal & Interpersonal Loss, 5*, 315–342.

Bargh, J. A., & Chartrand, T. L. (2000). A practical guide to priming and automaticity research. In H. Reis, & C. Judd (Eds.), *Handbook of research methods in social psychology* (pp. 253–285). New York, NY: Cambridge University Press.

Bargh, J. A., Schwader, K. L., Hailey, S. E., Dyer, R. L., & Boothby, E. J. (2012). Automaticity in social-cognitive processes. *Trends in Cognitive Science, 16,* 593–605.

Barone, L. (2003). Developmental protective and risk factors in borderline personality disorder: a study using the Adult Attachment Interview. *Attachment and Human Development, 5,* 64–77.

Bartels, A., & Zeki, S. (2004). The neural correlates of maternal and romantic love. *NeuroImage, 21,* 1155–1166.

Bartholomew, K. (1990). Avoidance of intimacy: an attachment perspective. *Journal of Social and Personal Relationships, 7,* 147–178.

Bartholomew, K., & Horowitz, L. (1991). Attachment styles among young adults: a test of a four category model. *Journal of Personality and Social Psychology, 61,* 226–244.

Bartholomew, K., Kwong, M. J., & Hart, S. D. (2001). Attachment. In J. W. Livesley (Ed.), *Handbook of personality disorders: Theory, research, and treatment* (pp. 196–230). New York, NY: Guilford Press.

Bartz, J. A., Zaki, J., Ochsner, K. N., Bolger, N., Kolevzon, A., Ludwig, N., & Lydon, J. E. (2010). Effects of oxytocin on recollections of maternal care and closeness. *Proceedings of the National Academy of Sciences USA, 107,* 21371–21375.

Batgos, J., & Leadbeater, B. J. (1994). Parental attachment, peer relations, and dysphoria in adolescence. In M. B. Sperling, & W. H. Berman (Eds.), *Attachment in adults: Clinical and developmental perspectives* (pp. 155–178). New York, NY: Guilford Press.

Batson, C. D., Fultz, J., & Schoenrade, P. A. (1987). Distress and empathy: two qualitatively distinct vicarious emotions with different motivational consequences. *Journal of Personality, 55,* 19–39.

Baumeister, R. F., & Leary, M. R. (1995). The need to belong: desire for interpersonal attachments as a fundamental human motivation. *Psychological Bulletin, 117,* 497–529.

Becker, S., Mosovitch, M., Behrmann, M., & Joordens, S. (1997). Long-term semantic priming: a computational account and empirical evidence. *Journal of Experimental Psychology: Learning, Memory, and Cognition, 23,* 1059–1082.

Beckes, L., & Simpson, J. A. (2009). Attachment, reproduction, and life history trade-offs: a broader view of human mating. *Behavioral and Brain Sciences, 32,* 23–24.

Beckes, L., & Coan, J. A. (2011). Social baseline theory: the role of social proximity in emotion and economy of action. *Social and Personality Psychology Compass, 5,* 976–988.

Beckes, L., & Coan, J. A. (2013). Toward an integrative neuroscience of relationships. In J. Simpson, & L. Campbell (Eds.), *The oxford handbook of close relationships* (pp. 685–710). New York, NY: Oxford University Press.

Beckes, L., IJzerman, H., & Tops, M. (2014). *Toward a radically embodied neuroscience of attachment and relationships?* Available from SSRN: http://papers.ssrn.com/sol3/papers. cfm?abstract_id=2429522. doi: 10.3389/fnhum.2015.00266.

Behringer, J., Reiner, I., & Spangler, G. (2011). Maternal representations of past and current attachment relationships, and emotional experience across the transition to motherhood: a longitudinal study. *Journal of Family Psychology, 25,* 210.

Belsky, J. (1996). Parent, infant, and social-contextual antecedents of father-son attachment security. *Developmental Psychology, 32,* 905–914.

Belsky, J. (1999). Modern evolutionary theory and patterns of attachment. In J. Cassidy, & P. R. Shaver (Eds.), *Handbook of attachment: Theory, research, and clinical applications* (pp. 141–161). New York, NY: Guilford Press.

Belsky, J., & Fearon, R. M. P. (2008). Precursors of attachment security. In J. Cassidy, & P. R. Shaver (Eds.), *Adult attachment: Theory, research, and clinical applications* (2nd ed., pp. 295–316). New York, NY: Guilford Press.

Belsky, J., & Isabella, R. (1998). Maternal, infant, and social-contextual determinants of attachment security. In J. Belsky, & T. Nezworski (Eds.), *Clinical implications of attachment* (pp. 41–94). Hillsdale, NJ: Erlbaum.

Belsky, J., Steinberg, L., & Draper, P. (1991). Childhood experience, interpersonal development, and reproductive strategy: an evolutionary theory of socialization. *Child Development, 62*, 647–670.

Belsky, J., Houts, R. M., & Fearon, R. P. (2010). Infant attachment security and the timing of puberty: testing an evolutionary hypothesis. *Psychological Science, 21*, 1195–1201.

Bennett, C. M., Baird, A. A., Miller, M. B., & Wolford, G. L. (2010). Neural correlates of interspecies perspective taking in the post-mortem Atlantic Salmon: an argument for multiple comparisons correction. *Journal of Serendipitous and Unexpected Results, 1*, 1–5.

Benetti, S., McCrory, E., Arulanantham, S., De Sanctis, T., McGuire, P., & Mechelli, A. (2010). Attachment style, affective loss and gray matter volume: a voxel-based morphometry study. *Human Brain Mapping, 31*, 1482–1489.

Benson, L. A., Sevier, M., & Christensen, A. (2013). The impact of behavioral couple therapy on attachment in distressed couples. *Journal of Marital and Family Therapy, 39*, 407–420.

Berant, E. (2009). Attachment styles, the Rorschach, and the Thematic Apperception Test: using traditional projective measures to assess aspects of adult attachment. In J. Obegi, & E. Berant (Eds.), *Attachment theory and research in clinical work with adults* (pp. 181–206). New York, NY: Guilford Press.

Berlin, L., Ziv, Y., Amaya-Jackson, L., & Greenberg, M. (2005). Enhancing early attachments: theory, research, intervention, and policy. In L. J. Berlin (Ed.), *Interventions to enhance early attachments: The state of the field today* (pp. 152–177). New York, NY: Guilford Press.

Berlin, L. J., Cassidy, J., & Appleyard, K. (2008). The influence of early attachments on other relationships. In J. Cassidy, & P. R. Shaver (Eds.), *Adult attachment: Theory, research, and clinical applications* (2nd ed., pp. 333–347). New York, NY: Guilford Press.

Berridge, K. C. (2007). The debate over dopamine's role in reward: the case for incentive salience. *Psychopharmacology, 191*, 391–431.

Berry, K., & Danquah, A. (2015). Attachment-informed therapy for adults: towards a unifying perspective on practice. *Psychology and Psychotherapy: Theory, Research and Practice*, Article first published online: July 14, 2015; doi: 10.1111/papt.12063.

Besser, A., Priel, B., & Wiznitzer, A. (2002). Childbearing depressive symptomatology in high-risk pregnancies: the roles of working models and social support. *Personal Relationships, 9*, 395–413.

Besser, A., & Priel, B. (2009). Emotional responses to a romantic partner's imaginary rejection: the roles of attachment anxiety, covert narcissism, and self-evaluation. *Journal of Personality, 77*, 287–325.

Besser, A., Neria, Y., & Haynes, M. (2009). Adult attachment, perceived stress, and PTSD among civilians exposed to ongoing terrorist attacks in Southern Israel. *Personality and Individual Differences, 47*, 851–857.

Bewernick, B. H., Hurlemann, R., Matusch, A., Kayser, S., Grubert, C., Hadrysiewicz, B., et al. (2010). Nucleus accumbens deep brain stimulation decreases ratings of depression and anxiety in treatment-resistant depression. *Biological Psychiatry, 67*, 110–116.

Bifulco, A., Figueiredo, B., Guedeney, N., Gorman, L. L., Hayes, S., & Muzik, M. (2004). Maternal attachment style and depression associated with childbirth: preliminary results from a European and US cross-cultural study. *British Journal of Psychiatry, 184*, 31–37.

Birnbaum, G. E., & Gillath, O. (2006). Measuring subgoals of the sexual behavioral system: what is sex good for? *Journal of Social and Personal Relationships, 23*, 675–701.

Birnbaum, G. E., Orr, I., Mikulincer, M., & Florian, V. (1997). When marriage breaks up: does attachment style contribute to coping and mental health? *Journal of Social and Personal Relationships, 14*, 643–654.

Bjorklund, D. F. (1997). The role immaturity in human development. *Psychological Bulletin, 122*, 153–169.

Blatz, W. (1940). *Hostages to peace: Parents and the children of democracy.* New York, NY: Morrow.

Boling, M. W., Barry, C. M., Kotchick, B. A., & Lowry, J. (2011). Relations among early adolescents' parent-adolescent attachment, perceived social competence, and friendship quality. *Psychological Reports, 109*, 819–841.

Boone, L. (2013). Are attachment styles differentially related to interpersonal perfectionism and binge eating symptoms? *Personality and Individual Differences, 54*, 931–935.

Bornstein, R. F. (1992). The dependent personality: developmental, social, and clinical perspectives. *Psychological Bulletin, 112*, 3–23.

Bosmans, G., Bowles, D. P., Dewitte, M., De Winter, S., & Braet, C. (2014). An experimental evaluation of the State Adult Attachment Measure: the influence of attachment primes on the content of state attachment representations. *Journal of Experimental Psychopathology, 5*, 134–150.

Bowlby, J. (1944). Forty-four juvenile thieves: their characters and home life. *International Journal of Psycho-Analysis, XXV*, 19–52.

Bowlby, J. (1951). *Maternal Care and Mental Health.* World Health Organization, Monograph Series No. 2. Geneva: World Health Organization.

Bowlby, J. (1969/1982) *Attachment and loss: Attachment* (Vol. 1). (2nd ed.). New York, NY: Basic Books.

Bowlby, J. (1973). *Attachment and loss: Vol. 2. Separation: Anxiety and anger.* New York, NY: Basic Books.

Bowlby, J. (1979). *The making and breaking of affectional bonds.* New York: Routledge, Taylor & Francis Group.

Bowlby, J. (1979). *The making and breaking of affectional bonds.* London: Tavistock.

Bowlby, J. (1980). *Attachment and loss: Vol. 3. Sadness and depression.* New York, NY: Basic Books.

Bowlby, J. (1988). *A secure base: Clinical applications of attachment theory.* London, UK: Routledge.

Bowlby, J., Robertson, J., & Rosenbluth, D. (1952). A two-year-old goes to hospital. *Psychoanalytic Study of the Child, 7*, 82–94.

Bradford, S. A., Feeney, J. A., & Campbell, L. (2002). Links between attachment orientations and dispositional and diary-based measures of disclosure in dating couples: a study of actor and partner effects. *Personal Relationships, 9*, 491–506.

Brassard, A., Shaver, P. R., & Lussier, Y. (2007). Attachment, sexual experience, and sexual pressure in romantic relationships: a dyadic approach. *Personal Relationships, 14*, 475–493.

Brennan, K. A. (1999). Searching for secure bases in attachment-focused group therapy: reaction to Kilmann et al. (1999). *Group Dynamics: Theory, Research, and Practice, 3*, 148–151.

Brennan, K. A., & Bosson, J. K. (1998). Attachment-style differences in attitudes toward and reactions to feedback from romantic partners: an exploration of the relational bases of self-esteem. *Personality and Social Psychology Bulletin, 24*, 699–714.

Brennan, K. A., & Morris, K. A. (1997). Attachment styles, self-esteem, and patterns of seeking feedback from romantic partners. *Personality and Social Psychology Bulletin, 23*, 23–31.

Brennan, K. A., & Shaver, P. R. (1995). Dimensions of adult attachment, affect regulation, and romantic relationship functioning. *Personality and Social Psychology Bulletin, 21*, 267–283.

Brennan, K. A., Clark, C. L., & Shaver, P. R. (1998). Self-report measurement of adult attachment: an integrative overview. In J. A. Simpson, & W. S. Rholes (Eds.), *Attachment theory and close relationships* (pp. 46–76). New York, NY: Guilford Press.

Bretherton, I. (1990). Communication patterns, internal working models, and the intergenerational transmission of attachment relationships. *Infant Mental Health Journal, 11*, 237–252.

Bretherton, I. (1992). The origins of attachment theory: John Bowlby and Mary Ainsworth. *Developmental Psychology, 28*, 759–775.

Bretherton, I., & Munholland, K. A. (1999). Internal working models revisited. In J. Cassidy, & P. R. Shave (Eds.), *Handbook of attachment: Theory, research, and clinical applications* (pp. 89–111). New York, NY: Guilford Press.

Bretherton, I., & Munholland, K. A. (2008). Internal working models in attachment relationships: elaborating a central construct in Attachment Theory. In J. Cassidy, & P. R. Shaver (Eds.), *Handbook of attachment: Theory, research, and clinical applications* (pp. 102–127). New York, NY: Guilford Press.

Briley, D. A., Harden, K. P., & Tucker-Drob, E. M. (2014). Child characteristics and parental educational expectations: evidence for transmission with transaction. *Developmental Psychology, 50*(12), 2614–2632.

Bringle, R. G., & Bagby, G. J. (1992). Self-esteem and perceived quality of romantic and family relationships in young adults. *Journal of Research in Personality, 26*, 340–356.

Brisch, K. H. (2012). *Treating attachment disorders: From theory to therapy.* New York, NY: Guilford Press.

Brown, A. S., Jones, T. C., & Mitchell, D. B. (1996). Single and multiple test repetition priming in implicit memory. *Memory, 4*, 159–173.

Brown, J., & Trevethan, R. (2010). Shame, internalized homophobia, identity formation, attachment style, and the connection to relationship status in gay men. *American Journal of Men's Health, 4*, 267–276.

Bruch, H. (1973). *Eating disorders: Obesity, anorexia nervosa, and the person within.* New York, NY: Basic Books.

Brumbaugh, C. C., & Fraley, R. C. (2006). Transference and attachment: how do attachment patterns get carried forward from one relationship to the next? *Personality and Social Psychology Bulletin, 32*, 552–560.

Brumbaugh, C. C., & Fraley, R. C. (2010). Adult attachment and dating strategies: how do insecure people attract mates? *Personal Relationships, 17*, 599–614.

Brumbaugh, C. C., Baren, A., & Agishtein, P. (2014). Attraction to attachment insecurity: flattery, appearance, and status's role in mate preferences. *Personal Relationships, 21*, 288–308.

Bruner, J. S. (1957). On perceptual readiness. *Psychological Review, 64*, 123–152.

Buchheim, A., Erk, S., George, C., Kächele, H., Ruchsow, M., Spitzer, M., ... & Walter, H. (2006). Measuring attachment representation in an fMRI environment: a pilot study. *Psychopathology, 39*, 144–152.

Buhl, H. M. (2008). Development of a model describing individuated adult child–parent relationships. *International Journal of Behavioral Development, 32*, 381–389.

Burkett, J. P., & Young, L. J. (2012). The behavioral, anatomical and pharmacological parallels between social attachment, love and addiction. *Psychopharmacology, 224*, 1–26.

Buss, D. M., & Kenrick, D. T. (1998). Evolutionary social psychology. In D. T. Gilbert, S. T. Fiske, & G. Lindzey (Eds.), *The handbook of social psychology* (4th ed., pp. 982–1026). Boston, MA: McGraw-Hill.

Buss, D. M., & Schmitt, D. P. (1993). Sexual strategies theory: an evolutionary perspective on human mating. *Psychological Review, 100*, 204–232.

Button, K. S., Ioannidis, J. P. A., Mokrysz, C., Nosek, B. A., Flint, J., Robinson, E. S. J., & Munafò, M. R. (2013). Power failure: why small sample size undermines the reliability of neuroscience: erratum. *Nature Reviews Neuroscience, 14*, 442.

Bylsma, W. H., Cozzarelli, C., & Sumer, N. (1997). Relation between adult attachment styles and global self-esteem. *Basic and Applied Social Psychology, 19*, 1–16.

Byrne, D. (1971). *The attraction paradigm.* New York: Academic Press.

Calhoun, V. D., Liu, J., & Adalı, T. (2009). A review of group ICA for fMRI data and ICA for joint inference of imaging, genetic, and ERP data. *NeuroImage, 45*, S163–S172.

Cameron, J. J., Finnegan, H., & Morry, M. M. (2012). Orthogonal dreams in an oblique world: a meta-analysis of the association between attachment anxiety and avoidance. *Journal of Research in Personality, 46*, 472–476.

Camprodon, J. A., Kaur, N., Deckersbach, T., Evans, K. C., Kopell, B. H., Halverson, J., et al. (2015). One step closer to patient-specific brain treatments: interleaved transcranial magnetic stimulation (TMS)/fMRI to assess the fMRI BOLD response before and after high frequency repetitive TMS treatment. *Abstracts/Brain Stimulation, 8*, 408.

Candelori, C., & Ciocca, A. (1998). Attachment and eating disorders. In P. Bria, A. Ciocca, & S. de Risio (Eds.), *Psychotherapeutic issues in eating disorders: Models, methods, and results* (pp. 139–153). Rome: Societa Editrice Universo.

Canterberry, M., & Gillath, O. (2012). Attachment and caregiving. In P. Noller, & G. C. Karantzas (Eds.), *The Wiley-Blackwell handbook of couples and family relationships* (pp. 207–219). Chichester, UK: Wiley-Blackwell.

Canterberry, M., & Gillath, O. (2013). Neural evidence for a multifaceted model of attachment security. *International Journal of Psychophysiology, 88*, 232–240.

Carnelley, K. B., & Rowe, A. C. (2007). Repeated priming of attachment security influences later views of self and relationships. *Personal Relationships, 14*, 307–320.

Carnelley, K. B., Pietromonaco, P. R., & Jaffe, K. (1994). Depression, working models of others, and relationship functioning. *Journal of Personality and Social Psychology, 66*, 127–140.

Carnelley, K. B., Otway, L. J., & Rowe, A. C. (2016). The effects of attachment priming on depressed and anxious mood. *Clinical Psychological Science*, 1–58.

Carpenter, B. D. (2001). Attachment bonds between adult daughters and their older mothers associations with contemporary caregiving. *The Journals of Gerontology Series B: Psychological Sciences and Social Sciences, 56*, 257–266.

Carter, C. S. (2005). Biological perspectives on social attachment and bonding. In C. Carter, L. Ahnert, K. Grossmann, S. Hrdy, M. Lamb, S. Porges, & N. Sachser (Eds.), *Attachment and bonding: A new synthesis* (pp. 85–100). Cambridge, MA: MIT Press.

Carter, C. S., Ahnert, L., Grossmann, K., Hrdy, S., Lamb, M., Proges, S., & Sachser, N. (Eds.). (2005). *Attachment and bonding: A new synthesis.* Cambridge, MA: MIT Press.

Carver, C. S., & Scheier, M. F. (1998). *On the self-regulation of behavior.* Cambridge, UK: Cambridge University Press.

Cash, T. F., Theriault, J., & Annis, N. M. (2004). Body image in an interpersonal context: adult attachment, fear of intimacy, and social anxiety. *Journal of Social and Clinical Psychology, 23*, 89–103.

Caspers, K. M., Paradiso, S., Yucuis, R., Troutman, B., Arndt, S., & Philibert, R. (2009). Association between the serotonin transporter promoter polymorphism (5-HTTLPR) and adult unresolved attachment. *Developmental Psychology, 45*, 64–76.

Caspi, A., & Roberts, B. W. (2001). Personality development across the life course: the argument for change and continuity. *Psychological Inquiry, 12*, 49–66.

Cassidy, J. (1994). Emotion regulation: influences of attachment relationships. *Monographs of the Society for Research in Child Development, 59*, 228–283.

Cassidy, J. (2008). The nature of the child's ties. In J. Cassidy, & P. R. Shaver (Eds.), *Handbook of attachment: Theory, research, and clinical applications* (2nd ed., pp. 3–22). New York, NY: Guilford Publications.

Cassidy, J., Ziv, Y., Mehta, T. G., & Feeney, B. C. (2003). Feedback seeking in children and adolescents: associations with self-perceptions, attachment representations, and depression. *Child Development, 74*, 612–628.

Cassidy, J., & Shaver, P. R. (Eds.). (2008). *Adult attachment: Theory, research, and clinical applications* (2nd ed.). New York, NY: Guilford Press.

Cassidy, J., Lichtenstein-Phelps, J., Sibrava, N. J., Thomas, C. L., & Borkovec, T. D. (2009). Generalized anxiety disorder: connections with self-reported attachment. *Behavior Therapy, 40*, 23–38.

Cave, C. B. (1997). Very long-lasting priming in picture naming. *Psychological Science, 8*, 322–325.

Cervone, D., & Shoda, Y. (Eds.). (1999). *The coherence of personality: Social-cognitive bases of consistency, variability, and organization.* New York, NY: Guilford Press.

Cesario, J. (2014). Priming, replication, and the hardest science. *Perspectives on Psychological Science, 9*, 40–48.

Champagne, F., Diorio, J., Sharma, S., & Meaney, M. (2001). Naturally occurring variations in maternal behavior in the rat are associated with differences in estrogen-inducible central oxytocin receptors. *Proceedings of the National Academy of Sciences of the United States of America, 98*, 12736–12741.

Chappell, K. D., & Davis, K. E. (1998). Attachment, partner choice, and perception of romantic partners: an experimental test of the attachment-security hypothesis. *Personal Relationships, 5*, 327–342.

Charles-Sire, V., Guéguen, N., Pascual, A., & Meineri, S. (2012). Words as environmental cues: the effect of the word "loving" on compliance to a blood donation request. *The Journal of Psychology, 146*, 455–470.

Chassler, L. (1997). Understanding anorexia nervosa and bulimia nervosa from an attachment perspective. *Clinical Social Work Journal, 25*, 407–423.

Chen, F. S., & Johnson, S. C. (2012). An oxytocin receptor gene variant predicts attachment anxiety in females and autism-spectrum traits in males. *Social Psychological and Personality Science, 3*, 93–99.

Chiao, J. Y. (2010). At the frontier of cultural neuroscience: introduction to the special issue. *Social Cognitive and Affective Neuroscience, 5*, 109–110.

Chisholm, K. (1998). A three year follow-up of attachment and indiscriminate friendliness in children adopted from Romanian orphanages. *Child Development, 69*, 1092–1106.

Chisholm, J. S., Quinlivan, J. A., Petersen, R. W., & Coall, D. A. (2005). Early stress predicts age at menarche and first birth, adult attachment, and expected lifespan. *Human Nature, 16*, 233–265.

Chopik, W. J., & Edelstein, R. S. (2014). Age differences in romantic attachment around the world. *Social Psychological and Personality Science, 5*, 892–900.

Chopik, W. J., Edelstein, R. S., & Fraley, R. C. (2013). From the cradle to the grave: age differences in attachment from early adulthood to old age. *Journal of Personality, 81*, 171–183.

Chopik, W. J., Moors, A. C., & Edelstein, R. S. (2014). Maternal nurturance predicts decreases in attachment avoidance in emerging adulthood. *Journal of Research in Personality, 53*, 47–53.

Chow, C. M., Ruhl, H., & Buhrmester, D. (2014). Reciprocal associations between friendship attachment and relational experiences in adolescence. *Journal of Social and Personal Relationships*, *33*, 122–146.

Cicchetti, D., & Serafica, F. C. (1981). Interplay among behavioral systems: illustrations from the study of attachment, affiliation, and wariness in young children with Down's syndrome. *Developmental Psychology*, *17*, 36–49.

Cicchetti, D., Rogosch, F. A., & Toth, S. L. (2011). The effects of child maltreatment and polymorphisms of the serotonin transporter and dopamine D4 receptor genes on infant attachment and intervention efficacy. *Development and Psychopathology*, *23*, 357–372.

Clark, C. L., Shaver, P. R., & Calverley, R. C. (1994, August). *Adult attachment styles, remembered childhood abuse, and self-concept structure.* Los Angeles, CA: Presented at the Annual Meetings of the American Psychological Association.

Clark, M. S., & Mills, J. (1979). Interpersonal attraction in exchange and communal relationships. *Journal of Personality and Social Psychology*, *37*, 12–24.

Cliff, M. (2015). 'How lucky I am to spend my life with the greatest woman I ever met': Johnny Cash's note to wife June voted greatest love letter of all time (and beats poet John Keats). Daily Mail. Available from: http://www.dailymail.co.uk/femail/article-2947362/Johnny-Cash-s-message-wife-June-beats-John-Keats-voted-greatest-love-letter-time.html

Clulow, C. (2001). Attachment theory and the therapeutic frame. In C. Clulow (Ed.), *Adult attachment and couple psychotherapy: The 'secure base' in practice and research* (pp. 85–104). London, UK: Routledge.

Coan, J. A. (2008). Toward a neuroscience of attachment. In J. Cassidy, & P. R. Shaver (Eds.), *Handbook of attachment: Theory, research, and clinical applications* (2nd ed., pp. 241–265). New York, NY: Guilford Press.

Coan, J. A. (2010). Adult attachment and the brain. *Journal of Social and Personal Relationships*, *27*, 210–217.

Cobb, R. J., & Davila, J. (2009). Internal working models and change. In J. H. Obegi, & E. Berant (Eds.), *Attachment theory and research in clinical work with adults* (pp. 209–233). New York, NY: Guilford Press.

Cohen, M. X., & Shaver, P. R. (2004). Avoidant attachment and hemispheric lateralization of the processing of attachment- and emotion-related words. *Cognition and Emotion*, *18*, 799–813.

Cohen, E., Dekel, R., & Solomon, Z. (2002). Long-term adjustment and the role of attachment among Holocaust child survivors. *Personality and Individual Differences*, *33*, 299–310.

Cole, T. (2001). Lying to the one you love: the use of deception in romantic relationships. *Journal of Social and Personal Relationships*, *18*, 107–129.

Cole-Detke, H., & Kobak, R. (1996). Attachment processes in eating disorder and depression. *Journal of Consulting and Clinical Psychology*, *64*, 282–290.

Colin, V. L. (1996). *Human attachment.* New York, NY: McGraw Hill.

Collins, N. L., & Allard, L. M. (2001). Cognitive representations of attachment: The content and function of working models. In G. J. O. Fletcher, & M. Clark (Eds.), *Blackwell handbook of social psychology: Interpersonal processes* (pp. 60–85). Malden: Blackwell.

Collins, N. L. (1996). Working models of attachment: implications for explanation, emotion, and behavior. *Journal of Personality and Social Psychology*, *71*, 810–832.

Collins, N. L., & Feeney, B. C. (2000). A safe haven: an attachment theory perspective on support-seeking and caregiving in adult romantic relationships. *Journal of Personality and Social Psychology*, *78*, 1053–1073.

Collins, N. L., Cooper, M., Albino, A., & Allard, L. (2002). Psychosocial vulnerability from adolescence to adulthood: a prospective study of attachment style differences in relationship functioning and partner choice. *Journal of Personality, 70,* 965–1008.

Collins, T. J., & Gillath, O. (2012). Attachment, breakup strategies, and associated outcomes: the effects of security enhancement on the selection of breakup strategies. *Journal of Research in Personality, 46,* 210–222.

Collins, N. L., & Feeney, B. C. (2004). Working models of attachment shape perceptions of social support: evidence from experimental and observational studies. *Journal of Personality and Social Psychology, 87,* 363–383.

Collins, N. L., Ford, M. B., Guichard, A. C., & Allard, L. M. (2006). Working models of attachment and attribution processes in intimate relationships. *Personality and Social Psychology Bulletin, 32,* 201–219.

Collins, N. L., & Read, S. J. (1990). Adult attachment, working models, and relationship quality in dating couples. *Journal of Personality and Social Psychology, 58,* 644–663.

Collins, N. L., & Read, S. J. (1994). Cognitive representations of attachment: the structure and function of working models. In K. Bartholomew, & D. Perlman (Eds.), *Advances in personal relationships: Attachment processes in adulthood* (pp. 53–92). (Vol. 5). London: Jessica Kingsley.

Condon, J., Corkindale, C., Boyce, P., & Gamble, E. (2013). A longitudinal study of father-to-infant attachment: antecedents and correlates. *Journal of Reproductive and Infant Psychology, 31,* 15–30.

Conradi, H. J., Gerlsma, C., van Duijn, M., & de Jonge, P. (2006). Internal and external validity of the experiences in close relationships questionnaire in an American and two Dutch samples. *The European Journal of Psychiatry, 20,* 258–269.

Consedine, N. S., & Magai, C. (2003). Attachment and emotion experience in later life: the view from emotions theory. *Attachment & Human Development, 5,* 165–187.

Corcoran, K. O., & Mallinckrodt, B. (2000). Adult attachment, self-efficacy, perspective taking, and conflict resolution. *Journal of Counseling and Development, 78,* 473–483.

Costa Jr., P. T., & McCrae, R. R. (1994). Set like plaster? Evidence for the stability of adult personality. In T. F. Heatherton, & J. L. Weinberger (Eds.), *Can personality change?* (pp. 21–40). Washington, DC: American Psychological Association.

Costa Jr., P. T., & McCrae, R. R. (2006). Age changes in personality and their origins: comments on Roberts, Walton, and Viechtbauer (2006). *Psychological Bulletin, 132,* 28–30.

Costa, B., Pini, S., Gabelloni, P., Abelli, M., Lari, L., Cardini, A., ... & Martini, C. (2009). Oxytocin receptor polymorphisms and adult attachment style in patients with depression. *Psychoneuroendocrinology, 34,* 1506–1514.

Couperus, J. W., & Nelson, C. A. (2008). Early brain development and plasticity. In K. McCartney, & D. Phillips (Eds.), *Blackwell handbook of early childhood development* (pp. 85–105). Malden, MA: Blackwell.

Cowan, P. A. (1997). Beyond meta-analysis: a plea for a family systems view of attachment. *Child Development, 68,* 601–603.

Coy, A. E., Green, J. D., & Davis, J. L. (2012). With or without you: the impact of partner presence and attachment on exploration. *Journal of Experimental Social Psychology, 48,* 411–415.

Cozolino, L. (2006). *The neuroscience of human relationships: Attachment and the developing social brain.* New York, NY: W. W. Norton & Co.

Cozzarelli, C., Sumer, N., & Major, B. (1998). Mental models of attachment and coping with abortion. *Journal of Personality and Social Psychology, 74,* 453–467.

Cozzarelli, C., Hoekstra, S. J., & Bylsma, W. H. (2000). General versus specific mental models of attachment: are they associated with different outcomes? *Personality and Social Psychology Bulletin, 26,* 605–618.

Crawford, T. N., Shaver, P. R., Cohen, P., Pilkonis, P. A., Gillath, O., & Kasen, S. (2006). Self-reported attachment, interpersonal aggression, and personality disorder in a prospective community sample of adolescents and adults. *Journal of Personality Disorders, 20,* 331–351.

Crawford, T. N., Livesley, W. J., Jang, K. L., Shaver, P. R., Cohen, P., & Ganiban, J. (2007). Insecure attachment and personality disorder: a twin study of adults. *European Journal of Personality, 21,* 191–208.

Craik, K. (1943). *The nature of explanation.* Cambridge, England: Cambridge University Press.

Creasey, G., & Jarvis, P. (2009). Attachment and marriage. In M. C. Smith, & N. DeFrates-Densch (Eds.), *Handbook of Research on Adult Learning and Development* (pp. 269–304). New York, NY: Routledge.

Crispi, E. L., Schiaffino, K., & Berman, W. H. (1997). The contribution of attachment to burden in adult children of institutionalized parents with dementia. *The Gerontologist, 37,* 52–60.

Csikszentmihalyi, M. (2014). *Flow and the foundations of positive psychology.* Dordrecht, The Netherlands: Springer.

Cummings, E. M., & Davies, P. T. (1994). Maternal depression and child development. *Journal of Child Psychology and Psychiatry, 35,* 73–112.

Cutrona, C. E. (2012). Recent advances in research on social support in couples. In P. Noller, & G. C. Karantzas (Eds.), *The Wiley-Blackwell handbook of couples and family relationships* (pp. 392–405). New York: Wiley-Blackwell.

Cyranowski, J. M., Bookwala, J., Feske, U., Houck, P., Pilkonis, P., Kostelnik, B., & Frank, E. (2002). Adult attachment profiles, interpersonal difficulties, and response to interpersonal psychotherapy in women with recurrent major depression. *Journal of Social and Clinical Psychology, 21,* 191–217.

Dakanalis, A., Timko, C.A., Zanetti, M.A., Rinaldi, L., Prunas, A., Carrà, G., ... & Clerici, M. (2014). Attachment insecurities, maladaptive perfectionism, and eating disorder symptoms: A latent mediated and moderated structural equation modeling analysis across diagnostic groups. *Psychiatry Research, 215,* 176–184.

Dalgleish, T. L., Johnson, S. M., Burgess Moser, M., Lafontaine, M. F., Wiebe, S. A., & Tasca, G. A. (2015). Predicting change in marital satisfaction throughout Emotionally Focused Couple Therapy. *Journal of Marital and Family Therapy, 41*(3), 276–291.

Dallos, R. (2006). *Attachment narrative therapy: Integrating narrative, systemic, & attachment therapies.* Maidenhead, UK: McGraw-Hill Education.

Dallos, R., & Vetere, A. (2009). *Systemic therapy and attachment narratives: Applications in a range of clinical settings.* London, UK: Routledge.

Dallos, R., & Vetere, A. (2010). Emotions, attachments and systems. *Context, 107,* 8–10.

Dalton, E. J., Greenman, P. S., Classen, C. C., & Johnson, S. M. (2013). Nurturing connections in the aftermath of childhood trauma: a randomized controlled trial of emotionally focused couple therapy for female survivors of childhood abuse. *Couple and Family Psychology: Research and Practice, 2,* 209.

Dan, O., & Raz, S. (2012). Adult attachment and emotional processing biases: an event-related potentials (ERPs) study. *Biological Psychology, 91,* 212–220.

Dandeneau, S. D., Baldwin, M. W., Baccus, J. R., Sakellaropoulo, M., & Pruessner, J. C. (2007). Cutting stress off at the pass: reducing vigilance and responsiveness to social threat by manipulating attention. *Journal of Personality and Social Psychology, 93,* 651–666.

Dandurand, C., Bouaziz, A. R., & Lafontaine, M. F. (2013). Attachment and couple satisfaction: the mediating effect of approach and avoidance commitment. *Journal of Relationships Research, 4,* e3.

Darwin, C. (1859). *On the origin of species.* London, UK: Murray.

Dasgupta, N., & Greenwald, A. G. (2001). On the malleability of automatic attitudes: combating automatic prejudice with images of admired and disliked individuals. *Journal of Personality and Social Psychology, 81*, 800–814.

Davidov, M., Zahn-Waxler, C., Roth-Hanania, R., & Knafo, A. (2013). Concern for others in the first year of life: theory, evidence, and avenues for research. *Child Development Perspectives, 7*, 126–131.

Davila, J. (2001). Refining the association between excessive reassurance seeking and depressive symptoms: the role of related interpersonal constructs. *Journal of Social and Clinical Psychology, 20*, 538–559.

Davila, J., & Cobb, R. J. (2003). Predicting change in self-reported and interviewer-assessed adult attachment: tests of the individual difference and life stress models of attachment change. *Personality and Social Psychology Bulletin, 29*, 859–870.

Davila, J., & Cobb, R. J. (2004). Predictors of changes in attachment security during adulthood. In W. S. Rholes, & J. A. Simpson (Eds.), *Adult attachment: Theory, research, and clinical implications* (pp. 133–156). New York, NY: Guilford Press.

Davila, J., Hammen, C., Burge, D., Daley, S. E., & Paley, B. (1996). Cognitive/interpersonal correlates of adult interpersonal problem-solving strategies. *Cognitive Therapy and Research, 20*, 465–480.

Davila, J., & Sargent, E. (2003). The meaning of life (events) predicts changes in attachment security. *Personality and Social Psychology Bulletin, 29*, 1383–1395.

Davila, J., Burge, D., & Hammen, C. (1997). Why does attachment style change? *Journal of Personality and Social Psychology, 73*, 826–838.

Davila, J., Karney, B. R., & Bradbury, T. N. (1999). Attachment change processes in the early years of marriage. *Journal of Personality and Social Psychology, 76*, 738–802.

Davis, D., Shaver, P. R., & Vernon, M. L. (2003). Physical, emotional, and behavioral reactions to breaking up: the roles of gender, age, emotional involvement, and attachment style. *Personality and Social Psychology Bulletin, 29*, 871–884.

Davis, D., Shaver, P. R., & Vernon, M. L. (2004). Attachment style and subjective motivations for sex. *Personality and Social Psychology Bulletin, 30*, 1076–1090.

Dawson, G., Ashman, S. B., Hessl, D., Spieker, S., Frey, K., Panagiotides, H., et al. (2001). Autonomic and brain electrical activity in securely- and insecurely attached infants of depressed mothers. *Infant Behavior and Development, 24*, 135–149.

De Dreu, C. K. W. (2012). Oxytocin modulates the link between adult attachment and cooperation through reduced betrayal aversion. *Psychoneuroendocrinology, 37*(7), 871–880.

Dekel, R., Solomon, Z., Ginzburg, K., & Neria, Y. (2004). Long-term adjustment among Israeli war veterans: the role of attachment style. *Anxiety, Stress and Coping: An International Journal, 17*, 141–152.

de Vaus, D. A. (2002). Marriage and mental health. *Family Matters, 62*, 26–32.

Del Giudice, M. (2009a). Sex, attachment, and the development of reproductive strategies. *Behavioral and Brain Sciences, 32*, 1–21.

Del Giudice, M. (2009b). Human reproductive strategies: an emerging synthesis. *Behavioral and Brain Sciences, 32*, 46–56.

Del Giudice, M. (2011). Sex differences in romantic attachment: a meta-analysis. *Personality and Social Psychology Bulletin, 37*, 193–214.

Del Giudice, M. (2016). Sex differences in romantic attachment: a facet-level analysis. *Personality and Individual Differences, 88*, 125–128.

Del Giudice, M., & Belsky, J. (2010). Sex differences in attachment emerge in middle childhood: an evolutionary hypothesis. *Child Development Perspectives, 4*, 97–105.

Del Giudice, M., Gangestad, S. W., & Kaplan, H. S. (2015). Life history theory and evolutionary psychology. *The handbook of evolutionary psychology* (2nd ed.). New York, NY: Wiley.

Dennett, D. C. (1993). *The intentional stance*. Cambridge, MA: MIT Press.

Dessaulles, A., Johnson, S. M., & Denton, W. H. (2003). Emotion-focused therapy for couples in the treatment of depression: a pilot study. *The American Journal of Family Therapy, 31*, 345–353.

DeWall, C. N., Masten, C. L., Powell, C., Combs, D., Schurtz, D. R., & Eisenberger, N. I. (2012). Do neural responses to rejection depend on attachment style?: an fMRI study. *Social Cognitive and Affective Neuroscience, 7*, 184–192.

DeWolff, M., & van IJzendoorn, M. (1997). Sensitivity and attachment: a meta-analysis on parental antecedents of infant attachment. *Child Development, 68*, 571–591.

Diamond, L. M., & Fagundes, C. P. (2010). Psychobiological research on attachment. *Journal of Social and Personal Relationships, 27*, 218–225.

Diamond, L. M., & Hicks, A. M. (2005). Attachment style, current relationship security, and negative emotions: the mediating role of physiological regulation. *Journal of Social and Personal Relationships, 22*, 499–518.

Diamond, G. S., Wintersteen, M. B., Brown, G. K., Diamond, G. M., Gallop, R., Shelef, K., & Levy, S. (2010). Attachment-based family therapy for adolescents with suicidal ideation: a randomized controlled trial. *Journal of the American Academy of Child & Adolescent Psychiatry, 49*, 122–131.

Diamond, G., Creed, T., Gillham, J., Gallop, R., & Hamilton, J. L. (2012). Sexual trauma history does not moderate treatment outcome in attachment-based family therapy (ABFT) for adolescents with suicide ideation. *Journal of Family Psychology, 26*, 595.

Didion, J. (2005). *The year of magical thinking*. New York, NY: Knopf.

Diehl, M., Elnick, A. B., Bourbeau, L. S., & Labouvie-Vief, G. (1998). Adult attachment styles: their relations to family context and personality. *Journal of Personality and Social Psychology, 74*, 1656.

DiFilippo, J. M., & Overholser, J. C. (2002). Depression, adult attachment, and recollections of parental caring during childhood. *Journal of Nervous and Mental Disease, 190*, 663–669.

Dinero, R. E., Conger, R. D., Shaver, P. R., Widaman, K. F., & Larsen-Rife, D. (2008). Influence of family of origin and adult romantic partners on romantic attachment security. *Journal of Family Psychology, 22*, 622–632.

Doherty, N. A., & Feeney, J. A. (2004). The composition of attachment networks throughout the adult years. *Personal Relationships, 11*, 469–488.

Doherty, R. W., Hatfield, E., Thompson, K., & Choo, P. (1994). Cultural and ethnic influences on love and attachment. *Personal Relationships, 1*, 391–398.

Domingue, R., & Mollen, D. (2009). Attachment and conflict communication in adult romantic relationships. *Journal of Social and Personal Relationships, 26*, 678–696.

Donnellan, M. B., Burt, S. A., Levendosky, A. A., & Klump, K. L. (2008). Genes, personality, and attachment in adults: a multivariate behavioral genetic analysis. *Personality and Social Psychology Bulletin, 34*, 3–16.

Donnellan, M. B., Lucas, R. E., & Cesario, J. (2015). On the association between loneliness and bathing habits: nine replications of Bargh and Shalev (2012) Study 1. *Emotion, 15*, 109.

Donovan, S., & Emmers-Sommer, T. M. (2012). Attachment style and gender as predictors of communicative responses to infidelity. *Marriage & Family Review, 48*, 125–149.

Downey, G., & Feldman, S. I. (1996). Implications of rejection sensitivity for intimate relationships. *Journal of Personality and Social Psychology, 70*, 1327–1343.

Doyen, S., Klein, O., Pichon, C. L., & Cleeremans, A. (2012). Behavioral priming: it's all in the mind, but whose mind? *PLoS ONE, 7*(1), e29081.

Dozier, M. (1990). Attachment organization and treatment use for adults with serious psychopathological disorders. *Development and Psychopathology, 2,* 47–60.

Dozier, M., Stovall-McClough, K., & Albus, K. (2008). Attachment and psychopathology in adulthood. In J. Cassidy, & P. R. Shaver (Eds.), *Handbook of attachment: Theory, research, and clinical applications* (2nd ed., pp. 718–744). New York, NY: Guilford Press.

Drevets, W. C. (2000). Neuroimaging studies of mood disorders. *Biological Psychiatry, 48,* 813–829.

Duck, S. (1994). Attaching meaning to attachment. *Psychological Inquiry, 5,* 34–38.

Duemmler, S. L., & Kobak, R. (2001). The development of commitment and attachment in dating relationships: attachment security as relationship construct. *Journal of Adolescence, 24,* 401–415.

Dunbar, R., & Machin, A. (2014). Sex differences in relationship conflict and reconciliation. *Journal of Evolutionary Psychology, 12,* 109–133.

Dunbar, R. I. M., & Spoors, M. (1995). Social networks, support cliques, and kinship. *Human Nature, 6,* 273–290.

Duncan, L. E., & Keller, M. C. (2011). A critical review of the first 10 years of candidate gene-by-environment interaction research in psychiatry. *The American Journal of Psychiatry, 168,* 1041–1049.

Dutton, L. B., & Winstead, B. A. (2006). Predicting unwanted pursuit: attachment, relationship satisfaction, relationship alternatives, and break-up distress. *Journal of Social and Personal Relationships, 23,* 565–586.

Dykas, M. J., & Cassidy, J. (2011). Attachment and the processing of social information across the life span: theory and evidence. *Psychological Bulletin, 137,* 19–46.

Dykas, M. J., Woodhouse, S. S., Cassidy, J., & Waters, H. S. (2006). Narrative assessment of attachment representations: links between secure base scripts and adolescent attachment. *Attachment & Human Development, 8,* 221–240.

Eagly, A. H., & Steffen, V. J. (1984). Gender stereotypes stem from the distribution of women and men into social roles. *Journal of Personality and Social Psychology, 46,* 735.

Eastwick, P. W., & Finkel, E. J. (2008). The attachment system in fledgling relationships: an activating role for attachment anxiety. *Journal of Personality and Social Psychology, 95,* 628–647.

Eastwick, P. W., & Finkel, E. J. (2012). The Evolutionary armistice attachment bonds moderate the function of ovulatory Cycle Adaptations. *Personality and Social Psychology Bulletin, 38,* 174–184.

Edelstein, R. S., & Gillath, O. (2008). Avoiding interference: adult attachment and emotional processing biases. *Personality and Social Psychology Bulletin, 34,* 171–181.

Edelstein, R. S., Stanton, S. J., Henderson, M. M., & Sanders, M. R. (2010). Endogenous estradiol levels are associated with attachment avoidance and implicit intimacy motivation. *Hormones and Behavior, 57,* 230–236.

Ein-Dor, T., Mikulincer, M., Doron, G., & Shaver, P. R. (2010). The attachment paradox: how can so many of us (the insecure ones) have no adaptive advantages? *Perspectives on Psychological Science, 5*(2), 123–141.

Ein-Dor, T., Mikulincer, M., & Shaver, P. R. (2011a). Attachment insecurities and the processing of threat-related information: studying the schemas involved in insecure people's coping strategies. *Journal of Personality and Social Psychology, 101,* 78–93.

Ein-Dor, T., Mikulincer, M., & Shaver, P. R. (2011b). Effective reaction to danger attachment insecurities predict behavioral reactions to an experimentally induced threat above and beyond general personality traits. *Social Psychological and Personality Science, 2,* 467–473.

Eisenberg, D. T. A., Apicella, C. L., Campbell, B. C., Dreber, A., Garcia, J. R., & Lum, J. K. (2010). Assortative human pair-bonding for partner ancestry and allelic variation of the dopamine receptor D4 (DRD4) gene. *Social Cognitive and Affective Neuroscience, 5*, 194–202.

Eisenberger, N. I., & Lieberman, M. D. (2004). Why rejection hurts: a common neural alarm system for physical and social pain. *Trends in Cognitive Sciences, 8*, 294–300.

Eisenberger, N. I., Master, S. L., Inagaki, T. K., Taylor, S. E., Shirinyan, D., Lieberman, M. D., et al. (2011). Attachment figures activate a safety signal-related neural region and reduce pain experience. *Proceedings of the National Academy of Sciences USA, 108*, 11721–11726.

Elliot, A. J., & Reis, H. T. (2003). Attachment and exploration in adulthood. *Journal of Personality and Social Psychology, 85*, 317–331.

Eng, W., Heimberg, R. G., Hart, T. A., Schneier, F. R., & Liebowitz, M. R. (2001). Attachment in individuals with social anxiety disorder: the relationship among adult attachment styles, social anxiety, and depression. *Emotion, 1*, 365.

Englund, M. M., Kuo, S. I., Puig, J., & Collins, W. A. (2011). Early roots of adult competence: the significance of close relationships from infancy to early adulthood. *International Journal of Behavioral Development, 35*, 490–496.

Epstein, S., & Meier, P. (1989). Constructive thinking: a broad coping variable with specific components. *Journal of Personality and Social Psychology, 57*, 332–350.

Erikson, E. H. (1968). Life cycle. *International encyclopedia of the social sciences, 9*, 286–292.

Evans, L., & Wertheim, E. H. (1998). Intimacy patterns and relationship satisfaction of women with eating problems and the mediating effects of depression, trait anxiety and social anxiety. *Journal of Psychosomatic Research, 44*, 355–365.

Evans, L., & Wertheim, E. H. (2005). Attachment styles in adult intimate relationships: comparing women with bulimia nervosa symptoms, women with depression and women with no clinical symptoms. *European Eating Disorders Review, 13*, 285–293.

Fagundes, C. P., & Schindler, I. (2012). Making of romantic attachment bonds: longitudinal trajectories and implications for relationship stability. *Personal Relationships, 19*, 723–742.

Farah, M. (2014). Brain images, babies, and bathwater: critiquing critiques of functional neuroimaging. *Hastings Center Report, 44*, S19–S30.

Fearon, P., Shmueli-Goetz, Y., Viding, E., Fonagy, P., & Plomin, R. (2014). Genetic and environmental influences on adolescent attachment. *Journal of Child Psychology and Psychiatry, 55*, 1033–1041.

Feeney, J. A., & Noller, P. (1992). Attachment style and romantic love: relationship dissolution. *Australian Journal of Psychology, 44*, 69–74.

Feeney, J. A. (1994). Attachment style, communication patterns, and satisfaction across the life cycle of marriage. *Personal Relationships, 1*, 333–348.

Feeney, J. A. (1998). Adult attachment and relationship-centered anxiety: responses to physical and emotional distancing. In J. A. Simpson, & W. S. Rholes (Eds.), *Attachment theory and close relationships* (pp. 189–219). New York: Guilford Press.

Feeney, J., Noller, P., & Callan, V. J. (1994). Attachment style, communication, and satisfaction in the early years of marriage. In K. Bartholomew, & D. Perlman (Eds.), *Advances in personal relationships: Attachment processes in adulthood* (pp. 269–308). (Vol. 5). London: Jessica Kingsley.

Feeney, J. A. (2000). Implications of attachment style for patterns of health and illness. *Child: Care, Health and Development, 26*, 277–288.

Feeney, J. A. (2003). The systemic nature of couple relationships: an attachment perspective. In P. Erdman, & T. Caffery (Eds.), *Attachment and family systems: Conceptual, empirical, and therapeutic relatedness* (pp. 139–164). New York: Brunner-Routledge.

Feeney, J. A. (2004). Transfer of attachment from parents to romantic partners: effects of individual and relationship variables. *Journal of Family Studies*, *10*, 220–238.

Feeney, J. A. (2005). Hurt feelings in couple relationships: exploring the role of attachment and perceptions of personal injury. *Personal Relationships*, *12*, 253–271.

Feeney, J. A. (2008). Adult romantic attachment: developments in the study of couple relationships. In J. Cassidy, & P. R. Shaver (Eds.), *Handbook of attachment: Theory, research, and clinical applications* (2nd ed., pp. 456–581). New York: Guilford Press.

Feeney, B. C., & Collins, N. L. (2001). Predictors of caregiving in adult intimate relationships: an attachment theoretical perspective. *Journal of Personality and Social Psychology*, *80*, 972–994.

Feeney, J. A., & Noller, P. (1996). *Adult attachment*. Thousand Oaks, CA: Sage.

Feeney, B. C., & Thrush, R. L. (2010). Relationship influences on exploration in adulthood: the characteristics and function of a secure base. *Journal of Personality and Social Psychology*, *98*, 57–76.

Feeney, J. A., Noller, P., & Hanrahan, M. (1994). Assessing adult attachment: developments in the conceptualization of security and insecurity. In M. B. Sperling, & W. H. Berman (Eds.), *Attachment in adults: Clinical and developmental perspectives* (pp. 128–152). New York, NY: Guilford Press.

Feeney, J. A., Noller, P., & Patty, J. (1993). Adolescents' interactions with the opposite sex: influence of attachment style and gender. *Journal of Adolescence*, *16*, 169–186.

Feeney, J., Alexander, R., Noller, P., & Hohaus, L. (2003). Attachment insecurity, depression, and the transition to parenthood. *Personal Relationships*, *10*, 475–493.

Feeney, J. A., & Fitzgerald, J. (2011). Facilitating apology, forgiveness, and relationship security following hurtful events. In P. Noller, & G. C. Karantzas (Eds.), *The Wiley-Blackwell handbook of couples and family relationships* (pp. 289–304). New York: Wiley-Blackwell.

Feeney, J. A., & Hohaus, L. (2001). Attachment and spousal caregiving. *Personal Relationships*, *8*, 21–39, Feeney, 2002.

Feeney, J. A., & Noller, P. (1990). Attachment style as a predictor of adult romantic relationships. *Journal of Personality and Social Psychology*, *58*, 281–291.

Feldman, R., Weller, A., Zagoory-Sharon, O., & Levine, A. (2007). Evidence for a neuroendocrinological foundation of human affiliation: plasma oxytocin levels across pregnancy and the postpartum period predict mother-infant bonding. *Psychological Science*, *18*, 965–970.

Felmlee, D. H. (1995). Fatal attractions: affection and disaffection in intimate relationships. *Journal of Social and Personal Relationships*, *12*, 295–311.

Ferenczi, N., & Marshall, T. C. (2013). Exploring attachment to the "homeland" and its association with heritage culture identification. *PloS One*, *8*, e53872.

Ferris, C. F., Kulkarni, P., Sullivan Jr., J. M., Harder, J. A., Messenger, T. L., & Febo, M. (2005). Pup suckling is more rewarding than cocaine: evidence from functional magnetic resonance imaging and three-dimensional computational analysis. *The Journal of Neuroscience*, *25*, 149–156.

Finkel, E. J., & Campbell, W. K. (2001). Self-control and accommodation in close relationships: an interdependence analysis. *Journal of Personality and Social Psychology*, *81*, 263–277.

Fiori, K. L., Consedine, N. S., & Magai, C. (2009). Late life attachment in context: patterns of relating among men and women from seven ethnic groups. *Journal of Cross-Cultural Gerontology*, *24*, 121–141.

Fishtein, J., Pietromonaco, P. R., & Barrett, L. -F. (1999). The contribution of attachment style and relationship conflict to the complexity of relationship knowledge. *Social Cognition*, *17*, 228–244.

Fitzgibbon, M. L., Sánchez-Johnsen, L. A., & Martinovich, Z. (2003). A test of the continuity perspective across bulimic and binge eating pathology. *International Journal of Eating Disorders, 34,* 83–97.

Fletcher, G. J., Simpson, J. A., Campbell, L., & Overall, N. C. (2015). Pair-bonding, romantic love, and evolution the curious case of homo sapiens. *Perspectives on Psychological Science, 10,* 20–36.

Florian, V., Mikulincer, M., & Bucholtz, I. (1995). Effects of adult attachment style on the perception and search for social support. *Journal of Psychology: Interdisciplinary and Applied, 129,* 665–676.

Fodor, J. A. (1983). *The modularity of mind.* Cambridge, MA: MIT Press.

Fodor, J. A. (2005). Reply to Steven Pinker 'so how does the mind work?'. *Mind & Language, 20,* 25–32.

Fonagy, P., Leigh, T., Steele, M., Steele, H., Kennedy, R., Mattoon, G., Target, M., & Gerber, A. (1996). The relation of attachment status, psychiatric classification, and response to psychotherapy. *Journal of Consulting and Clinical Psychology, 64,* 22–31.

Fonagy, P., Luyten, P., & Strathearn, L. (2011). Borderline personality disorder, mentalization, and the neurobiology of attachment. *Infant Mental Health Journal, 32,* 47–69.

Fossati, A., Feeney, J. A., Donati, D., Donini, M., Novella, L., Bagnato, M., Carreta, I., Leonardi, B., Mirabelli, S., & Maffei, C. (2003a). On the dimensionality of the Attachment Style Questionnaire in Italian clinical and nonclinical participants. *Journal of Social and Personal Relationships, 20,* 55–79.

Fossati, A., Feeney, J. A., Donati, D., Donini, M., Novella, L., Bagnato, M., Carreta, I., Leonardi, B., Mirabelli, S., & Maffei, C. (2003b). Personality disorders and adult attachment dimensions in a mixed psychiatric sample: a multivariate study. *Journal of Nervous and Mental Disease, 191,* 30–37.

Fowler, J. C., Allen, J. G., Oldham, J. M., & Frueh, B. C. (2013). Exposure to interpersonal trauma, attachment insecurity, and depression severity. *Journal of Affective Disorders, 149,* 313–318.

Fraley, R. C., Davis, K. E., & Shaver, P. R. (1998). Dismissing-avoidance and the defensive organization of emotion, cognition, and behaviour. In J. A. Simpson, & W. S. Rholes (Eds.), *Attachment theory and close relationships* (pp. 249–279). New York: Guilford Press.

Fraley, R. C. (2002). Attachment stability from infancy to adulthood: meta-analysis and dynamic modeling of developmental mechanisms. *Personality and Social Psychology Review, 6,* 123–151.

Fraley, R. C., & Bonanno, G. A. (2004). Attachment and loss: a test of three competing models on the association between attachment-related avoidance and adaptation to bereavement. *Personality and Social Psychology Bulletin, 30,* 878–890.

Fraley, R. C., & Brumbaugh, C. C. (2004). A dynamical systems approach to understanding stability and change in attachment security. In W. S. Rholes, & J. A. Simpson (Eds.), *Adult attachment: Theory, research, and clinical implications* (pp. 86–132). New York, NY: Guilford Press.

Fraley, R. C. (2007). A connectionist approach to the organization and continuity of working models of attachment. *Journal of Personality, 75,* 1157–1180.

Fraley, R. C., & Brumbaugh, C. C. (2007). Adult attachment and preemptive defenses: converging evidence on the role of defensive exclusion at the level of encoding. *Journal of Personality, 75,* 1033–1050.

Fraley, R. C., & Davis, K. E. (1997). Attachment formation and transfer in young adults' close friendships and romantic relationships. *Personal Relationships, 4,* 131–144.

Fraley, R. C., & Roberts, B. W. (2005). Patterns of continuity: a dynamic model for conceptualizing the stability of individual differences in psychological constructs across the life course. *Psychological Review, 112,* 60–74.

Fraley, R. C., & Roisman, G. I. (2015). Early attachment experiences and romantic functioning: developmental pathways, emerging issues, and future directions. In J. A. Simpson, & W. S. Rholes (Eds.), *Attachment theory and research: New directions and emerging themes* (pp. 9–38). New York, NY: Guilford.

Fraley, R. C., & Shaver, P. R. (1998). Airport separations: a naturalistic study of adult attachment dynamics in separating couples. *Journal of Personality and Social Psychology*, *75*, 1198–1212.

Fraley, R. C., & Shaver, P. R. (1999). Loss and bereavement: attachment theory and recent controversies concerning "grief work" and the nature of detachment. In J. Cassidy, & P. R. Shaver (Eds.), *Handbook of attachment: Theory, research, and clinical applications* (pp. 735–759). New York, NY: Guilford Press.

Fraley, R. C., & Shaver, P. R. (2000). Adult romantic attachment: theoretical developments, emerging controversies, and unanswered questions. *Review of General Psychology*, *4*, 132–154.

Fraley, R. C., & Shaver, P. R. (2008). Attachment theory and its place in contemporary personality theory and research. In O. P. John, R. W. Robins, & L. A. Pervin (Eds.), *Handbook of personality: Theory and research* (3rd ed., pp. 518–541). New York, NY: Guilford Press.

Fraley, R.C., & Shaver, P.R. (2015). Attachment, loss, and grief: Bowlby's views, new developments, and current controversies. In J. Cassidy & P.R. Shaver (Eds.), *Handbook of attachment: Theory, research, and clinical applications* (3rd ed.). New York, NY: Guilford Press.

Fraley, R. C., & Spieker, S. J. (2003). What are the differences between dimensional and categorical models of individual differences in attachment? Reply to Cassidy (2003), Cummings (2003), Sroufe (2003), and Waters and Beauchaine (2003). *Developmental Psychology*, *39*, 423–429.

Fraley, R. C., & Waller, N. G. (1998). Adult attachment patterns: a test of the typological model. In J. A. Simpson, & W. S. Rholes (Eds.), *Attachment theory and close relationships* (pp. 77–114). New York, NY: Guilford Press.

Fraley, R. C., Waller, N. G., & Brennan, K. A. (2000). An item response theory analysis of self-report measures of adult attachment. *Journal of Personality and Social Psychology*, *78*, 350–365.

Fraley, R. C., Brumbaugh, C. C., & Marks, M. J. (2005). The evolution and function of adult attachment: a comparative and phylogenetic analysis. *Journal of Personality and Social Psychology*, *89*, 731–746.

Fraley, R. C., Fazzari, D. A., Bonanno, G. A., & Dekel, S. (2006). Attachment and psychological adaptation in high exposure survivors of the September 11th attack on the World Trade Center. *Personality and Social Psychology Bulletin*, *32*, 538–551.

Fraley, R. C., Heffernan, M. E., Vicary, A. M., & Brumbaugh, C. C. (2011a). The Experiences in Close Relationships-Relationship Structures questionnaire: a method for assessing attachment orientations across relationships. *Psychological Assessment*, *23*, 615–625.

Fraley, R. C., Vicary, A. M., Brumbaugh, C. C., & Roisman, G. I. (2011b). Patterns of stability in adult attachment: an empirical test of two models of continuity and change. *Journal of Personality and Social Psychology*, *101*, 974–992.

Fraley, R. C., Roisman, G. I., & Haltigan, J. D. (2013a). The legacy of early experiences in development: formalizing alternative models of how early experiences are carried forward over time. *Developmental Psychology*, *49*, 109–126.

Fraley, R. C., Roisman, G. I., Booth-LaForce, C., Owen, M. T., & Holland, A. S. (2013b). Interpersonal and genetic origins of adult attachment styles: a longitudinal study from infancy to early adulthood. *Journal of Personality and Social Psychology*, *104*, 817–838.

Fraley, R. C., Hudson, N. W., Heffernan, M. E., & Segal, N. (2015). Are adult attachment styles categorical or dimensional? A taxometric analysis of general and relationship-specific attachment orientations. *Journal of Personality and Social Psychology*, *109*, 354–368.

Frazier, P. A., Byer, A. L., Fischer, A. R., Wright, D. M., & DeBord, K. A. (1996). Adult attachment style and partner choice: correlational and experimental findings. *Personal Relationships*, *3*, 117–136.

Fredrickson, B. L. (2001). The role of positive emotions in positive psychology: the broaden-and-build theory of positive emotions. *American Psychologist, 56*, 218–226.

Freeman, H., & Brown, B. B. (2001). Primary attachment to parents and peers during adolescence: differences by attachment style. *Journal of Youth and Adolescence, 30*, 653–674.

Frei, J. R., & Shaver, P. R. (2002). Respect in close relationships: prototype definition, self-report assessment, and initial correlates. *Personal Relationships, 9*, 121–139.

Freud, S. (1900). The interpretation of dreams. In J. Strachey (Ed. & Trans.), *The standard edition of the complete psychological works of Sigmund Freud* (Vols. 4 and 5). London: Hogarth Press.

Fricker, J., & Moore, S. (2002). Relationship satisfaction: the role of love styles and attachment styles. *Current Research in Social Psychology, 7*, 182–204.

Friedlmeier, W., & Granqvist, P. (2006). Attachment transfer among Swedish and German adolescents: a prospective longitudinal study. *Personal Relationships, 13*, 261–279.

Fry, R. (2014). A rising share of young adults live in their parents' home. *Pew Research Centers Social Demographic Trends Project RSS. Pew Social Trends, 1 Aug. 2013.* Available from < http://www.pewsocialtrends.org/2013/08/01/a-rising-share-of-young-adults-live-in-their-parents-home/>.

Furman, W., Simon, V. A., Shaffer, L., & Bouchey, H. A. (2002). Adolescents' working models and styles with parents, friends, and romantic partners. *Child Development, 73*, 241–255.

Gable, S. L. (2012). Regulating incentives and threats in close relationships. In P. Noller, & G. C. Karantzas (Eds.), *The Wiley-Blackwell handbook of couples and family relationships* (pp. 193–206). New York: Wiley-Blackwell.

Gabriel, S., Carvallo, M., Dean, K. K., Tippin, B., & Renaud, J. (2005). How I see me depends on how I see we: the role of attachment style in social comparison. *Personality and Social Psychology Bulletin, 31*, 1561–1572.

Gailliot, M. T., Baumeister, R. F., DeWall, C. N., Maner, J. K., Plant, E. A., Tice, D. M., ... & Schmeichel, B. J. (2007). Self-control relies on glucose as a limited energy source: Willpower is more than a metaphor. *Journal of Personality and Social Psychology, 92*, 325–336.

Galton, F. (1894). *Natural inheritance.* London, UK: Macmillan.

Galynker, I. I., Yaseen, Z. S., Katz, C., Zhang, X., Jennings-Donovan, G., Dashnaw, S., ... & Winston, A. (2012). Distinct but overlapping neural networks subserve depression and insecure attachment. *Social Cognitive and Affective Neuroscience, 7*, 896–908.

Gamble, S. A., & Roberts, J. E. (2005). Adolescents' perceptions of primary caregivers and cognitive style: the roles of attachment security and gender. *Cognitive Therapy and Research, 29*, 123–141.

Gentzler, A. L., & Kerns, K. A. (2004). Associations between insecure attachment and sexual experiences. *Personal Relationships, 11*, 249–265.

Gentzler, A. L., & Kerns, K. A. (2006). Adult attachment and memory of emotional reactions to negative and positive events. *Cognition and Emotion, 20*, 20–42.

George, C., & Solomon, J. (2008). The caregiving system: a behavioral system approach to parenting. In J. Cassidy, & P. R. Shaver (Eds.), *Handbook of attachment: Theory, research, and clinical applications* (2nd ed., pp. 833–857). New York, NY: Guilford Press.

Ghafoori, B., Hierholzer, R. W., Howsepian, B., & Boardman, A. (2008). The role of adult attachment, parental bonding, and spiritual love in the adjustment to military trauma. *Journal of Trauma & Dissociation, 9*(1), 85–106.

Gilbert, P. (2000). Varieties of submissive behavior as forms of social defense: evolution and psychopathology. In L. Sloman, & P. Gilbert (Eds.), *Subordination: Evolution and mood disorders* (pp. 3–45). New York, NY: Lawrence Erlbaum.

Gillath, O., & Collins, T. (2016). Unconscious desire: the affective and motivational aspects of subliminal sexual priming. *Archives of Sexual Behavior, 45*(1), 5–20.

Gillath, O., & Hart, J. J. (2010). The effects of psychological security and insecurity on political attitudes and leadership preferences. *European Journal of Social Psychology, 40*, 122–134.

Gillath, O., & Karantzas, G. (2015). Insights into the formation of attachment bonds from a social network perspective. In V. Zayas, & C. Hazan (Eds.), *Bases of adult attachment* (pp. 131–156). New York, NY: Springer.

Gillath, O., & Schachner, D. A. (2006). How do sexuality and attachment interrelate?: goals, motives, and strategies. In M. Mikulincer, & G. Goodman (Eds.), *Dynamics of romantic love: Attachment, caregiving, and sex* (pp. 337–355). New York, NY: Guilford Press.

Gillath, O., & Shaver, P. R. (2007). Effects of attachment style and relationship context on selection among relational strategies. *Journal of Research in Personality*, *41*, 968–976.

Gillath, O., Bunge, S. A., Shaver, P. R., Wendelken, C., & Mikulincer, M. (2005a). Attachment-style differences in the ability to suppress negative thoughts: exploring the neural correlates. *NeuroImage*, *28*, 835–847.

Gillath, O., Gregersen, S. C., Canterberry, M., & Schmitt, D. P. (2014). The consequences of high levels of attachment security. *Personal Relationships*, *21*, 497–514.

Gillath, O., Karantzas, G. C., & Karantzas, K. (2016). Effects of attachment security: a meta-analysis. Manuscript submitted for publication.

Gillath, O., Shaver, P. R., & Mikulincer, M. (2005b). An attachment-theoretical approach to compassion and altruism. In P. Gilbert (Ed.), *Compassion: Its nature and use in psychotherapy* (pp. 121–147). London, UK: Brunner-Routledge.

Gillath, O., Mikulincer, M., Fitzsimons, G. M., Shaver, P. R., Schachner, D. A., & Baragh, J. A. (2006). Automatic activation of attachment-related goals. *Personality and Social Psychology Bulletin*, *32*, 1375–1388.

Gillath, O., Mikulincer, M., Birnbaum, G. E., & Shaver, P. R. (2008a). When sex primes love: subliminal sexual priming motivates relationship goal pursuit. *Personality and Social Psychology Bulletin*, *34*, 1057–1069.

Gillath, O., Selcuk, E., & Shaver, P. R. (2008b). Moving toward a secure attachment style: can repeated security priming help? *Social and Personality Psychology Compass*, *2*, 1651–1666.

Gillath, O., Giesbrecht, B., & Shaver, P. R. (2009a). Attachment, attention, and cognitive control: attachment style and performance on general attention tasks. *Journal of Experimental Social Psychology*, *45*, 647–654.

Gillath, O., Hart, J., Noftle, E. E., & Stockdale, G. D. (2009b). Development and validation of a state adult attachment measure (SAAM). *Journal of Research in Personality*, *43*, 362–373.

Gillath, O., Sesko, A. K., Shaver, P. R., & Chun, D. S. (2010). Attachment, authenticity, and honesty: dispositional and experimentally induced security can reduce self-and other-deception. *Journal of Personality and Social Psychology*, *98*(5), 841–855.

Gillath, O., Landau, M. J., Selcuk, E., & Goldenberg, J. L. (2011). Effects of low survivability cues and participant sex on physiological and behavioral responses to sexual stimuli. *Journal of Experimental Social Psychology*, *47*, 1219–1224.

Gillath, O., Canterberry, M., & Collins, T. J. (2012). A multilevel, multimethod interdisciplinary approach to the understanding of attachment. In O. Gillath, G. Adams, & A. Kunkel (Eds.), *Relationship science: Integrating evolutionary, neuroscience, and sociocultural approaches* (pp. 219–240). Washington, DC: American Psychological Association.

Gillath, O., Atchley, R., Imran, A., & El-Hodiri, M. (2016a). *Attachment, game theory, and neuroscience: examining the enhancement and experience of generous behavior.* Manuscript submitted for publication.

Gillath, O., Karantzas, G. C., & Karantzas, K. (2016b). *Effects of attachment security: A meta-analysis.* Manuscript submitted for publication.

Gillath, O., Pressman, S. D., Schoermann, A. M., Moskovitz, J., & Stetler, D. (2016c). *Attachment security primes, oxytocin levels, and reactions to stress.* Manuscript submitted for publication.

Gillath, O., Pressman, S., Stetler, D., & Moskovitz, J. (2016d). *Attachment security and metabolic energy: Enhancement of security results with increased blood glucose*. Manuscript submitted for publication.

Goodwin, I., Holmes, G., Cochrane, R., & Mason, O. (2003). The ability of adult mental health services to meet clients' attachment needs: the development and implementation of the service attachment questionnaire. *Psychology and Psychotherapy, 76*, 145–161.

Gould, J. L., & Gould, C. G. (2007). *Animal architects: Building and the evolution of intelligence*. New York, NY: Basic.

Green, J. D., & Campbell, W. K. (2000). Attachment and exploration in adults: chronic and contextual accessibility. *Personality and Social Psychology Bulletin, 26*(4), 452–461.

Green, B. L., Furrer, C. J., & McAllister, C. L. (2011). Does attachment style influence social support or the other way around? A longitudinal study of Early Head Start mothers. *Attachment & Human Development, 13*, 27–47.

Griffin, D. W., & Bartholomew, K. (1994a). The metaphysics of measurement: the case of adult attachment. In K. Bartholomew, & D. Perlman (Eds.), *Advances in personal relationships: Vol. 5. Attachment processes in adulthood* (pp. 17–52). London, UK: Jessica Kingsley.

Griffin, D. W., & Bartholomew, K. (1994b). Models of the self and other: fundamental dimensions underlying measures of adult attachment. *Journal of Personality and Social Psychology, 67*, 430–445.

Groh, A. M., Roisman, G. I., van IJzendoorn, M. H., Bakermans-Kranenburg, M. J., & Fearon, R. (2012). The significance of insecure and disorganized attachment for children's internalizing symptoms: a meta-analytic study. *Child Development, 83*, 591–610.

Gross, C., Zhuang, X., Stark, K., Ramboz, S., Oosting, R., Kirby, L., et al. (2002). Serotonin 1A receptor acts during development to establish normal anxiety like behavior in the adult. *Nature, 416*, 396–400.

Grossmann, K., Grossmann, K. E., Spangler, G., Suess, G., & Unzner, L. (1985). Maternal sensitivity and newborns' orientation responses as related to quality of attachment in northern Germany. *Monographs of the Society for Research in Child Development, 50*(1–2), 233–256.

Gutzwiller, J., Oliver, J. M., & Katz, B. M. (2003). Eating dysfunctions in college women: the roles of depression and attachment to fathers. *Journal of American College Health, 52*, 27–32.

Hadden, B. W., Smith, C. V., & Webster, G. D. (2014). Relationship duration moderates associations between attachment and relationship quality meta-analytic support for the temporal adult romantic attachment model. *Personality and Social Psychology Review, 18*, 42–58.

Haggbloom, S. J., Warnick, R., Warnick, J. E., Jones, V. K., Yarbrough, G. L., Russell, T. M., ... & Monte, E. (2002). The 100 most eminent psychologists of the 20th century. *Review of General Psychology, 6*, 139–152.

Haggerty, G., Hilsenroth, M. J., & Vala-Stewart, R. (2009). Attachment and interpersonal distress: examining the relationship between attachment styles and interpersonal problems in a clinical population. *Clinical Psychology & Psychotherapy, 16*, 1–9.

Halchuk, R. E., Makinen, J. A., & Johnson, S. M. (2010). Resolving attachment injuries in couples using emotionally focused therapy: a three-year follow-up. *Journal of Couple & Relationship Therapy, 9*, 31–47.

Han, S., & Pistole, M. C. (2014). College student binge eating: insecure attachment and emotion regulation. *Journal of College Student Development, 55*(1), 16–29.

Hardy, G. E., & Barkham, M. (1994). The relationship between interpersonal attachment styles and work difficulties. *Human Relations, 47*, 263–281.

Harlow, H. F. (1958). The nature of love. *American Psychologist, 13*, 673–685.

Harris, C. R., Coburn, N., Rohrer, D., & Pashler, H. (2013). Two failures to replicate high-performance-goal priming effects. *PLoS ONE, 8*, e72467.

Havighurst, R. J. (1972). *Developmental tasks and education*. New York, NY: David McKay Company. Inc.

Haydon, K. C., Roisman, G. I., Marks, M. J., & Fraley, R. C. (2011). An empirically derived approach to the latent structure of the Adult Attachment Interview: additional convergent and discriminant validity evidence. *Attachment & Human Development, 13*, 503–524.

Hazan, C., & Shaver, P. R. (1987). Romantic love conceptualized as an attachment process. *Journal of Personality and Social Psychology, 52*, 511–524.

Hazan, C., & Shaver, P. R. (1992). Broken attachments: relationship loss from the perspective of attachment theory. In T. Orbuch (Ed.), *Close relationship loss* (pp. 90–108). New York, NY: Springer.

Hazan, C., & Shaver, P. R. (1994). Attachment as an organizational framework for research on close relationships. *Psychological Inquiry, 5*, 1–22.

Hazan, C., & Zeifman, D. (1994). Sex and the psychological tether. In D. Perlman & K. Bartholomew (Eds.), *Advances in personal relationships* (pp. 151–180). London, UK: Jessica Kingsley.

Hazan, C., Hutt, M. J., Sturgeon, J., & Bricker, T. (1991, April). The process of relinquishing parents as attachment figures. Paper presented at the *Biennial meeting of the Society for Research in Child Development, Seattle, WA*.

Heatherton, T. F., & Baumeister, R. F. (1991). Binge eating as escape from self-awareness. *Psychological Bulletin, 110*, 86.

Heaven, P. C. L., Da Silva, T., Carey, C., & Holen, J. (2004). Loving styles: relationships with personality and attachment styles. *European Journal of Personality, 18*, 103–113.

Heffernan, M. E., Fraley, R. C., Vicary, A. M., & Brumbaugh, C. C. (2012). Attachment features and functions in romantic relationships. *Journal of Social and Personal Relationships, 29*, 671–693.

Hellige, J. B. (1993). *Hemispheric asymmetry*. Cambridge, MA: Harvard University Press.

Henderson, A. J. Z., Bartholomew, K., & Dutton, D. G. (1997). He loves me; he loves me not: attachment and separation resolution of abused women. *Journal of Family Violence, 12*, 169–191.

Hendrick, C., & Hendrick, S. S. (1989). Research on love: does it measure up? *Journal of Personality and Social Psychology, 56*, 784–794.

Hepper, E. G., & Carnelley, K. B. (2010). Adult attachment and feedback-seeking patterns in relationships and work. *European Journal of Social Psychology, 40*(3), 448–464.

Higgins, E. T., & Eitam, B. (2014). Priming…shmiming: it's about knowing when and why stimulated memory representations become active. *Understanding Priming Effects in Social Psychology, 32*, 234.

Higgins, E. T., & King, G. (1981). Accessibility of social constructs: information processing consequences of individual and contextual variability. In N. Cantor, & J. Kihlstrom (Eds.), *Personality, cognition, and social interaction* (pp. 69–121). Hillsdale, NJ: Erlbaum.

Hillyard, S. A., Teder-Sälejärvi, W. A., & Münte, T. F. (1998). Temporal dynamics of early perceptual processing. *Current Opinion in Neurobiology, 8*, 202–210.

Hinde, R. A. (1970). *Animal behaviour: A synthesis of ethology and comparative psychology* (2nd ed.). New York, NY: McGraw-Hill.

Hinde, R. (1982). *Ethology, its nature and relations with other sciences*. New York, NY: Oxford University Press.

Hinde, R. A. (2005). Ethology and attachment theory. In K. E. Grossmann, K. Grossmann, & E. Waters (Eds.), *Attachment from infancy to adulthood: The major longitudinal studies* (pp. 6). New York, NY: Guilford Press.

Hoeve, M., Stams, G. J. J., van der Put, C. E., Dubas, J. S., van der Laan, P. H., & Gerris, J. R. (2012). A meta-analysis of attachment to parents and delinquency. *Journal of Abnormal Child Psychology, 40*, 771–785.

Hoffman, K. T., Marvin, R. S., Cooper, G., & Powell, B. (2006). Changing toddlers' and preschoolers' attachment classifications: the Circle of Security intervention. *Journal of Consulting and Clinical Psychology, 74,* 1017–1026.

Hofstra, J., van Oudenhoven, J. P., & Buunk, B. P. (2005). Attachment styles and majority members' attitudes towards adaptation strategies of immigrants. *International Journal of Intercultural Relations, 29,* 601–619.

Holland, A. S., Fraley, R. C., & Roisman, G. I. (2012). Attachment styles in dating couples: predicting relationship functioning over time. *Personal Relationships, 19,* 234–246.

Holman, T. B., Galbraith, R. C., Timmons, N. M., Steed, A., & Tobler, S. B. (2009). Threats to parental and romantic attachment figures' availability and adult attachment insecurity. *Journal of Family Issues, 30,* 413–429.

Holt-Lunstad, J., Birmingham, W., & Jones, B. Q. (2008). Is there something unique about marriage? The relative impact of marital status, relationship quality, and network social support on ambulatory blood pressure and mental health. *Annals of Behavioral Medicine, 35,* 239–244.

Holmes, B. M., & Johnson, K. R. (2009). Adult attachment and romantic partner preference: a review. *Journal of Social and Personal Relationships, 26,* 833–852.

Holtzworth-Munroe, A., Stuart, G. L., & Hutchinson, G. (1997). Violent versus nonviolent husbands: differences in attachment patterns, dependency, and jealousy. *Journal of Family Psychology, 11,* 314–331.

Horowitz, L. M., Rosenberg, S. E., & Bartholomew, K. (1993). Interpersonal problems, attachment styles, and outcome in brief dynamic psychotherapy. *Journal of Consulting and Clinical Psychology, 61,* 549.

Horvath, A. O., & Greenberg, L. (1989). Development and validation of the Working Alliance Inventory. *Journal of Counseling Psychology, 36,* 223–232.

Howes, C., Rodning, C., Galluzzo, D. C., & Myers, L. (1988). Attachment and child care: relationships with mother and caregiver. *Early Childhood Research Quarterly, 3,* 403–416.

Hrdy, S. B. (1992). Fitness tradeoffs in the history and evolution of delegated mothering with special reference to wet-nursing, abandonment, and infanticide. *Ethology and Sociobiology, 13,* 409–442.

Hudson, N. W., Fraley, R. C., Vicary, A. M., & Brumbaugh, C. C. (2014). Coregulation in romantic partners' attachment styles: a longitudinal investigation. *Personality and Social Psychology Bulletin, 40,* 845–857.

Hudson, N.W., Fraley, R.C., Chopik, W.J., & Heffernan, M.E. (2015). Not all attachment relationships change alike: normative cross-sectional age trajectories in attachment to romantic partners, best friends, and parents across the lifespan. *Journal of Research in Personality, 59,* 44–55.

Hurlemann, R., Patin, A., Onur, O. A., Cohen, M. X., Baumgartner, T., Metzler, S., et al. (2010). Oxytocin enhances amygdala-dependent, socially reinforced learning and emotional empathy in humans. *The Journal of Neuroscience, 30,* 4999–5007.

Illing, V., Tasca, G. A., Balfour, L., & Bissada, H. (2010). Attachment insecurity predicts eating disorder symptoms and treatment outcomes in a clinical sample of women. *The Journal of Nervous and Mental Disease, 198,* 653–659.

Insel, T. R., & Young, L. J. (2001). The neurobiology of attachment. *Nature Reviews Neuroscience, 2,* 129–136.

Irons, C., Gilbert, P., Baldwin, M. W., Baccus, J., & Palmer, M. (2006). Parental recall, attachment relating, and self-attacking/self-reassurance: their relationship with depression. *British Journal of Clinical Psychology, 45,* 1–12.

Jackson, J. J., & Kirkpatrick, L. A. (2007). The structure and measurement of human mating strategies: toward a multidimensional model of sociosexuality. *Evolution and Human Behavior, 28,* 382–391.

Jang, S. A., Smith, S. W., & Levine, T. R. (2002). To stay or to leave? The role of attachment styles in communication patterns and potential termination of romantic relationships following discovery of deception. *Communication Monographs, 69,* 236–252.

Johnson, S. M. (2002). *Emotionally focused couple therapy with trauma survivors: Strengthening attachment bonds.* New York, NY: Guilford Press.

Johnson, S. M. (2004). *The practice of emotionally focused marital therapy: Creating the connection.* New York, NY: Bruner & Routledge.

Johnson, S. M. (2009). Attachment theory and emotionally focused therapy for individuals and couples. In J. Obegi, & E. Berant (Eds.), *Attachment theory and research in clinical work with adults* (pp. 410–433). New York, NY: Guilford Press.

Johnson, S. M., & Rheem, K. D. (2012). Surviving Trauma. In P. Noller, & G. C. Karantzas (Eds.), *The Wiley-Blackwell handbook of couples and family relationships* (pp. 333–344). New York, NY: Wiley-Blackwell Publishing.

Joordens, S., & Becker, S. (1997). The long and short of semantic priming effects in lexical decision. *Journal of Experimental Psychology: Learning, Memory, and Cognition, 23,* 1083–1105.

Kachadourian, L. K., Fincham, F., & Davila, J. (2004). The tendency to forgive in dating and married couples: the role of attachment and relationship satisfaction. *Personal Relationships, 11,* 373–393.

Kafetsios, K., & Sideridis, G. D. (2006). Attachment, social support and well-being in young and older adults. *Journal of Health Psychology, 11,* 863–875.

Kafetsios, K., Andriopoulos, P., & Papachiou, A. (2014). Relationship status moderates avoidant attachment differences in positive emotion decoding accuracy. *Personal Relationships, 21,* 191–205.

Kanninen, K., Punamaki, R. L., & Qouta, S. (2003). Personality and trauma: adult attachment and posttraumatic distress among former political prisoners. *Peace and Conflict: Journal of Peace Psychology, 9,* 97–126.

Karantzas, G. C. (2012). Family caregiving. In P. Noller, & G. C. Karantzas (Eds.), *The Wiley-Blackwell handbook of couples and family relationships* (pp. 82–96). Chichester, UK: Wiley-Blackwell.

Karantzas, G. C., & Cole, S. F. (2011). Arthritis and support seeking tendencies: the role of attachment. *Journal of Social and Clinical Psychology, 30,* 404–440.

Karantzas, G. C., & Simpson, J. A. (2015). Attachment and aged care. In J. A. Simpson, & W. S. Rholes (Eds.), *Attachment theory and research: New directions and emerging themes* (pp. 319–345). New York, NY: Guilford.

Karantzas, G. C., Feeney, J. A., & Wilkinson, R. (2010). Is less more? Confirmatory factor analysis of the Attachment Style Questionnaires. *Journal of Social and Personal Relationships, 27,* 749–780.

Karantzas, G. C., Feeney, J. A., Goncalves, C. V., & McCabe, M. P. (2014). Towards an integrative attachment-based model of relationship functioning. *British Journal of Psychology, 105,* 413–434.

Karantzas, G. C., Feeney, J., Bale, R., & Hoyle, L. (2015a). *An attachment theory perspective on coping.* Unpublished manuscript.

Karantzas, G. C., Kamboroupoulos, N., & Ure, K. (2015b). *An integration of attachment theory and Reinforcement Sensitivity Theory.* Unpublished manuscript.

Karantzas, G. C., Karantzas, K.M., & McCormack, M. (2015c). *For the love of food: Role of food in attachment functions – the case of binge eating.* Unpublished manuscript.

Karantzas, G. C., McCabe, M. P., Karantzas, K. M., Pizzirani, B., Campbell, H., & Mullins, E. R. (2016). Attachment style and less severe forms of sexual coercion: a systematic review. *Archives of Sexual Behavior*. doi: 10.1007/s10508-015-0600-7.

Karen, R. (1994). *Becoming attached: First relationships and how they shape our capacity to love.* New York, NY: Warner Books.

Karremans, J. C., Heslenfeld, D. J., van Dillen, L. F., & Van Lange, P. A. (2011). Secure attachment partners attenuate neural responses to social exclusion: an fMRI investigation. *International Journal of Psychophysiology*, *81*, 44–50.

Keating, L., Tasca, G. A., & Hill, R. (2013). Structural relationships among attachment insecurity, alexithymia, and body esteem in women with eating disorders. *Eating Behaviors*, *14*, 366–373.

Keefer, L. A., Landau, M. J., Rothschild, Z. K., & Sullivan, D. (2012). Attachment to objects as compensation for close others' perceived unreliability. *Journal of Experimental Social Psychology*, *48*, 912–917.

Keelan, J. R., Dion, K. K., & Dion, K. L. (1998). Attachment style and relationship satisfaction: test of a self-disclosure explanation. *Canadian Journal of Behavioral Science*, *30*, 24–35.

Kennedy, J. H. (1999). Romantic attachment style and ego identity, attributional style, and family of origin in first-year college students. *College Student Journal*, *33*, 171–180.

Kennedy, P. J., & Shapiro, M. L. (2004). Retrieving memories via internal context requires the hippocampus. *Journal of Neuroscience*, *24*, 6979–6985.

Kenny, M. E., & Hart, K. (1992). Relationship between parental attachment and eating disorders in an inpatient and a college sample. *Journal of Counseling Psychology*, *39*, 521–526.

Kenny, D. A., & Zautra, A. (2001). The trait-state models for longitudinal data. In L. Collins, & A. Sayer (Eds.), *New methods for the analysis of change* (pp. 243–263). Washington, DC: American Psychological Association.

Kenny, M. E., Lomax, R., Brabeck, M., & Fife, J. (1998). Longitudinal pathways linking adolescent reports of maternal and paternal attachments to psychological well-being. *Journal of Early Adolescence*, *18*, 221–243.

Kerns, K. A., Mathews, B. L., Koehn, A. J., Williams, C. T., & Siener-Ciesla, S. (2015). Assessing both safe haven and secure base support in parent–child relationships. *Attachment & Human Development, 7*(4), 337–353.

Kestenbaum, R., Farber, E., & Sroufe, L. A. (1989). Individual differences in empathy among preschoolers' concurrent and predictive validity. In N. Eisenberg (Ed.), *Empathy and related emotional responses: No. 44. New directions for child development* (pp. 51–56). San Francisco, CA: Jossey-Bass.

Kidd, T., & Sheffield, D. (2005). Attachment style and symptom reporting: examining the mediating effects of anger and social support. *British Journal of Health Psychology*, *10*, 531–541.

Kilmann, P. R. (1996). *Attachment-based group preventive intervention.* Unpublished manual, University of South Carolina.

Kilmann, P. R., Laughlin, J. E., Carranza, L. V., Downer, J. T., Major, S., & Parnell, M. M. (1999). Effects of an attachment-focused group preventive intervention on insecure women. *Group Dynamics: Theory, Research, and Practice*, *3*, 138.

Kilmann, P. R., Urbaniak, G. C., & Parnell, M. M. (2006). Effects of attachment-focused versus relationship skills-focused group interventions for college students with insecure attachment patterns. *Attachment & Human Development*, *8*, 47–62.

Kim, I. J., & Zane, N. W. (2004). Ethnic and cultural variations in anger regulation and attachment patterns among Korean American and European American male batterers. *Cultural Diversity and Ethnic Minority Psychology*, *10*, 151.

Kirkpatrick, L. A., & Davis, K. E. (1994). Attachment style, gender, and relationship stability: a longitudinal analysis. *Journal of Personality and Social Psychology, 66,* 502–512.

Kirkpatrick, L. A. (1998). Evolution, pair-bonding, and reproductive strategies: a reconceptualization of adult attachment. In J. A. Simpson, & W. S. Rholes (Eds.), *Attachment theory and close relationships* (pp. 353–393). New York, NY: Guilford Press.

Kirkpatrick, L. A. (2005). *Attachment, evolution, and the psychology of religion.* New York, NY: Guilford Press.

Kirkpatrick, L. A., & Hazan, C. (1994). Attachment styles and close relationships: a four-year prospective study. *Personal Relationships, 1,* 123–142.

Klohnen, E. C., & John, O. P. (1998). Working models of attachment: a theory-based prototype approach. In J. A. Simpson, & W. S. Rholes (Eds.), *Attachment theory and close relationships* (pp. 115–140). New York, NY: Guilford Press.

Klohnen, E. C., & Luo, S. (2003). Interpersonal attraction and personality: what is attractive—self similarity, ideal similarity, complementarity or attachment security? *Journal of Personality and Social Psychology, 85,* 709–722.

Klohnen, E. C., Weller, J. A., Luo, S., & Choe, M. (2005). Organization and predictive power of general and relationship-specific attachment models: one for all, and all for one? *Personality and Social Psychology Bulletin, 31,* 1665–1682.

Kobak, R. (2009). Defining and measuring of attachment bonds: comment on Kurdek (2009). *Journal of Family Psychology, 23,* 447–449.

Kobak, R. R., & Hazan, C. (1991). Attachment in marriage: effects of security and accuracy of working models. *Journal of Personality and social Psychology, 60,* 861–869.

Kobak, R. R., & Sceery, A. (1988). Attachment in late adolescence: working models, affect regulation, and representations of self and others. *Child Development, 59,* 135–146.

Korfmacher, J., Adam, E., Ogawa, J., & Egeland, B. (1997). Adult attachment: implications for the therapeutic process in a home visitation intervention. *Applied Developmental Science, 1,* 43–52.

Kunce, L. J., & Shaver, P. R. (1994). An attachment-theoretical approach to caregiving in romantic relationships. In K. Bartholomew, & D. Perlman (Eds.), *Attachment processes in adulthood. Advances in personal relationships* (pp. 205–237). London, UK: Jessica Kingsley Publishers.

Kurdek, L. A. (2008). Pet dogs as attachment figures. *Journal of Social and Personal Relationships, 25,* 247–266.

La Guardia, J. G., Ryan, R. M., Couchman, C. E., & Deci, E. L. (2000). Within-person variation in security of attachment: a self-determination theory perspective on attachment, need fulfillment, and well-being. *Journal of Personality and Social Psychology, 79,* 367–384.

Laible, D., & Thompson, R. (1998). Attachment and emotional understanding in preschool children. *Developmental Psychology, 34,* 1038–1045.

Lakatos, K., Nemoda, Z., Toth, I., Ronai, Z., Ney, K., Sasvari-Szekely, M., et al. (2002). Further evidence for the role of the dopamine D4 receptor (DRD4) gene in attachment disorganization: interaction of the exon III 48-bp repeat and the 521-C/T promoter polymorphisms. *Molecular Psychiatry, 7,* 27–31.

Lamb, M. E., Thompson, R. A., Gardner, W. P., Charnov, E. L., & Estes, D. (1984). Security of infantile attachment as assessed in the "strange situation": its study and biological interpretation. *Behavioral and Brain Sciences, 7,* 127–147.

Larose, S., & Boivin, M. (1998). Attachment to parents, social support expectations, and socioemotional adjustment during the high school-college transition. *Journal of Research on Adolescence, 8,* 1–27.

Latty-Mann, H., & Davis, K. E. (1996). Attachment theory and partner choice: preference and actuality. *Journal of Social and Personal Relationships, 13,* 5–23.

LeBel, E. P., & Campbell, L. (2013). Heightened sensitivity to temperature cues in individuals with high anxious attachment: real or elusive phenomenon? *Psychological Science, 24,* 2128–2130.

Leedom, L. J. (2014). Human social behavioral systems: ethological framework for a unified theory. *Human Ethology Bulletin, 29,* 39–65.

Lemche, E., Giampietro, V. P., Surguladze, S. A., Amaro, E. J., Andrew, C. M., Williams, S. C. R., et al. (2006). Human attachment security is mediated by the amygdala: evidence from combined fMRI and psychophysiological measures. *Human Brain Mapping, 27,* 623–635.

Le Poire, B. A., Shepard, C., & Duggan, A. (1999). Nonverbal involvement, expressiveness, and pleasantness as predicted by parental and partner attachment style. *Communication Monographs, 66,* 293–311.

Levinger, G. (1994). Figure versus ground: micro- and macro perspectives on the social psychology of personal relationships. In R. Erber, & R. Gilmour (Eds.), *Theoretical frameworks for personal relationships* (pp. 1–28). Hillsdale, NJ: Erlbaum.

Levinson, D. J. (1986). A conception of adult development. *American Psychologist, 41,* 3–13.

Levy, M. B., & Davis, K. E. (1988). Lovestyles and attachment styles compared: their relations to each other and to various relationship characteristics. *Journal of Social and Personal Relationships, 5,* 439–471.

Levy, K. N., Ellison, W. D., Scott, L. N., & Bernecker, S. L. (2011). Attachment style. *Journal of Clinical Psychology, 67,* 193–203.

Lieberman, M. D. (2007). Social cognitive neuroscience: a review of core processes. *Annual Review of Psychology, 58,* 259–289.

Lieberman, M. D., & Cunningham, W. A. (2009). Type I and type II error concerns in fMRI research: re-balancing the scale. *Social Cognitive and Affective Neuroscience, 4,* 423–428.

Lim, M. M., & Young, L. J. (2006). Neuropeptidergic regulation of affiliative behavior and social bonding in animals. *Hormones and Behavior, 50,* 506–517.

Litman-Ovadia, H. (2004). An attachment perspective on the career counseling process and career exploration. Unpublished doctoral dissertation, Bar-Ilan University, Ramat Gan, Israel.

Locke, K. D. (2008). Attachment styles and interpersonal approach and avoidance goals in everyday couple interactions. *Personal Relationships, 15,* 359–374.

Lopez, F. G. (2001). Adult attachment orientations, self-other boundary regulation, and splitting tendencies in a college sample. *Journal of Counseling Psychology, 48,* 440–446.

Lopez, F. G., & Gormley, B. (2002). Stability and change in adult attachment style over the first-year college transition: relations to self-confidence, coping, and distress patterns. *Journal of Counseling Psychology, 49,* 355–364.

Lopez, F. G., & Rice, K. G. (2006). Preliminary development and validation of a measure of relationship authenticity. *Journal of Counseling Psychology, 53,* 362–371.

Lopez, F. G., Melendez, M. C., & Rice, K. G. (2000). Parental divorce, parent-child bonds, and adult attachment orientations among college students: a comparison of three racial/ethnic groups. *Journal of Counseling Psychology, 47,* 177–186.

Lorenz, K. Z. (1937). The companion in the bird's world. *The Auk, 54,* 245–273.

Lorenz, K. Z. (1970). *Studies in animal and human behavior* (Vol. 1). Cambridge, MA: Harvard University Press.

Lowery, B. S., Eisenberger, N. I., Hardin, C. D., & Sinclair, S. (2007). Long-term effects of subliminal priming on academic performance. *Basic and Applied Social Psychology, 29,* 151–157.

Luke, M. A., Maio, G. R., & Carnelley, K. B. (2004). Attachment models of the self and others: relations with self-esteem, humanity-esteem, and parental treatment. *Personal Relationships, 11*, 281–303.

Lyddon, W. J., & Sherry, A. (2001). Developmental personality styles: an attachment theory conceptualization of personality disorders. *Journal of Counseling and Development, 79*, 405–414.

MacDonald, G., & Leary, M. R. (2005). Why does social exclusion hurt? The relationship between social and physical pain. *Psychological Bulletin, 131*, 202–223.

Macdonald, K., & Macdonald, T. M. (2010). The peptide that binds: a systematic review of oxytocin and its prosocial effects in humans. *Harvard Review of Psychiatry, 18*, 1–21.

MacDonald, K., & MacDonald, T. M. (2011). The peptide that binds: a systematic review of oxytocin and its prosocial effects in humans. *Harvard Review of Psychiatry, 18*, 1–21.

Madey, S. F., & Jilek, L. (2012). Attachment style and dissolution of romantic relationships: breaking up is hard to do, or is it? *Individual Differences Research, 10*, 202–210.

MacIntosh, H., Reissing, E. D., & Andruff, H. (2010). Same-sex marriage in Canada: the impact of legal marriage on the first cohort of gay and lesbian Canadians to wed. *Canadian Journal of Human Sexuality, 19*, 79–90.

Magai, C. (2008). Attachment in middle and later life. In J. Cassidy, & P. R. Shaver (Eds.), *Handbook of attachment: Theory, research, and clinical applications* (2nd ed., pp. 532–551). New York, NY: Guilford.

Magai, C., Hunziker, J., Mesias, W., & Culver, L. C. (2000). Adult attachment styles and emotional biases. *International Journal of Behavioral Development, 24*, 301–309.

Magai, C., Cohen, C., Milburn, N., Thorpe, B., McPherson, R., & Peralta, D. (2001). Attachment styles in older European American and African American adults. *The Journals of Gerontology Series B: Psychological Sciences and Social Sciences, 56*, S28–S35.

Main, M. (1981). Avoidance in the service of attachment: a working paper. *Behavioral development: The Bielefeld interdisciplinary project* (pp. 651–693).

Main, M., & Hesse, E. (1990). Parents' unresolved traumatic experiences are related to infant disorganized attachment status: is frightened and/or frightening parental behavior the linking mechanism? In M. T. Greenberg, D. Cicchetti, & E. M. Cummings (Eds.), *Attachment in the preschool years: Theory, research, and intervention* (pp. 161-18). Chicago and London: University of Chicago Press.

Main, M., & Solomon, J. (1990). Procedures for identifying infants as disorganized-disoriented during the Ainsworth Strange Situation. In M. T. Greenberg, D. Cicchetti, & E. M. Cummings (Eds.), *Attachment in the preschool years: Theory, research and intervention* (pp. 121–160). Chicago, IL: University of Chicago Press.

Main, M., Kaplan, N., & Cassidy, J. (1985). Security of infancy, childhood, and adulthood: a move to the level of representation. *Monographs of the Society for Research in Child Development, 50*, 66–106.

Mak, M., C., K., Bond, M. H., Simpson, J. A., & Rholes, W. S. (2010). Adult attachment, perceived support, and depressive symptoms in Chinese and American cultures. *Journal of Social and Clinical Psychology, 29*, 144–165.

Mallinckrodt, B., & Wei, M. (2005). Attachment, social competencies, social support, and psychological distress. *Journal of Counseling Psychology, 52*, 358–367.

Man, K. O., & Hamid, P. (1998). The relationship between attachment prototypes, self-esteem, loneliness, and causal attributions in Chinese trainee teachers. *Personality and Individual Differences, 24*, 357–371.

Marganska, A., Gallagher, M., & Miranda, R. (2013). Adult attachment, emotion dysregulation, and symptoms of depression and generalized anxiety disorder. *American Journal of Orthopsychiatry, 83*, 131–141.

Markiewicz, D., Lawford, H., Doyle, A. B., & Haggart, N. (2006). Developmental differences in adolescents' and young adults' use of mothers, fathers, best friends, and romantic partners to fulfill attachment needs. *Journal of Youth and Adolescence, 35,* 121–134.

Markus, H. R., & Kitayama, S. (1991). Culture and the self: implications for cognition, emotion, and motivation. *Psychological Review, 98,* 224–253.

Marmarosh, C. L., & Tasca, G. A. (2013). Adult attachment anxiety: using group therapy to promote change. *Journal of Clinical Psychology, 69,* 1172–1182.

Masten, A. S., & Cicchetti, D. (Eds.), (2010). Developmental cascades (Special Issue), *Development and Psychopathology, Part 1, 22,* 491–715; *Part 2, 22,* 717–983.

Masten, A. S., Roisman, G. I., Long, J. D., Burt, K. B., Obradović, J., Riley, J. R., Boelcke-Stennes, K., & Tellegen, A. (2005). Developmental cascades: linking academic achievement and externalizing and internalizing symptoms over 20 years. *Developmental Psychology, 41,* 733–746.

Masterson, J. F. (1977). Primary anorexia nervosa. In P. Hartocollis (Ed.), *Borderline personality disorders* (pp. 475–494). New York, NY: International Universities Press.

Maxwell, H., Tasca, G. A., Ritchie, K., Balfour, L., & Bissada, H. (2014). Change in attachment insecurity is related to improved outcomes 1-year post group therapy in women with binge eating disorder. *Psychotherapy, 51,* 57.

Mayseless, O. (2004). Home leaving to military service: attachment concerns, transfer of attachment functions from parent to peers, and adjustment. *Journal of Adolescent Research, 19,* 533–558.

McCarthy, G. (1999). Attachment style and adult love relationships and friendships: a study of a group of women at risk of experiencing relationship difficulties. *British Journal of Medical Psychology, 72,* 305–321.

McClure, M. J., & Lydon, J. E. (2014). Anxiety doesn't become you: how attachment anxiety compromises relational opportunities. *Journal of Personality and Social Psychology, 106,* 89–111.

McElwain, N. L., Cox, M. J., Burchinal, M. R., & Macfie, J. (2003). Differentiating among insecure mother-infant attachment classifications: a focus on child-friend interaction and exploration during solitary play at 36 months. *Attachment and Human Development, 5,* 136–164.

McElwain, N. L., Booth-LaForce, C., & Wu, X. (2011). Infant-mother attachment and children's friendship quality: maternal mental-state talk as an intervening mechanism. *Developmental Psychology, 47,* 1295–1311.

McNeil, C., & Hembree-Kigin, T. L. (2010). *Parent-child interaction therapy.* New York, NY: Springer Science & Business Media.

McRae, K. (2006). Johnny Cash [Reordered by Kelly McRae]. *Never Be [CD].* Louisville, Kentucky: Sonablast Records-The song was released in 2006 so I believe you should sight the year the song was released.Meehl, P. E., & Yonce, L. J. (1996). Taxometric analysis: II. Detecting taxonicity using covariance of two quantitative indicators in successive intervals of a third indicator (MAXCOV procedure). *Psychological Reports, 78,* 1091–1227.

Meyer, B., & Pilkonis, P. A. (2005). An attachment model of personality disorders. In M. F. Lenzenweger, & J. F. Clarkin (Eds.), *Major theories of personality disorder* (2nd ed., pp. 231–281). New York, NY: Guilford Press.

Meyer, D., & Schvaneveldt, R. W. (1971). Facilitation in recognizing pairs of words: evidence of dependence between retrieval operations. *Journal of Experimental Psychology, 90,* 227–234.

Meyer, B., Pilkonis, P. A., & Beevers, C. G. (2004). What's in a (neutral) face? Personality disorders, attachment styles, and the appraisal of ambiguous social cues. *Journal of Personality Disorders, 18,* 320–336.

Mickelson, K. D., Kessler, R. C., & Shaver, P. R. (1997). Adult attachment in a nationally representative sample. *Journal of Personality and Social Psychology, 73,* 1092–1106.

Mikulincer, M. (1995). Attachment style and the mental representation of the self. *Journal of Personality and Social Psychology, 69,* 1203–1215.

Mikulincer, M. (1997). Adult attachment style and information processing: individual differences in curiosity and cognitive closure. *Journal of Personality and Social Psychology, 72,* 1217.

Mikulincer, M. (1998a). Attachment working models and the sense of trust: an exploration of interaction goals and affect regulation. *Journal of Personality and Social Psychology, 74,* 1209–1224.

Mikulincer, M. (1998b). Adult attachment style and affect regulation: strategic variations in self-appraisals. *Journal of Personality and Social Psychology, 75,* 420–435.

Mikulincer, M., & Arad, D. (1999). Attachment working models and cognitive openness in close relationships: a test of chronic and temporary accessibility effects. *Journal of Personality and Social Psychology, 77,* 710–725.

Mikulincer, M., & Florian, V. (1998). The relationship between adult attachment styles and emotional and cognitive reactions to stressful events. In J. A. Simpson, & W. S. Rholes (Eds.), *Attachment theory and close relationships* (pp. 143–165). New York, NY: Guilford Press.

Mikulincer, M., & Nachshon, O. (1991). Attachment styles and patterns of self-disclosure. *Journal of Personality and Social Psychology, 61,* 321–331.

Mikulincer, M., & Orbach, I. (1995). Attachment styles and repressive defensiveness: the accessibility and architecture of affective memories. *Journal of Personality and Social Psychology, 68,* 917–925.

Mikulincer, M., & Selinger, M. (2001). The interplay between attachment and affiliation systems in adolescents' same-sex friendships: the role of attachment style. *Journal of Social and Personal Relationships, 18,* 81–106.

Mikulincer, M., & Shaver, P. R. (2001). Attachment theory and intergroup bias: evidence that priming the secure base schema attenuates negative reactions to out-groups. *Journal of Personality and Social Psychology, 81,* 97–115.

Mikulincer, M., Orbach, I., & Iavnieli, D. (1998). Adult attachment style and affect regulation: strategic variations in subjective self-other similarity. *Journal of Personality and Social Psychology, 75,* 436–448.

Mikulincer, M., & Shaver, P. R. (2003). The attachment behavioral system in adulthood: activation, psychodynamics, and interpersonal processes. In M. P. Zanna (Ed.), *Advances in experimental social psychology* (pp. 53–152). New York, NY: Academic Press.

Mikulincer, M., & Shaver, P. R. (2004). Security-based self-representations in adulthood: contents and processes. In W. S. Rholes, & J. A. Simpson (Eds.), *Adult attachment: Theory, research, and clinical implications* (pp. 159–195). New York, NY: Guilford Press.

Mikulincer, M., & Shaver, P. R. (2005). Mental representations of attachment security: theoretical foundation for a positive social psychology. In M. W. Baldwin (Ed.), *Interpersonal cognition* (pp. 233–266). New York: Guilford Press.

Mikulincer, M., & Shaver, P. R. (2007). *Adult attachment: Structure, dynamics, and change.* New York: Guilford Press.

Mikulincer, M., & Shaver, P. R. (2007a). *Attachment patterns in adulthood: Structure, dynamics and change.* New York, NY: Guilford Press.

Mikulincer, M., & Shaver, P. R. (2007b). Boosting attachment security to promote mental health, prosocial values, and inter-group tolerance. *Psychological Inquiry, 18,* 139–156.

Mikulincer, M., & Shaver, P. R. (2008). Adult attachment and affect regulation. In J. Cassidy, & P. R. Shaver (Eds.), *Handbook of attachment: Theory, research, and clinical applications* (2nd ed., pp. 503–531). New York: Guilford Press.

Mikulincer, M., & Shaver, P. R. (2003). The attachment behavioral system in adulthood: activation, psychodynamics, and interpersonal processes. In P. Mark, & Zanna (Eds.), *Advances in experimental social psychology* (pp. 53–152). (Vol. 35). San Diego, CA: Elsevier Academic Press.

Mikulincer, M., & Shaver, P. R. (2009). An attachment and behavioral systems perspective on social support. *Journal of Social and Personal Relationships, 26*, 7–19.

Mikulincer, M., Shaver, P. R., Sapir-Lavid, Y., & Avihou-Kanza, N. (2009). What's inside the minds of securely and insecurely attached people? The secure-base script and its associations with attachment-style dimensions. *Journal of Personality and Social Psychology, 97*, 615–633.

Mikulincer, M., & Shaver, P. R. (2012). An attachment perspective on psychopathology. *World Psychiatry, 11*, 11–15.

Mikulincer, M., & Sheffi, E. (2000). Adult attachment style and cognitive reactions to positive affect: a test of mental categorization and creative problem solving. *Motivation and Emotion, 24*, 149–174.

Mikulincer, M., Florian, V., & Weller, A. (1993). Attachment styles, coping strategies, and posttraumatic psychological distress: the impact of the Gulf War in Israel. *Journal of Personality and Social Psychology, 64*, 817–826.

Mikulincer, M., Horesh, N., Eilati, I., & Kotler, M. (1999). The association between adult attachment style and mental health in extreme life-endangering conditions. *Personality and Individual Differences, 27*, 831–842.

Mikulincer, M., Gillath, O., Halevy, V., Avihou, N., Avidan, S., & Eshkoli, N. (2001a). Attachment theory and reactions to others' needs: evidence that activation of the sense of attachment security promotes empathic responses. *Journal of Personality and Social Psychology, 81*, 1205–1224.

Mikulincer, M., Hirschberger, G., Nachmias, O., & Gillath, O. (2001b). The affective component of the secure base schema: affective priming with representations of proximity maintenance. *Journal of Personality and Social Psychology, 81*, 305–321.

Mikulincer, M., Gillath, O., & Shaver, P. R. (2002). Activation of the attachment system in adulthood: threat-related primes increase the accessibility of mental representations of attachment figures. *Journal of Personality and Social Psychology, 83*, 881–895.

Mikulincer, M., Gillath, O., Sapir-Lavid, Y., Yaakobi, E., Arias, K., Tal-Aloni, L., & Bor, G. (2003). Attachment theory and concern for others' welfare: evidence that activation of the sense of secure base promotes endorsement of self-transcendence values. *Basic and Applied Social Psychology, 25*, 299–312.

Mikulincer, M., Dolev, T., & Shaver, P. R. (2004). Attachment-related strategies during thought suppression: ironic rebounds and vulnerable self-representations. *Journal of Personality and Social Psychology, 87*, 940–956.

Mikulincer, M., Shaver, P. R., Gillath, O., & Nitzberg, R. A. (2005). Attachment, caregiving, and altruism: boosting attachment security increases compassion and helping. *Journal of Personality and Social Psychology, 89*, 817–839.

Mikulincer, M., Shaver, P. R., & Horesh, N. (2006). Attachment bases of emotion regulation and posttraumatic adjustment. In D. K. Snyder, J. A. Simpson, & J. N. Hughes (Eds.), *Emotion regulation in families: Pathways to dysfunction and health* (pp. 77–99). Washington, DC: American Psychological Association.

Mikulincer, M., Ein-Dor, T., Solomon, Z., & Shaver, P. R. (2011). Trajectories of attachment insecurities over a 17-year period: a latent growth curve analysis of the impact of war captivity and posttraumatic stress disorder. *Journal of Social and Clinical Psychology, 30*, 960–984.

Mikulincer, M., Solomon, Z., Shaver, P. R., & Ein-Dor, T. (2014). Attachment-related consequences of war captivity and trajectories of posttraumatic stress disorder: a 17-year longitudinal study. *Journal of Social and Clinical Psychology, 33*, 207–228.

Mikulincer, M., Shaver, P. R., & Solomon, Z. (2015). An attachment perspective on traumatic and posttraumatic reactions. In M. Saffir, H. Wallach, & A. Rizzo (Eds.), *Future directions in posttraumatic stress disorder: Prevention, diagnosis, and treatment* (pp. 79–96). New York, NY: Springer.

Miller, E. K., & Cohen, J. D. (2001). An integrative theory of prefrontal cortex function. *Annual Review of Neuroscience, 24*, 167–202.

Miller, G. A., Galanter, E., & Pribram, K. H. (1960). *Plans and the structure of behavior*. New York, NY: Holt, Rinehart, & Winston.

Millon, T., & Davis, R. D. (1996). *Disorders of personality: DSM-IV and beyond*. New York, NY: Wiley.

Milyavskaya, M., & Lydon, J. E. (2013). Strong but insecure: examining the prevalence and correlates of insecure attachment bonds with attachment figures. *Journal of Social and Personal Relationships, 30*, 529–544.

Mitchell, D. B. (2006). Nonconscious priming after 17 years: invulnerable implicit memory? *Psychological Science, 17*, 925–929.

Mitchell, J. P., Macrae, C. N., & Banaji, M. R. (2006). Dissociable medial prefrontal contributions to judgements of similar and dissimilar other. *Neuron, 50*, 655–663.

Molden, D. C. (2014). Understanding priming effects in social psychology: an overview and integration. *Social Cognition, 32*, 243–249.

Montague, D. P., Magai, C., Consedine, N. S., & Gillespie, M. (2003). Attachment in African American and European American older adults: the roles of early life socialization and religiosity. *Attachment & Human Development, 5*, 188–214.

Muller, R. T., & Lemieux, K. E. (2000). Social support, attachment, and psychopathology in high risk formerly maltreated adults. *Child Abuse and Neglect, 24*, 883–900.

Muller, R. T., Sicoli, L. A., & Lemieux, K. E. (2000). Relationship between attachment style and posttraumatic stress symptomatology among adults who report the experience of childhood abuse. *Journal of Traumatic Stress, 13*, 321–332.

Murphy, B., & Bates, G. W. (1997). Adult attachment style and vulnerability to depression. *Personality and Individual Differences, 22*, 835–844.

Nash, K., Prentice, M., Hirsh, J., McGregor, I., & Inzlicht, M. (2014). Muted neural response to distress among securely attached people. *Social Cognitive and Affective Neuroscience, 9*, 1239–1245.

Nedelisky, A., & Steele, M. (2009). Attachment to people and to objects in obsessive-compulsive disorder: an exploratory comparison of hoarders and non-hoarders. *Attachment and Human Development, 11*, 365–383.

Nelson, E. E., & Panksepp, J. (1998). Brain substrates of infant–mother attachment: contributions of opioids, oxytocin, and norepinephrine. *Neuroscience and Biobehavioral Reviews, 22*, 437–452.

Neria, Y., Guttmann-Steinmetz, S., Koenen, K., Levinovsky, L., Zakin, G., & Dekel, R. (2001). Do attachment and hardiness relate to each other and to mental health in real-life stress? *Journal of Social and Personal Relationships, 18*, 844–858.

Nickerson, A. B., & Nagle, R. J. (2005). Parent and peer attachment in late childhood and early adolescence. *The Journal of Early Adolescence, 25*, 223–249.

Niedenthal, P. M., Brauer, M., Robin, L., & Innes-Ker, A. H. (2002). Adult attachment and the perception of facial expression of emotion. *Journal of Personality and Social Psychology, 82*, 419–433.

Noller, P. (2012). Conflict in family relationships. In P. Noller, & G. C. Karantzas (Eds.), *The Wiley-Blackwell handbook of couples and family relationships* (pp. 129–143). New York: Wiley-Blackwell.

Noftle, E. E., & Shaver, P. R. (2006). Attachment dimensions and the big five personality traits: associations and comparative ability to predict relationship quality. *Journal of Research in Personality, 40*, 179–208.

Nye, E. C., Katzman, J., Bell, J. B., Kilpatrick, J., Brainard, M., & Haaland, K. Y. (2008). Attachment organization in Vietnam combat veterans with posttraumatic stress disorder. *Attachment & Human Development, 10*, 41–57.

O'Connor, T. G., & Croft, C. M. (2001). A twin study of attachment in preschool children. *Child Development, 72*, 1501–1511.

Obegi, J. H., & Berant, E. (Eds.). (2009). *Attachment theory and research in clinical work with adults*. New York, NY: The Guilford Press.

Obegi, J. H., & Berant, E. (2010). *Attachment theory and research in clinical work with adults*. New York, NY: Guilford Press.

Ognibene, T. C., & Collins, N. L. (1998). Adult attachment styles, perceived social support, and coping strategies. *Journal of Social and Personal Relationships, 15*, 323–345.

Oliver, L. E., & Whiffen, V. E. (2003). Perceptions of parents and partners and men's depressive symptoms. *Journal of Social and Personal Relationships, 20*, 621–635.

Onishi, M., Gjerde, P. F., & Block, J. (2001). Personality implications of romantic attachment patterns in young adults: a multi-method, multi-informant study. *Personality and Social Psychology Bulletin, 27*, 1097–1110.

Orzolek-Kronner, C. (2002). The effect of attachment theory in the development of eating disorders: can symptoms be proximity-seeking? *Child and Adolescent Social Work Journal, 19*, 421–435.

Overall, N. C., Fletcher, G. J. O., & Friesen, M. D. (2003). Mapping the intimate relationship mind: comparisons between three models of attachment representations. *Personality and Social Psychology Bulletin, 29*, 1479–1493.

Pace, U., Cacioppo, M., & Schimmenti, A. (2012). The moderating role of father's care on the onset of binge eating symptoms among female late adolescents with insecure attachment. *Child Psychiatry & Human Development, 43*, 282–292.

Palazzoli, M. (1978). *Self-starvation*. New York, NY: Aronson.

Panksepp, J. (1998). *Affective neuroscience: The foundations of human and animal emotions*. New York, USA: Oxford University Press.

Pantin, C.F. A. (1965). Learning, world-models and pre-adaptation. In W. H. Thorpe & D. Davenport (Eds.), *Learning and associated phenomena in invertebrates*. London, UK: Bailliere, Tindal & Cassell.

Parish, M., & Eagle, M. N. (2003). Attachment to the therapist. *Psychoanalytic Psychology, 20*, 271–286.

Parker, J. G., & Asher, S. R. (1993). Friendship and friendship quality in middle childhood: links with peer group acceptance and feelings of loneliness and social dissatisfaction. *Developmental Psychology, 29*, 611–621.

Parkes, C. M., & Weiss, R. S. (1983). *Recovery from bereavement*. New York, NY: Basic Books.

Pearce, Z. J., & Halford, W. (2008). Do attributions mediate the association between attachment and negative couple communication? *Personal Relationships, 15*, 155–170.

Penke, L. (2009). Adaptive developmental plasticity might not contribute much to the adaptiveness of reproductive strategies. *Behavioral and Brain Sciences, 32*, 38–39.

Pereg, D., & Mikulincer, M. (2004). Attachment style and the regulation of negative affect: exploring individual differences in mood congruency effects on memory and judgment. *Personality and Social Psychology Bulletin, 30*, 67–80.

Perry, B. D. (2001). Bonding and attachment in maltreated children. *The Child Trauma Center, 3*, 1–17.

Phelps, E. A., & LeDoux, J. E. (2005). Contributions of the amygdala to emotion processing: from animal models to human behavior. *Neuron, 48*, 175–187.

Piaget, J. (1937/1954). *The construction of reality in the child*. New York, NY: Basic Books.

Pickles, A., Hill, J., Breen, G., Quinn, J., Abbott, K., Jones, H., & Sharp, H. (2013). Evidence for interplay between genes and parenting on infant temperament in the first year of life: monoamine oxidase: a polymorphism moderates effects of maternal sensitivity on infant anger proneness. *Journal of Child Psychology and Psychiatry, 54*, 1308–1317.

Pierce, T., & Lydon, J. (2001). Global and specific relational models in the experience of social interactions. *Journal of Personality and Social Psychology, 80*, 613–631.

Pietromonaco, P. R., & Barrett, L. F. (1997). Working models of attachment and daily social interactions. *Journal of Personality and Social Psychology, 73*, 1409–1423.

Pietromonaco, P. R., & Barrett, L. F. (2000). The internal working models concept: what do we really know about the self in relation to others? *Review of General Psychology, 4*, 155–175.

Pietromonaco, P. R., & Carnelley, K. B. (1994). Gender and working models of attachment: consequences for perceptions of self and romantic relationships. *Personal Relationships, 1*, 63–82.

Pincus, A. L., & Ansell, E. B. (2003). Interpersonal theory of personality. *Handbook of Psychology: Two* (pp. 209–229). New York, NY: Wiley.

Pincus, A. L., & Wiggins, J. S. (1990). Interpersonal problems and conceptions of personality disorders. *Journal of Personality Disorders, 4*, 342–352.

Pinker, S. (1997). *How the Mind Works*. New York, NY: W. W. Norton & Company.

Pinker, S. (2005). So how does the mind work? *Mind & Language, 20*, 1–24.

Pistole, M. (1995). Adult attachment style and narcissistic vulnerability. *Psychoanalytic Psychology, 12*, 115–126.

Pitman, R., & Scharfe, E. (2010). Testing the function of attachment hierarchies during emerging adulthood. *Personal Relationships, 17*, 201–216.

Poldrack, R. A. (2012). The future of fMRI in cognitive neuroscience. *NeuroImage, 62*, 1216–1220.

Powers, S. I., Pietromonaco, P. R., Gunlicks, M., & Sayer, A. (2006). Dating couples' attachment styles and patterns of cortisol reactivity and recovery in response to a relationship conflict. *Journal of Personality and Social Psychology, 90*, 613–628.

Priel, B., Mitrany, D., & Shahar, G. (1998). Closeness, support and reciprocity: a study of attachment styles in adolescence. *Personality and Individual Differences, 25*, 1183–1197.

Proksch, M., Orth, U. R., & Bethge, F. (2013). Disentangling the influence of attachment anxiety and attachment security in consumer formation of attachments to brands. *Journal of Consumer Behaviour, 12*, 318–326.

Quirin, M., Gillath, O., Eggert, L., Pruessner, J., Kuestermann, E., & Kuhl, J. (2010). Attachment insecurity and cell density in the hippocampus. *Social Cognitive and Affective Neuroscience, 5*, 39–47.

Raby, K. L., Roisman, G. I., Fraley, R. C., & Simpson, J. A. (2015). The predictive significance of early maternal sensitivity in the Minnesota Longitudinal Study of Risk and Adaptation: academic and social competence through age 32 years. *Child Development, 86*, 695–708.

Raleigh, M. J., Brammer, G. L., & McGuire, M. T. (1983). Male dominance, serotonergic systems, and the behavioral and physiological effects of drugs in vervet monkeys (Cercopithecus aethiops sabaeus). In K. A. Miczek (Ed.), *Ethopharmacology: Primate models of neuropsychiatric disorders* (pp. 185–197). New York, NY: Alan R. Liss.

Ray, R. D., Shelton, A. L., Hollon, N. G., Matsumoto, D., Frankel, C. B., Gross, J. J., & Gabrieli, J. D. E. (2010). Interdependent self-construal and neural representations of self and mother. *Social Cognitive and Affective Neuroscience, 5*, 318–323.

Redgrave, P., Prescott, T. J., & Gurney, K. (1999). The basal ganglia: a vertebrate solution to the selection problem? *Neuroscience, 89*, 1009–1023.

Reeve, J. M. (2015). *Understanding motivation and emotion* (6th ed.). New York, NY: Wiley.

Reis, H. T., & Shaver, P. R. (1988). Intimacy as an interpersonal process. In S. Duck (Ed.), *Handbook of research in personal relationships* (pp. 367–389). London: Wiley.

Reis, S., & Grenyer, B. F. S. (2004). Fear of intimacy in women: relationship between attachment styles and depressive symptoms. *Psychopathology, 37*, 299–303.

Reiter, M. J., & Gee, C. B. (2008). Open communication and partner support in intercultural and interfaith romantic relationships: a relational maintenance approach. *Journal of Social and Personal Relationships, 25*(4), 539–559.

Reynolds, K. J., & Branscombe, N. R. (Eds.). (2014). *Psychology of change: Life contexts, experiences, and identities*. New York, NY: Psychology Press.

Rholes, W., Simpson, J. A., & Blakely, B. S. (1995). Adult attachment styles and mothers' relationships with their young children. *Personal Relationships, 2*, 35–54.

Roberts, B. W., Harms, P. D., Smith, J., Wood, D., & Webb, M. (2006). Methods in personality psychology. In M. Eid, & E. Diener (Eds.), *Handbook of psychological assessment: A multimethod perspective* (pp. 321–335). Washington, DC: American Psychological Association.

Roche, D. N., Runtz, M. G., & Hunter, M. A. (1999). Adult attachment: a mediator between child sexual abuse and later psychological adjustment. *Journal of Interpersonal Violence, 14*, 184–207.

Rockliff, H., Karl, A., McEwan, K., Gilbert, J., Matos, M., & Gilbert, P. (2011). Effects of intranasal oxytocin on 'compassion focused imagery'. *Emotion, 11*, 1388–1396.

Rogers, W. S., Bidwell, J., & Wilson, L. (2005). Perception of and satisfaction with relationship power, sex, and attachment styles: a couple level analysis. *Journal of Family Violence, 20*, 241–251.

Roisman, G. I., Holland, A., Fortuna, K., Fraley, R. C., Clausell, E., & Clarke, A. (2007). The Adult Attachment Interview and self-reports of attachment style: an empirical rapprochement. *Journal of Personality and Social Psychology, 92*, 678–697.

Rosenstein, D. S., & Horowitz, H. A. (1996). Adolescent attachment and psychopathology. *Journal of Consulting and Clinical Psychology, 64*, 244.

Rosenthal, N. L., & Kobak, R. (2010). Assessing adolescents' attachment hierarchies: differences across developmental periods and associations with individual adaptation. *Journal of Research on Adolescence, 20*, 678–706.

Roth, G. (1992). *When food is love: Exploring the relationship between eating and intimacy*. California, CA: Plume.

Rothbaum, F., Weisz, J., Pott, M., Miyake, K., & Morelli, G. (2000). Attachment and culture: security in the United States and Japan. *American Psychologist, 55*, 1093–1104.

Rowe, A., & Carnelley, K. B. (2003). Attachment style differences in the processing of attachment-relevant information: primed-style effects on recall, interpersonal expectations, and affect. *Personal Relationships, 10*, 59–75.

Rowe, A. C., & Carnelley, K. B. (2005). Preliminary support for the use of a hierarchical mapping technique to examine attachment networks. *Personal Relationships, 12*, 499–519.

Rusbult, C. E. (1980). Commitment and satisfaction in romantic associations: a test of the investment model. *Journal of Experimental Social Psychology, 16*, 172–186.

Ruvolo, A. P., Fabin, L. A., & Ruvolo, C. M. (2001). Relationship experiences and change in attachment characteristics of young adults: the role of relationship breakups and conflict avoidance. *Personal Relationships, 8*, 265–281.

Sack, A., Sperling, M. B., Fagen, G., & Foelsch, P. (1996). Attachment style, history, and behavioral contrasts for a borderline and nomal sample. *Journal of Personality Disorders, 10*, 88–102.

Sakaluk, J. K., & Gillath, O. (2016). The causal effects of relational security and insecurity on condom use attitudes and acquisition behavior. *Archives of Sexual Behavior, 45*(2), 339–352.

Salasoo, A., Shiffrin, R. M., & Feustel, T. C. (1985). Building permanent memory codes-codification and repetition effects in word identification. *Journal of Experimental Psychology: General, 114*, 50–77.

Salo, J., Jokela, M., Lehtimäki, T., & Keltikangas-Järvinen, L. (2011). Serotonin receptor 2A gene moderates the effect of childhood maternal nurturance on adulthood social attachment. *Genes Brain and Behavior, 10*, 702–709.

Salzman, J. P. (1996). Primary attachment in female adolescents: association with depression, self-esteem, and maternal identification. *Psychiatry: Interpersonal and Biological Processes, 59*, 20–33.

Sandberg, D. A. (2010). Adult attachment as a predictor of posttraumatic stress and dissociation. *Journal of Trauma & Dissociation, 11*, 293–307.

Sbarra, D. A. (2006). Predicting the onset of emotional recovery following nonmarital relationship dissolution: survival analyses of sadness and anger. *Personality and Social Psychology Bulletin, 32*, 298–312.

Sbarra, D. A., & Hazan, C. (2008). Coregulation, dysregulation, self-regulation: an integrative analysis and empirical agenda for understanding adult attachment, separation, loss, and recovery. *Personality and Social Psychology Review, 12*, 141–167.

Scannell, L., & Gifford, R. (2013). Comparing the theories of interpersonal and place attachment. In L. Manzo, & P. Devine-Wright (Eds.), *Place attachment. Advances in theory, methods and applications* (pp. 23–36). New York, NY: Routledge.

Scarr, S., & McCartney, K. (1983). How people make their own environments: a theory of genotype → environment effects. *Child Development, 54*, 424–435.

Schachner, D. A., & Shaver, P. R. (2004). Attachment dimensions and sexual motives. *Personal Relationships, 11*, 179–195.

Schachner, D. A., Shaver, P. R., & Gillath, O. (2008). Attachment style and long-term singlehood. *Personal Relationships, 15*, 479–491.

Schaller, M., & Duncan, L. A. (2007). The behavioral immune system: its evolution and social psychological implications. In J. P. Forgas, M. G. Haselton, & W. von Hippel (Eds.), *Evolution and the social mind: Evolutionary psychology and social cognition* (pp. 293–307). New York, NY: Psychology Press.

Schaller, M., & Park, J. H. (2011). The behavioral immune system (and why it matters). *Current Directions in Psychological Science, 20*, 99–103.

Scharfe, E., & Bartholomew, K. I. M. (1994). Reliability and stability of adult attachment patterns. *Personal Relationships, 1*, 23–43.

Scharfe, E., & Bartholomew, K. (1998). Do you remember? Recollections of adult attachment patterns. Personal Relationships, 5, 219–234.

Scharfe, E., & Cole, V. (2006). Stability and change of attachment representations during emerging adulthood: an examination of mediators and moderators of change. *Personal Relationships, 13*, 363–374.

Scher, A., & Mayseless, O. (2000). Mothers of anxious/ambivalent infants: maternal characteristics and child-care context. *Child Development, 71*, 1629–1639.

Schmitt, D. P. (2005). Sociosexuality from Argentina to Zimbabwe: a 48-nation study of sex, culture, and strategies of human mating. *Behavioral and Brain Sciences, 28*, 247–275.

Schmitt, D. P. (2008). Evolutionary perspectives on romantic attachment and culture: how ecological stressors influence dismissing orientations across genders and geographies. *Cross-Cultural Research, 42*, 220–247.

Schmitt, D. P. (2011). Romantic attachment from Argentina to Zimbabwe: patterns of adaptive variation across contexts, cultures, and local ecologies. In P. Erdman, & K. Ng (Eds.), *Attachment: Expanding the cultural connection*. London, UK: Taylor & Francis.

Schmitt, D. P., & Pilcher, J. J. (2004). Evaluating evidence of psychological adaptation: how do we know one when we see one? *Psychological Science, 15*, 643–649.

Schmitt, D.P., Alcalay, L., Allensworth, M., Allik, J., Ault, L., Austers, I., ... & Kardum, I. (2004). Patterns and universals of adult romantic attachment across 62 cultural regions: are models of self and of other pancultural constructs? *Journal of Cross-Cultural Psychology, 35*, 367–402.

Schneier, F. R., Liebowitz, M. R., Abi-Dargham, A., Zea-Ponce, Y., Lin, S. H., & Laruelle, M. (2000). Low dopamine D2 receptor binding potential in social phobia. *American Journal of Psychiatry, 157*, 457–459.

Schwartz, S. H. (1999). Cultural value differences: some implications for work. *Applied Psychology: An International Review, 48*, 23–47.

Scott, S., & Babcock, J. C. (2010). Attachment as a moderator between intimate partner violence and PTSD symptoms. *Journal of Family Violence, 25*, 1–9.

Segal, D. L., Needham, T. N., & Coolidge, F. L. (2009). Age differences in attachment orientations among younger and older adults: evidence from two self-report measures of attachment. *International Journal of Aging and Human Development, 69*, 119–132.

Seibert, A. C., & Kerns, K. A. (2009). Attachment figures in middle childhood. *International Journal of Behavioral Development, 33*, 347–355.

Selcuk, E., & Gillath, O. (2009). Attachment and depression. In R. Ingram (Ed.), *Encyclopedia of depression* (pp. 32–37). New York, NY: Springer.

Selcuk, E., Gunaydin, G., Sumer, N., Harma, M., Salman, S., Hazan, C., ... & Ozturk, A. (2010). Self-reported romantic attachment style predicts everyday maternal caregiving behavior at home. *Journal of Research in Personality, 44*, 544–549.

Shakory, S., Van Exan, J., Mills, J. S., Sockalingam, S., Keating, L., & Taube-Schiff, M. (2015). Binge eating in bariatric surgery candidates: the role of insecure attachment and emotion regulation. *Appetite, 91*, 69–75.

Shaver, P., & Hazan, C. (1987). Being lonely, falling in love: perspectives from attachment theory. *Journal of Social Behavior & Personality, 2*, 105–124.

Shaver, P. R., & Hazan, C. (1988). A biased overview of the study of love. *Journal of Social and Personal Relationships, 5*, 473–501.

Shaver, P. R., Hazan, C., & Bradshaw, D. (1988). Love as attachment: the integration of three behavioral systems. In R. J. Steinberg, & M. L. Barnes (Eds.), *The psychology of love* (pp. 68–99). New Haven, CT: Yale University Press.

Shaver, P. R., Collins, N., & Clark, C. L. (1996). Attachment styles and internal working models of self and relationship partners. In G. J. O. Fletcher, & J. Fitness (Eds.), *Knowledge structures in close relationships: a social psychological approach* (pp. 25–61). Mahwah, NJ: Erlbaum.

Shaver, P. R., Schachner, D. A., & Mikulincer, M. (2005). Attachment style, excessive reassurance seeking, relationship processes, and depression. *Personality and Social Psychology Bulletin, 31*, 343–359.

Shaver, P. R., & Mikulincer, M. (2006). Attachment theory, individual psychodynamics, and relationship functioning. *The Cambridge Handbook of Personal Relationships*, 251–271.

Shaver, P. R., Mikulincer, M., Lavy, S., & Cassidy, J. (2009). Understanding and altering hurt feelings: an attachment-theoretical perspective on the generation and regulation of emotions. In A. Vangelisti (Ed.), *Feeling hurt in close relationships* (pp. 92–122). New York, NY: Cambridge University Press.

Shaver, P. R., Segev, M., & Mikulincer, M. (2011). A behavioral systems perspective on power and aggression. In P. R. Shaver, & M. Mikulincer (Eds.), *Human aggression and violence: Causes, manifestations, and consequences* (pp. 71–87). Washington, DC: American Psychological Association.

Shaver, P. R., & Mikulincer, M. (2012). Adult attachment and sexuality. In P. Noller, & G. Karantzas (Eds.), *The Wiley-Blackwell handbook of couples and family relationships* (pp. 159–174). Chichester, UK: Wiley-Blackwell.

Sheldon, A. E., & West, M. (1990). Attachment pathology and low social skills in avoidant personality disorder: an exploratory study. *Canadian Journal of Psychiatry, 35*, 596–599.

Shi, L. (2003). The association between adult attachment styles and conflict resolution in romantic relationships. *American Journal of Family Therapy, 31*, 143–157.

Shorey, H. S. (2010). Attachment theory as a social-developmental psychopathology framework for the practice of psychotherapy. In J. E. Maddux, & J. P. Tangney (Eds.), *Social psychological foundations of clinical psychology* (pp. 157–176). New York, NY: Guilford.

Shulman, S., Elicker, J., & Sroufe, L. A. (1994). Stages of friendship growth in preadolescence as related to attachment history. *Journal of Social and Personal Relationships, 11*, 341–361.

Sibley, C. G., Fischer, R., & Liu, J. H. (2005). Reliability and validity of the revised experiences in close relationships (ECR-R) self-report measure of adult romantic attachment. *Personality and Social Psychology Bulletin, 31*, 1524–1536.

Sibley, C. G., & Overall, N. C. (2008). Modeling the hierarchical structure of attachment representations: a test of domain differentiation. *Personality and Individual Differences, 44*, 238–249.

Silverman, L. H. (1983). The subliminal psychodynamic activation method: overview and a comprehensive listing of studies. *Empirical Studies of Psychoanalytic Theories, 1*, 69–100.

Silverman, L. H., & Weinberger, J. (1985). Mommy and I are one: implications for psychotherapy. *American Psychologist, 40*, 1296–1308.

Simpson, J. A. (1990). The influence of attachment styles on romantic relationships. *Journal of Personality and Social Psychology, 59*, 971–980.

Simpson, J. A., & Belsky, J. (2008). Attachment theory within a modern evolutionary framework. In J. Cassidy, & P. R. Shaver (Eds.), *Adult attachment: Theory, research, and clinical applications* (2nd ed., pp. 131–157). New York, NY: Guilford Press.

Simpson, J. A., Rholes, W. S., & Nelligan, J. S. (1992). Support seeking and support giving within couples in an anxiety-provoking situation: the role of attachment styles. *Journal of Personality and Social Psychology, 62*, 434–446.

Simpson, J. A., Rholes, W. S., & Phillips, D. (1996). Conflict in close relationships: an attachment perspective. *Journal of Personality and Social Psychology, 71*, 899–914.

Simpson, J. A., Rholes, W. S., Orina, M., & Grich, J. (2002). Working models of attachment, support giving, and support seeking in a stressful situation. *Personality and Social Psychology Bulletin, 28*, 598–608.

Simpson, J. A., Rholes, W. S., Campbell, L., & Wilson, C. L. (2003a). Changes in attachment orientations across the transition to parenthood. *Journal of Experimental Social Psychology, 39*, 317–331.

Simpson, J. A., Rholes, W. S., Campbell, L., Tran, S., & Wilson, C. L. (2003b). Adult attachment, the transition to parenthood, and depressive symptoms. *Journal of Personality and Social Psychology, 84*, 1172.

Simpson, J. A., Collins, W. A., Tran, S., & Haydon, K. C. (2007). Attachment and the experience and expression of emotions in romantic relationships: a developmental perspective. *Journal of Personality and Social Psychology, 92*, 355–367.

Simpson, J. A., Rholes, W. S., & Winterheld, H. A. (2010). Attachment working models twist memories of relationship events. *Psychological Science, 21*, 252–259.

Simpson, J. A., Kim, J. S., Fillo, J., Ickes, W., Rholes, W. S., Oriña, M. M., & Winterheld, H. A. (2011). Attachment and the management of empathic accuracy in relationship-threatening situations. *Personality and Social Psychology Bulletin, 37*, 242–254.

Simpson, J. A., Rholes, W. S., & Shallcross, S. (2012). Attachment and depression across the transition to parenthood. In P. Noller, & G. C. Karantzas (Eds.), *Wiley-Blackwell handbook of couple and family relationships* (pp. 377–391). New York, NY: Wiley-Blackwell Publishing.

Simpson, J. A., & Overall, N. C. (2014). Partner buffering of attachment insecurity. *Current Directions in Psychological Science, 23*, 54–59.

Simpson, J. A., Collins, W. A., Farrell, A. K., & Raby, K. L. (2015). Attachment and relationships across time: an organizational-developmental perspective. In V. Zayas, & C. Hazan (Eds.), *Bases of adult attachment: Linking brain, mind, and behavior* (pp. 61–78). New York, NY: Springer.

Slavich, G. M., & Cole, S. W. (2013). The emerging field of human social genomics. *Clinical Psychological Science, 1*, 331–348.

Snyder, M., & Swann, W. B. (1978). Behavioral confirmation in social interaction: from social perception to social reality. *Journal of Experimental Social Psychology, 14*, 148–162.

Sohlberg, S., & Birgegard, A. (2003). Persistent complex subliminal activation effects: first experimental observations. *Journal of Personality and Social Psychology, 85*, 302–316.

Solomon, Z., Dekel, R., & Mikulincer, M. (2008). Complex trauma of war captivity: a prospective study of attachment and post-traumatic stress disorder. *Psychological Medicine, 38*, 1427–1434.

Soltani, M., Shairi, M. R., Roshan, R., & Rahimi, C. R. (2014). The impact of emotionally focused therapy on emotional distress in infertile couples. *International Journal of Fertility & Sterility, 7*, 337.

Sörensen, S., Webster, J., & Roggman, L. (2002). Preparation for care giving and adult attachment. *Attachment and Human Development, 4*, 84–106.

Specht, J., Bleidorn, W., Denissen, J. J., Hennecke, M., Hutteman, R., Kandler, C., ... & Zimmermann, J. (2014). What drives adult personality development? A comparison of theoretical perspectives and empirical evidence. *European Journal of Personality, 28*, 216–230.

Sroufe, L. A., & Jacobvitz, D. (1989). Diverging pathways, developmental transformations, multiple etiologies and the problem of continuity in development. *Human Development, 32*, 196–203.

Sroufe, L. A., & Waters, E. (1977a). Attachment as an organizational construct. *Child Development, 48*, 1184–1199.

Sroufe, L. A., & Waters, E. (1977b). Heart rate as a convergent measure in clinical and developmental research. *Merrill-Palmer Quarterly of Behavior and Development, 23*, 3–27.

Sroufe, L. A., Egeland, B., & Kreutzer, T. (1990). The fate of early experience following developmental change: longitudinal approaches to individual adaptation in childhood. *Child Development, 61*, 1363–1373.

Sroufe, L. A., Egeland, B., Carlson, E. A., & Collins, W. A. (2005). *The development of the person: The Minnesota study of risk and adaptation from birth to adulthood*. New York, NY: Guilford.

Srull, T. K. (1981). Person memory: some tests of associative storage and retrieval models. *Journal of Experimental Psychology: Human Learning and Memory, 7*, 440–463.

Srull, T. K., & Wyer, R. S. (1980). Category accessibility and social perception: some implications for the study of person memory and interpersonal judgements. *Journal of Personality and Social Psychology, 38*, 841–856.

Stalker, C. A., & Davies, F. (1998). Working models of attachment and representations of the object in a clinical sample of sexually abused women. *Bulletin of the Menninger Clinic, 62*, 334–335.

Steele, H., Phibbs, E., & Woods, R. T. (2004). Coherence of mind in daughter caregivers of mothers with dementia: links with their mothers' joy and relatedness on reunion in a strange situation. *Attachment and Human Development, 6*, 439–450.

Steele, H., & Steele, M. (Eds.), (2008). *Clinical applications of the adult attachment interview*. New York, NY: Guilford Press.

Steele, R. D., Waters, T. E., Bost, K. K., Vaughn, B. E., Truitt, W., Waters, H. S., ... & Roisman, G. I. (2014). Caregiving antecedents of secure base script knowledge: a comparative analysis of young adult attachment representations. *Developmental Psychology, 50,* 2526–2538.

Steinberg, L. (2014). *Age of opportunity: Lessons from the new science of adolescence.* New York, NY: Houghton Mifflin Harcourt.

Steiner-Pappalardo, N. L., & Gurung, R. A. R. (2002). The femininity effect: relationship quality, sex, gender, attachment, and significant-other concepts. *Personal Relationships, 9,* 313–325.

Strauss, C., Morry, M. M., & Kito, M. (2012). Attachment styles and relationship quality: actual, perceived, and ideal partner matching. *Personal Relationships, 19,* 14–36.

Strathearn, L., Fonagy, P., Amico, J., & Montague, P. R. (2009). Adult attachment predicts maternal brain and oxytocin response to infant cues. *Neuropsychopharmacology, 34,* 2655–2666.

Strodl, E., & Noller, P. (2003). The relationship of adult attachment dimensions to depression and agoraphobia. *Personal Relationships, 10,* 171–185.

Suldo, S. M., & Sandberg, D. A. (2000). Relationship between attachment styles and eating disorder symptomatology among college women. *Journal of College Student Psychotherapy, 15,* 59–73.

Sumer, N., & Cozzarelli, C. (2004). The impact of adult attachment on partner and self-attributions and relationship quality. *Personal Relationships, 11,* 355–371.

Sutcliffe, A., Dunbar, R., Binder, J., & Arrow, H. (2012). Relationships and the social brain: integrating psychological and evolutionary perspectives. *British Journal of Psychology, 103,* 149–168.

Sutin, A. R., & Gillath, O. (2009). Autobiographical memory phenomenology and content mediate attachment style and psychological distress. *Journal of Counseling Psychology, 56,* 351–364.

Surra, C. A., Gray, C. R., Boettcher, T. M., Cottle, N. R., & West, A. R. (2006). From courtship to universal properties: research on dating and mate selection, 1950 to 2003. In A. Vangelisti, & D. Perlman (Eds.), *The Cambridge handbook of personal relationships* (pp. 113–130). Cambridge: Cambridge University Press.

Swann, W. B., & Read, S. J. (1981). Self-verification processes: how we sustain our self-conceptions. *Journal of Experimental Social Psychology, 17,* 351–372.

Swann, W. B. (1983). Self-verification: bringing social reality into harmony with the self. *Social Psychological Perspectives on the Self, 2,* 33–66.

Swann, W. B., Jr. (1990). To be adored or to be known: the interplay of self-enhancement and self-verification. In R. M. Sorrentino, & E. T. Higgins (Eds.), *Motivation and cognition* (pp. 33–66). (Vol. 2). New York: Guilford Press.

Talegaonkar, S., & Mishra, P. R. (2004). Intranasal delivery: an approach to bypass the blood brain barrier. *Indian Journal of Pharmacology, 36,* 140–147.

Tancredy, C. M., & Fraley, R. C. (2006). The nature of adult twin relationships: an attachment-theoretical perspective. *Journal of Personality and Social Psychology, 90,* 78–93.

Tarabulsy, G. M., Larose, S., Bernier, A., Trottier-Sylvain, K., Girard, D., Vargas, M., & Noël, C. (2012). Attachment states of mind in late adolescence and the quality and course of romantic relationships in adulthood. *Attachment & Human Development, 14,* 621–643.

Tasca, G. A., Kowal, J., Balfour, L., Ritchie, K., Virley, B., & Bissada, H. (2006a). An attachment insecurity model of negative affect among women seeking treatment for an eating disorder. *Eating Behaviors, 7,* 252–257.

Tasca, G. A., Ritchie, K., Conrad, G., Balfour, L., Gayton, J., Lybanon, V., & Bissada, H. (2006b). Attachment scales predict outcome in a randomized controlled trial of two group therapies for binge eating disorder: an aptitude by treatment interaction. *Psychotherapy Research, 16,* 106–121.

Tasca, G.A., Szadkowski, L., Illing, V., Trinneer, A., Grenon, R., Demidenko, N., ... & Bissada, H. (2009). Adult attachment, depression, and eating disorder symptoms: the mediating role of affect regulation strategies. *Personality and Individual Differences, 47,* 662–667.

Taube-Schiff, M., Van Exan, J., Tanaka, R., Wnuk, S., Hawa, R., & Sockalingam, S. (2015). Attachment style and emotional eating in bariatric surgery candidates: the mediating role of difficulties in emotion regulation. *Eating Behaviors, 18*, 36–40.

Taubman-Ben-Ari, O., Findler, L., & Mikulincer, M. (2002). The effects of mortality salience on relationship strivings and beliefs: the moderating role of attachment style. *British Journal of Social Psychology, 41*, 419–441.

Taylor, P., Rietzschel, J., Danquah, A., & Berry, K. (2015). Changes in attachment representations during psychological therapy. *Psychotherapy Research, 25*, 222–238.

Teti, D. M., & Ablard, K. E. (1989). Security of attachment and infant-sibling relationships: a laboratory study. *Child Development, 60*, 1519–1528.

Teti, D. M., Gelfand, D. M., Messinger, D. S., & Isabella, R. (1995). Maternal depression and the quality of early attachment: an examination of infant, preschoolers and their mothers. *Developmental Psychology, 31*, 364–376.

Tharner, A., Herba, C. M., Luijk, M. P., van IJzendoorn, M. H., Bakermans-Kranenburg, M. J., Govaert, P. P., et al. (2011). Subcortical structures and the neurobiology of infant attachment disorganization: a longitudinal ultrasound imaging study. *Social Neuroscience, 6*, 336–347.

Thomas, B. H., Ciliska, D., Dobbins, M., & Micucci, S. (2004). A process for systematically reviewing the literature: providing the research evidence for public health nursing interventions. *Worldviews on Evidence-based Nursing/Sigma Theta Tau International, Honor Society of Nursing, 1*, 176–184.

Tinbergen, N. (1951). *The study of instinct*. New York, NY: Oxford University Press.

Tinbergen, N. (1963). On aims and methods of ethology. *Zeitschrift für Tierpsychologie, 20*, 410–433.

Trentini, C., Foschi, R., Lauriola, M., & Tambelli, R. (2015). The State Adult Attachment Measure (SAAM): a construct and incremental validity study. *Personality and Individual Differences, 85*, 251–257.

Trillingsgaard, T., Elklit, A., Shevlin, M., & Maimburg, R. D. (2011). Adult attachment at the transition to motherhood: predicting worry, health care utility and relationship functioning. *Journal of Reproductive and Infant Psychology, 29*, 354–363.

Trinke, S. J., & Bartholomew, K. (1997). Hierarchies of attachment relationships in young adulthood. *Journal of Social and Personal Relationships, 14*, 603–625.

Troisi, A., Di Lorenzo, G., Alcini, S., Nanni, R. C., Di Pasquale, C., & Siracusano, A. (2006). Body dissatisfaction in women with eating disorders: relationship to early separation anxiety and insecure attachment. *Psychosomatic Medicine, 68*, 449–453.

Troisi, A., Frazzetto, G., Carola, V., Di Lorenzo, G., Coviello, M., Siracusano, A., & Gross, C. (2012). Variation in the µ-opioid receptor gene (OPRM1) moderates the influence of early maternal care on fearful attachment. *Social Cognitive and Affective Neuroscience, 7*, 542–547.

Troy, M., & Sroufe, L. A. (1987). Victimization among preschoolers: the role of attachment relationship history. *Journal of the American Academy of Child and Adolescent Psychiatry, 26*, 166–172.

Tulving, E. (1983). *Elements of episodic memory* (Vol. 2). New York, NY: Oxford University Press.

Tulving, E., & Schacter, D. L. (1990). Priming and human memory systems. *Science, 247*, 301–305.

Turner, H., Bryant-Waugh, R., & Peveler, R. (2009). An approach to sub-grouping the eating disorder population: adding attachment and coping style. *European Eating Disorders Review, 17*, 269–280.

Uecker, J. E. (2012). Marriage and mental health among young adults. *Journal of Health and Social Behavior, 53*, 67–83.

Umemura, T., Lacinová, L., & Macek, P. (2014). Is emerging adults' attachment preference for the romantic partner transferred from their attachment preferences for their mother, father, and friends? *Emerging Adulthood, 3,* 179–193.

Van Assche, L., Luyten, P., Bruffaerts, R., Persoons, P., van de Ven, L., & Vandenbulcke, M. (2013). Attachment in old age: theoretical assumptions, empirical findings and implications for clinical practice. *Clinical Psychology Review, 33,* 67–81.

Van den Boom, D. (1990). Preventive intervention and the quality of mother-infant interaction and infant exploration in irritable infants. In W. Koops, H. J. G. Soppe, J. L. van der Linden, P. C. M. Molenaar, & J. J. F. Schroots (Eds.), *Developmental psychology behind the dikes: An outline of developmental psychological research in the Netherlands.* Delft, Netherlands: Uitgeverij Eburon.

van den Boom, D. C. (1994). The influence of temperament and mothering on attachment and exploration: an experimental manipulation of sensitive responsiveness among lower-class mothers with irritable infants. *Child Development, 65,* 1457–1477.

van IJzendoorn, M. H. (1997). Attachment, emergent morality, and aggression: toward a developmental socioemotional model of antisocial behaviour. *International Journal of Behavioral Development, 21,* 703–727.

van IJzendoorn, M. H., & Bakermans-Kranenburg, M. J. (1996). Attachment representations in mothers, fathers, adolescents, and clinical groups: a meta-analytic search for normative data. *Journal of Consulting and Clinical Psychology, 64,* 8.

van IJzendoorn, M. H., & Bakermans-Kranenburg, M. J. (2010). Invariance of adult attachment across gender, age, culture, and socioeconomic status? *Journal of Social and Personal Relationships, 27,* 200–208.

van IJzendoorn, M. H., Goossens, F. A., Tavecchio, L. W. C., Vergeer, M. M., & Hubbard, F. O. A. (1983). Attachment to soft objects: its relationship with attachment to the mother and with thumbsucking. *Child Psychiatry and Human Development, 14,* 97–105.

van IJzendoorn, M. H., Juffer, F., & Duyvesteyn, M. G. (1995). Breaking the intergenerational cycle of insecure attachment: a review of the effects of attachment-based interventions on maternal sensitivity and infant security. *Journal of Child Psychology and Psychiatry and Allied Disciplines, 36,* 225–248.

van IJzendoorn, M. H., Feldbrugge, J., Derks, F. C. H., de Ruiter, C., Verhagen, M. F., Philipse, M. W., van der Staak, C. P., & Riksen-Walraven, J. M. (1997). Attachment representations of personality-disordered criminal offenders. *American Journal of Orthopsychiatry, 67,* 449–459.

Van Schaik, C. P., & Dunbar, R. I. M. (1990). The evolution of monogamy in large primates: a new hypothesis and some crucial tests. *Behaviour, 115,* 30–61.

Vicary, A. M., & Fraley, R. C. (2007). Choose your own adventure: attachment dynamics in a simulated relationship. *Personality and Social Psychology Bulletin, 33,* 1279–1291.

Vrticka, P., & Vuilleumier, P. (2012). Neuroscience of human social interactions and adult attachment style. *Frontiers in Human Neuroscience, 6,* 212.

Vrticka, P., Andersson, F., Grandjean, D., Sander, D., & Vuilleumier, P. (2008). Individual attachment style modulates human amygdala and striatum activation during social appraisal. *PLoS ONE, 3,* e2868.

Vul, E., Harris, C., Winkielman, P., & Pashler, H. (2009). Puzzlingly high correlations in fMRI studies of emotion, personality, and social cognition. *Perspectives on Psychological Science, 4,* 274–290.

Waddington, C. H. (1967). *The strategy of the genes: A discussion of some aspects of theoretical biology.* London, UK: Allen & Unwin.

Waller, N. G., & Meehl, P. E. (1998). *Multivariate taxometric procedures: Distinguishing types from continua*. Thousand Oaks, CA: Sage Publications, Inc.

Wallin, D. (2007). *Attachment and psychotherapy*. New York, NY: Guilford Press.

Waroquier, L., Klein, O., Marchiori, D., & Cleeremans, A. (2008, September). Is unconscious thought more efficient than conscious thought when choosing among complex alternatives? In *Paper Presented at the tenth ESCON Transfer of Knowledge Conference*. Volterra, Italy.

Waroquier, L., Marchiori, D., Klein, O., & Cleeremans, A. (2009). Methodological pitfalls of the unconscious thought paradigm. *Judgment and Decision Making, 4*, 601–610.

Warren, S.L., Bost, K.K., Roisman, G.I., Silton, R.L., Spielberg, J.M., Engels, A.S., ... & Heller, W. (2010). Effects of adult attachment and emotional distractors on brain mechanisms of cognitive control. *Psychological Science, 21*, 1818–1826.

Waters, E., & Sroufe, L. A. (1983). Social competence as a developmental construct. *Developmental Review, 3*, 79–97.

Waters, E., Crowell, J., Elliott, M., Corcoran, D., & Treboux, D. (2002). Bowlby's secure base theory and the social/personality psychology of attachment styles: work (s) in progress. *Attachment & Human Development, 4*, 230–242.

Waters, H. S., Rodrigues, L. M., & Ridgeway, D. (1998). Cognitive underpinnings of narrative attachment assessment. *Journal of Experimental Child Psychology, 71*, 211–234.

Waters, H. S., & Rodrigues-Doolabh, L. (2004). *Manual for decoding secure base narratives*. Unpublished manuscript, State University of New York at Stony Brook.

Waters, H. S., & Waters, E. (2006). The attachment working models concept: among other things, we build script-like representations of secure base experiences. *Attachment & Human Development, 8*, 185–197.

Wautier, G., & Blume, L. B. (2004). The effects of ego identity, gender role, and attachment on depression and anxiety in young adults. *Identity, 4*, 59–76.

Webster, J. D. (1997). Attachment style and well-being in elderly adults: a preliminary investigation. *Canadian Journal on Aging/La Revue canadienne du vieillissement, 16*, 101–111.

Wegner, D. M., Schneider, D. J., Carter, S. R., & White, T. L. (1987). Paradoxical effects of thought suppression. *Journal of Personality and Social Psychology, 53*, 5–13.

Wei, M., Russell, D. W., Mallinckrodt, B., & Zakalik, R. A. (2004). Cultural equivalence of adult attachment across four ethnic groups: factor structure, structured means, and associations with negative mood. *Journal of Counseling Psychology, 51*, 408–417.

Wei, M., Vogel, D. L., Ku, T. Y., & Zakalik, R. A. (2005). Adult attachment, affect regulation, negative mood, and interpersonal problems: the mediating roles of emotional reactivity and emotional cutoff. *Journal of Counseling Psychology, 52*, 14–24.

Wei, M., & Ku, T. Y. (2007). Testing a conceptual model of working through self-defeating patterns. *Journal of Counseling Psychology, 54*, 295–305.

Wei, M., Russell, D. W., Mallinckrodt, B., & Vogel, D. L. (2007). The Experiences in Close Relationship Scale (ECR)-short form: reliability, validity, and factor structure. *Journal of Personality Assessment, 88*, 187–204.

Weiss, R. S. (1975). *Marital separation*. New York, NY: Basic Books.

Weiss, R. S. (1982). Attachment in adult life. In C. M. Parkes, & J. Stevenson-Hinde (Eds.), *The place of attachment in human behavior* (pp. 171–184). New York, NY: Basic Books.

Weiss, R. S. (1998). A taxonomy of relationships. *Journal of Social and Personal Relationships, 15*, 671–683.

Wensauer, M., & Grossmann, K. E. (1995). Quality of attachment representation, social integration and use of social network resources in advanced age. *Zeitschrift für Gerontologie und Geriatrie, 28*, 444–456.

West, M., Rose, S. M., & Sheldon-Keller, A. E. (1994). Assessment of patterns of insecure attachment in adults and application to dependent and schizoid personality disorders. *Journal of Personality Disorders, 8*, 249–256.

Whiffen, V. E. (2005). The role of partner characteristics in attachment insecurity and depressive symptoms. *Personal Relationships, 12*, 407–423.

White, R. W. (1959). Motivation reconsidered: the concept of competence. *Psychological Review, 66*, 297–333.

Whitehead, C. (2010). The culture ready brain. *Social Cognitive and Affective Neuroscience, 5*, 168–179.

Widiger, T. A., & Frances, A. (1985). The DSM-III personality disorders: perspectives from psychology. *Archives of General Psychiatry, 42*, 615–623.

Wilkinson, L. L., Rowe, A. C., Bishop, R. J., & Brunstrom, J. M. (2010). Attachment anxiety, disinhibited eating, and body mass index in adulthood. *International Journal of Obesity, 34*, 1442–1445.

Williams, N. L., & Riskind, J. H. (2004). Adult romantic attachment and cognitive vulnerabilities to anxiety and depression: examining the interpersonal basis of vulnerability models. *Journal of Cognitive Psychotherapy, 18*, 7–24.

Wilson, E. O. (1998). *Consilience: The unity of knowledge*. New York, NY: Knopf.

Wilson, M. (2010). The re-tooled mind: how culture re-engineers cognition. *Social Cognitive and Affective Neuroscience, 5*, 180–187.

Woody, E. Z., & Szechtman, H. (2011). Adaptation to potential threat: the evolution, neurobiology, and psychopathology of the security motivation system. *Neuroscience & Biobehavioral Reviews, 35*(4), 1019–1033.

Woody, E. Z., & Szechtman, H. (2013). A biological security motivation system for potential threats: are there implications for policy-making? *Frontiers in Human Neuroscience, 7*, 1–5.

Xu, J. H., & Shrout, P. E. (2013). Assessing the reliability of change: a comparison of two measures of adult attachment. *Journal of Research in Personality, 47*, 202–208.

You, H. S., & Malley-Morrison, K. (2000). Young adult attachment styles and intimate relationships with close friends: a cross-cultural study of Koreans and Caucasian Americans. *Journal of Cross-Cultural Psychology, 31*, 528–534.

You, J., Huang, J. L., Ho, M. Y., Leung, H., Li, C., & Bond, M. (2015). Perceived support and relational conflict as mediators linking attachment orientations with depressive symptoms: a comparison of dating individuals from Hong Kong and the United States. *Personality and Individual Differences, 73*, 50–55.

Young, J. Z. (1964). *A model for the brain*. London: Oxford University Press.

Young, A., & Acitelli, L. (1998). The role of attachment style and relationship status of the perceiver in the perceptions of romantic partner. *Journal of Social and Personal Relationships, 15*, 161–173.

Young, L. J., & Wang, Z. (2004). The neurobiology of pair bonding. *Nature Neuroscience, 7*, 1048–1054.

Youngblade, L. M., & Belsky, J. (1992). Parent-child antecedents of 5-year-olds' close friendships: a longitudinal analysis. *Developmental Psychology, 28*, 700–713.

Zakin, G., Solomon, Z., & Neria, Y. (2003). Hardiness, attachment style, and long-term psychological distress among Israeli POWs and combat veterans. *Personality and Individual Differences, 34*, 819–829.

Zayas, V., Shoda, Y., Mischel, W., Osterhout, L., & Takahashi, M. (2009). Neural responses to partner rejection cues. *Psychological Science, 20*, 813–821.

Zayas, V., Mischel, W., Shoda, Y., & Aber, J. L. (2011). Roots of adult attachment: maternal caregiving at 18 months predicts adult attachment to peers and partners. *Social Psychological and Personality Science, 2,* 289–297.

Zeifman, D., & Hazan, C. (2008). Pair bonds as attachments: re-evaluating the evidence. In J. Cassidy, & P. R. Shaver (Eds.), *Adult attachment: Theory, research, and clinical applications* (2nd ed., pp. 436–455). New York, NY: Guilford Press.

Zhang, F. (2009). The relationship between state attachment security and daily interpersonal experience. *Journal of Research in Personality, 43,* 511–515.

Zhang, F., & Hazan, C. (2002). Working models of attachment and person perception processes. *Personal Relationships, 9,* 225–235.

Zhang, F., & Labouvie-Vief, G. (2004). Stability and fluctuation in adult attachment style over a 6-year period. *Attachment and Human Development, 6,* 419–437.

Zhang, X., Li, T., & Zhou, X. (2008). Brain responses to facial expressions by adults with different attachment-orientations. *NeuroReport, 19,* 437–441.

Zhang, H., Chan, D. K., & Teng, F. (2011). Transfer of attachment functions and adjustment among young adults in China. *The Journal of Social Psychology, 151,* 257–273.

Zilber, A., Goldstein, A., & Mikulincer, M. (2007). Adult attachment orientations and the processing of emotional pictures–ERP correlates. *Personality and Individual Differences, 43,* 1898–1907.

Zuroff, D. C., & Fitzpatrick, D. K. (1995). Depressive personality styles: implications for adult attachment. *Personality and Individual Differences, 18,* 253–365.

Subject Index